PUBLIC LIABILITY IN EU LAW

Over the last two decades public law liability for breach of European Union law has been subject to remarkable developments. This book examines the convergence between its two constituent systems: the damages liability of the EU and that of its Member States for failing to comply with EU rules. Member State liability, based as it is on the *Francovich* case (1991) and *Brasserie du Pêcheur and Factortame* (1996) judgments of the European Court of Justice (ECJ) is well established. But it is yet to be closely scrutinised by reference to the detailed rules on the liability of the European Union.

The focus of the book is on the two key legal criteria that are common to both systems, namely the grant of rights to individuals by EU law and the notion of sufficiently serious breach of such rights. The analysis concentrates on developments in the case law of the ECJ and the General Court since the *Bergaderm* judgment (2000), which consolidated the convergence of the two liability systems that was first indicated in *Brasserie du Pêcheur and Factortame.* These two criteria are set side by side to evaluate the extent, in real terms, of the convergence of Member State and EU institutional damages liability, and to determine the extent to which one has influenced the other.

This book shows that although full convergence between the two liability systems is not likely, each stream of case law should look to the other more actively as this important element of EU remedial law develops. Convergence in EU law public liability is supported by developments in adjacent areas, most notably European tort law and European administrative law. This study also illustrates how convergence in the EU liability systems to date has had spill-over effects into national public liability law.

Volume 27 in the series Modern Studies in European Law

Modern Studies in European Law
Recent titles in this series:

EU Criminal Law *Valsamis Mitsilegas*

Effective Judicial Protection and the Environmental Impact Assessment Directive in Ireland *Áine Ryall*

Network-Based Governance in EC Law: The Example of EC Competition and EC Communications Law *Maartje de Visser*

Legitimacy in EU Cartel Control *Ingeborg Simonsson*

Mixed Agreements Revisited: The EU and its Member States in the World *Edited by Christophe Hillion and Panos Koutrakos*

Reflexive Governance: Redefining the Public Interest in a Pluralistic World *Edited by Olivier De Schutter and Jacques Lenoble*

The Impact of EU Law on Minority Rights *Tawhida Ahmed*

Direct Investment, National Champions and EU Treaty Freedoms: From Maastricht to Lisbon *Frank S Benyon*

The Cyprus Issue: The Four Freedoms in a Member State under Siege *Nikos Skoutaris*

The European Union and Global Emergencies: A Law and Policy Analysis *Edited by Antonis Antoniadis, Robert Schütze and Eleanor Spaventa*

Public Liability in EU Law: *Brasserie, Bergaderm* and Beyond *Pekka Aalto*

For the complete list of titles in this series, see 'Modern Studies in European Law' link at www.hartpub.co.uk/books/series.asp

Public Liability in EU Law

Brasserie, *Bergaderm* and Beyond

Pekka Aalto

• HART •
PUBLISHING

OXFORD AND PORTLAND, OREGON
2011

Published in the United Kingdom by Hart Publishing Ltd
16C Worcester Place, Oxford, OX1 2JW
Telephone: +44 (0)1865 517530
Fax: +44 (0)1865 510710
E-mail: mail@hartpub.co.uk
Website: http://www.hartpub.co.uk

Published in North America (US and Canada) by
Hart Publishing
c/o International Specialized Book Services
920 NE 58th Avenue, Suite 300
Portland, OR 97213-3786
USA
Tel: +1 503 287 3093 or toll-free: (1) 800 944 6190
Fax: +1 503 280 8832
E-mail: orders@isbs.com
Website: http://www.isbs.com

British Library Cataloguing in Publication Data
Data Available

ISBN: 978-1-84946-133-7

Typeset by Hope Services, Abingdon
Printed and bound in Great Britain by
TJ International Ltd, Padstow, Cornwall

Acknowledgements

Twelve years ago, when I published my previous book on EU public liability, it was appropriate to discuss the liability of the Member States as a stand-alone subject. However, things have changed since then and the liability of the European Union now plays an ever increasing role in Member State liability. Therefore, providing a complete picture of the systems meant covering both areas. The new approach has also made writing more challenging this time round.

This dissertation project, which was started with the late Professor Kari Joutsamo, has not been pursued under a single-hand. Several individuals have contributed to it, directly or indirectly. I would like to thank some of them here; those not mentioned I will thank personally.

Professor Tuomas Ojanen of University of Turku supervised the work. Professors Olli Mäenpää and Juha Raitio of the University of Helsinki, as the preliminary examiners appointed by the Law Faculty, assessed the original version of the manuscript. Professor Jukka Snell of Swansea University kindly agreed to be my opponent in the public examination in Turku. Thank you all very much.

When writing this book, I was a member of the graduate school of the law faculty of University of Turku. I would like to thank Professor Veli-Pekka Viljanen, Professor Jukka Mahonen and the members of the graduate school for useful discussions. In addition, I am grateful to Professor Juha Karhu and to Dr. Suvianna Hakalehto-Wainio for their encouragment and help.

Most of the work was written when I was working in the Legal Service of the European Commission. This is a very stimulating environment for any EU lawyer, even if combining work and academic activities can sometimes be a challenge. I wish to thank my colleagues, and especially my superiors, Hans Peter Hartvig and Patrick Hetsch, for crucial support and advice. The research was finalised while working at the Chambers of Advocate General Niilo Jääskinen at the Court of Justice in Luxembourg.

Over the years, it has been very useful to see EU law from different vantage points. My experiences in the Ministry of Justice, the Parliament of Finland, the European Commission, and the ECJ have been essential. I feel that I have learnt a lot working with Niilo Jääskinen, Sten Palmgren, the late Heikki Karapuu, Tiina Astola, Kirsti Rissanen, Leif Sevón, and Allan Rosas. Needless to say this book presents my own views, and not necessarily those of the institutions themselves, or of the persons mentioned.

I am particularly grateful to Hart Publishing and Richard Hart for publishing the book in the series 'Modern Studies in European Law'. Throughout the publication process, it has been a pleasure working with the competent and friendly people of Hart Publishing. I am thankful to Peter Oliver who first put me in contact with Richard Hart.

I would like to thank my wife Minna for leading by example and relentlessly encouraging me to finalise the work, and our children Aarne and Onerva for being there. My parents Leena and Jorma S Aalto have provided unfailing support since the very beginning. This book is dedicated to all of them.

Financial support from *Jenny and Antti Wihuri Foundation* and *Finnish Lawyers' Society* is also gratefully acknowledged.

Finally, I owe a special thanks to David Allen and his book *Getting Things Done.* It seems unlikely that I would have been able to write the book while working full-time if I had not found, by accident, his excellent study on GTD methods. It should be on the reading list of anyone planning to write a dissertation.

Incidentally, the publication of this book coincides with an anniversary of the *Francovich* judgment, which in 1991 consolidated the foundations of EU damages liability law. It remains to be seen whether the years to come will prove as interesting as those to date. I think they will.

Luxembourg September 2011
Pekka Aalto

Contents

Abbreviations

CFI	Court of First Instance (of the European Union)
CDE	Cahiers de droit européen
ch	Chapter
CST	Civil Service Tribunal (of the European Union)
EC	(Treaty establishing the) European Community
ECHR	European Convention on Human Rights
ECJ	European Court of Justice
ECR	European Court Reports
ECSC	(Treaty establishing the) European Coal and Steel Community
ECtHR	European Court of Human Rights
EEA	European Economic Area
EEC	(Treaty establishing the) European Economic Community
EFTA	European Free Trade Association
EU	European Union
GC	General Court (of the European Union)
OJ	Official Journal
s	Section
TEU	Treaty on the European Union (as amended by the Lisbon Treaty)
TFEU	Treaty on the Functioning of the European Union (as amended by the Lisbon Treaty)
WTO	World Trade Organisation

List of Tables and Figures

Tables

Figures

Table of Cases

European Court of Justice

Court of First Instance (CFI) –2009

General Court (GC) 2009–

Civil Service Tribunal (CST)

Other Courts

European Court of Human Rights

Finland

France

Germany

Spain

UK

EFTA Court

Table of Statutes

Regulations

Directives

Decisions

Other sources

1

Introduction

THIS BOOK ADDRESSES the convergence effort concerning EU public liability law. While presenting the two constituent systems, it proposes that the two sets of EU public liability case-law form an operational whole. When these two sets are taken together, they form, it is submitted, a sufficient critical mass of case-law which forms a viable basis for its future development

This introductory chapter will set out briefly the essential development of the two EU public liability systems (section I), present the themes of the book (section II) and its structure (section III).

I. EU PUBLIC LIABILITY LAW AND ITS CONVERGENCE

A. Liability of the European Union

The non-contractual damages liability of the European Union stems from the original Treaty Establishing the European Economic Community (1957). The provision concerning non-contractual liability of the Community, which first appeared in Article 215(2) EEC, later became Article 288(2) EC. The current provision, following the entry into force of the Lisbon Treaty,[1] is now in Article 340(2) of the Treaty on the Functioning of the European Union ('TFEU').[2] Despite changes in the Article number, the substance of the current Article 340(2) TFEU is the same as in the original Treaty, with the exception that the Lisbon Treaty extended the coverage of liability from Community to Union as of 1 December 2009. The current treaty provision in Article 340(2) TFEU now obliges the Union, in the case of non-contractual liability, to make good any damage caused by its institutions in the performance of their duties, in accordance with the general principles common to the laws of the Member States. Exclusive competence to rule on liability has always been attributed to the Courts of the European Union in Luxembourg,

[1] The Lisbon Treaty which entered into force on 1 December 2009 brought about several changes which also affect damages liability (the European Community was fully replaced by the European Union, the Treaties were renamed and articles renumbered, and the Courts got new names). The changes resulting from that Treaty have been taken into account as appropriate.

[2] The 'Treaty establishing the European Community' (EC) was renamed by the Lisbon Treaty as the 'Treaty on the Functioning of the European Union' (TFEU), and the articles were renumbered. A correspondence table is attached to the final act.

namely the Court of Justice of the European Union ('ECJ'), the General Court of the European Union ('GC', ex-Court of First Instance 'CFI') and the Civil Service Tribunal ('CST)'.[3]

Since the creation of the Communities, the ECJ has worked out a restrictive set of liability criteria for the liability of the Community, starting from the *Schöppenstedt* case-law (ECJ 1971).[4] However, during the last two decades, the restrictive and much criticised liability criteria developed by the ECJ have been opened up and some almost astounding judgments on liability have been delivered. The development has been incremental, based on individual judgments. For example, *Mulder* (ECJ 1992 and 2000), a well-known series of damages cases relating to the Community milk quota regime, marked a turning point in the number of applicants.[5] The first *Schneider* case (CFI 2002), a competition law case relating to annulment of a Commission decision declaring a merger incompatible with the Treaty, was followed by a damages claim of more than 1663 million euros, largely accepted at first instance (CFI 2007), although reduced considerably on appeal (ECJ 2009).[6] Before its extension to the Union, the overarching coverage of the liability principle was confirmed to include all of the Community, including the actions of the European Ombudsman in *Lamberts* (CFI 2002; ECJ 2004).[7] Finally, in *FIAMM* (CFI 2003, ECJ 2006), the two Courts considered the issue of strict liability in EU public liability law.[8]

B. Liability of the Member States

The development of the damages liability criteria of the Member States for breaches of EU law has been even more remarkable. This form of liability was also the

[3] These names apply since the Treaty of Lisbon. In the text, preference is given to the new name, which will be used as a generic term, save when the text refers to a specific judgment handed down by a given court; then of course the name of the court as it then was is used, ie the CFI until 30 November 2009.

[4] ECJ Case 5/71 *Zuckerfabrik Schöppenstedt v Council* (damages claim dismissed) [1971] ECR 975 [11]. In this book, the number in square brackets after the page number refer to paragraph of the judgment. Moreover, references to the cases in the corpus text will include the abbreviation of the EU court and the year. They are made to help the reader, as the study contains frequent references to case-law and created over a period of time, and there have been recent important changes. It would appear somewhat awkward and maybe too demanding for the reader to recall that AG Roemer gave his opinion in *Vloeberghs* (ECJ 1962), whereas *Arizmendi* (GC 2009) is from a different court, another century – and post-*Bergaderm* (ECJ 2000).

[5] ECJ Joined Cases C-104/89 and C-37/90 *Mulder (No 1) and others v Council and Commission* (liability established) [1992] ECR I-3061, ECJ Joined Cases C-104/89 and C-37/90 *Mulder (No 2) and others v Council and Commission* (quantum) [2000] ECR I-203.

[6] CFI Case T-310/01 *Schneider Electric v Commission* (annulment action; annulled, no appeal) [2002] ECR II-4071; CFI Case T-351/03 *Schneider Electric v Commission* (damages action; liability established, appealed C-440/07 P) [2007] ECR II-2237; ECJ Case C-440/07 P *Commission v Schneider Electric (No 1 extent of liability)* (liability reduced on appeal to less than €2m) [2009] ECR I-6413 and ECJ Case C-440/07 P *Commission v Schneider (No 2 quantum)* (damages awarded €50000) [2010] ECR I-0000.

[7] CFI Case T-209/00 *Lamberts v Ombudsman* (dismissed, appealed C-234/02 P) [2002] ECR II-2203; ECJ Case C-234/02 P *Médiateur (Ombudsman) v Lamberts* (appeal dismissed) [2004] ECR I-2803.

[8] CFI Case T-69/00 *FIAMM and FIAMM Technologies v Council and Commission* (dismissed, appealed C-120/06 P) [2005] ECR II-5393, ECJ Joined Cases C-120/06 P and C-121/06 P *FIAMM and Fedon v Council and Commission* (appeal dismissed) [2008] ECR I-6513.

creation of the ECJ, but in contrast to the liability of the Union, the Treaty contained no express legal basis for such Member State liability. The existence of that principle was laid down in *Francovich* (ECJ 1991).[9] The Court based the liability of the Member States on the effectiveness of Community rules. Effectiveness would be impaired, and protection of rights which individuals derive directly from Community law weakened, if they would not be able to obtain redress from breaches by Member States. The court laid down three criteria which must be fulfilled for liability.

The jurisdiction to rule on Member State liability lies with the Member State courts, applying in part EU law, in part national damages law. The applicability of this principle in all sectors of Member State activity when applying EU law has been progressively and expressly confirmed in the case-law: first for legislative action in *Brasserie du Pêcheur* (ECJ 1996),[10] then for administrative action in *Norbrook* (ECJ 1996)[11] and *Hedley Lomas* (ECJ 1996)[12] and finally, and more controversially, for judicial action, in *Köbler* (ECJ 2003) and *Traghetti* (ECJ 2006).[13]

C. Convergence as an Approach to get 'Beyond *Brasserie* and *Bergaderm*'?

The convergence and mutual alignment of these two liability systems is the most recent issue. Albeit the three essential conditions for liability were the same in the two liability systems (breach of an EU law obligation, existence of actual damage, and a direct causal link between the two), the detailed criteria in the two systems originally developed in different directions. The criteria for Community liability for legislative acts – which in reality has been the main category of liability situations – were laid down by the ECJ in the restrictive criteria of the *Schöppenstedt* judgment (1971).[14] The criteria for Member State liability as established in the *Francovich* judgment (1991) were less strict.[15] However, some years later, in *Brasserie du Pêcheur* (1996), the ECJ ruled that the criteria for the two liability systems should not, 'in the absence of particular justification' be different in like circumstances. The Court of Justice affirmed in *Brasserie du Pêcheur* a statement of principle that protection of the rights which individuals derive from European Union law cannot vary depending on whether a national authority or a Union authority is responsible for the damage.[16] The first case concerning liability of the Union where this alignment of conditions was put into practice was *Bergaderm* (ECJ 2000).[17] It was here

[9] ECJ Joined Cases C-6/90 and C-9/90 *Francovich and Bonifaci* [1991] ECR I-5357 [33], [40].
[10] ECJ Joined Cases C-46/93 and C-48/93 *Brasserie du Pêcheur and Factortame* [1996] ECR I-1029.
[11] ECJ Case C-127/95 *Norbrook Laboratories* [1998] ECR I-1531.
[12] ECJ Case C-5/94 *Hedley Lomas* [1996] ECR I-2553.
[13] ECJ Case C-224/01 *Köbler* [2003] ECR I-10239 and ECJ Case C-173/03 *Traghetti del Mediterraneo* [2006] ECR I-5177.
[14] ECJ *Zuckerfabrik Schöppenstedt v Council* (n 4) [11].
[15] ECJ *Francovich and Bonifaci* (n 9).
[16] ECJ *Brasserie du Pêcheur and Factortame* (n 10) [42].
[17] ECJ Case C-352/98 P *Bergaderm and Goupil v Commission* (appeal dismissed) [2000] ECR I-5291.

that the *objective of convergence of the two liability systems*, which forms the focus of this study, was first established by the ECJ.

Convergence of the two public liability systems will be used here as an approach to enhance the understanding of their functioning. One of the fundamental purposes of European integration is to increase *coherence* in the European legal arena by reducing and flattening *divergences*, through various mechanisms in different areas. To present, in schematic form, how convergence works in general within European integration, this interactive process can be simplified so as to make the different relationships more clearly visible. Figure 1.1 depicts EU law as the upper level, and Member State law as the lower level.

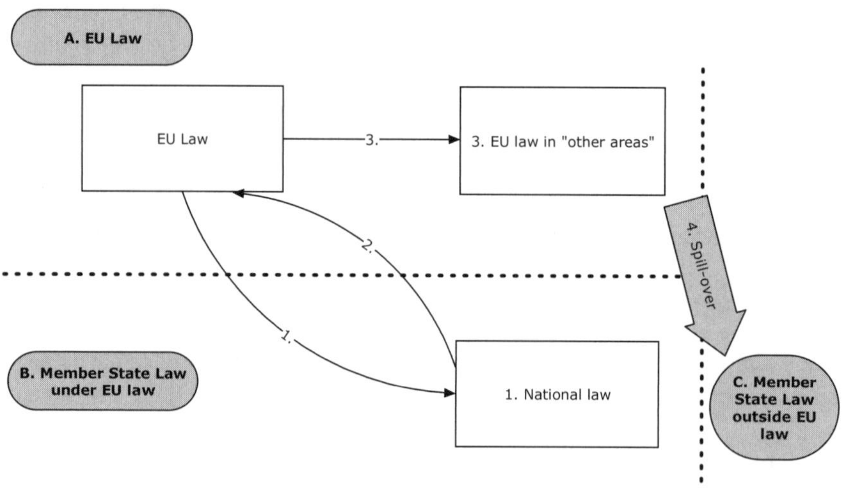

Figure 1.1 Basic Relationship Between EU Law and National Law

The basic interactions can be described through the following phases. The (1) first phase relates to the general effects of EU law in Member States: direct effect, primacy and interpretation in conformity. The (2) second phase, or relationship, is thus the 'refined feedback' effect on EU law. This could result for example from difficulties which become apparent in implementing a directive. When a directive is amended on the basis of a new Commission proposal, a Member State can suggest amendments to the Commission proposal based on its national law/problems, which, when adopted, become EU law. Further, a (3) third relationship is the convergence between various areas within the different sectors of EU law.

An assessment of convergence and divergence would necessarily have to be completed by an assessment of what happens at national level as a whole. Apparently this analysis should consist of two elements: what has taken place in a Member State in implementing this one specific remedy, and what effects that has had beyond the specific area in question (4), in terms of convergence spill-over.

The construction presented above can be transposed to the law concerning public liability in damages. Mutual interaction between national public liability law and two public liability systems created at EU level could be schematised as follows.

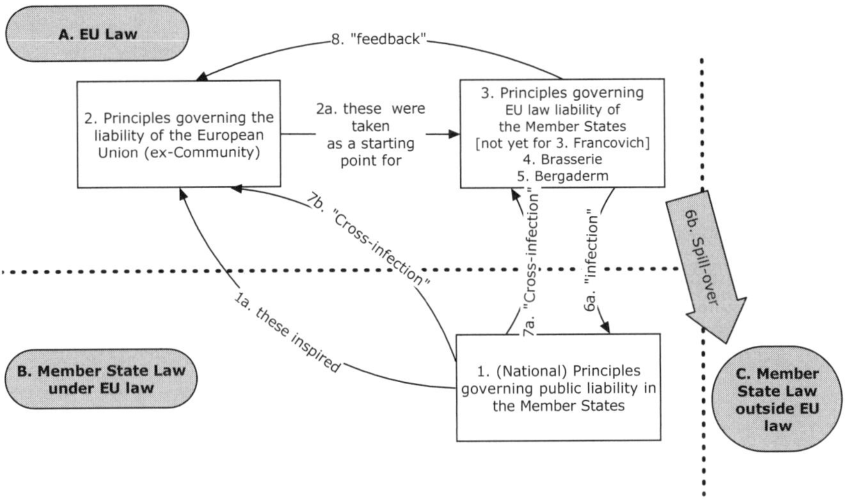

Figure 1.2 Cross-infection (Cross-fertilisation) of the Public Liability Law of the Member States and that of the European Union

Although the picture becomes slightly more complicated, three essential relationships should be noted, namely the relationship between EU law and national law, the mutual relationships between the two liability systems within EU law, and the spill-over effect on Member State law outside the EU law field.

In the picture, the starting point is (1) national principles governing public liability in damages in Member States. These inspired the (2) principles governing the liability of the Community (now: Union), the famous *Schöppenstedt/Adams* conditions. In turn, these principles influenced the formulation of conditions for Member State liability for breaches of EU law, even if not yet in (3) *Francovich*, but already in (4) *Brasserie du Pêcheur* and (5) *Bergaderm*. Oddly enough, in the current situation EU liability principles (6a) 'infect' national systems, which again provide (7a) 'cross-infection' to EU level, both to Member State liability conditions, as well as (7b) conditions governing Union liability. What is more, the 'infection' (6a) and the 'cross-infection' (7a) have a spill-over effect on national law (6b), going beyond the field of application of EU law.

One of the characteristics of public liability in damages in EU law is that all convergence and approximation of law takes place *without the intervention of the EU legislator*. In view of the democratic legitimacy or democratic deficit of the European Union, the role of democratic processes and public participation in policy-making is important. Here, however, EU level policy is formulated by the EU courts in Luxembourg without intervention by the Union legislator. In this respect it is clearly different from legislation-driven areas, such as the internal market, where the essential part of legal norms is enacted by the EU legislator, nowadays increasingly with the participation of the European Parliament. For public liability law in the EU, no external institution exists which can encourage or inhibit, promote or prevent, development of the law. This is carried out solely by the EU courts.

II. RESEARCH ISSUES

A. The Aim and the Research Questions

The aim of this study is to present the two public liability systems established in EU law from the standpoint of their parallel assessment. In view of that, the study purports to discuss and find answers to the three following research questions:

> *Systematisation.* The first research question is to make visible and present the law at the current state of development of the two public liability systems in EU law, including systematising case-law (the law) and through applying some specific tools and approaches to better grasp future issues.
>
> *Parallel assessment.* The second question is to assess the similarities and differences between the two systems, discuss the roles of the EU courts and the procedural differences. An attempt should also be made to find out how potential new issues in each system could be solved by learning from the 'other' system. This would also include highlighting problems in application of the criteria and practical application of the criteria ('law in action'), such as an overview of successful cases, success rate of damages cases, observations on applicants and nature of the cases.
>
> *Contextualisation.* Thirdly, the question is to place public liability for breaches of EU law in context, beyond *Bergaderm* and to show the connections with convergent developments in general, including the more general convergence based on European Union law and others, and the role of this area of law in the context of the constitutionalisation of the European Union.

The choice of subject matter of the study, and the choice of approach, builds upon earlier research I have done in respect of public liability in EU law.[18]

B. Added Value: is it Still Worth a Try to Dig into *Francovich*, and EU liability?

Studies concerning various aspects of EU public liability law would seem to be numerous, in fact all too numerous to be cited or listed in full.[19] By taking a more

[18] Although I have been working with Member State liability for some time, it was the convergence aspect which re-ignited my interest in this area. My initial interest in public liability in damages started with Member State liability in the mid-1990s. The research done at that time concentrated on Member State liability and one of the key purposes was to systematise Member State liability case-law, see P Aalto, *Jäsenvaltion vahingonkorvausvastuu EY-oikeudessa [Damages Liability of the Member States in EC Law]* (Helsinki, Kauppakaari, 1999); P Aalto, 'Twelve Years of Francovich in the European Court of Justice: A survey of the Case-law on the Interpretation of the Three Conditions of Liability' in S Moreira de Sousa and W Heusel (eds), *Enforcing Community Law from Francovich to Köbler: Twelve Years of the State Liability Principle* (Cologne, Bundesanzeiger, 2004) and P Aalto, 'Valtion korvausvastuu yksilölle unionin oikeuden rikkomisesta [State Liability for Individuals for Breaches of Union Law]' in H Kaila and E Pirjatanniemi et al (eds), *Yksilön oikeusasema Euroopan unionissa – Individens rättsställning inom Europeiska Unionen: Juhlakirja Allan Rosas – Festskrift Allan Rosas* (Turku/Åbo, 2008).

[19] In this respect, the visionary works made before the two systems even existed are very interesting, see eg, P Pescatore, 'Responsabilité des États membres en cas de manquement aux règles communautaires'

narrow starting point, and limiting the assessment to some of the published doctoral dissertations in this field (without any attempt at being exhaustive, or even representative), the following groups emerge.[20]

Liability of the European Community (now: Union) has given rise to the first group of dissertations, which include the works of Lysén (1976), Fines (1990), Czaja (1996), Wakefield (2002) and Patrão (2008).[21]

The liability of Member States has given rise to the second group which consists of works treating Member State liability in general terms. Such works, focusing on *Francovich* and preceding *Brasserie du Pêcheur*, include for example dissertations by Albers (1995), Cornils (1995), Henrichs (1995), Seltenreich (1997) and Zenner (1995).[22] For the post-Brasserie period, there are dissertations by Hidien (1999), Beljin (2000), Schoißwohl (2002), Säuberlich (2005) and Nacimiento (2006).[23]

Certain authors have concentrated on a specific sector: Fetzer (1994) and Sencovic (2000) analysed liability of the national legislator,[24] while Bertelman (2005), Wollbrandt (2005) and Scherr (2009) examined judicial liability.[25]

(1972) (Parta Quarta) *Il Foro Padano* 9–24 and D Simon and A Barav, 'La responsabilité de l'administration nationale en cas de violation du droit communautaire' (1987) *Revue du Marché Commun et de l'Union Européenne* 165–74.

[20] This presentation attempts to cover some of the doctoral dissertations published in English, French, German and Swedish regarding either component of EU damages liability.

[21] The year in parenthesis refers to the publication year, which is in many cases later than the year the work was actually defended. G Lysén, *The Non-Contractual and Contractual Liability of the European Economic Communities* (Uppsala, 1976); F Fines, *Étude de la responsabilité extracontractuelle de la Communauté économique européenne* (Paris, LGDJ, 1990); A Czaja, *Die Außervertragliche Haftung der EG für ihre Organe* (Baden Baden, Nomos, 1996) and J Wakefield, *Judicial Protection through the Use of Article 288(2) EC* (The Hague, Kluwer Law International, 2002) and A Patrão, *Responsabilidade Extracontratual da Comunidade Europeia* (Coimbra, Almedina, 2008).

[22] C Albers, *Die Haftung der Bundesrepublik Deutschland für die Nichtumsetzung von EG-Richtlinien* (Baden-Baden, Nomos, 1995); M Cornils, *Der gemeinschaftsrechtliche Staatshaftungsanspruch. Rechtsnatur und Legitimität eines richterrechtlichen Haftunginstituts* (Baden-Baden, Nomos, 1995); C Henrichs, *Haftung der EG-Mitgliedstaaten für Verletzung von Gemeinschaftsrecht* (Baden-Baden, Nomos, 1995); S Seltenreich, *Die Francovich-Rechtsprechung des EuGH und ihre Auswirkungen auf das deutsche Staatshaftungsrecht: ein Rückblick fünf Jahre nach dem Ergehen des Francovich-Urteils* (Constance, Hartung-Gorre, 1997) and M Zenner, *Die Haftung der EG-Mitgliedstaaten für die Anwendung europarechtswidriger Rechtsnormen* (Munich, V. Florenz, 1995).

[23] JW Hidien, *Die Gemeinschaftsrechtliche Staatshaftung der EU-Mitgliedstaaten* (Baden-Baden, Nomos, 1999); S Beljin, *Staatshaftung im Europarecht. Konturen des Haftungsinstituts, Mitgliedstaaliche Pflichen und subjektive Gemeinschaftsrechte, Innerstaatliche Durchführung* (Cologne, Carl Heymanns Verlag KG, 2000); B Schoißwohl, *Staatshaftung wegen Gemeinschaftsrechtsverletzung: Anspruchsgrundlage und materielle Voraussetzungen (f. Österreich)* (Vienna, Springer, 2002); U Säuberlich, *Die außervertragliche Haftung im Gemeinschaftsrecht: Eine Untersuchung der Mehrpersonenverhältnisse*, 2005) and P Nacimiento, *Gemeinschaftsrechtliche und nationale Staatshaftung in Deutschland, Italien und Frankreich* (Baden-Baden, Nomos, 2006).

[24] R Fetzer, *Die Haftung des Staates für legislatives Unrecht: zugleich ein Beitrag zum Staatshaftungsrecht der Europäischen Gemeinschaften, der EG-Mitgliedstaaten, der Schweiz und Österreichs* (Berlin, Duncker & Humblot, 1994) and P Senkovic, *L'évolution de la responsabilité de l'État législateur sous l'influence du droit communautaire* (Brussels, Bruylant, 2000).

[25] H Bertelmann, *Die Europäisierung des Staatshaftungsrechts* (Frankfurt, Lang, 2005); J Wollbrandt, *Gemeinschaftshaftung für judikatives Unrecht* (Osnabrück, dissertation.de, 2005) and KM Scherr, *The Principle of State Liability for Judicial Breaches. The case Gerhard Köbler v. Austria under European Community Law and from a comparative national law perspective* (Florence, European University Institute, 2008).

Some thematic studies on Member State liability are closely connected with recent events: Gratias (1999), Böhme (2009) and Emsinghoff (2009) examined state liability for bank supervision.[26]

One recurring theme has been the liability of the European Union for legal action, in particular in the context of the rules regarding the World Trade Organisation (WTO). This was examined eg by Görgens (2005), Held (2006), Höher (2006), Steinbach (2009) and Thies (2009).[27]

The obvious question that any study relating to Member State liability faces is what added value, if any, can it offer? It is well-known that for Member State liability, *Francovich* and *Brasserie du Pêcheur/Factortame* have for some time been the two judgments which have given rise to a considerable number of books, articles and case comments.[28] Even if liability of the Community/Union has been more in the margins of research interest for some time, comments on specific questions at least have been abundant. Despite the large number of comments, it is submitted that this study could bring some new elements and approaches to the discussion, for the following reasons.

The first reason is that in the post-*Bergaderm* commentaries, rather surprisingly, the convergence aspect of the two systems does not seem to be sufficiently addressed. In fact, there does not appear to be any overarching study from the convergence point of view. One explanation for this can be that, speaking from experience, dwelling on the case-law of the two systems is rather a laborious task. It is easier to concentrate on just one system.

The second reason justifying the subject matter is that considerable new case-law is available under the two systems, which would benefit from an attempt at systematisation.

The third justification is that existing systematic assessments of one or both systems are inevitably becoming outdated, in particular due to *Bergaderm*. So far, there seems to be no up-to-date work covering the convergence aspect of the two liability systems.[29]

[26] M Gratias, *Staatshaftung für fehlerhafte Banken- und Versicherungsaufsicht im Europäischen Binnenmarkt* (Baden-Baden, Nomos, 1999); M Böhme, *Staatshaftung für fehlerhafte Bankenaufsicht nach deutschem und europäischem Recht* (Baden-Baden, Nomos, 2009) and JF Emsinghoff, *Entschädigung für Eigentumseingriffe infolge rechtmäßiger Rechtsetzungsakte der Europäischen Gemeinschaft* (Baden-Baden, Nomos, 2009).

[27] S Görgens, *Die außervertragliche Haftung der Europäischen Gemeinschaft für Verletzungen des WTO-Rechts durch ihre Organe. Die Haftung bei Nichtumsetzung von Entscheidungen des Streitbeilegungsgremiums der WTO* (Berlin, Duncker & Humblot, 2005); S Held, *Die Haftung der EG für die Verletzung von WTO-Recht* (Tübingen, Mohr Siebeck, 2006); K Höher, *Die Haftung der Europäischen Gemeinschaft für Verstöße gegen das WTO-Recht: eine Untersuchung am Beispiel des WTO-Bananenstreitverfahrens* (Baden-Baden, Nomos, 2006); A Steinbach, *Die Haftung der EG und ihrer Mitgliedsstaaten für WTO-Rechtsverletzungen aus rechtswissenschaftlicher und ökonomischer Perspektive* (Berlin, Duncker & Humblot, 2009) and A Thies, *The Liability of the European Community for Conduct in the Context of International Trade Disputes* (Munich, 2009).

[28] See eg, the case notes listed on the database 'Notes aux arrets de la Cour', available on the Court's website.

[29] See eg, T Heukels and A McDonnell (eds), *The Action for Damages in Community Law* (The Hague, Kluwer Law International, 1997) or a more recent book discussing the two systems (but not from the convergence aspect) A Biondi and P Farley, *The Right to Damages in European Law* (Alphen aan der Rijn, Kluwer Law International, 2009).

Despite the quantity, parallel studies on the two systems are very rare, and the good ones are, at best, somewhat ageing, or even outdated.[30]

In addition to the systemic aspect relating to convergence, several reasons explain why public liability for breaches of EU law in general as such does well merit a study.

In the first place, the rule of law consists of several elements and also includes the damages liability of public authorities. Public damages liability is one aspect of the web of remedies available to a person whose EU law rights have been infringed. The mere existence of this remedy is one of the elements that contribute to the unique expression of a system of rule of law that the European Union represents through the constitutionalisation process.[31]

Secondly, public liability is an important remedy for many applicants: it is at the same time a remedy of last resort after all other remedies have been exhausted and a remedy in which applicants are called upon to quantify in monetary terms the losses claimed in a more or less substantiated manner and sometimes in mind-boggling figures.[32] It is also an important remedy: it is often invoked and it has also led to regular litigation before the EU courts.

Thirdly, apart from the question of 'alignment' of the two EU public liability systems and the fact there has been considerable case-law on both of them at EU level, public liability is also an area that has been rapidly developing lately in national legal systems.[33] Public liability for breaches of EU law has an inextricable link with Member State public liability systems (as to its origins, as to the application of Member State liability which takes place in the Member State) and it has in all likelihood had an effect on those systems and led to their adjustment.

Fourthly, this study could also function as a building block in an area which is expressly left out of the scope of this study. That is, the presentation and findings of this study could be useful when preparing the accession of the European Union to the European Convention of Human Rights. This is a very complex issue which involves various delicate legal and institutional questions, but also some pragmatic issues, such as those relating to the interplay of two (or more) compensation systems based on the treaties.

Finally, a number of other reasons could be used to justify this subject matter. In fact, changes in case-law and treaty structure call for an up-to-date analysis of the 'current state of state liability'.[34] Moreover, public liability can also be analysed as an example of how constitutionalisation of the Union works in practice.

[30] P Aubin, *Die Haftung der Europäischen Wirtschaftsgemeinschaft und ihrer Mitgliedstaaten bei gemeinschaftsrechtswidrigen nationalen Verwaltungsakten* (Baden-Baden, Nomos, 1982).

[31] See below ch 3, s I.

[32] eg, in CFI Case T-212/03 *MyTravel v Commission* (damages action dismissed, no appeal) [2008] ECR II-1967, the original damages claim was £518 m. In CFI Case *Schneider Electric v Commission* ECR, it was some €1663 m.

[33] See ch 3, s II below.

[34] To use an expression from C Harlow, 'The Current State of State Liability' (2002) (4) *Rivista trimestrale di diritto pubblico* 915–33.

III. STRUCTURE AND TERMINOLOGY

A. Structure

In order to examine the three issues set out in section II.A above, this study has been organised in the following way. First, general issues of the two liability systems are analysed through a common structure, thus highlighting the similarities and inherent differences. Second, the core convergence in EU public liability law is examined through two parameters. These correspond to the two harmonised conditions laid down for EU public liability in both liability systems, namely (1) the granting of rights to individuals and (2) sufficiently serious breach.[35] The structure of the study is presented in Figure 1.3 in summary form.

Ch 1 - Introduction
Ch 2 - Parameters of convergence *... s IV Structural aspects - s V Rights - s VI Breach ...*
Ch 3 - Contexts of convergence
Ch 4 - Alignment of the two systems
Ch 5 - Liability of the European Union *s I Structural aspects - s II Rights - s III Breach ...*
Ch 6 - Liability of the Member States *s I Structural aspects - s II Rights - s III Breach ...*
Ch 7 - Conclusions on convergence *s I Structural aspects - s II Rights - s III Breach ...*

Figure 1.3 Structure of the Research

After the introductory chapter one, chapter two examines the parameters of 'convergence' and its function in this study. It also sets out the methodological issues, and the general framework for the subsequent presentation and assessment of the convergence parameters of the two liability systems. In other words, the methodological issues presented in this chapter are applied when the liability law of the European Union is presented in chapter five, and when the liability law concerning the Member States is presented in chapter six. Most importantly, assessment of convergence in concluding chapter seven follows the structure presented in the methodological sections.

Chapter three sets out the world surrounding EU law public liability, ie its operational context. It also examines the constitutionalisation of EU law and its relation

[35] ECJ *Brasserie du Pêcheur and Factortame* (n 10).

to EU law on public damages liability. Chapter four presents and analyses the process as a result of which convergence was attained. Chapters five and six, respectively, set out and assess the law relating to liability of the European Union and to liability of the Member States, following the structures and parameters laid down in the methodological sections.

Chapter seven presents the results, the conclusions on convergence, by regrouping the assessment criteria of the two systems in a vertical manner (one section on rights in EU and Member State liability, the other on breach in EU and Member State liability, and so on).

The basic structural approach chosen here is to examine the two key criteria of damages liability in both liability systems. The two elements chosen are the essential criteria for any damages liability. Therefore, it could be expected that most convergence – if any – should have been reached on these essential elements. In addition, the courts proceed in their analysis so that it is most often on the basis of these three criteria that liability is rejected. It is thus likely that one of these criteria is assessed or addressed in some way in most case-law. They are also the criteria on which there appears to be most case-law, both for EU liability and for Member State liability, emanating both from the ECJ and the CFI.

Causation, the third element, is not treated in this study. It is somewhat different in nature. In the first place, it is the only element on which the ECJ has said that there is no convergence, as Member State liability causation (or 'direct causation') is defined in national law. Thus there is very little ECJ case-law on causation concerning the Member States. Moreover, causation in both systems is also a highly fact-intensive criterion.[36]

[36] On causation, see eg, F Smith and L Woods, 'Causation in *Francovich*: The Neglected Problem' (1997) *ICLQ* 925–41, AG Toth, 'The Concepts of Damage and Causality as Elements of Non-Contractual Liability' in T Heukels and A McDonnell (eds), *The Action for Damages in Community Law* (The Hague, Kluwer Law International, 1997). For case-law see eg, CFI Case T-138/03 *E.R. et al v Council and Commission* (no causal link, appealed C-100/07 P) [2006] ECR II-4923, [99]–[140], ECJ Case C-100/07 P *E.R. et al v Council and Commission* (appeal dismissed) [2007] ECR I-136*, Summ.pub. (order of 4 October 2007); ECJ *Commission v Schneider Electric (No 1 extent of liability)* (n 6), [190]–[205], [221] and [222]; GC Case T-440/03, T-121/04, T-171/04, T-208/04, T-365/04 and T-484/04 *Arizmendi and others v Council and Commission* (damages claim dismissed, no appeal) [2009] ECR II-4883 [85]–[94]; GC Joined Cases T-252/07, T-271/07 and T-272/07 *Sungro v Council and Commission* (damages claim dismissed, no appeal) [2010] ECR II-55 and GC Case T-452/05 *BST v Commission* (damages claim dismissed, no appeal) [2010] ECR II-0000 (judgment of 28 April 2010). Of particular interest are also contributions where causation is analysed beyond the two public law liability systems assessed in this book, ie by including an 'EU tort law aspect' (causation in EU damages liability directives) and national systems; see on this aspect eg IC Durant, 'Causation' in H Koziol and R Schulze (eds), *Tort Law of the European Community* (Vienna, SpringerWienNewYork, 2008); W van Gerven and J Lever et al, *Cases, Materials and Text on National, Supranational and International Tort Law* (Oxford, Hart Publishing, 2000) 395–466 and W Wurmnest, *Grundzüge eines europäischen Haftungsrechts: eine rechtsvergleichende Untersuchung des Gemeinschaftsrechts* (Tübingen, Mohr Siebeck, 2003), 159–91.

B. Some Terminological Points and Limitations

i. 'Public Liability in EU Law'

In this study, 'public liability in EU law' is used as a joint term referring to the two EU law-based systems of non-contractual liability, namely that of the European Union and that of the Member States of the European Union, for breaches of European Union law. The choice of term was not straightforward and its two constituent parts, 'public authorities' and 'liability' should be explained.

'Public [authorities]', instead of 'government', 'crown' or 'state'. The subject matter of this study covers both the public liability in damages of the European Union for breaches of EU law, and the damages liability of the Member States of the European Union for breach of EU law. This coverage has posed some problems as to finding an appropriate term to describe the scope of the work. The joint term '*public authorities*' seems appropriate to cover them both. Even if the terms 'governmental liability'[37] or 'state liability'[38] could well be used to describe the liability situation of the Member States, the word 'crown'[39] would clearly be inappropriate for that purpose. The European Union can be called many things, but to refer to it as government, state, or even crown, would be inaccurate and misleading.

Starting from the Member State level, the Court has been called on to define what is covered by the concept of 'state' in an EU context. According to the constant case-law of the Court the obligations arising from Community directives are binding, inter alia, on bodies or entities subject to the authority or control of a public authority or the state.[40]

This is of course a very clear and workable EU level concept. It can easily be used at Member State level, and reference can be made to state liability, both under national and EU law.[41] The only problem is that the state as a legal entity does not exist everywhere. Therefore in some states or third countries the corresponding

[37] *cf* P Schuck, *Suing Government* (New Haven, Yale University Press, 1983) or J Bell and AW Bradley (eds), *Governmental Liability: A Comparative Study* (London, The United Kingdom National Committee of Comparative Law, 1991).

[38] *cf* D Fairgrieve, *State Liability in Tort. A Comparative Law Study* (Oxford, Oxford University Press, 2003) and C Harlow, *State Liability: Tort Law and Beyond* (Oxford, Oxford University Press, 2004).

[39] *cf* PW Hogg and PJ Monahan, *Liability of the Crown*, 3rd edn (Toronto, Carswell Thomson Professional Publishing, 2000).

[40] ECJ Case C-6/05 *Medipac – Kazantzidis* [2007] ECR I-4557 [43]; ECJ Case 152/84 *Marshall v Southampton and South-West Hampshire Area Health Authority* [1986] ECR 723 [49]; ECJ Case 103/88 *Fratelli Costanzo v Comune di Milano* [1989] ECR 1839 [30] and [31]; ECJ Case C-188/89 *Foster and others v British Gas* [1990] ECR I-3313 [18]; ECJ Case C-297/03 *Sozialhilfeverband Rohrbach* [2005] ECR I-4305 [27]. See also V Kvjatkovski, 'What is an 'Emanation of the State'? An Educated Guess' (1997) *European Public Law* 329–38.

[41] *cf* Fairgrieve, *State Liability in Tort. A Comparative Law Study* (n 38); Harlow, *State Liability: Tort Law and Beyond* (n 38); F Ossenbühl, *Staatshaftungsrecht. 5., neu bearbeitete und erweiterte Auflage* (Munich, Beck, 1998); Senkovic, *L'évolution de la responsabilité de l'État législateur sous l'influence du droit communautaire* (n 24) – State responsibility on the other hand refers to liability under public international law, *cf* J Crawford, *The International Law Commission's Articles on State Responsibility. Introduction, Text and Commentaries* (Cambridge, 2002).

liability is that of 'the crown'[42] or that of 'the government'.[43] A further complication was that this work also covers the liability of the European Union. Even if one of the above terms could be used with some force as a generic descriptor of the state, it would still not cover the European Union. Therefore 'public authorities' is used as the generic term. This concept seems to be fairly neutral and widely in use.[44] Accordingly, for liability, reference is be made to '*public liability*'.

'Liability', instead of 'tort' or 'non-contractual liability in damages'. As to the second part of the term: for the liability of the European Union, the TFEU mentions 'non-contractual liability in damages', while another possibility is 'tort'. The doctrine has used both terms.[45] Even if 'tort' is handy and short, it is not fully accurate.[46] Thus preference has been given to 'liability'.

In all, the term '*public liability in EU law*' has been chosen to describe the subject matter of the study, with synonyms such as 'EU law public liability', 'EU public liability'. This term refers to EU law and, it contains the public elements and the notion of liability. It is thus distinguished from public liability in damages under national public liability systems in Member States, and from 'private' tort law liability, either under EU or national systems. It also contains the subliminal distinction between the rights and remedies approaches. It puts forward the liability aspect: public authorities are to bear the consequences of their action. It is not so much about what 'I' can do, or what 'I' have the right to, but rather about a duty owed to individuals and economic operators by public authorities.

Changes following from the entry into force of the Lisbon Treaty on 1 December 2009 have been taken into account.[47] As the European Community ceased to exist and was replaced by the European Union, it has been necessary to define a somewhat consistent approach to the distinction 'Community'/'Union'. 'Liability of the European Union' is used as a generic term, even if in formal terms a distinction

[42] Hogg and Monahan, *Liability of the Crown* (n 39).

[43] Bell and Bradley (eds), *Governmental Liability: A Comparative Study* (n 37); For United States, see Schuck, *Suing Government* (n 37).

[44] eg D Fairgrieve and M Andenas et al (eds), *Tort Liability of Public Authorities in Comparative Perspective* (London, BIICL, 2002) and C Booth QC and D Squires, *The Negligence Liability of Public Authorities* (Oxford, Oxford University Press, 2006).

[45] See eg, G Lysén, *The Non-Contractual and Contractual Liability of the European Economic Communities* (n 21), C Van Dam, *European Tort Law* (Oxford, Oxford University Press, 2006) or H Koziol and R Schulze (eds), *Tort Law of the European Community* (Vienna, SpringerWienNewYork, 2008).

[46] The problems of choosing between 'tort' and 'non-contractual liability' can be highlighted by the choices of Professor Christian von Bar. His comprehensive study on damages liability was about 'torts' (C von Bar, *The Common European Law of Torts. Volume One* (Oxford, Clarendon, 1998), C von Bar, *The Common European Law of Torts. Volume Two* (Oxford, Clarendon, 2000)). Some 10 years later he produced a voluminous study on the same area, now about 'non-contractual liability' (C von Bar (ed), *Principles of European Law: Non-Contractual Liability Arising out of Damage Caused to Another: v. 7 (European Civil Code Series)* (Oxford, Oxford University Press, 2009)). In the latter he explained the change of term as follows (p xiii): 'The title of this volume "Non-contractual liability arising out of damage caused to another" was suggested by Professor Eric Clive, Edinburgh. We have gratefully taken it up. The expression "tort law" is too tied to the Common Law tradition, while "law of delict" is too closely allied to the latin tradition and, moreover, no longer entirely correct, semantically considered, in view of the widespread forms of liability without intention or negligence'.

[47] For a concise analysis of the amendments, see M Dougan, 'The Treaty of Lisbon 2007: winning minds, not hearts' (2008) *Common Market Law Review* 617–703.

should be made for the liability of the European Community (up to 30 November 2009).[48] Equally, reference is made to EU law, together with other 'union'-based derivatives ('union law rights', 'acquis of the Union', 'Union law').[49] For specific facts or legal situations relating to the time before entry into force of the Lisbon Treaty, reference is made to the 'Community'. References to Treaty Articles are given to the Articles as applied at the time of the facts of the case (EEC/EC Treaty, TFEU), with additional reference to current numbering of the TFEU, where appropriate.

ii. Limitations

As to the *liability of the European Union*, the focus is on its non-contractual liability, and issues of *contractual* liability, foreseen now in Article 340(1) TFEU, are not addressed.[50] Moreover, for Union liability, the emphasis is on its liability towards the 'outside'. There is no systematic discussion of *staff cases* and damages issues in that context. However, there are references to staff cases when they appear appropriate to illustrate certain developments.[51]

The Community, whenever used, means the *European Community*. Specific liability issues of the two other Treaties, namely liability under the European Coal and Steel Community Treaty (*ECSC*), which came to an end in 2002, and the *Euratom* Treaty, which continues to exist separately even after the entry into force of the Lisbon Treaty, are not discussed.[52]

[48] Of course, to be fully precise, one should speak of the liability of the European Economic Community, when discussing the liability before the entry into force of the Treaty of Maastricht.

[49] Even if, once again, a distinction could timewise be made between the Community and Union based expressions, such as *acquis communautaire*.

[50] For contractual liability, see eg, T Heukels, 'The Contractual Liability of the European Community Revisited', in T Heukels and A McDonnell (eds), *The Action for Damages in Community Law* (The Hague, Kluwer Law International, 1997).

[51] For the specificities of the staff rules, see eg, S Dalle-Crode, *Le fonctionnaire communautaire: droits, obligations et régime disciplinaire* (Brussels, Bruylant, 2008).

[52] On ECSC liability see eg, G Bebr, 'The Non-contractual Liability of the European Coal and Steel Community' in T Heukels and A McDonnell (eds), *The Action for Damages in Community Law* (The Hague, Kluwer Law International, 1997) and for Euratom see eg, L Hancher, 'Issues of Non-Contractual Liability under the EAEC Treaty' in T Heukels and A McDonnell (eds), *The Action for Damages in Community Law* (The Hague, Kluwer Law International, 1997).

2

Parameters of Convergence

THIS CHAPTER SETS out the key parameters for the purposes of analysing convergence. We examine first the concept of convergence at a more strategic level by analysing the various characterisations, by defining four types of convergence and by taking up the dichotomy 'convergence/divergence' (section I). After that the core methodological issues are explained (section II). As the EU public liability is based on case-law, certain questions in particular for the assessment and qualification of the case-law are set out (section III).

The essential element of this chapter is the definition of a table on parameters for comparing the two systems (section IV) and setting out the underlying thinking for the two converging that will be assessed in the following chapters, namely granting of rights to individuals (section V) and sufficient serious breach of EU law and its intriguing relation to 'fault' (section VI).

I. CONVERGENCE AND DIVERGENCE IN EUROPEAN PUBLIC LIABILITY LAW

A. Characterising 'Convergence' and Adjacent Concepts

The discussion in this study is mainly limited to convergence and divergence in the EU legal system between the Member State level and EU level liability; these two-way developments are of course present in other areas, too.[1] The purpose of this section is to give a more general context for convergence, and convergence in public liability law is specifically discussed in the following chapters.

To start with, it appears useful to explore initially what certain authors mean by convergence. For Lyons, it 'refers to an ongoing process, within the realm of national and supranational (public) law of the EU, whereby those laws are mutually influenced and which has resulted in shared or common principles'.[2]

[1] Another good example would be the effects of the European Convention of Human Rights.

[2] C Lyons, 'Perspectives on Convergence Within the Theatre of European Integration' in P Beaumont and C Lyons et al (eds), *Convergence and Divergence in European Public Law* (Oxford, Hart Publishing, 2002) 81.

Another definition is provided by Harlow: for her, convergence simply denotes 'the coming together of legal systems through mutual interest and common development'.[3]

Van Gerven gives an even wider definition of convergence in the following terms:[4]

> Convergence, by contrast, is here understood as a generic term comprising two components, that is, not only harmonisation through an institutionalised (legislative or judicial) process but also the growing together of rules through voluntary or even spontaneous action – and therefore not necessarily occurring because of a legal obligation but for reasons of consistency, natural justice, or simply convenience.

All of these characterisations are useful here. In particular, the definition proposed by van Gerven successfully encapsulates the two main types of convergence, namely 'institutionalised' convergence and 'growing together' convergence. When dealing with developments in public liability for breaches of EU law, the main driver is the ECJ; this process could thus be characterised as institutionalised convergence. When looking at harmonious developments in national law public liability law outside the EU law context, it is rather the second type of convergence, the 'growing together' convergence between various national legal systems, that happens through voluntary or spontaneous action – it does not occur as a result of a legal obligation but 'for reasons of consistency, natural justice, or simply convenience'.

What is important in Harlow's definition is the idea that 'mutual interest and common development' bring together the legal criteria applicable in various areas of a legal system. Furthermore, when Lyons notes that convergence is an ongoing process where the national and supranational public law of the EU mutually influence each other and results 'in shared or common principles', she gets very close to the essence of convergence in public liability law in EU law. Therefore, her definition is kept in mind when referring to 'convergence' in this study.

Harlow further distinguishes two dimensions: by '*vertical convergence*' she refers to a gradual process of harmonisation of national legal principles and procedure brought about by the case-law of the ECJ. This brings to light another aspect, namely '*horizontal divergence*', which is used to describe the variance between the legal principles and procedures of the Member States in relation to the application of EU law.[5]

[3] C Harlow, 'Voices of Difference in a Plural Community' in P Beaumont and C Lyons et al (eds), *Convergence and Divergence in European Public Law* (Oxford, Hart Publishing, 2002) 202. Wakefield refers to '*harmonising responsibility*', see J Wakefield, *Judicial Protection through the Use of Article 288(2) EC* (The Hague, Kluwer Law International, 2002) 272ff.

[4] W van Gerven, 'Two Twin Principles of EU Law: Democracy and Accountability, Consistency and Convergence' in U Bernitz and J Nergelius et al (eds), *General principles of EC law in a process of development: reports from a conference in Stockholm, 23–24 March 2007, organised by the Swedish Network for European Legal Studies* (Alphen aan den Rijn, Kluwer Law International, 2008) 44. In a later text, he uses 'coherence' seemingly in a more narrow sense, calling the first component above approximation and limiting convergence only to the second component above. *cf* W van Gerven, 'Judicial Convergence of Laws and Minds in European Tort law and Related Matters' in A Colombi Ciacchi and C Godt et al (eds), *Haftungsrecht im dritten Millenium – Liability in the Third Millenium: Liber Amicorum Gert Brüggemeier* (Baden-Baden, Nomos, 2009) 29.

[5] C Harlow, 'Voices of Difference in a Plural Community' (n 3) 202.

Overall, it would seem that '*convergence*' best describes developments in public liability in damages. The term '*alignment*' can be used as a synonym for 'convergence'.[6] Some authors have also used terms such as '*cross-fertilisation*' or '*legal transplants*'[7], or '*mutual permeation*'[8] of EU and national rules, or even '*europeanisation*'.[9] Yet '*harmonisation*' is best reserved for 'a conscious and negotiated process of harmonisation, culminating in a rulemaking procedure or a legislative act'.[10]

'*Coherence*', in contrast, would seem to denote a somewhat different situation. Coherence and related concepts have been used widely in legal theory, and with different meanings.[11] Tuori discusses why coherence should be required of the law and notes that this question can be approached from several angles. He underlines the role of legal science in creating, or in fact producing, coherence. The possibilities of coherence have been questioned, from the point of view of single sectors of law, or from the fact that the current understanding of law is characterised by polycentrism of sources of law and by pluralism of legal orders.[12]

By way of conclusion, Prechal makes the connection between the two concepts: 'European legal order, just like any other legal order . . . requires a special kind of *coherence*, namely *convergence*.'[13] As a matter of fact, no excessive importance should be attached to these definitions; they are here to facilitate description of the subject matter but are not an end in themselves.

B. Four Types of Convergence: Top-down, Bottom-up, Horizontal and Spill-over

The complex mutual interaction leading to similar legal rules and their similar application as regards public liability for breaches of EU law could be hidden behind expressions such as 'convergence' or 'europeanisation'. As these concepts are difficult to grasp, four relationships could be distinguished in convergence as a

[6] M Wathelet and S Van Raepenbusch, 'La responsabilité des États membres en cas de violation du droit communautaire. Vers un alignement de l'État sur celle de la Communauté ou l'inverse?' (1997) *Cahiers de droit européen* 13–65.

[7] See eg, JWF Allison, 'Transplantation and Cross-fertilisation' in J Beatson and T Tridimas (eds), *New Directions in European Public Law* (Oxford, Hart Publishing, 1998), who analyses the contributions following the classical debate between Kahn-Freund and Watson.

[8] See W van Gerven, 'Mutual Permeation of Public and Private Law at the National and Supranational Level' (1998) *Maastricht Journal of European and Comparative Law* 7–24; J Lever, 'Mutual Permeation of Community and National Tort Rules' in J Wouters and J Stuyck et al (eds), *Principles of Proper Conduct for Supranational, State and Private Actors in the European Union: Towards a Ius Commune. Essays in Honour of Walter van Gerven* (Antwerp, Intersentia, 2001).

[9] JH Jans and R de Lange et al (eds), *Europeanisation of Public Law* (Groningen, Europa Law Publishing, 2007).

[10] C Harlow, 'Voices of Difference in a Plural Community' (n 3) 201.

[11] See eg, N MacCormick, *Rhetoric and the Rule of Law. A Theory of Legal Reasoning* (Oxford, Oxford University Press, 2005) 189ff on 'normative coherence', and the concepts of 'local coherence/global coherence', 'coherence of case law' and the idea that law works as an integrity. See also J Schwarze, *European Administrative Law*, revised 1st edn (London, Sweet and Maxwell, 2006) cxxxvi.

[12] K Tuori, *Oikeuden ratio ja voluntas* (Vantaa, WSOYpro, 2007) 123–32.

[13] S Prechal and B van Roermund, 'Binding Unity in EU Legal Order: An Introduction' in S Prechal and B van Roermund (eds), *Coherence in EU Law. The Search for Unity in Divergent Concepts* (Oxford, Oxford University Press, 2008) 1 (emphasis added).

process in order to better understand the whole in slices,[14] thus radically simplifying complex and nuanced relations.[15] Such an approach seems adequate for the purposes of this study.[16]

i. Two Forms of Vertical Convergence

The first type of convergence is created by legislated provisions of EU law which are aimed at bringing about change in national law. Convergence is created by imposing '*top-down*' norms (EU to national) which are to be implemented and applied in all Member States.[17]

The second type of convergence is '*bottom-up*' convergence (national to EU). This refers to 'feedback' from national systems to EU law. Elements from one or several systems mount from national level to influence the EU level.

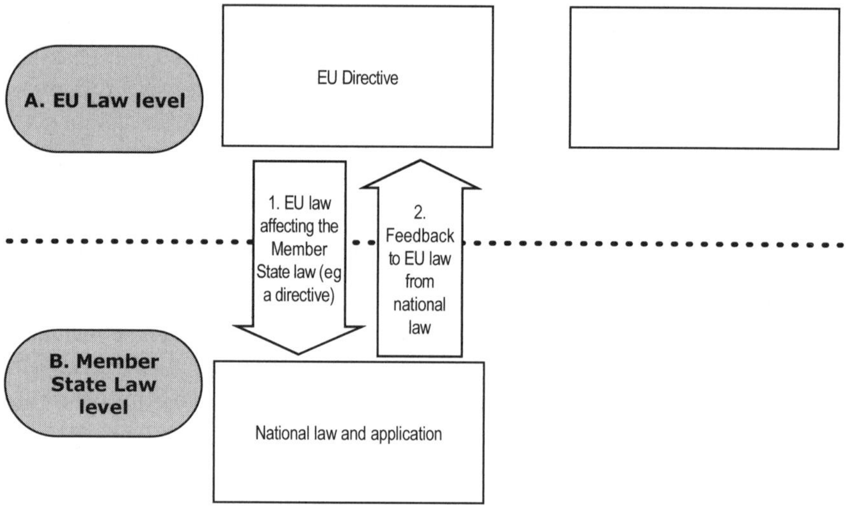

Figure 2.1 Two-way Train between EU Law and National Law

[14] Convergence as a word also appears in the Treaty, in a very specific context though, in the provisions concerning Economic and Monetary Union. Under Art 121(3) TFEU, the Member States aim to enhance the convergence of their economic policies, while under Art 140(1) TFEU a high degree of sustainable convergence is mentioned as one of the conditions for the introduction of the euro.

[15] Such mutual relation has been referred to as *Wechselwirkung*, see eg, J Schwarze, 'Rechtstaatliche Grundsätze für das Verwaltungshandeln in der "alten" und "neuen" Europäischen Union' in J Iliopoulos-Strangas and H Bauer (eds), *Die Neue Europäische Union* (Athens, Ant. N. Sakkoulas, 2006) 173.

[16] The model presented here is a simple one, where many nuances are set aside. A compact and clear presentation of in what ways legal systems can be overlapping is made by T Mylly, *Intellectual Property and European Economic Constitutional Law – The Trouble with Private Informational Power* (Vaajakoski, IPR University Center, 2009). While underlining the pluralistic and polycentric nature of modern law, he also notes that in the current situation of interlegality, the mutual relations between legal institutions cannot always be arranged hierarchically, but they can rather be collaborative or complementary, see 103–08.

[17] As noted by P Beaumont and C Lyons et al (eds), *Convergence and Divergence in European Public Law* (Oxford, Hart Publishing, 2002) v, it is overly simplistic to see this relation as one-way train.

Relationships (1) and (2) can be analysed at two levels. The first level is that of *legislation*. As stated above, European Union legislation is supposed to bring about change in national law. However, feedback to EU level can also occur from national legal systems. The second level is that of *judicial dialogues*. Albeit the ECJ can have a considerable effect on national systems, in particular in areas where EU law is applied, it is also true that national courts can have a smaller or greater influence on the deliberations of the ECJ, most directly as a source of preliminary references.[18]

ii. Two Forms of Horizontal Convergence

There are two further types of horizontal convergence, both of which relate to the unintended effects on the relevant legal system of ideas received from outside.

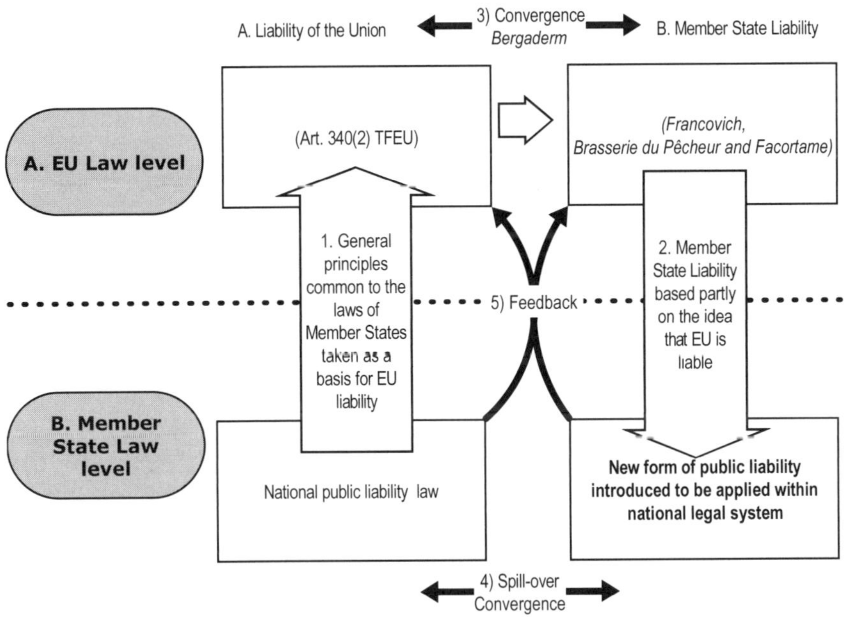

Figure 2.2 'Commuter Train' between EU and National Public Liability Law

In this diagram, the interaction between the two types of EU law-based liability is described as the third relationship (3). It has been elegantly described by Berrod as the 'boomerang effect'.[19] It could be described as pure *horizontal convergence* (EU to EU). It is an idea which came into expression in *Bergaderm* (ECJ 2000):[20] similar rights should be protected in a similar manner, unless specific justification exists for differential treatment.

[18] *cf* A-M Slaughter and A Stone Sweet et al (eds), *The European Court and National Courts – Doctrine and Jurisprudence. Legal Change in Its Social Context* (Oxford, Hart Publishing, 1998) xii-xiii.

[19] See F Berrod, 'Plaidoyer pour une Union de droit dans la diversité des systèmes judiciaires nationaux', *Chemins d'Europe. Mélanges en l'honneur de Jean Paul Jacqué* (Paris, LGDJ, 2010) 97.

[20] ECJ Case C-352/98 P *Bergaderm and Goupil v Commission* (appeal dismissed) [2000] ECR I-5291.

However, probably the most unexpected and most spectacular effect of 'europeanisation' is the fourth relationship (4). It is some kind of 'cross-over effect' or 'cross-fertilisation': it is the phenomenon that EU law acts as a source of inspiration for national law in fields not covered by EU law. It could be characterised as horizontal convergence *spill-over* effect (EU to national non-EU-related Areas),

The following example may be helpful: in EU law, the principle of the legislator's liability for breaches of EU law has been firmly established, ever since *Schöppenstedt* (ECJ 1971).[21] Now, on the basis of 'convergence thinking', in a Member State where such liability under national law does not exist, the idea of the legislator's liability starts floating. Because of the example given by EU law, the idea is fed into various internal discussions. It can be debated by academia, it can be invoked in court practices or traces of it may appear even at the legislative level. There is no EU law obligation to do this: the 'pressure' to do so may flow from striving for convergence. Simple questions can be asked: 'why should certain legislative breaches (where the conditions are fulfilled) be actionable when a breach of EU law occurs, but not when 'only' a breach of national law occurs'?[22] This spill-over effect to other than EU systems (ie to national systems) enhances convergence.

C. Convergence v Divergence and Risks of 'Convergence Fundamentalism'

Legal systems tend inherently to strive towards their own inner *coherence within* themselves. It is also true that *convergence between* legal systems is seen by many as a virtue and arguments can be advanced for rapprochement/harmonisation in general.[23]

Convergence of laws *within* the *European Union* is something which is fundamentally present in the European Union legal system. The basic idea underlying integration and thus the original Treaties was to jointly establish rules by which a multitude of divergences would be reduced in various areas, first by establishing a customs union and a common market. At a later stage, with the establishment of the internal market, economic arguments were also advanced to support convergence and unity.[24]

The basic mechanisms for bringing about coherence in EU law and thus *between* legal systems are well-known: the Treaties have set objectives and interdictions. These, in turn, are completed by secondary legislation to render provisions more precise or to stretch the divergence-abolishing effects of EU law to new areas. The

[21] ECJ Case 5/71 *Zuckerfabrik Schöppenstedt v Council* (damages claim dismissed) [1971] ECR 975 [11].

[22] See, in this respect, eg P Craig, 'The Domestic Liability of Public Authorities in Damages: Lessons from the European Community?' in J Beatson and T Tridimas (eds), *New Directions in European Public Law* (Oxford, Hart Publishing, 1998) 83ff. W van Gerven and J Lever et al, *Cases, Materials and Text on National, Supranational and International Tort Law* (Oxford, Hart Publishing, 2000) 889ff, 946–56.

[23] An interesting contribution also covering cultural aspects of private law harmonisation, and a historical aspect on the rivalry between Savigny and Thibault is offered by S Paasilehto, *Constellations – A New Approach to Legal Culture and European Integration of Private Law* (Helsinki, 2002) 171ff.

[24] *cf* the so-called Cecchini report.

role of the ECJ in bringing about harmonisation cannot be underestimated. In addition, academia, including various joint research projects, has helped in 'uncovering' common features.

Convergence can be seen to have many positive aspects. Is divergence then a negative connotation? Should one think that harmony is always good, whereas disharmony is bad? Or could divergence sometimes (or always) be a better option? Several authors, for example Teubner and Legrand, have proposed detailed arguments why the attempted unification of law in a given question does not yield the purported result, or how the rapprochement of European legal systems is not taking place, despite the efforts of the European Union.[25]

Moreover, even if one would agree that convergence may bring about certain benefits, it may go too far. There is something which has been described as '*convergence fundamentalism*', which refers to 'the belief amongst many academics, politicians and bureaucrats, as often implicit as explicit, that the convergence of systems of public law is essentially and so generally a good thing'.[26] This type of 'convergence overkill' or 'convergence getting out of hand' is not so rare. The introduction of the principle of subsidiarity by the Maastricht Treaty (now Article 5(3) TFEU), alongside the principle of proportionality (now Article 5(4) TFEU), could also be seen as an attempt to underline the importance of keeping in mind alternatives to harmonisation and imposed convergence. This trend continued with the Lisbon Treaty, by which specific mention of the principle of conferral was added to Article 5(2) TFEU.[27] There are also interesting studies on how rights created at the European level affect national legal systems and national legal cultures in particular – how far can *ius commune* go?[28]

II. CONVERGENCE APPROACH AND GENERAL METHODOLOGICAL ISSUES

A. The Added Value of the 'Convergence Approach' in this Study

With the development of case-law it has become clear that mere analysis of Member State liability case-law does not lead very far. A fresh approach is needed. Indeed,

[25] See eg, P Legrand, 'European Legal Systems Are Not Converging' (1996) *ICLQ* 52–81 or G Teubner, 'Legal Irritants: Good Faith in British Law or How Unifying Law Ends Up in New Divergences' (1998) *MLR* 11–32; P Legrand, 'A Diabolical Idea' in A Hartkamp and M Hesselink et al (eds), *Towards a European Civil Code. Third Fully Revised and Expanded Edition* (The Hague, Kluwer Law International, 2004); see also T Wilhelmsson and E Paunio et al, *Private law and the many cultures of Europe* (The Hague, Kluwer, 2006).

[26] N Walker, 'Culture, Democracy and the Convergence of Public Law: Some Scepticisms about Scepticism' in N Walker (ed), *Convergence and Divergence in European Public Law* (Oxford, Hart Publishing, 2002) 257.

[27] For a critical contribution, see P Giliker, 'European Tort Law: Five Key Questions for Debate' (2009) *European Review of Private Law* 285–304.

[28] M Aziz, *The Impact of European Rights on National Legal Cultures* (Oxford, Hart Publishing, 2004). In the field of liability law, see C Van Dam, 'European Tort Law and the Many Cultures of Europe' in T Wilhelmsson and E Paunio et al (eds), *Private law and the many cultures of Europe* (The Hague, Kluwer, 2006) 61ff.

following *Bergaderm*, the aspect of convergence seems like an interesting approach to deepen understanding of the two systems. A study of these two systems in parallel, focusing on some essential themes, looks promising in many ways.

In the first place, the convergence aspect appears to be something new, as this has been relatively unexploited in the doctrine (see above chapter one). Secondly, both systems are based on case-law and thus constitute a patchwork type of fabric. A parallel study could help to see if the two systems would be able to mutually fill one another's gaps: for example, could some elements be transposed from Union liability to Member State liability (such as the case-law on assessing sufficient seriousness of breach, which the ECJ in principle does not do for Member State liability)? Or could some issues already treated in the context of Member State liability be interesting in the context of Union liability, such as liability for judicial action, following the *Köbler* case-law? Thirdly, the time appears ripe for such parallel analysis. There have been major developments in subsequent steps, in 1991, in 1996, and in 2000, and by now there appears to be sufficient case-law so that some conclusions could be drawn. Moreover, interesting judgments have been handed down recently to complete the legal frame which has gradually been emerging. Thereby it has now become possible to assess whether and under what conditions convergence operates and how that objective has been attained.

Some explanation is required of the role of 'convergence' (and 'divergence') in this study. Convergence first appeared as an argument in the field of public liability for breach of EU law at the time of *Francovich* (ECJ 1991).[29] The damages liability of the original Community was created on the basis of principles common to the legal systems of the Member States. However, it was only in 1991 that a potential problem of convergence appeared, when a new type of damages liability for Member States was established by the ECJ in *Francovich*.

This study concentrates on the 'internal' European Union law question of convergence within EU law, instead of comparing, for example, EU law-based Member State liability and national law-based state liability. In a national system, our approach might come close to comparing the liability issues of two similar yet different public entities. One could think of comparing the liability grounds of state and municipalities in Finland, or the liability of the Bundesrepublik and Bundesstaat/Kommunalhaftung in Germany. Albeit none of these accurately correspond to the differences between Member State liability and Union liability for breaches of EU law, they may help to understand the vantage point chosen.[30]

Recourse to 'convergence' as an argument to justify change in law leads to a number of questions: Was it appropriate and justified to use convergence as a criterion for change in 1996/2000? Is it 'useful'? Is it still applied? The last question merits

[29] ECJ Joined Cases C-6/90 and C-9/90 *Francovich and Bonifaci* [1991] ECR I-5357.

[30] *cf* F Ossenbühl, *Staatshaftungsrecht. 5., neu bearbeitete und erweiterte Auflage* (Munich, Beck, 1998), K-O Bergmann and H Schumacher, *Die Kommunalhaftung. Ein Handbuch des Staatshaftungsrechts* (Cologne, Carl Heymanns Verlag, 2007). In a way, the comparison with state/municipal liability is rather interesting. Both are public authorities, and in principle many of the liability conditions are similar. However, their respective areas of action do not coincide fully. This is also true of the relationship between the EU and Member States.

particular attention. It should be noted that the Court had recourse to convergence as a key element in changing the system. Some authors have now concluded that the Court has already abandoned convergence as a touchstone of development of the two systems.[31] If that was the case, it could mean that the idea of convergence was used mainly as a temporary justification.

B. Methods and Approaches

One of the tasks when writing a legal dissertation is to put in writing the methods used in carrying out the research. The researcher may have the impression that most research 'just happens': books are read, cases are studied and new text appears on the screen. The invisible framework that guides this procedure is operating mostly in the background.

In EU law studies, methodological questions often remain implicit. This is not to say that works are carried out without methods, but rather that methodological issues are not set out explicitly or not in detail.[32] The characteristic elements relating to methodological issues of EU law studies are the underlining of the strong role of case-law, of the supranational and independent role of the EU legal system and also its multilingual and multicultural nature.

The methods by which research in the EU law area has been carried out in this study can be characterised as conventional. The main sources studied are case-law in particular, legislation to some extent, and doctrine.[33] In fact, the approaches in works where the emphasis is on some other areas of law (even if EU law were in the picture) are distinct, and this difference underlines the specific features of the EU law method, which for an EU law researcher may seem self-evident or banal.

Two approaches can be distinguished in EU law studies. One is to analyse the effects of EU law on national law. The other is to analyse EU law at the EU level, and see how it is applied in Member States.[34] The emphasis here is clearly on the latter, but through contextual elements the effects of EU public liability in national laws are also addressed.

This study is based on an EU law approach. This means that the approach adopted in this study towards public liability for breaches of EU law is that of EU

[31] eg C Hilson, 'The Role of Discretion in EC Law on Non-Contractual Liability' (2005) *Common Market Law Review* 677–95.

[32] In fact, works on 'pure' EU law methodology would appear to be rather rare. For two examples, see F Müller and R Christensen, *Juristische Methodik. Band II. Europarecht Zweite, neu bearbeitete und stark erweiterte Auflage* (Berlin, Duncker & Humblot, 2007) and J Hettne and I Otken Eriksson (eds), *EU-rättslig metod: teori och genomslag i svensk rättstillämpning* (Stockholm, Norstedts juridik, 2005).

[33] For other studies with somewhat similar approach see eg T Ojanen, *The European Way. The Structure of National Court Obligation under EC Law* (Saarijärvi, 1998), J Raitio, *The principle of legal certainty in EC law* (Dordrecht, Kluwer Academic Publishers, 2003); N Jääskinen, *Eurooppalaistuvan oikeuden oikeusteoreettisia ongelmia [The Europeanisation of Law – Jurisprudential Problems]* (Helsinki, 2008) and A Guimaraes-Purokoski, *Vertikaalinen toimivallanjako EU-oikeudessa [The Vertical Division of Competences in EU Law]* (Jyväskylä, Suomalainen Lakimiesyhdistys, 2009).

[34] cf J Raitio, 'Eurooppaoikeus, tieto ja sivistys' (2008) *Lakimies* 288–93, 291.

law,[35] ie the method the EU courts are using.[36] Although the subject matter of the research relates to damages liability, this subject is not treated from the tort law[37] or comparative law approach.[38]

One way of extending the classic EU law method is to add to the analysis of 'law in books' some elements from 'law in action'. The study has been extended from pure analysis of EU level case-law and doctrine to certain other elements. Some statistical information from the EU courts is introduced and analysed (eg the seemingly low success rate of damages actions). For Member State liability, not only are EU level rulings examined, but also (even if to a very limited extent) the application of the principle at national level.

C. Doctrine on EU Law Public Liability

As mentioned above, doctrine on the liability of the Member States is immense. This doctrine has been used as a starting point for the study, but it is difficult to point to a single author or work as a key source for Member State liability. The same applies for Community liability, albeit the dissertations of Fines and Wakefield have been important sources of inspiration.[39] However, both of these predate *Bergaderm*. In particular, the fact that works addressing the two liability systems in one study are even rarer, has directed interest towards making such a study. As to the idea of convergence in European (public) tort law, a most important source has been the work of van Gerven.[40]

In general, as regards doctrine, one could distinguish three periods: the first is *recent* doctrine, ie doctrine less than eg five years old. The second category is doctrine which is post-*Bergaderm*, less than 10 years old (ie since 2000). The third category is 'old' doctrine over 10 years old, and thus predating *Bergaderm*. Such works should be used with great care, in particular as regards Community liability. As regards languages, the works cited are mainly in English, French, German, Finnish and Swedish.

[35] On the EU law approach, see eg, J Raitio, 'Eurooppaoikeus on kehittyvä oikeudenala' (2006) *Lakimies* 813–17.

[36] J Hettne, *Rättsprinciper som styrmedel: Allmänna rättsprinciper i EU:s domstol* (Stockholm, Norstedts Juridik, 2008) 35–38.

[37] For examples of the 'tort law approach' see C von Bar, *The Common European Law of Torts. Volume One* (Oxford, Clarendon, 1998); C von Bar, *The Common European Law of Torts. Volume Two* (Oxford, Clarendon, 2000); *C Van Dam,* European Tort Law (Oxford, Oxford University Press, 2006).

[38] For examples of the 'comparative law approach' to (public) tort law, see eg, W Wurmnest, *Grundzüge eines europäischen Haftungsrechts: eine rechtsvergleichende Untersuchung des Gemeinschaftsrechts* (Tübingen, Mohr Siebeck, 2003); D Fairgrieve, *State Liability in Tort. A Comparative Law Study* (Oxford, Oxford University Press, 2003) and D Fairgrieve and M Andenas et al (eds), *Tort Liability of Public Authorities in Comparative Perspective* (London, BIICL, 2002).

[39] F Fines, *Étude de la responsabilité extracontractuelle de la Communauté économique européenne* (Paris, LGDJ, 1990); Wakefield, *Judicial protection* (n 3).

[40] See bibliography.

D. Situating the Study in the Field of EU Law

This study relates to the institutional law of the European Union. First of all, the origins of Member State liability lie in the principles of direct effect, primacy and effectiveness of EU law. Member State liability is an extension of those principles, all created by the Court. The existence and development of both liability systems is also an expression of constitutionalisation of the EU legal system, part of the mechanisms that ensure that action by the EU and Member States is 'legal' and in particular that appropriate remedial tools are available, when needed.

Apart from aspects of constitutionalisation, this study interacts with convergent developments within and outside EU law in general. Approximation of laws through the European Union has been carried out formally and informally. Informal approximation has been very active in the field of private law of the Member States, including law on non-contractual liability.

The subject matter has close connections with EU administrative law, both as it applies to EU institutions and as it limits and guides action by Member States when they apply EU law. It has further links with a fundamental question of EU law, namely the relationship between EU law and national law. It also has links with the effectiveness of EU law in Member States, directly how individuals can claim their rights from the state through damages actions, but it is also linked to the question of 'private enforcement' of EU law.

Going beyond the EU and its Member States, the subject matter also touches the responsibility of states in international law, between themselves and towards individuals. This is an area with numerous recent developments. Not to be excluded are links with the liability grounds of other international organisations – all of which would currently seem to lack at least some of the elements that have made the EU legal order unique, elements that underlie the catchword 'constitutionalisation'. Links exist, too, to liability of yet a different type, based on the European Convention of Human Rights (ECHR), including the rules concerning 'just satisfaction' for breaches of the rights guaranteed by that convention. Public liability for breaches of EU law is clearly not a phenomenon that should or even could be examined in isolation.

III. CRITERIA FOR ASSESSING THE CASE-LAW

A. EU Public Liability Law as Case-law

It is necessary to set out some issues relating to the use of case-law as a source of law and the corresponding assessment criteria. The focus is first on how the sources of law in EU law are understood in this study and how one can find out what is the 'law', in particular for public liability issues. The underlying thinking also sketches out the limits of how to verify the 'validity' of EU law. Clearly this is one of the central issues when EU law is studied and criticised. This study relies heavily on the case-law of the Community courts in Luxembourg, as hardly any legislation exists on either liability system.

The purpose of this section is to set out the criteria applied throughout the study as regards case-law. These criteria underlie the analysis and presentation of different cases throughout the study, albeit not expressly explained each time a case is cited.

In many Member States, non-contractual liability law, both private and public, consists, at least to a certain degree, of legislative provisions, case-law, and doctrine. The proportionate importance of these sources varies, but it is clear that questions on legislative interpretation are commonplace.

In contrast, the distinguishing feature of public liability in EU law is that there is no legislation, either for Member State liability following *Francovich*, or for Union liability following *Bergaderm*. Legal rules come into expression in case-law. Indeed the 'only' source of law for public liability in EU law is case-law.[41] Various stages of development can easily be distinguished in the development of public liability case-law: the *Schöppenstedt* formula (ECJ 1971),[42] its further definition in *Bayerische HNL* (ECJ 1978),[43] its extreme forms (eg arbitrariness requirement for liability in *Amylum* ECJ 1979),[44] their neutralisation, *Francovich* (ECJ 1991)[45] and the challenge for Community liability, *Brasserie* (ECJ 1996)[46] and the objective of alignment, *Bergaderm* (ECJ 2000),[47] the practice of alignment, and so on.

B. Locating the Sources of Law for EU Public Liability Law

The main function of the Court of Justice is to ensure that the law is observed in the interpretation and application of the Treaties.[48] What is the 'law' and what are the sources of law in the public liability damages field? To explain what the 'law' is in EU public liability law, it is useful to present the approach in three textbooks, by Schermers and Waelbroeck, Arnull and Lenaerts et al.

[41] At this juncture, we should mention that public liability in Member State laws has been, if not solely, at least in non-negligible part, relying on case-law even in many 'continental' systems. To cite another example, in Finland there are provisions on public liability in the Damages Act of 1974, but liability existed long before the specific legislation, which has been largely clarified and completed by case-law. See S Hakalehto-Wainio, *Valta ja vahinko. Julkisen vallan käyttäjän vastuu vahingonkorvauslaissa [Power and Liability. Tort Liability of the Public Authorities under the Tort Liability Act]* (Hämeenlinna, Talentum, 2008) throughout.

[42] ECJ *Zuckerfabrik Schöppenstedt* (n 21).

[43] ECJ Case 83/76 *Bayerische HNL and Others v Council and Commission* (damages action dismissed) [1978] ECR 1209 [4] and [5].

[44] ECJ Joined Cases 116/77 and 124/77 *Amylum v Council and Commission* (damages claim dismissed) [1979] ECR 3497 [21].

[45] ECJ *Francovich and Bonifaci* (n 29).

[46] ECJ Joined Cases C-46/93 and C-48/93 *Brasserie du Pêcheur and Factortame* [1996] ECR I-1029.

[47] ECJ *Bergaderm and Goupil* (n 20).

[48] See Art 19(1) TEU [ex-Art 220 EC].

In their textbook on judicial remedies, Schermers and Waelbroeck (2001) have classified the sources of Community law, as it then was, into five categories:[49] (1) founding Treaties and acts of Community institutions; (2) general principles of law; (3) case-law of the Court of Justice; (4) custom and (5) other legal orders.

The importance of written sources of law varies from one legal order to another, but it is clear that no legal order is solely composed of written sources of law. However, in European Union law, unwritten sources and general principles of law and the case-law of the courts enjoy a particularly prominent role. In fact, in the European Union legal order, case-law may often be the most important source of law.[50]

As regards the two forms of public damages liability, no substantive legislation exists on either of the two forms of EU law liability. The only exceptions to this with respect to Union liability are a reference in Article 340(2) TFEU and the rules of a procedural nature concerning the attribution of competence to the EU courts and certain time limits. These are laid down at the level of primary law (the Treaty and the Statute of the Court of Justice) and their wording is not very detailed. In this respect, research on these two forms of public liability recalls studying the general principles of European Union law, such as direct effect, primacy, principle of proportionality, or the like.

The result is that in this area case-law is the exclusive source of law. When it comes to the case-law of the Court, Schermers and Waelbroeck distinguish three functions for case-law, ie (1) filling the gaps; (2) refining the law; and (3) interpreting the law. One can agree that in the field of non-contractual liability, case-law has the function of filling a gap expressly left for it in primary law.

On closer analysis, it seems that the dichotomy proposed by Arnull for case-law would fit better into this setting. Arnull speaks of interpretation and norm-setting.[51]

For Arnull, interpretation concerns written provisions of law and 'how the ECJ determines the meaning and effect of the written provisions it is called on to apply'. However, that is not the question here: there are no written provisions to be interpreted, only a very generic and generous reference to the legal systems of the Member States. The effect of drafting the provisions of European Union law or the effect of the multilingual nature of the Union does not play a prominent role here.

Public liability case-law fits best in Arnull's second category, which pertains to the normative status of case-law.[52] In fact, in the framework of the rules relating to Union liability, one is faced with the Court's capacity to 'make law visible'. In general terms, it is possible to agree with Arnull who argues that 'judicial decisions do not constitute a source of law in the civilian tradition, they do not bind lower courts but are persuasive only'. Arnull concludes as follows (footnote omitted):

[49] HG Schermers and DF Waelbroeck, *Judicial Protection in the European Communities* 6th edn (The Hague, Kluwer Law International, 2001) 7ff.

[50] HG Schermers and DF Waelbroeck, *Judicial Protection* (n 49) 133.

[51] A Arnull, *The European Union and its Court of Justice*, 2nd edn (Oxford, Oxford University Press, 2006) 607.

[52] Arnull, *The European Union and its Court of Justice* (n 51) 622, 625, 633.

> The imprecision of the EC Treaty would have made it wholly implausible for the Court of Justice to purport to be merely the mouthpiece of the written law. There was in any event no reason why it should. The authors of the Treaties seemed motivated less by controlling judicial excesses than by ensuring observance of the law. The establishment of the CFI on the same model as the Court and the endorsement of both Courts' case law by the Constitutional Treaty show that their motivation has not changed, whatever their criticisms of individual cases.

In general, it is true that new legal rules are brought into expression by the judiciary, within certain (narrow) and (clearly) defined limits. Freeman has aptly captured the different positions of the legislator and the judge.[53] He notes that the legislator is at least in principle free to make innovations as it sees fit and deal in an abstract way with all future cases; a court, on the other hand, is limited to the actual issues and the parties before it. What Freeman says seems true. Yet it appears that in some cases only a limited difference exists between legislator and judge, as the legislator is never completely free to choose, while the judge is not completely bound. Equally, open texture entails discretion for the judge.

What is also true, however, is that neither of the two damages liability systems would ever have been created by the legislator, owing to the impossibility of agreeing on the rules or procedures to be followed. The advantage of a case-law-based liability system is that judges can be asked questions which the legislator would not be asked and they may have to reply to questions which the legislator would never be able to answer in the abstract – or would never even take up, such as specific issues of the relationship between European Union law and national law (eg direct effect, primacy). The 'downside' of the case-law approach can then be the weakness and lack of clarity of case-law, its incompleteness, and problems relating to its legitimacy.

In comparison to the categories proposed by Schermers and Waelbroeck in 2001, it is interesting to note the differences with respect to the presentation made by Lenaerts and van Aerschot in 2005.[54] For them, the appropriate order starts with primary Community law, but then at the second level are general principles of Community law, analysed in two categories, namely general principles of law and fundamental rights. After that come sources in international law (international agreements concluded by the Community, by Member States with non-Member States, and other rules of international law). Only after this come autonomous measures adopted by institutions and bodies, and the case-law of the ECJ and the CFI.

It is not clear where the liability of the Member States for breaches of EU law should appear in this system. Nor is the position of Union liability very clear. Still, this qualification has an important bearing when defining the hierarchical level of the rule of law(s). If these principles are qualified as 'case-law of the courts', it means that at a hierarchical level they stand at the very bottom of the legal sources. In fact,

[53] MDA Freeman, *Lloyd's Introduction to Jurisprudence*, 7th edn (London, Sweet & Maxwell, 2005 (2001)) 1403, 1405.

[54] K Lenaerts and P van Aerschot et al, *Constitutional Law of the European Union*, 2nd edn (London, Sweet and Maxwell, 2005) 703–94.

this is a possible qualification: there is no written provision in European Union law: they could be qualified as 'simple' case-law. On the other hand, it could be claimed that they are general principles of EU law: some support for this could already be found in *Francovich* (ECJ 1991).[55] Even if the liability of the EU were not expressly qualified as a principle, under Article 340(2) TFEU, the Union is obliged, in accordance with the general principles common to the laws of the Member States, to make good any damage caused by its institutions or by its servants in the performance of their duties. Therefore, the liability of the Union could be qualified, for the purposes of sources of law, at the level of case-law, as a principle, or as a treaty provision.[56] This is also consonant with the development relating to constitutionalisation, and the position of that principle there.

The reason why it would be important to try to define the proper place of the two liability systems is that their 'placement' has a bearing on assessment of the key legal source: are we discussing here the Treaty and its interpretation, or are we faced with general principles of law which come into expression in the courts' case-law, or is it just 'normal' case-law?

As an interim conclusion, the following could be proposed.

The damages liability of the European Union is a general principle of EU law, which has its origins in the principles common to the laws of the Member States. Albeit the court has fairly unlimited jurisdiction to establish the conditions thereof under the wide task conferred upon it under current Article 340(2) TFEU, some limits can be traced. In *FIAMM* (2008), the ECJ found that

> it is clear that, while comparative examination of the Member States' legal systems enabled the Court to make at a very early stage the finding recalled in paragraph 170 of the present judgment concerning *convergence* of those legal systems in the establishment of a principle of liability in the case of unlawful action or an unlawful omission of the authority, including of a legislative nature, *that is in no way the position as regards the possible existence of a principle of liability in the case of a lawful act or omission of the public authorities,* in particular where it is of a legislative nature.[57]

Strict liability of the public authorities was thus not subject to any such *convergence.* For that reason, the Court refused to establish non-fault liability for breaches of WTO rules.

Member State liability, on the other hand, is 'inherent' in the Treaty, but there is nothing in the case-law which would directly allow qualifying it as a general principle of European Union law. Be that as it may, it seems that there is nothing preventing such qualification either. Given that the two liability systems should

[55] ECJ *Francovich and Bonifaci* (n 29) [35]: 'It follows that the principle whereby a State must be liable for loss and damage caused to individuals as a result of breaches of Community law for which the State can be held responsible is inherent in the system of the Treaty'.

[56] See *Raitio* who discusses whether Member State liability is a rule or a principle, but he also assesses briefly the justification process in the ECJ, on the basis of Klami's contributions. J Raitio, 'Mistä EY:n jäsenvaltion vahingonkorvausvastuu jäsenvelvoitteidensa rikkomisesta yksityisille aiheutuneista vahingoista voidaan johtaa?' (1998) *Lakimies* 630–50, 649–50.

[57] ECJ Joined Cases C-120/06 P and C-121/06 P *FIAMM and Fedon v Council and Commission* (appeal dismissed) [2008] ECR I-6513 [175], emphasis added.

have similar conditions, it appears logical to justify the 'principle' nature of Member State liability also by reference to the 'sister' liability system of the Union.

C. Some Criteria for Assessing the Case-law on EU Public Liability Law

i. Introduction

There is rather abundant case-law by the three EU jurisdictions on Community and Union liability since the 1950s, while the case-law on Member State liability is somewhat more limited.[58] This section attempts to lay out some elements to help in assessing the relative importance of various cases.

The first element to help in identifying the relevant cases is the passing of time. Timewise, as regards Community liability, the study focuses on the case-law of the last 10 years, ie on post-*Bergaderm* case-law of the courts.[59] For Member State liability, we examine the case-law since 1991. This approach necessitates rather extensive explanation and references to the relevant judgments. Cases from the ECJ and CFI have been chosen on the basis of cases where the applicant has invoked damages liability. Whether the claim was finally successful or not, or whether it was rejected as inadmissible, has not been a decisive factor for selection.

When assessing the importance of the different sources of written law, the doctrine distinguishes, without much problem, a hierarchical order for different sources, either expressly or concludently (eg Treaty → Council Directive → Commission Regulation, adopted in Comitology → Commission Decision).

However, it seems that this aspect is often missing when dealing with case-law. Yet not all documents signed by judges bear the same value. In the course of the research for this study it has appeared necessary to set out some elements and criteria to appreciate the importance of the various cases in the abundant case-law.

As the Treaties and secondary legislation have a very limited direct role in public liability in EU law, the 'law' is solely construed from 'precedents'.[60] However, in the field of state liability, the EU courts have not been expressly granted any such powers. What the ECJ has done is basically the same as it did for primacy, direct effect and direct applicability.

If, in general, one wishes to criticise Union legislation and advocate for its change, the message should be addressed to the legislator, or better yet, to the Commission, which makes proposals for secondary legislation. If one wishes to criticise or assess the conditions for Union liability, or those of Member State liability, the right addressee is the Court. The limits for the Court's action here are different from

[58] For more details, see ch 5, s I and ch 6, s I below. For Member State liability, national case-law is not explored systematically.

[59] Staff cases with a damages aspect are not systematically examined. Reference is made to some important judgments.

[60] For an interesting theoretical contribution on judicial legislation, see *R Siltala,* A Theory of Precedent. From analytical positivism to a post-analytical philosophy of law (Oxford, Hart Publishing, 2000) 80ff.

Jégo-Quéré (ECJ 2004), where the Court found the limits in the Treaty.[61] For EU law public liability, the Court has fairly ample room for manoeuvre.[62]

ii. Matters to be Taken into Account in Direct Actions (Liability of the European Union)

For direct actions on liability of the European Union, there are two groups of questions. The first group concerns the competent court, ie whether this is the ECJ, the General Court, the Civil Service Tribunal, or a national court.

The mutual roles of the two principal damages courts for EU law-based liability should not be forgotten. The ECJ and the GC[63] are similar and yet very different courts with differences in jurisdiction and procedures. The ECJ created original restrictive jurisprudence as regards Community liability, which the CFI (now GC) has applied since its creation. It was the ECJ which in 1991 established Member State liability, and which remains the master on this point. Furthermore, in 1996/2000 it was again the ECJ which decided to reorient the case-law on Community liability, and in cases where the CFI (GC) has misapplied the case-law the ECJ has corrected the course. In view of this, the ECJ has the final say and that cases where it has had the last word should be treated with appropriate weight.[64] Yet the bulk of EU liability case-law emanates from the CFI (now the GC). Even for appeal cases before the ECJ it should be remembered that full examination of the facts of the case can only be done at first instance.

Not every damages ruling of the CFI is appealed to the ECJ – in fact, on average less than one third of cases are appealed – while in the cases appealed clearly less than half of appeals result in any substantive change.[65] In addition, for personnel cases with a damages aspect which are decided by the CST, the CFI in practice becomes the court of final instance, with such cases only exceptionally ending up in the ECJ.[66]

[61] ECJ Case C-263/02 P *Commission v Jégo-Quéré* [2004] ECR I-3425 [36] (emphasis added): 'Although the condition that a natural or legal person can bring an action challenging a regulation only if he is concerned both directly and individually must be interpreted in the light of the principle of effective judicial protection by taking account of the various circumstances that may distinguish an applicant individually, *such an interpretation cannot have the effect of setting aside the condition in question, expressly laid down in the Treaty. The Community Courts would otherwise go beyond the jurisdiction conferred by the Treaty* (see Unión de Pequeños Agricultores v Council, paragraph 44)'.

[62] In addition to the rejection of strict liability in EU public liability law, see ECJ *FIAMM and Fedon* (n 57), and for stringent interpretation of limitation periods see ECJ Case C-51/05 P *Commission v Cantina sociale di Dolianova and Others* (CFI judgment set aside; damages action dismissed as inadmissible) [2008] ECR I-5341 and ECJ Case C-335/08 P *Transports Schiocchet - Excursions v Commission* (appeal dismissed) [2009] ECR I-104*, Summ.pub. (judgment of 11 June 2009).

[63] And CST, for personnel cases.

[64] *cf* eg CFI Case T-69/00 *FIAMM and FIAMM Technologies v Council and Commission* (dismissed, appealed C-120/06 P) [2005] ECR II-5393 and ECJ *FIAMM and Fedon* (n 57); and CFI Case T-166/98 *Cantina sociale di Dolianova and Others v Commission* (liability established; appealed C-51/05 P) [2004] ECR II-3991 and ECJ *Commission v Cantina Sociale di Dolianova* (n 62).

[65] See Annual Reports of the Court.

[66] For such a case, see ECJ Case C-197/09 RX-II *Review of the judgment in Case T-12/08P – M v EMEA* [2009] ECR (unpublished judgment of 17 December 2009); *cf* also ECJ Case C-17/11 RX-II *Decision*

The ECJ now functions as an appeal court in cases concerning the damages liability of the Union. Therefore, the ECJ, which originally dealt with all damages cases, since the establishment of the CFI deals with EU liability cases only on a secondary level and adjudicates only on a fraction of all damages cases. What is more, it will adjudicate on such cases always as a second instance, which results in automatic limitation of its jurisdiction (appeal to the ECJ depending on the parties' decision whether to litigate further, with appeal and jurisdiction limited only to points of law).[67] Even if the ECJ only plays a limited role since the establishment of the CFI in cases relating to damages liability of the Union – as regards the number of cases at least – the consequences can be important when it enters into the picture on appeal.

iii. Matters to be Taken into Account for Preliminary Rulings (Member State Liability)

Next, certain issues should be taken into account when assessing cases as sources of law for Member State liability. First, the preliminary rulings procedure, through which Member State liability cases come before the ECJ, is always only a step in the procedure before that national court. Judgments in preliminary rulings are already for this reason less 'fact-intensive'. The ECJ does not, and in principle cannot, rule on the facts, but can limit itself to the legal question raised by the national court; it can and normally will leave appreciation of the complete factual situation to the national court. The multilingual and multi-jurisdictional dimension which is created once the case is brought before the ECJ is highlighted by the fact that Member States can automatically participate in preliminary references and present written and oral observations and they do exercise this right too. Member States contribute to the court proceedings through presentation of legal arguments based not only on EU law, but also on national law. In particular, the Member State concerned may offer the Court complementary legal and factual materials for the consideration of the case. The participation of Member States and the Commission extends the legal input to the Court's decisions and 'europeanises' the originally purely national procedure.

To date, the ECJ has retained monopoly to rule on Member State liability, as all preliminary rulings are decided by that court. The GC has thus been out of that procedure. However, following changes in the Statute of the Court, it is now possible to further amend the Statute so as to transfer certain categories of preliminary reference cases to the GC. Even if this is done in limited form only, it would open up a whole new area for judicial action by the GC, which would certainly not occur without effects, and could also affect liability case-law.[68] The jurisdiction of the three courts can be summarised in a table as follows:

concerning review of the judgment in Case T-143/09 P Commission v Petrilli (no review) [2011] ECR I-0000 (Decision of 8 February 2011), where the Court decided not to proceed to review suggested by the First Advocate General.

[67] The ECJ may be called on to give a preliminary ruling on validity of a EU instrument, which can lead to a subsequent damages action before the GC.

[68] As the courts are not very keen to make mutual references to their case-law, the situation where the GC would be in charge both of damages actions and preliminary rulings could make a change.

Table 2.1 Jurisdiction of the Three EU Courts and National Courts in Damages Cases

Type of case	Court			
	CST – Civil Service Tribunal	GC – General Court	ECJ – European Court of Justice	**National courts**
Damages actions against Member States (*Francovich/ Brasserie* case-law)	–	–	ECJ involved only through preliminary rulings procedure, when initiated by national court	National courts primarily competent
Damages actions against the European Union (excl. staff cases) Article 340(2) TFEU	–	GC as first instance	ECJ only as appeal court	–
Staff cases including a claim for damages	CST as first instance	GC only as appeal court	ECJ involved only very exceptionally (re-examination procedure)	–

As to argumentation, there is also a difference in the addressees of the argumentation of the different courts and different cases. For cases relating to the liability of the Union, it is in principle sufficient for the CFI to convince the parties, itself and the ECJ (in the case of an appeal) of the well-foundedness of the reasoning and the outcome. However, for Member State liability cases, the ECJ may have to make a precise effort of reasoning when it intends to convey a convincing message to the national court that will give the final judgment (and academia) which will attempt to discover the 'law' on the basis of the judgment.

The second group of questions concerns appeals (and exceptionally re-examination) within the EU court system. A number of procedural issues are linked to appeals. As a rule, any of the parties to the original proceedings can introduce an appeal, ie in a damages claim, the original applicant that is seeking damages, or the original defendant institution. It is also possible that an intervener can introduce an appeal, albeit this is rather rare, at least in damages cases.[69] Any appeal to the ECJ is limited to 'questions of law', chosen and argued by the applicant.[70] On appeal the

[69] For an appeal introduced by an intervening party before the CFI, see ECJ Joined Cases C-39/05 P and C-52/05 P *Sweden and Turco v Council* (CFI judgment set aside) [2008] ECR I-4723.

[70] However, where the ECJ decides to annul a judgment of the CFI, it has the possibility to rule itself on the substance of the case or return it to the CFI for ruling. Where the ECJ rules itself on the case, it has full powers to examine the case, as in ECJ Case C-198/03 P *Commission v CEVA and Pfizer* (CFI judgment set aside, damages action dismissed on appeal) [2005] ECR I-6357.

ECJ does not have competence to examine the factual findings made by the CFI. In addition, the ECJ can only take up issues that have been invoked by the applicant. Conversely, if the applicant takes up issues which were not discussed before the General Court, they are inadmissible and the ECJ will not rule upon them, even if they were important.[71]

An appeal has various effects. After the General Court has handed down its judgment, this should be regarded as 'provisional' until the deadline for appeal has run out or the Court above has ruled on the appeal. Where an appeal has been lodged, the General Court judgment is subject to change before the ECJ. In such cases, the outcome before the General Court can be presented, not as the final ruling, but rather as 'law in the making', subject to change. That is why this study attempts to indicate precisely whether a judgment of the CFI/General Court is being appealed or has been judged by the ECJ on appeal.

A judgment of the General Court which has been appealed may have various legal values after the ECJ has ruled on the appeal.[72] Probably the clearest case is where the appeal has been rejected as inadmissible by the ECJ. In this case the judgment of the General Court retains its full value.[73] Where the ECJ examines the substance of the appeal but upholds the conclusion of the General Court, we can distinguish two categories. The first is that the ECJ rejects the appeal having come to the same *legal* conclusion as the General Court but on different legal grounds. The second is that the ECJ rejects the appeal having come to the same *substantive* conclusion on different legal grounds.[74] Finally, there is the situation where the appeal is successful and the ECJ overrules the judgment of the General Court.[75] Moreover, the fact that the ECJ on appeal has ruled on something should also be examined carefully. If a point of law in the General Court judgment was not appealed, it cannot be examined by the ECJ. Thus it is fully possible that an appeal judgment affects the General Court judgment only in part.

However, even 'final' judgments of the court below should be examined with care. The fact that a judgment of the General Court (or CST) was not appealed *may* indicate that the parties agree with that court on the interpretation given. On the other hand, such a situation may equally well indicate that the parties – expressly or impliedly – did not want to continue the procedure, for any conceivable practical, legal, or policy reasons. One must also keep in mind that a formally

[71] In ECJ Case C-93/02 P *Biret International v Council* (appeal dismissed) [2003] ECR I-10497, the applicant took up the issue of strict liability for breaches of WTO rules. This issue is mentioned in the judgment of the ECJ, but the ECJ did not rule on it precisely as it was taken up only at the appeal stage. The ECJ's position was clarified only some years later in ECJ *FIAMM and Fedon* (n 57).

[72] For precedent value, see N MacCormick and RS Summers (eds), *Interpreting Precedents. A Comparative Study* (Aldershot, Ashgate, 1997) throughout.

[73] See for such a situation CFI Case T-138/03 *E.R. et al v Council and Commission* (no causal link, appealed C-100/07 P) [2006] ECR II-4923 and ECJ Case C-100/07 P *E.R. et al v Council and Commission* (appeal dismissed) [2007] ECR I-136*, Summ.pub. (order of 4 October 2007).

[74] CFI Case T-199/96 *Bergaderm and Goupil v Commission* (damages claim dismissed, appealed C-352/98 P) [1998] ECR II-2805 and ECJ *Bergaderm and Goupil* (n 20).

[75] ECJ *Commission v Cantina Sociale di Dolianova* (n 62).

final judgment may have been de facto overruled in a similar and maybe even contemporary case.[76]

iv. Categories of Public Liability Case-law

Various aspects should be taken into account when considering the legal value of a EU court judgment. The first formal criterion to assess the weight of the ruling is the composition of the competent court. Judgments are nowadays typically handed down by chambers of three or five judges. Particular attention should be given to cases which are decided in the ECJ by the Grand Chamber (currently 11 judges) or which have been decided in the past by the full court, grand or petit plenum. Conversely, statements relating to damages issues in rulings given by the president functioning as the judge for interim measures may not give a full picture of the law applicable in the damages field.[77]

Another aspect is the age of the judgment and the point in time when it was handed down. Timewise, between 'old' and 'new' cases there can be considerable differences. Even if it was possible to find elements of convergence between 'old' and 'new' cases, it is important to keep in mind that the world and the law have changed between the ground-breaking judgment in *Humblet* (ECJ 1960)[78] and post-*Bergaderm* (ECJ 2000) case-law. Therefore, the emphasis in this study is on the latter, as stated above.

The way judgments are reasoned has also evolved over time. The judgment in *Schöppenstedt* (ECJ 1971) consisted of 16 paragraphs, while in the more recent *Schneider* damages action (CFI 2007) the mere dispositive part contained as many as 11 paragraphs while the judgment itself some 352 paragraphs. It is evident that the justification of judgments by EU courts has been considerably developing.

Another element which has to be taken into account when assessing damages case-law is the division between cases where the whole argumentation is concentrated around the issue of public liability. The relative value of such judgments for damages purposes is of course much greater than that of cases which just have some paragraphs briefly addressing the damages issues. More generally, it is important

[76] eg in CFI Case T-383/00 *Beamglow v European Parliament, Council and Commission* (damages claim dismissed, no appeal) [2005] ECR II-5459, the CFI addressed questions relating to strict liability in the WTO context, but found that the conditions were not fulfilled. The judgment was not appealed. However, the judgment in CFI Case *FIAMM and FIAMM Technologies v Council and Commission* ECR of the same day came to the same conclusion. That judgment, was, in contrast, appealed and eventually quashed by ECJ *FIAMM and Fedon* (n 57). Therefore, albeit *Beamglow* appears formally intact, it no longer reflects the current situation. The same applies to all pre-*Bergaderm* CFI judgments, which are solely built on the dichotomy of administrative act/legislative act.

[77] One of the elements assessed for an order for interim measures is the risk of irreparable damage, *cf* F Castillo de la Torre, 'Interim measures in Community courts: recent trends' (2007) *Common Market Law Review* 273–353. The composition of the Court is not a unequivocal factor either; it is also an indication of the potential importance of the case as assessed by the Court before it starts its deliberations.

[78] ECJ Case 6/60 *Humblet v Belgian State* [1960] ECR 559, 569.

to understand the specifities of the context and the way the courts of the Union operate.[79]

The following classification attempts to single out the most important judgments from the rest.

a. Rulings of Principle, or Constitutional Judgments

The 'leading cases' in the field of public liability in damages are those where the principle of liability has been established or its conditions have been considerably revised. These cases are *Francovich, Brasserie du Pêcheur* and *Bergaderm.* This category would also include cases where the limits of liability have been considered (such as *FIAMM* on the existence of strict liability).

b. Habitual Cases – Clarifying Law

'Habitual cases' could be characterised as cases where essential choices or definitions as to the scope of public liability have been established. Examples of such cases are *Haim* (for Member State liability, a question concerning liability for breaches attributable to a public-law body of a Member State) or *Dolianova* (for liability of the European Union, strict interpretation of the limitation period). Further examples are *Schneider* (liability in merger control) or *M v Ombudsman*, confirming the damages liability of the Ombudsman.

c. Routine Cases – Applying the Law

Normal cases or statistical cases is a category which covers 'normal damages cases', ie cases where the damages criteria are assessed and applied by a court in a 'normal' manner. This category would readily contain the post-*Mulder* milk quota cases where that judgment was applied in individual damages actions brought by farmers.

d. Non-serious Cases

Finally, analysis of the case-law shows a surprisingly high number of cases that might be classified as damages cases, but which do not contain any real substantive ruling on the application of damages criteria or in which the damages action is declared simply inadmissible or manifestly unfounded. These 'non-serious damages cases' often lack the elementary basic components of any successful damages action.[80] This category may, at least in part, explain the vague success rate of damages cases.

[79] A very interesting and complete analysis is made by L Coutron, 'Style des arrêts de la Cour de justice et normativité de la jurisprudence communautaire' (2009) *Revue trimestrielle de droit européen* 643, where the author discusses the cultural context in which the Court functions, consquences of absence of binding precedents, various classes of obiter dicta and how the Court distinguishes between the cases.

[80] CFI Case T-228/02 *Organisation des Modjahedines du Peuple d'Iran v Council (No 1)* (damages claim dismissed, no appeal) [2006] ECR II-4665 [180]: '. . . the claim for damages contained in the application lacks even the most basic detail and must, accordingly, be declared inadmissible, especially given that the applicant did not even attempt to remedy that defect in its reply'.

In proportionate terms, one could estimate that 'rulings of principle' and 'habitual cases' form one fifth of the cases introduced, while the remaining four fifths is the 'routine cases' and 'non-serious cases'.

e. A Category of Their Own: Personnel Cases

It would seem justified to distinguish personnel cases as a category of their own. They are not treated systematically in this study and they relate to the internal workings of the institution, rather than to the 'external' aspect. They also have a separate legal basis in the Treaty, while the damages awarded can also be the symbolic sum of one Euro.[81]

v. Periodisation of Case-law: 'the Traffic Lights'

Periodisation of case-law is a useful tool to get to grips with a mass of cases. This method has been frequently used by EC researchers.[82] To give an idea of the time aspect of public liability case-law, the case-law can be divided into three periods, marked by the well-known 'traffic lights' metaphor:

a. 'Green Period'

Case-law back till July 2000: presumption that they are 'good law' (*Bergaderm* and post-*Bergaderm*). This study thus mainly concentrates on 'green period' case-law, ie case-law from the post-*Bergaderm* era.

b. 'Red Period'

Case law that is 30 years and older (1978 and before): these cases should be examined with considerable care. Many things have changed since the Community of nine Member States. These cases are mainly quoted as examples of application of original parameters or as factual situations which can be interesting (even if the factual circumstances of damages liability have considerably changed since, for example, the 1970s)

c. 'Yellow Period'

The period falling between the two other periods (ie 1978–2000) contains very heterogenic elements. It may have cases which are still undoubtedly 'good law' (eg when they relate to causation, or heads of damage), but may as well contain cases which have been superseded by later case-law (eg on the decisive importance of the administrative/legislative distinction).

[81] These cases are also distinguished as a separate group by J-M Favret, *Les influences réciproques du droit communautaire et du droit national de la responsabilité publique extracontractuelle* (Paris, Pedone, 2000).

[82] See eg, JHH Weiler, 'The Transformation of Europe' (1991) *Yale Law Journal* 2403–83, Ojanen, *The European* Way (n 33) and N Jääskinen, 'Kolme aaltoa – miten Suomen oikeusjärjestys eurooppalaistui?' (2001) *Defensor Legis* 603–19.

IV. STRUCTURAL ASPECTS FOR COMPARING THE MAIN FEATURES OF THE TWO LIABILITY SYSTEMS

As the two liability systems are analysed in separate chapter five (for EU liability) and chapter six (for Member State liability), it is appropriate to present the underlying common analytical framework in one place, so as to avoid repeating it. The table below represents the structure and parameters according to which each system is assessed (ie EU liability in chapter five, section I and Member State liability in chapter six, section I). It should assist, already by the joint structure, to highlight the similarities and differences of the two systems.

Table 2.2 Structural Aspects Regarding the Liability of the European Union and of its Member States for Breaches of EU Law

Aspect	**Liability of the European Union (ch 5)** ('*Schöppenstedt/Bergaderm*')	**Liability of Member States (ch 6)** ('*Francovich/Brasserie/Factortame*')
Development	*When and how was this type of liability established?*	
Aims of liability system	*What is the primary purpose of this liability system?*	
Source of rules governing liability	*What are the sources of law for this liability system? (case-law, enacted provisions, EU or national?)*	
Finding law: Availability of cases, Statistics, number of cases	*Where to find the law? How many cases are there?*	
Alternative remedies	*What is the role of damages liability in respect of other remedies available?*	
Open or closed nature of the legal framework for the system	*Is this liability system independent or does it depend on some other system in its operation?*	
Institutional coverage	*What bodies are subject to this type of liability?*	
Sectors of liability	*In what sectors, typically, has this type of liability been invoked?*	
Applicants	*Who has been invoking this type of liability?*	
Heads of damage	*What are the heads of damage typically requested/awarded?*	
Successful cases	*How many successful cases are there? Proportionate relation to all cases? Quantum of damages awarded?*	

V. INTRODUCTION TO 'RIGHTS'

A. 'Rights', 'a Rule of Law Granting Rights to Individuals', 'Individual Rights' and 'Subjective Rights'

This section sets out the common criteria for assessment of the *rights* criterion. This criterion is analysed for each liability system in its context, ie in chapter five, section II for EU liability and in chapter six, section II for Member State liability. Comparative conclusions on convergence of this criterion in the two systems are then made in chapter seven, section II.

One of the fundamental features uncovered by the Court from the newly created European Community legal order in the 1960s was the idea that, in relations between the Community legal order and national legal orders, Community law can grant rights directly to individuals, and not only affect the legal position of its Member States. Since the seminal case of *Van Gend en Loos* (ECJ 1963),[83] an ever increasing amount of case-law of the European Court of Justice has been dealing with how these rights are granted to individuals and how these rights can be invoked in Member States. The rights discussion has also played a key role in the constitutionalisation process.[84]

Despite its central role in EU law, the concept of 'right' is rather confused and not very structured. One reason contributing to this situation is that the concept of right has been gradually created in case-law, and depending on the relationships in question, it may have various meanings. It is thus not easy to characterise *what is meant by 'right'* in EU law: it is an amorphous concept difficult to capture. Van Gerven proposed in 2000 that it

> refers to the *general right*, and accompanying remedy, to have a court set aside national measures which conflict with the requirements of a directive, but may also refer to a *specific right* which a directive grants to private parties, and which, together with other conditions, gives rise . . . to a right and an accompanying remedy for compensation in respect of harm sustained.[85]

[83] ECJ Case 26/62 *Van Gend en Loos* [1963] ECR 1, 12.

[84] One essential element of this development has been the position of fundamental rights. In this respect the following two articles have been very important: JHH Weiler and NJS Lockhart, '"Taking Rights Seriously" Seriously: The European Court and its Fundamental Rights Jurisprudence I' (1995) *Common Market Law Review* 51–94 and JHH Weiler and NJS Lockhart, '"Taking Rights Seriously" Seriously: The European Court and its Fundamental Rights Jurisprudence II' (1995) *Common Market Law Review* 579–627. The rights discussion returned to the scene in 2008 in the *Kadi* appeals judgment, see ECJ Joined Cases C-402/05 P and C-415/05 P *Kadi and Al Barakaat International Foundation v Council and Commission* (CFI judgment set aside) [2008] ECR I-6351, see [283], [285]. In that case the relationship between fundamental rights and the restrictive measures imposed by the UN Security Council was addressed. The Court recalled, inter alia, that fundamental rights form an integral part of the general principles of law whose observance the Court ensures and that even the obligations imposed by an international agreement cannot have the effect of prejudicing the constitutional principles of the EC Treaty, which include the principle that all Community acts must respect fundamental rights, that respect constituting a condition of their lawfulness which it is for the Court to review in the framework of the complete system of legal remedies established by the Treaty.

[85] W van Gerven, 'Of Rights, Remedies and Procedures' (2000) *Common Market Law Review* 501–36, 507.

Another definition offered by van Gerven in the same article is the following:

> The concept of right refers, in my view, to a legal position which a person recognised as such by the law – thus a legal 'subject' (hence the name 'subjective' right) – may have and which in its normal state can be enforced by that person against (some or all) others before a court of law by means of one or more remedies[86]

In EU public liability law, the rights discourse also has a prominent place, as following *Brasserie du Pêcheur/Bergaderm*, the liability of the European Union and of the Member States both require that the rule of law infringed must have been intended to give rights to individuals. This requirement is far more complicated than one might think at first glance.[87] It can be 'easy' to establish in explicit cases, but then explicit cases are becoming more and more rare. Naturally, in each system, a person claiming responsibility for damages must first identify the rule of law said to have been breached.

It has been noted that one of the consequences of the Court's case-law on Member State liability was that it triggered a broader discussion in the 1990s on the concept of rights in Community law.[88] Moreover, the concept of 'rights' does not necessarily fully coincide in the two contexts, namely at European Union level and at Member State level. Member State liability started in *Francovich* with very concrete rights; rights which could be identified on the basis of the Wage Guarantee Directive 80/987[89] whereas the liability of the Community started from a higher level of abstraction, as the rights breached had to be 'superior rules of law for the protection of the individual'. Therefore, for Member State liability, we are most often talking about a right expressed in the Treaties or in legislation, while Community liability is more about breaching principles.

One terminological issue should be noted. The concept of '*rights*' appears in the doctrine and in the case-law with various qualifiers. The Court uses the phrase 'a rule of law granting *rights to individuals*'. Many authors talk about '*individual rights*' and those with links to the Germanic legal system often refer to '*subjective rights*'. In this text all these expressions are in principle used interchangeably. Preference is given to 'individual rights' as this is a fairly straightforward shorthand for the phrase used by the Court in post-*Bergaderm* case-law.[90]

[86] W van Gerven, 'Of Rights, Remedies and Procedures' (n 85) 502.

[87] See, in contrast, Jans who seems to suggest that the granting of rights to individuals is a clear matter to be decided on the basis of European law: for him, the 'rule infringed' contains 'rights for individuals or not', JH Jans, 'State Liability: In Search of a Dividing Line between National and European Law' in D Obradovic and N Lavranos (eds), *Interface between EU Law and National Law* (Groningen, Europa Law Publishing, 2007) 288. cf ECJ Case C-222/02 *Paul and others* [2004] ECR I-9425 where the granting of rights was discussed in some detail, and ECJ Case C-201/02 *Wells* [2004] ECR I-723.

[88] S Prechal, 'Member State liability and direct effect: what's the difference after all?' (2007) *European Business Law Review* 299–316, 303. She makes a useful summary of that discussion in S Prechal, 'Protection of Rights: How Far?' in S Prechal and B van Roermund (eds), *Coherence in EU Law. The Search for Unity in Divergent Concepts* (Oxford, Oxford University Press, 2008), 157–63.

[89] Council Directive 80/987/EEC of 20 October 1980 on the approximation of the laws of the Member States relating to the protection of employees in the event of the insolvency of the employer [1980] OJ L283/23.

[90] See also ECJ Case C-445/06 *Opinion of Advocate General Trstenjak – Danske Slagterier* [2009] ECR I-2119 [64].

The variations in terminology can be explained in different ways. One explanation is that in English a distinction exists between 'law' and 'rights' whereas in French, for example, both are based on the same expression 'droit', which has to be qualified for different purposes, ie 'droit' as such which corresponds to 'law' in English and 'droit subjectif' which corresponds to 'right' in English. The same distinction can be found in German. Therefore, in principle, it would not be necessary to talk about 'subjective rights' as the concept of 'right', in contrast to 'law', already covers the personal, subjective element.[91]

The concept of rights in EU law, including for the purposes of damages liability, might benefit from a more analytical and theoretical approach. One example of a beneficial change of paradigm which could be used as a model in this context was Finnish analytical legal positivism, which, in its forms from the 1950s to the early 1970s deconstructed the traditional system of subjective rights and replaced it with various correlative and opposite legal positions, inspired by WN Hohfeld's basic legal oppositions.[92] We will attempt to see if this approach could be helpful, in chapter six, section II below, in view of the rights invoked in the Member State liability context.

B. Path to Convergence for the Condition Concerning 'Rights'

Bergaderm established the presumption of *convergence* for the 'rights' criterion, too. Here, apparently for the first time in the context of the Community liability, the Court gave up the concept of 'superior rule for the protection of the individual' and replaced it with 'rights language', namely with a '*rule of law infringed must be intended to confer rights on individuals*'. The requirements of protection and superiority, as presented since *Zuckerfabrik* (ECJ 1971),[93] were gone, at least expressly; from now on the examination should only concentrate on the issue whether the rule in question intends to confer rights on individuals. This should be clear from the judgment in *San Pedro* (CFI 2005),[94] relating to Community liability, where the CFI noted, contrary to the Council's submissions in the case, that it was unimportant whether or not the rule of law infringed constitutes a higher-ranking rule of law, and it referred expressly to *Bergaderm.*

It is also useful to recall that originally, for the liability of Member States in *Francovich* (ECJ 1991), the condition was that 'the result prescribed by the directive should entail the grant of rights to individuals'. Moreover, the

[91] S Beljin, 'Rights in EU Law' in S Prechal and B van Roermund (eds), *Coherence in EU Law. The Search for Unity in Divergent Concepts* (Oxford, Oxford University Press, 2008) 95. See also van Gerven et al, *Tort law* (n 22), 63–64.

[92] See N Jääskinen, 'Back to the *Begriffshimmel?* A Plea for an Analytical Perspective in European Law' in S Prechal and B van Roermund (eds), *Coherence in EU Law. The Search for Unity in Divergent Concepts* (Oxford, Oxford University Press, 2008).

[93] ECJ *Zuckerfabrik Schöppenstedt* (n 21) [11].

[94] CFI Case T-415/03 *Cofradía de pescadores 'San Pedro' de Bermeo and others v Council* (damages claim dismissed, appealed C-6/06 P) [2005] ECR II-4355 [85].

result required by that directive entails the grant to employees of a right to a guarantee of payment of their unpaid wage claims. As is clear from examination of the first part of the first question, the content of that right can be identified on the basis of the provisions of the directive.[95]

C. Hypothesis for Assessment of the Rights Criterion in Chapter Five and Chapter Six

The main purpose of the rights sections in chapters five and six is to examine the convergence of the granting of rights criterion, both as regards liability of the European Union and liability of the Member States, as interpreted for the purposes of liability of its predecessor, the European Community. For the purposes of these sections the following hypothesis concerning the differences between the Member State level rights discussion and the Community level rights discussion serve as a starting point.

As regards *Member State liability* (chapter six) the relationship between grant of rights, direct effect, remedies and Member State liability could be outlined in summary form as follows. The *original rights discourse* was initially triggered through *Van Gend and Loos* case-law (ECJ 1962)[96] and the question of 'direct effect' was there from the beginning. That discussion concerned the position of Community law in the Member States. Community law rights so established enjoyed 'primacy' in Member States.[97] Albeit originally no new remedies were meant to be created for protecting these rights (*Rewe, Comet* ECJ 1976),[98] the new remedy in damages was established through *Francovich* (ECJ 1991).[99] This was based on 'rights' and breach thereof. It was created as an extension of the principles of direct effect and primacy. Therefore, the relationship between Community law and Member State law is anchored firmly to the concept of rights. What *Francovich/Brasserie du Pêcheur* did was merely to 'complete' the picture as regards the remedy of damages for breach of those rights.

However, as regards the *liability of the Union [ex-Community]* (chapter five) the situation is somewhat different. The concepts of direct effect and primacy had – naturally – no role to play within the liability system of the Community, as those concepts were established in relation to Community law in Member States. Thus the question of upholding Community law rights at Community level was never such an important issue; at Member State level it was a crucial issue, the existential question. The case-law on Community liability started to develop with the criterion concerning 'superior rule of law for the protection of the individual' (*Schöppenstedt*;

95 ECJ *Francovich and Bonifaci* (n 29) [40] and [44].
96 ECJ *Van Gend en Loos* (n 83) 12.
97 ECJ Case 6/64 *Costa v ENEL* [1964] ECR 585, 594.
98 ECJ Case 33/76 *Rewe v Landwirtschaftskammer für das Saarland* [1976] ECR 1989 [6] and ECJ Case 45/76 *Comet BV v Produktschap voor Siergewassen* [1976] ECR 2043 [19].
99 ECJ *Francovich and Bonifaci* (n 29).

ECJ 1971). That condition was firmly established by the time of *Brasserie du Pêcheur*, but until then no similar 'language redolent of rights' attached to the liability of the Community, as for Member State liability, existed. With *Brasserie du Pêcheur*, and by the latest with *Bergaderm*, the condition of 'superior rule of law for the protection of the individual' was replaced with the 'rule of law conferring rights on individuals'.

Therefore, *Brasserie du Pêcheur* and *Bergaderm* actually marked the final entrée of the rights discourse to the realm of Community liability. This coincided with the establishment of the EU Charter of Fundamental Rights in 2000, which related to the rights individuals can claim before Community institutions and Member States, when they apply Community law.[100] This development was also an integral part of the constantly evolving case-law of the EU courts on fundamental rights.

VI. INTRODUCTION TO 'BREACH' AND 'FAULT'

A. Overview

This section lays down joint criteria for assessment of the criteria concerning sufficient seriousness of *breach*. As above, this criterion is analysed for each liability system in its context, ie in chapter five, section III for EU liability and in chapter six, section III for Member State liability. Comparative conclusions on convergence of this criterion in the two systems are then made in chapter seven, section III.

The second condition for public liability in EU law is that the breach must be *sufficiently serious*. This qualification of breach was one of the novelties of the test established in *Brasserie* (ECJ 1996).[101] This condition consists of two limbs: (1) there must be a breach of an EU rule of law by a public authority, and (2) the breach must be sufficiently serious. Since *Bergaderm* (ECJ 2000), this criterion applies both to liability of Member States and to liability of the Union. Of the three liability conditions, this second condition relating to breach and its qualification, and in particular its second limb, is the most problematic. It deals with the existence and degree of the breach.

'Sufficiently serious breach' is an EU law concept. For the purposes of examining convergence it is a highly interesting and illuminating concept. In fact we are faced with a triangular situation which is illustrated in Figure 2.3.

[100] Charter of Fundamental Rights of the European Union, proclaimed in Nice on 7 December 2000 and as adapted at Strasbourg on 12 December 2007 [2007] OJ C303/1.

[101] The change which has taken place with the introduction of this condition is addressed in ch 5. It is noteworthy that the Court gives the following clarification in ECJ Joined Cases C-178/94, C-179/94, C-189/94 and C-190/94 *Dillenkofer and others v Bundesrepublik Deutschland* [1996] ECR I-4845 ([23], emphasis added): 'In substance, the conditions laid down in that group of judgments [*Brasserie* and *Hedley Lomas*] are the same, *since the condition that there should be a sufficiently serious breach, although not expressly mentioned in Francovich, was nevertheless evident from the circumstances of that case*'.

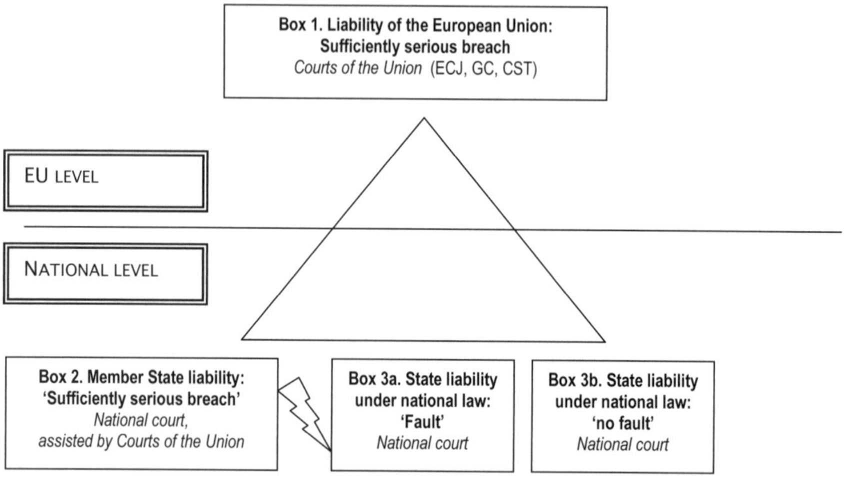

Figure 2.3 Public Liability in Triangular Setting

The liability criteria for the Union (see Box 1 in the figure) were originally based on national systems (see Box 3a). Following *Bergaderm*, the liability criteria for the Union and Member States, including the one related to the breach, should be the same ('Box 1 = Box 2'). For the liability of the Union, which is decided solely by the EU courts, this should not be a major problem, but for national courts the use of this EU law concept requires special attention. For the national judge the first question may be: how does this differ from the fault concept required in my national law?

As the concept of sufficiently serious breach was introduced in 1996/2000 for Member State and EU liability respectively, the case-law before those dates cannot be used directly to assess this criterion. However, before delving into case-law, it is necessary to take a more general look at the question of breach/fault in order to set the context for analysis of the Luxembourg case-law. Here we start with a procedural question as to establishment of illegality in the two systems, before addressing the core issue of fault and discretion.

B. Procedures for Establishing Breach of EU Law in the Two Liability Systems

For *the liability of the Union*, a breach of EU law by EU institutions for damages purposes can be established in three ways. First, the most clear-cut means is the damages action under Article 340(2) TFEU where the General Court[102] assesses both the existence of a breach and its seriousness in the specific context of the damages action and the position of the applicant, alongside all other pertinent criteria.

[102] Save for staff cases, the CST.

Second, in general, the way to establish a breach of EU law by EU institutions *par excellence* is of course an action for annulment. Third, a breach by EU institutions can also be established in a preliminary reference from a Member State court where the validity of an EU measure is examined.[103] In the two latter situations the ECJ does not assess the seriousness of the breach for damages purposes, as that is not the object of those procedures, but that issue needs to be assessed in a separate damages action to be introduced on the basis of Article 340(2) TFEU.

The three actions are partly overlapping and partly exclusive. There are no particular procedural hurdles to initiate a damages action against the European Union, whereas for action for annulment the criterion of 'directly and individually concerned' presented a major limitation until the Article was amended by the Lisbon Treaty. Thus, for example, an action for damages resulting from a EU Regulation can easily be initiated, but damages cannot be prevented by initiating an action for annulment, as the procedural rules make this impossible in practice. However, where an action for annulment is available (eg damage resulting from a decision addressed to the party), the party should avail itself of the possibility to introduce an action for annulment, as a damages action cannot be used to circumvent eg the short deadline established for introduction of an annulment action.[104]

As regards *Member State liability*, breach for damages liability purposes can also be established in three ways. The primary way to establish breach of EU law by Member State authorities for this purpose is in fact a damages action against the Member State in question in a national court. The national court should be in a position to assess whether the criteria of *Brasserie du Pêcheur* (ECJ 1996)[105] are fulfilled. A second way of establishing breach is an *infringement action*, which can be initiated by the Commission and where the ECJ can formally establish the incompatibility of national legislation with EU law.[106] Third, the incompatibility of national law can be indirectly revealed in a reply to a *preliminary reference*.[107]

For Member State liability, it should be noted that these three actions are partly overlapping and partly exclusive. The procedural requirements for initiating a damages action are set by national law. An infringement action is solely at the discretion of the Commission and an individual or company cannot force the Commission to

[103] In national proceedings, where the national court makes a preliminary reference to the ECJ, the illegality of Community measure can be invoked through a *plea of illegality*. This was the case in the milk quota cases, see *cf* ECJ Case 120/86 *Mulder* [1988] ECR 2321, ECJ Case 170/86 *Von Deetzen v Hauptzollamt Hamburg-Jonas* [1988] ECR 2355 [17] which led to the milk quota damages cases, most notably ECJ Joined Cases C-104/89 and C-37/90 *Mulder (No 1) and others v Council and Commission* (liability established) [1992] ECR I-3061 [22] and ECJ Joined Cases C-104/89 and C-37/90 *Mulder (No 2) and others v Council and Commission* (quantum) [2000] ECR I-203.

[104] ECJ Case 25/62 *Plaumann v Commission EEC* (damages claim dismissed) [1963] ECR 95, 108 and E Cujo, 'L'autonomie du recours en indemnité par rapport au recours en annulation – évolutions jurisprudentielles' (1999) *Revue du Marché Commun et de l'Union Européenne* 414–20.

[105] ECJ *Brasserie du Pêcheur and Factortame* (n 46).

[106] See now Art 258 and 260 TFEU. For a direct action underlying a damages case, see ECJ Case 178/84 *Commission v Germany* [1987] ECR 1227 [54], which preceded ECJ *Brasserie du Pêcheur* (n 46).

[107] See now Art 267 TFEU. For a preliminary ruling underlying a damages case, see ECJ Case C-31/92 *Larsy (No 1)* [1993] ECR I-4543, which preceded the second *Larsy* case, namely ECJ Case C-118/00 *Larsy (No 2)* [2001] ECR I-5063.

take a Member State to the Court.[108] A request for preliminary reference is a matter for the national court. Even if the EU courts may at most assist when fulfilment of the various conditions is assessed, the final decision on assessment of fulfilment of the criteria and damages award always belongs to the national court. Establishing breach in the two systems could be summarized in a table as follows.

Table 2.3 Means of Asserting Breach of EU Law for the Purposes of a Damages Claim

	Establishing breach for the purposes of liability of the EU (ch 5 s III)	**Establishing breach for the purposes of Member State liability (ch 6 s III)**
Primary means	1. Damages action under Article 340(2) TFEU before the GC	1. Damages action in Member State court
Supportive means	2. Action for annulment under Article 263 TFEU before GC	2. Action for annulment against a national measure in national court under national law (for breach of EU law)
		3. Enforcement action against Member State under Articles 260 TFEU (by Commission) and 262 TFEU (by another Member State)
	3. Preliminary ruling under Article 267 TFEU	4. Preliminary ruling under Article 267 TFEU
	4. General case-law of the EU courts	5. General case-law of the EU courts

The 'primary means' in the table reflects the procedure under which the full and final qualification for damages purposes can be made. The 'other means' refers to categories which either can assist in that finding, or sometimes precede it, one way or the other. However, they are secondary in the sense that those findings, even if qualified as 'breaches' sufficient eg for annulment of an EU act or condemnation of a Member State for breach of a Treaty obligation, are not in themselves sufficient to qualify the breach as sufficiently serious for damages purposes.[109] But the contrary is not true either: damages liability cannot arise without an annulment or finding of illegality, because the existence of a breach is a necessary condition for liability.[110] This is evidenced by the case-law, discussed in more detail later in chapter five, section III and chapter six, section III.

[108] CFI Case T-202/02 *Makedoniko Metro and Michaniki v Commission* (inadmissible, no appeal) [2004] ECR II-181 [43].

[109] ECJ Case 22/88 *Vreugdenhil (No 1) and another v Minister van Landbouw en Visserij* (preliminary ruling) [1989] ECR 2049, ECJ Case C-282/90 *Vreugdenhil (No 2) v Commission* (damages action, dismissed) [1992] ECR I-1937.

[110] ECJ *FIAMM and Fedon* (n 57).

Finally, the courts proceed to assess breach for damages purposes in two steps: first they examine whether there is a breach or not.[111] If there is no breach, the case is examined no further. If there is a breach, then the courts will proceed to qualify it: by first establishing the scope of discretion for the case at hand (wide discretion/narrow discretion), after which they will analyse whether the limits of discretion have been breached in a sufficiently serious manner (when liability will be incurred) or not (when there will be no liability).[112]

C. Qualifying Breach for Damages Purposes

i. Various Forms of 'Fault' in National Public Liability Law

Starting from Member State liability, it is clear from Figure 2.3 that assessment of breach of applicable rules is done by a national judge. Most national judges, under most national public liability systems, include in their assessment the concept of 'fault' (Box 3 in Figure 2.3).[113] However, when looking at Member State liability under EU law, there is no 'fault' (Box 2 in Figure 2.3): European Union law mentions 'sufficiently serious breach'. This is explained further in the next section (VI.D) below, but in this section it is necessary to examine the concept of 'fault' in national systems.

We will not be able to tackle national public liability 'fault' satisfactorily in this context. What we would try to do is to revisit briefly some of its forms to mark the pertinent differences in relation to EU law 'breach'. What should be recalled at the outset is that in Member States where 'fault' is essential for *public* liability, it is often a kind of specific extension of 'fault' in *private* liability.[114] Therefore, doctrinal works which treat 'fault' in general national liability law cannot necessarily be used without reserve in the public liability context.[115] Ideally, specialised works on 'public liability fault' should be used.[116] Van Dam offers a succinct comparative overview of three states, by presenting first the 'fault' condition with its variations in the general systems of liability in France, Germany and England, and then, separately, the 'fault' condition with its variations in the specific public liability systems in the same states.[117]

[111] See below ch 5 s III.2 and ch 6 s III.1.

[112] See below ch 5 s III.3 and ch 6 s III.2.

[113] We have also added, for the sake of completeness, 'Box 3a' for no-fault liability for Member State national public liability law, to have a 'marker' for this additional difference between the two systems.

[114] Where such a difference exists (not in the UK for example).

[115] An interesting overview of the use of 'fault' in EC law instruments pertaining to private law area (company law, electronic commerce, environmental liability) is provided by M Lukas, 'Fault Liability' in H Koziol and R Schulze (eds), *Tort Law of the European Community* (Vienna, SpringerWienNewYork, 2008).

[116] For fault liability of public authorities in English and French law, see Fairgrieve, *State Liability in Tort. A Comparative Law Study* (n 38) 58-135. For Germany, Italy and France, see also P Nacimiento, *Gemeinschaftsrechtliche und nationale Staatshaftung in Deutschland, Italien und Frankreich* (Baden-Baden, Nomos, 2006) 84–129.

[117] Van Dam, *European Tort Law* (n 37); for France see section 302; for Germany see sections 402–404; for England (tort of negligence) see section 503. Thereafter he sets out the liability of public authorities; for France see section 1802; for Germany see sections 1803 and for England (tort of negligence) see section 1804.

At the general level, two components can be distinguished, namely illegality and fault.[118] *Illegality* ('Rechtswiedrigkeit', 'illegalité') is the objective element of activity not in conformity with applicable norms. *Fault* ('Verschulden', 'culpable behaviour on the part of the defendant') and similar concepts are of course mainly present in private tort law liability in national systems.[119] To assess the level of breach which may lead to damages liability there are different national concepts of fault.[120] Additional fault concepts can be found, for example, in criminal law. Now, what further complicates matters somewhat is that in different legal systems illegality and fault (1) have various meanings; (2) cannot be distinguished from one another or simply (3) one of them does not really exist. Zweigert and Kötz explain the key elements of the German system as follows (emphasis in the original):

> The requirement of *unlawfulness*... is satisfied by any invasion of one of the legal interests specified in § 823 par. I BGB which is not justified by any of the few special privileges such as self defence, necessity, and so on. The requirement of *culpability* or fault is satisfied if the harmful conduct is either intentional, that is, accompanied by the intention of invading the protected legal interest, or negligent.[121]

This level of detail can be contrasted with the French system, where the

> French lawyers draw no clear distinction between unlawfulness and fault. Both are contained in the concept of 'faute'.... neither the French courts nor the French writers draw any subtle doctrinal distinctions or even enter the lists on the 'concepts of unlawfulness' so familiar to German controversialists.[122]

In the English system, the concept of fault as such is a strange animal.[123] In Finland, it appears that 'public law fault' is often very close to 'private law fault', but in many liability situations the fault of public authorities is appreciated on somewhat different grounds.[124]

ii. Why Should 'Fault' not be Used in EU Law Liability?

In European Union public liability law, the concept of fault should not be pertinent as such. Instead, the more neutral, and at least partly different, concept of 'sufficiently serious breach' is used. 'Sufficiently serious breach' is detached from fault, although it bears strong resemblances to it in some respects.

[118] See generally, H Koziol (ed), *Unification of Tort Law: Wrongfulness* (The Hague, Kluwer Law International, 1998).

[119] For basic question in relation to provisions governing liability for fault, see eg, K Zweigert and H Kötz, *An Introduction to Comparative Law*, 3rd revised edn (Oxford, Clarendon, 1998) 559ff; von Bar, *The Common European Law of Torts. Volume One* (n 37) 20ff.

[120] See eg, Van Dam, *European Tort law* (n 37) throughout.

[121] Zweigert and Kötz, *An Introduction to Comparative Law* (n 119) 599.

[122] Zweigert and Kötz, *An Introduction to Comparative Law* (n 119) 619. On 'faute' in French public liability law, see B Delaunay, *La faute de l'administration* (Paris, LGDJ, 2007) 131.

[123] Zweigert and Kötz, *An Introduction to Comparative Law* (n 119) 605.

[124] For fault liability of public authorities in Finnish law, see Hakalehto-Wainio, *Valta ja vahinko* (n 41) 201–366.

However, fault is not absent from the case-law. Even if it seems that in the current practice the EU courts use the concept of 'sufficiently serious breach' fairly consistently, they have also used the concept of 'fault' in the past. In certain situations there have been good reasons for this. In the European Coal and Steel Community Treaty, which ceased to be in force in 2002, the distinction was made at Treaty level between two different types of 'fault', namely *faute de service* and *faute personnelle.*[125] Yet it is not difficult to find case-law where the Court has analysed in the EEC/EC or Euratom context whether the Community has committed a 'fault'.[126] In particular, the concept of fault is almost systematically present in cases where issues relating to possible 'no-fault liability' (or 'strict liability') of the Community are discussed.[127]

Fault, moreover, has been used in doctrine, too. This seems to be the case in particular when authors discuss 'no-fault liability' (rather than 'liability in the absence of sufficiently serious breach').

Advocate General Mischo discussed the concepts of 'illegality' and 'fault' in his opinion in *Francovich* (ECJ 1991).[128] He was considering whether unlawful conduct on the part of the State is sufficient to make it liable in damages. He noted that there had been some developments as regards the concepts of 'illegality' and 'fault' in the case-law of the Court. He pointed out that in *Les Assurances du Crédit* (ECJ 1991)[129] the Court held that in respect of legislative acts involving choices of economic policy, the unlawfulness of a coordinating directive is not in itself sufficient to establish Community non-contractual liability. Mr Mischo then suggested that apparently

[125] See G Bebr, 'The Non-contractual Liability of the European Coal and Steel Community' in T Heukels and A McDonnell (eds), *The Action for Damages in Community Law* (The Hague, Kluwer Law International, 1997) and the following articles of the Treaty establishing the European Coal and Steel Community (ECSC):

Art 34 ECSC: 'If the Court declares a decision or recommendation void, it shall refer the matter back to the Commission. The Commission shall take the necessary steps to comply with the judgment. If direct and special harm is suffered by an undertaking or group of undertakings by reason of a decision or recommendation held by the Court to involve a fault of such a nature as to render the Community liable, the Commission shall, using the powers conferred upon it by this Treaty, take steps to ensure equitable redress for the harm resulting directly from the decision or recommendation declared void and, where necessary, pay appropriate damages.

If the Commission fails to take within a reasonable time the necessary steps to comply with the judgment, proceedings for damages may be instituted before the Court'.

Under Art 40 ECSC the Court had jurisdiction to order pecuniary reparation from the Community, so as to make good any injury caused in carrying out the Treaty by *a wrongful act or omission* on the part of the Community in the performance of its functions. It also had jurisdiction to order the Community to make good any injury caused by *a personal wrong by a servant of the Community* in the performance of his duties.

[126] One of the reasons why 'fault' has been discussed in cases outside the ECSC Treaty – where it would have not been strictly speaking necessary – may be that when in Court cases the applicant's lawyers have argued against the fact that action or inaction by the Community institution constituted a fault, the Court had to reply to such arguments, without necessarily having to convert the reasoning to 'sufficiently serious breach or not'.

[127] See eg, ECJ Joined Cases C-120/06 P and C-121/06 P *Opinion of Advocate General Poiares Maduro – FIAMM and Fedon v Council and Commission* [2008] ECR I-6513.

[128] ECJ Joined Cases C-6/90 and C-9/90 *Opinion of Advocate General Mischo – Francovich and Bonifaci* [1991] ECR I-5357 [74] and [75].

[129] ECJ Case C-63/89 *Assurances du crédit v Council and Commission* (damages claim dismissed) [1991] ECR I-1799 [12] and [13].

in the eyes of the Court, the concepts of unlawfulness and fault, or wrongful conduct, are *synonymous in the case of normative measures.*

> It follows that even where the law of a Member State requires, in addition to illegality, the proof of fault, the national court need not (in relation to normative measures) seek to determine whether such fault exists and need merely consider whether the other conditions laid down by the case-law of the Court are met.

In EU public liability doctrine, some support can be found for the idea that fault has been replaced with wrongfulness.[130] Case-law has been somewhat fluctuating: in *Plaumann* (ECJ 1963)[131] and *Kampffmeyer* (ECJ 1967)[132] fault was required; in *Lütticke* (ECJ 1971[133] and *Zuckerfabrik* (ECJ 1971)[134] the question is unclear. *Cobrecaf* (CFI 1995)[135] mentions 'administrative fault' in the EEC, while in *Quiller* (CFI 1997)[136] and *Perillo* (CFI 1997)[137] fault is no longer mentioned. Then again in *Schneider* (CFI 2007) it pops up again all of a sudden.[138]

A further issue is whether 'fault' refers to an objective or a subjective element: is it unlawfulness or is it culpa? This issue has been discussed by Mulders as regards translations of the judgment in *Dekker* (ECJ 1990).[139]

However, as for Member State liability case-law of the ECJ such 'fault discussion' is rare, if not non-existent. But for the national judge the starting point is the inverse: the national judge is likely to start from fault and more precisely from the concept of fault in national law.

But, finally, what is wrong with 'fault' as a concept in EU law? The Court was directly confronted with the question in *Brasserie du Pêcheur.*[140] One of the questions which the Bundesgerichtshof seeked to establish was whether the national court is entitled to make reparation conditional upon the existence of fault (whether intentional or negligent) on the part of the organ of the State to which the infringement is attributable.

[130] F Schockweiler and G Vivenes et al, 'Le régime de la responsabilité extra-contractuelle du fait d'actes juridiques dans la Communauté européenne' (1990) *Revue trimestrielle de droit européen* 27–74, 51 and S Grossrieder Tissot, 'La responsabilité de la Communauté européenne du fait de l'activité normative de la Commission' (2001) *Revue trimestrielle de droit européen* 91–121, 100.

[131] ECJ *Plaumann v Commission EEC* (n 104) 108.

[132] ECJ Case 5/66 *Kampffmeyer v Commission* [1967] ECR 245, 262.

[133] ECJ Case 4/69 *Lütticke v Commission* (damages claim dismissed) [1971] ECR 325 [19].

[134] ECJ *Zuckerfabrik Schöppenstedt*, (n 21) [11].

[135] CFI Case T-514/93 *Cobrecaf and others v Commission* (damages awarded, no appeal) [1995] ECR II-621.

[136] CFI Joined Cases T-195/94 and T-202/94 *Quiller and Heusmann v Council and Commission* (damages awarded, no appeal) [1997] ECR II-2247.

[137] CFI Case T-7/96 *Perillo v Commission* (dismissed, no appeal) [1997] ECR II-1061.

[138] CFI Case T-351/03 *Schneider Electric v Commission* (damages action; liability established, appealed C-440/07 P) [2007] ECR II-2237.

[139] L Mulders, 'Translation at the Court of Justice of the European Communities' in S Prechal and B van Roermund (eds), *Coherence in EU Law. The Search for Unity in Divergent Concepts* (Oxford, Oxford University Press, 2008) 51–2 and ECJ Case 177/88 *Dekker v Stichting Vormingscentrum voor Jong Volwassenen* [1990] ECR I-3941.

[140] ECJ *Brasserie du Pêcheur and Factortame* (n 46) [75]–[80].

The ECJ noted first that the concept of fault does not have the same content in the various legal systems, and then went on as follows (emphasis added):

> 77 Next, it follows from the reply to the preceding question that, where a breach of Community law is attributable to a Member State acting in a field in which it has a wide discretion to make legislative choices, a finding of a right to reparation on the basis of Community law will be conditional, inter alia, upon the breach having been sufficiently serious.
>
> 78 So, certain objective and subjective factors connected with the concept of fault under a national legal system may well be relevant for the purpose of determining whether or not a given breach of Community law is serious (see the factors mentioned in paragraphs 56 and 57 above).
>
> 79 The obligation to make reparation for loss or damage caused to individuals cannot, however, depend upon a condition based on any concept of fault going beyond that of a sufficiently serious breach of Community law. Imposition of such a supplementary condition would be tantamount to calling in question the right to reparation founded on the Community legal order.
>
> 80 Accordingly, the reply to the question from the national court must be that, pursuant to the national legislation which it applies, reparation of loss or damage cannot be made conditional upon fault (intentional or negligent) on the part of the organ of the State responsible for the breach, going beyond that of a sufficiently serious breach of Community law.

It is submitted that the ECJ correctly disconnected 'EU fault' from the national systems. A different solution would have meant the express or implicit acceptance of 27 different basic concepts of fault – each of which has been amply refined in national case-law in relation to different sectors. However, the Court left it open as to what 'breach' actually means in the EU system. The only way to find out what it means is to go through the case-law. Of particular interest are cases where breach was established but was not considered to be sufficiently serious.

The conclusion from the above elements should thus be that owing to heavy risks of misunderstandings, use of the concept of 'fault' should be avoided in the EU system. Ideally, for the sake of clarity, the concept of 'fault', if used in the EU context, should be coupled with a 'EU-qualifier'. One could suggest using it with a qualifier to link it to EU-based liability, such as '*Francovich* type fault', 'European Union law fault' or 'EU law fault'.

D. 'Sufficiently Serious Breach' as an Autonomous EU Law Concept, and the Role of 'Discretion'

Sufficiently serious breach is an autonomous EU law concept. It is 'EU-speak', an expression like 'economic operator'. Sufficiently serious breach very much recalls unlawfulness or fault in national systems (or a combination of the two), but it is not necessarily the same. Sufficiently serious breach is basically independent of whatever 'national' weight fault, negligence, or any other similar expression in national law might carry with it; it excludes the national burden. In practical terms, sufficiently serious breach may sometimes coincide with the national law concept – and sometimes not.

In *Brasserie* (ECJ 1996), the Court established the following *five criteria* for the competent court in evaluating breach: (1) the clarity and precision of the rule breached; (2) the measure of discretion left by that rule to the national or Community authorities; (3) whether the infringement and the damage caused was intentional or involuntary; (4) whether any error of law was excusable or inexcusable; and (5) the fact that the position taken by a Community institution may have contributed towards the omission, and the adoption or retention of national measures or practices contrary to Community law.[141]

In addition there were two further categories, in which assessment was supposed to be more straightforward. Breach of Community law is clearly sufficiently serious if it has persisted despite a judgment finding the infringement in question, or a preliminary ruling or settled case-law of the Court on the matter from which it is clear that the conduct in question constituted an infringement.[142]

Furthermore, it is clear since *Francovich* (ECJ 1991) that non-transposition of a directive within the deadline was in itself sufficiently serious breach. It seems that the criteria relating to clarity of the EU law rule have played a key role in this respect. The following diagram attempts to present the various types of breach in relation to each other in order to determine their relative 'gravity'.

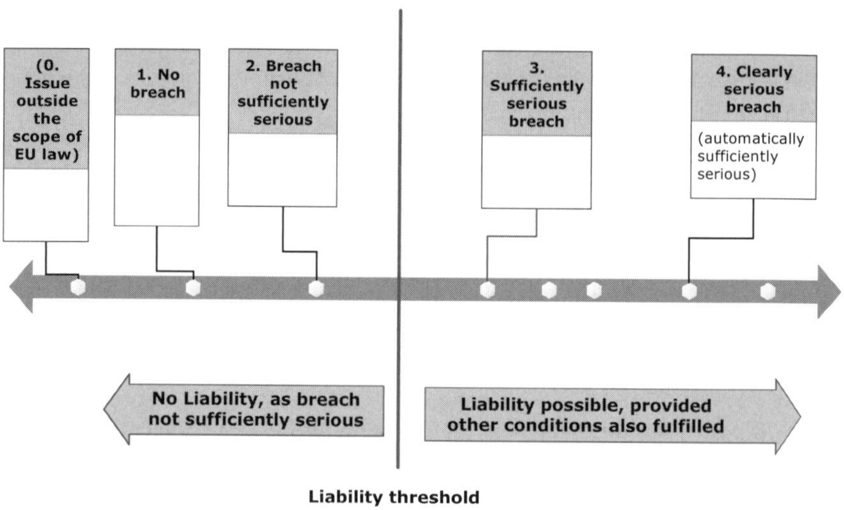

Figure 2.4 Degree of Breach and the Liability Threshold

[141] ECJ *Brasserie du Pêcheur and Factortame* (n 46) [56].
[142] Arts 258 TFUE and 267 TFUE, respectively.

In the diagram, the situations at both ends of the vector do not present major problems. It is in the middle that the devil lies: how to decide whether there is a breach which is not sufficiently serious or whether there is a sufficiently serious breach which may trigger liability. We examine the replies given in the case-law in chapter five, section III (European Union) and chapter six, section III (Member States).

Finally there is the question of discretion. It was the choice of the ECJ to replace the dichotomy between administrative and legislative acts with the concept of discretion. The ECJ requires that discretion be defined, whether wide or narrow. In this respect, Caranta has distinguished three levels, based on national legal systems. He notes that national systems have evolved beyond the generic notion of discretion when describing the room for manoeuvre left for decision makers by a higher-ranking legal rule. He calls the categories '*discrI*', '*discrII*' and '*discrIII*'.[143] The first group is *discrI* meaning 'policy decision linked to the weighing of *conflicting private and public interest*'. The second group, *discrII*, contains 'decisions involving complex *factual* situations' and the third, *discrIII*, relates to 'decisions involving the interpretation of complex and/or unclear *legal* rules'. However, it seems that this division should be completed by a situation without any discretion, ie. '*discr0*'. A summary listing of cases on this basis appears in the table below:

Table 2.4 Discretion Split into Four Levels

	Liability of the European Union	**Liability of the Member States**
discr0: no discretion	*Fresh Marine*	*Francovich*, *Dillenkofer*
discrI: policy decision linked to the weighing of conflicting *private and public interests*		*Schmidberger*
discrII: decisions involving complex *factual* situations	*CEVA/Pfizer* *Candiotte*	
discrIII: decisions involving interpretation of complex and/or unclear *legal* rules		*British Telecom (No 1)* *British Telecom (No 2)*

Even if such categorisation can be helpful, it remains rather general, and the limits of each group are not very clear. Obviously there would seem to be a number of issues outside these categories, too.[144]

[143] R Caranta, 'On Discretion' in S Prechal and B van Roermund (eds), *Coherence in EU Law. The Search for Unity in Divergent Concepts* (Oxford, Oxford University Press, 2008) 195.

[144] For an example outside the damages context, see ECJ Case C-531/06 *Commission v Italy* [2009] ECR I-4103, where the Court allowed rather large discretion for Member States as regards the organisation of measures concerning public health and pharmacies, see [36], [63], [64], [84] and [103].

At first sight discretion looks tempting, as it allows a more nuanced approach to different liability situations. The 'revirement' was an attempt to get rid of the old weight, but the current system still bears much of the old baggage with it. One question is whether it is more helpful to adopt a distance from national systems and have discretion as an autonomous concept of EU law, or stay close to national systems. However, some authors have argued that introduction of discretion may be more unhelpful than helpful and this aspect should be kept in mind when assessing the case-law in the following sections.[145]

In conclusion, one could say that one of the main issues in assessing the degree of breach is its relation to 'fault'. This is almost an automatic problem in Member State liability, as that form of liability is applied by national courts within national systems, but can very easily pop up in EU level liability, too. As to the concept of fault, it should be used with caution: it cannot be universally defined and it can, has and will be used for different purposes. The conceptual position of 'fault' indeed resembles that of one EU law concept, namely that of 'direct effect': a uniform, universally accepted, or acceptable definition of fault appears impossible to establish. At best we can flag a warning for its use to say that content may vary and that there are many ways to understand what it 'really' means.

[145] For criticism, see Caranta, 'On Discretion' (n 143). *cf* also C Hilson, 'Liability of Member States in Damages: The Place of Discretion' (1997) *ICLQ* 941–47 and Hilson, 'The Role of Discretion in EC Law on Non-Contractual Liability' (n 31).

3

Contexts of Convergence

THE CONVERGENCE WITHIN EU public law liability is not developing in isolation. This chapter presents the operational context when discussing convergent developments within EU public law liability. It is useful to start with the general constitutional context (section I) and then to proceed to areas which are more closely linked with the liability issues.

The national public liability laws, upon which the two EU public liability systems are based, and their mutual convergence, play an important part (section II). In addition, there is also a rather heterogeneous group of the 'other' relevant public liability systems (section III). The three last contexts relate to the counterparts of state liability for breaches of EU law, namely private liability for breaches of EU law under the *Courage* case-law (section IV), the convergence of private law in general in the EU (section V) and convergence of administrative law in the EU in general (section VI).

I. CONSTITUTIONAL CONTEXT OF EU PUBLIC LIABILITY

The development of EU law-based public liability is linked to constitutionalisation of the European Union in two ways: it is a constituent part of the process, and has itself evolved as a result of that process. Therefore it should be treated in the first place when explaining the context of EU public liability.

What is constitutionalisation?[1] In one article (originally published in 1997), Weiler offers a handy version, which contains in a condensed and plain form a number of dimensions of constitutionalisation.[2] Weiler notes that the European Economic Community was originally conceived as a legal order founded by international treaties creating an international organisation. What the constitutionalism thesis claims

[1] The gradual constitutionalisation of the current European Union is presented in JHH Weiler, *The Constitution of Europe. 'Do the New Clothes Have an Emperor?' and Other Essays on European Integration* (Cambridge, Cambridge University Press, 1999), 10–101 (reprinting inter alia. JHH Weiler, 'The Transformation of Europe' (1991) *Yale Law Journal* 2403–83). Constitutionalisation in the EU context was already evoked in the 1950s by Stein, whose late collection offers an insight into development, see E Stein, *Thoughts from a Bridge. A Retrospective of Writings on New Europe and American Federalism* (Ann Arbor, The University of Michigan Press, 2000) Constitutionalisation from the human rights perspective is assessed eg by T Ojanen, *The European Way. The Structure of National Court Obligation under EC Law* (Saarijärvi, 1998).

[2] Weiler, *The Constitution of Europe* (n 1) 221.

is that the Community has in certain essential aspects evolved and acts as if it was founded on a constitutional form of constitutional law, not on an ordinary international treaty. According to him, constitutionalism is the key element that differentiates the European Community from other transnational systems and, within the Union, from the other 'pillars'.

In more narrow terms, constitutionalisation is characterised by van Gerven as a process where 'constitutional values and principles underlying the constitutional law and/or constitutional traditions of a specific legal system . . . spread through all branches of that legal system, including principles of private and criminal law'.[3] This aspect highlights one constituent feature of constitutionalisation: it works at two levels (at least), and in interaction. The European Union has become more like a state through constitutionalisation, by incorporating, importing and imitating statal elements. Conversely, the Union forms a level playing field, which affects the legal systems with which it interacts. This is clearly visible for example in the accession processes to the European Union, where the applicant countries must fulfil certain constitutionalised accession criteria.[4]

The relationship between the different levels of constitutinalisation has also been referred to as two narratives, one told by the case-law of the ECJ, underlining the supreme authority of the European Union legal system and the role of the ECJ in it, the other by the highest national courts emphasising their role as final arbiter. One way of better apprehending these levels and putting the elements of the constitutional pluralism in action is to analyse these initially opposing approaches through a more nuanced framework. Maduro's thoughts about contrapunctual law could also be used to describe and analyse the development of public liability in EU law.[5]

Snyder analyses constitutionalisation through three dimensions: constitutional principles, constitutionalising processes and constitutional culture. In my view, they all have corresponding elements with the public liability law of the European Union.[6] First, constitutional principles consist of constituent principles of the integration process, and of the legal system it has set up. To counterbalance the transfer of powers, liability in damages is one of the essential elements to legitimise the powers of the Union. Second, as for constitutionalising processes: they are by nature dynamic and in constant development. The same also characterises damages liability, which develops all the time, and according to the general trend,

[3] W van Gerven, 'Judicial Convergence of Laws and Minds in European Tort law and Related Matters' in A Colombi Ciacchi and C Godt et al (eds), *Haftungsrecht im dritten Millenium – Liability in the Third Millenium: Liber Amicorum Gert Brüggemeier* (Baden-Baden, Nomos, 2009) 45.

[4] The criteria fixed at the Copenhagen European Council in 1993 include the stability of institutions guaranteeing democracy, the rule of law, human rights and respect for and protection of minorities; the existence of a functioning market economy as well as the capacity to cope with competitive pressure and market forces within the Union and the ability to take on the obligations of membership including adherence to the aims of political, economic and monetary union.

[5] M Poiares Maduro, 'Contrapunctual Law: Europe's Constitutional Pluralism in Action' in N Walker (ed) *Sovereignity in Transition* (Oxford, Hart Publishing, 2003).

[6] F Snyder, 'The unfinished constitution of the European Union: principles, processes and culture' in JHH Weiler and M Wind (eds), *European Constitutionalism Beyond the State* (Cambridge, Cambridge University Press, 2003) 60ff.

towards more extensive liability, rather than towards limitation. Third, constitutional culture (not compensation culture) is the more profound, underlying layer which advancement of the system builds upon. For damages liability, it is part of this deeper layer, as an overarching principle, and not just as a punctual ad hoc remedy available only in a limited number of cases.

Mylly construes an overarching critical view of private informational power, by a detailed reading of the doctrinal ideas presented in the constitutional context. For him the constitutionalism aspect forms an instrument to open up the rights discussion carried out by highly specialised experts in their own areas to deeper levels of law, common to all sectors.[7]

Jääskinen examines constitutionalisation from four different angles: namely through codification of the constituent treaties, through development of the institutional system, through the increasing bindingness of EU law and through development of the external identity of the Union.[8] Damages liability can also be seen as an important element in these four aspects. First, in codification of the constituent treaties, damages liability has not only been maintained but has been extended to cover all activities of the Union. Second, the liability of institutions has not only provided a readily available remedy, but also a useful reminder mechanism for the institutions on their responsibilities as public authorities. Third, to match the increasingly binding nature of EU law the creation of a new remedy in the Member States has enhanced the enforcement of EU law rights. Lastly, development of an external identity has been carried out with regular references to responsibility issues in relation to acts in external fields, for example in the ever recurring theme of damages liability for breach of the WTO rules. Moreover, the ECJ was probably the only court which could have taken the bold position expressed in *Kadi* (ECJ 2008) as regards judicial control of decisions of the United Nations Security Council in the fight against terrorism: that judgment is clearly one of the central building blocks of the current constitutional agenda.[9]

Overall, damages liability for breaches of EU law, both for EU institutions as well as for Member States, was a necessary element of the EU constitutional order. As for the liability of the institutions, it was logical to foresee this in the original treaties, alongside the transfer of competencies and other remedies. It is plausible that this is what the founding fathers and drafters of the Treaty thought: when competencies are transferred to the Community, and if the Community causes some damage, then it should repair the damage, just as national public authorities would do. In this regard, the damages liability of the current Union functions as a shield against illegal EU action.

[7] T Mylly, *Intellectual Property and European Economic Constitutional Law – The Trouble with Private Informational Power* (Vaajakoski, IPR University Center, 2009) 37, 151.

[8] N Jääskinen, *Euroopan unioni – oikeudelliset perusteet [European Union – Legal Foundations]* (Jyväskylä, Talentum, 2007) 70–81.

[9] ECJ Joined Cases C-402/05 P and C-415/05 P *Kadi and Al Barakaat International Foundation v Council and Commission* (CFI judgment set aside) [2008] ECR I-6351, J Nergelius, *The Constitutional Dilemma of the European Union* (Groeningen, Europa Law Publishing, 2009) 11.

However, the damages liability of Member States was completely different in nature. There is nothing on it in the Treaty. The idea of the Treaty drafters was to give competence for the Commission to sue Member States in the ECJ for a declaration of non-fulfilment of their obligations. It soon turned out that the Court interpreted its competences for the preliminary rulings procedure more extensively, by uncovering legal principles, such as primacy and direct effect, which existed in the system even if they were not expressly mentioned. Damages liability, the existence of which is a logical part of the EU legal system, then became a different type of instrument, a sword if you wish, against the Member States. In this respect an interesting question is whether conditions for use of the sword and shield are the same.

Timewise, recent constitutional developments can be regrouped in three periods: the first which through establishment of the Charter of Fundamental Rights (2000)[10] led to the Convention establishing a Constitution for Europe, its solemn signature in Rome under the Italian Presidency (2004) and its sudden rejection in two referenda in the Netherlands and France (2005). The second period, in diplomatic terms the 'reflection period', formed a kind of 'half-time' in the match. Tactical and political wisdom in Europe was gathered together to find a way forward from the impasse. The third period started with only moderate optimism with signature of the Lisbon Treaty (2007) and ended with the entry into force, almost by stealth, of the Treaty on 1 December 2009. In reading the first assessments of the post-Lisbon situation, one gets the impression that despite the finally adopted amendments in black-letter law, which for some issues are truly substantial, the whole decade of constitutional reforms rather witnesses the dramatic decline of political constitutionalism, and that hopes for a brighter future should still be addressed to the Court, the initiator and genuine developer of judicial constitutionalism.[11]

The constitutional context must be kept in mind when analysing past, current and future developments in the public liability area. Over a relatively short period, discussion on constitutional issues has extended from sovereign relations towards rights.[12] Rights have of course always been an underlying factor in this discourse, but it can be asserted that the argument has changed in nature. In fact, as regards the role of fundamental rights and human rights, Ojanen has argued that their importance in the constitutional discussion is on the rise, not so much as new super-principles which can supersede the fundamental economic rights (freedoms) on which the Community was originally built, but rather as equals – rights at the levels of the classic four freedoms.[13] If this development actually takes place,

[10] Charter of Fundamental Rights of the European Union, proclaimed in Nice on 7 December 2000 and as adapted at Strasbourg on 12 December 2007 [2007] OJ C303/1 and Art 6(1) TEU.

[11] J Wouters and L Verhey et al (eds), *European Constitutionalism Beyond Lisbon* (Antwerp, Intersentia, 2009).

[12] See N Walker (ed) *Sovereignity in Transition* (Oxford, Hart Publishing, 2003) and C Barnard, 'Introduction: The Constitutional Treaty, the Constitutional Debate and the Constitutional Process' in C Barnard (ed) *The Fundamentals of EU Law Revisited: Assessing the Impact of the Constitutional Debate* (Oxford, Oxford University Press, 2007).

[13] T Ojanen, 'Perus- ja ihmisoikeudet – eurooppalaisen konstitutionalismin Akilleen kantapää?' (2009) *Lakimies* 1106–24, 1108, 1113, 1116 and 1123.

then such rights could potentially also form a basis for damages actions more often in the future. Ojanen also refers to Tuori's 'four constitutions': in the contexts of economic constitution, juridico-political constitution, social constitution and security constitution, damages liability has played the main part in the economic constitution, but clearly it is on the rise in the other constitutional settings, too.[14]

Finally, to see the big picture, a concise book on post-Lisbon EU Constitutional law may well describe the place of public liability in this whole. Rosas and Armati present the EU constitutional law in a concise form, underlining its core values, principles and objectives.[15] In that book, questions of liability are one, not very lengthy, but equally essential part as all the other elements. Expounding on the thoughts of Oliver, one could say that public liability in damages for breaches of EU law should not be seen in isolation and certainly not only as a part of the web of remedies available to aggrieved parties through EU courts and national courts, but also and more profoundly as an active ingredient for, and an eager recipient of, the fruits of the constitutionalisation process in Europe.[16]

II. PUBLIC LIABILITY IN NATIONAL LAW

A. Overview of National Public Liability Laws

To start with public liability in national law, it should be examined at the outset whether the public authorities are a special case, subject to differential treatment in national liability law systems. What are the grounds for liability of public authorities in Member States? Are public authorities and governments equated with private parties as regards damages liability or are there some specific rules or even structures for this purpose?

In many Member States, special rules apply to liability of public authorities. That is the situation for example in France, Germany and Finland. However, in some countries, like the United Kingdom, general liability law (including tort) applies equally to governmental action.[17] Moreover, even if national public liability law may contain special rules, it is clearly not an isolated watertight compartment. Albeit public liability law forms a part of liability law, in text books public liability often appears as a secondary or rather more a marginal issue in relation to the core

[14] K Tuori, 'The Many Constitutions of Europe' in K Tuori and S Sankari (eds), *The Many Constitutions of Europe* (Farnham, Ashgate, 2010) 9ff (for the taxonomy of constitutions).

[15] *A Rosas and L Armati,* EU Constitutional Law (Oxford, Hart Publishing, 2010) 12–17 (discussing EU's state-like features and the non-state-like features).

[16] P Oliver, 'State Liability in Damages following Factortame III: A Remedy Seen in Context' in J Beatson and T Tridimas (eds), *New Directions in European Public Law* (Oxford, Hart Publishing, 1998) 61.

[17] Hogg discusses Dicey's idea of equality in his comprehensive study on the liability of the Crown in several Common law countries, see PW Hogg and PJ Monahan, *Liability of the Crown*, 3rd edn (Toronto, Carswell Thomson Professional Publishing, 2000) 1. See also T Cornford, *Towards a Public Law of Tort* (Aldershot, Ashgate, 2008) 9ff.

area of private law liability (ie tort).[18] Public liability law does not appear to stand at the core of (general) liability law studies.

What are the main features of the principal systems of liability for conduct of public authorities in certain EU Member States? The basic approaches of the English, German and French systems have been neatly summarised as follows:[19]

> English law . . ., in principle, subjects the conduct of public authorities to the same tort rules as those that are applicable to individuals. German law regulates the conduct of civil servants in the BGB [Civil Code], the liability of public authorities in the GG [Constitution]. In both legal systems . . . liability for wrongful legislative or judicial acts is but an exceptional occurrence. French law, on the contrary, is characterised by a sharp distinction between private and public law, not least because of the existence of a well-developed administrative court system, which has resulted in the development of a special form of liability without fault (in addition to fault-based liability).

It is thus clear that national public liability systems and a detailed study of their features may not be *the* solution to the EU law public liability puzzle, but their interaction with the Union system and their mutual permeation are essential in trying to grasp the essence of the various facets of the EU public law liability system.[20]

General non-contractual liability law is in many Member States at least in part founded on legislative provisions.[21] However, even if public law liability is in many Member States connected to a basic law or constitution, which may be completed by ordinary legislative provisions[22] or even a state liability act, regulation of public law liability is even in these states based mainly on case-law.[23] State liability law typically relies less on legislation, so that national state liability laws in many

[18] W van Gerven and J Lever et al, *Cases, Materials and Text on National, Supranational and International Tort Law* (Oxford, Hart Publishing, 2000) 358–94. For Finland, see eg, M Hemmo, *Vahingonkorvausoikeus [Law of Damages]* (Porvoo, 2006) 79–90; E Routamo and P Ståhlberg et al, *Suomen vahingonkorvausoikeus [Finnish Law of Damages]* (Helsinki, 2006) 223–36.

[19] van Gerven et al, *Tort Law* (n 18) 358.

[20] There are thorough studies concerning different aspects of liability of public authorities under national law for each legal system. For example, as regards Germany, see F Ossenbühl, *Staatshaftungsrecht. 5., neu bearbeitete und erweiterte Auflage* (Munich, Beck, 1998); for England C Booth QC and D Squires, *The Negligence Liability of Public Authorities* (Oxford, Oxford University Press, 2006); for France C Broyelle, *La responsabilité de l'Etat du fait des lois* (Paris, LGDJ, 2003), B Delaunay, *La faute de l'administration* (Paris, LGDJ, 2007) and KM Scherr, 'Public Liability for Administrative Acts under French Law' (2008) (2) *European Public Law* 213–36; for Finland S Hakalehto-Wainio, *Valta ja vahinko. Julkisen vallan käyttäjän vastuu vahingonkorvauslaissa [Power and Liability. Tort Liability of the Public Authorities under the Tort Liability Act]* (Hämeenlinna, Talentum, 2008) and for Sweden B Bengtsson, *Det allmännas ansvar enligt skadeståndslagen. Andra upplagan* (Stockholm, Norstedts, 1996).

[21] For a concise comparative study of the EU 12 Member States, see F Schockweiler and G Vivenes et al, 'Le régime de la responsabilité extra-contractuelle du fait d'actes juridiques dans la Communauté européenne' (1990) *Revue trimestrielle de droit européen* 27–74. The basic findings of this article appear still valid, although it was written some 20 years ago. Naturally, it only covers less than half of the current Member States. See also R Rebhahn, 'Public Liability in Comparison – England, France, Germany' in BC Steininger (ed), *European Tort law 2005* (Vienna, SpringerWienNewYork, 2006).

[22] For Germany, for example, there is 'one pillar' of the state liability law (*Amtshaftungsanspruch*) which is based on law Art 34 GG and §839 BGB, see Ossenbühl, *Staatshaftungsrecht* (n 20) 3.

[23] Again for Germany, a specific State Liability Law was drafted and even adopted in 1981 (*Staatshaftungsgesetz*), but it was annulled by the Bundesverfassungsgericht in a judgment of 19 October 1982 for lack of competence, see F Ossenbühl, *Staatshaftungsrecht* (n 20) 438–56.

Member States is something which develops through case-law. Specific rules also relate to the question whether separate courts exist for damages liability of public authorities.

Public liability in Member States can be analysed from two perspectives, namely from that of grounds of liability or from that of sectors of liability.

What liability sectors are normally meant when reference is made to public liability, or state liability, in national laws of Member States? It seems that it is in fact used to refer as a form of shorthand to a multitude of situations where the public authority is to be held liable in damages for its actions or omissions. Apart from the public authorities being liable in the habitual private law type of relationships, the specific feature of public liability lies in areas where public authorities exercise public powers. As examples, the following areas can be mentioned:[24] education; award of social benefits; rescue services; planning; environment; banking supervision; restriction or termination of parental responsibility; surveillance and supervision; advice and dissemination of information; roads, land-use, and planning; provision of health care; police and public prosecution service; judicial activities; detention; questions related to the armed forces.

Many of these areas are such that they do not in any way belong to public liability for breaches of EU law. Moreover, it would appear that national systems rarely involve a single uniform 'system' of public liability, but rather a multitude of punctual 'subsystems', more or less developed or embryonic in form, depending on the area.

What all national public liability systems have in common is that the liability of public authorities is limited in various ways. These immunities are linked to various sectors of governmental activity, for example: (1) immunities relating to administration of justice; (2) immunities relating to the legislative process and (3) immunities relating to executive action. However, none of these immunities is absolute; they are in turn limited in various ways. Bell and Bradley wrote in 1991 that the general picture which was then emerging from the contributions to the volume they had edited on governmental liability was the widening of governmental liability.[25]

Furthermore, a distinction should be drawn between reparation for planned consequences of governmental action and reparation for unplanned consequences.[26] Specific rules may apply for example, to expropriation.

The basic functions of liability law are a complicated and controversial subject, but for the purposes of this study it suffices to refer to Van Gerven et al[27] who list

[24] Examples of specific areas are also in the figure 4.1 below. Further and more detailed examples can be found from the national public law liability commentaries. See B Bengtsson, *Skadestånd vid myndighetsutövning I* (Stockholm, Norstedt, 1976); Booth and Squires, *The Negligence Liability of Public Authorities*(n 20); *cf* F Ossenbühl, *Staatshaftungsrecht* (n 20), and K-O Bergmann and H Schumacher, *Die Kommunalhaftung. Ein Handbuch des Staatshaftungsrechts* (Cologne, Carl Heymanns Verlag, 2007) and Hakalehto-Wainio, *Valta ja vahinko* (n 20) 267.

[25] J Bell and AW Bradley (eds), *Governmental Liability: A Comparative Study* (London, The United Kingdom National Committee of Comparative Law, 1991) 15.

[26] J Bell, 'Introduction' in D Fairgrieve and M Andenas, et al (eds), *Tort Liability of Public Authorities in Comparative Perspective* (London, BIICL, 2002) xxi.

[27] van Gerven et al, *Tort Law* (n 18) 18ff with references to basic works.

four main functions of general liability law which operate with other compensation systems (such as private insurance and social security). According to them, the basic functions of tort law are: (1) compensation, (2) loss-shifting/loss-spreading, (3) deterrence of undesirable behaviour and (4) avoidance of inefficient behaviour. Wurmnest has made a comparative analysis to the same effect.[28]

As to governmental liability, Bell and Bradley note that the key function of this area of law is to provide compensation for injury caused.[29] Further, 'assigning blame' can detect malfunctioning in the system or individuals and can also influence the conduct of officials as they become more aware of liability. The loss-spreading function, in particular when connected with litigation, is not a primary function of governmental liability.

B. Convergence of National Public Liability Laws

Moving one step above each and every individual national system, it is worthwhile considering the emerging convergence between national public liability laws.

Article 340(2) TFEU is one of the rare examples where the Treaty expressly refers to national law as a source of EU law norms, in this instance for formulation of the liability norm. Numerous studies have shown that the EU public liability system based on this article is not the arithmetic mean of Member State liability systems.[30] It has been shown that it was and is difficult to find 'general principles common to the laws of the Member States' regarding liability of public authorities. However, this does not mean that no importance whatsoever should be attached to national systems. The connection to national systems is there, on a formal and factual level. In order to gain some further understanding as to why the Court has created the criteria the way it has and how the criteria may be justified, one of the main reliable sources could be the national systems.[31]

For the purposes of the current study, research work of a comparative nature is most interesting. Some works compare liability of public authorities in two or more legal systems from a more general or a more specific perspective. Other works, like the one edited by Vandersanden and Dony, analyse the functioning of *Francovich*

[28] W Wurmnest, *Grundzüge eines europäischen Haftungsrechts: eine rechtsvergleichende Untersuchung des Gemeinschaftsrechts* (Tübingen, Mohr Siebeck, 2003) 94–106.

[29] Bell and Bradley (eds), *Governmental Liability* (n 25) 11.

[30] eg J-M Favret, *Les influences réciproques du droit communautaire et du droit national de la responsabilité publique extracontractuelle* (Paris, Pedone, 2000).

[31] eg, in *FIAMM*, the ECJ noted that in its view, strict liability of the public authorities was not a general principle of law common to the law of the Member States. See ECJ Joined Cases C-120/06 P and C-121/06 P *FIAMM and Fedon v Council and Commission* (appeal dismissed) [2008] ECR I-6513 [175]: 'Finally, it is clear that, while comparative examination of the Member States' legal systems enabled the Court to make at a very early stage the finding recalled in paragraph 170 of the present judgment concerning convergence of those legal systems in the establishment of a principle of liability in the case of unlawful action or an unlawful omission of the authority, including of a legislative nature, that is in no way the position as regards the possible existence of a principle of liability in the case of a lawful act or omission of the public authorities, in particular where it is of a legislative nature'.

liability in several Member States.[32] In that book, each chapter discussing the situation in a given Member State is based on a structure where first the (purely) national liability system is analysed, followed by a section on the application of EU law-based Member State liability in that system. The book thus provides a concise – and by its structure comparative – overview of the systems. Granger has published an impressive overview of national case-law in relation to Member State liability for breaches of EU law. The particular merit of that article lies is in its exceptional breadth, while it still covers the cases and their background in sufficient depth.[33] Examples of detailed comparative studies of two or more national public liability systems can also be found.[34]

One additional aspect makes this issue specific and that is the spill-over effects from the EU public liability system to public liability under national systems and the resulting convergent developments at national level and in various national legal systems.[35] This is a kind of *'unintended rapprochement'* of national public tort law. It is this aspect which makes EU law-based public liability relevant even for lawyers who are not dealing directly with EU law and whose clients are not damaged by the (in)action of EU institutions and who – for the time being, at least – do not derive rights from EU law, which would be infringed by the national authorities.

It is true that, in formal terms, the EU system is based on conferral of competencies, which conferral, at least initially, took place only in limited fields. However, experience shows that when considerable developments occur at EU level affecting both the European Union itself and the Member States (when they apply EU law), it is almost reasonable to suppose that there would be 'supplementary' or 'additional' effects at national level too, outside the scope of application of EU law. Indeed, it appears that a number of recent developments have occurred in national legislation on public liability in Member States. It can be supposed that these developments, at least in part, have been taking place under the influence of developments at Community level.[36] The Court's case-law has undoubtedly facilitated such cross-fertilisation. A study, even if concentrating primarily at EU law level, may thus

[32] G Vandersanden and M Dony (eds), *La responsabilité des États membres en cas de violation du droit communautaire. Études de droit communautaire et de droit national comparé* (Brussels, Bruylant, 1997).

[33] M-PF Granger, 'National applications of *Francovich* and the construction of a European administrative *ius commune*' (2007) *European Law Review* 157–92.

[34] D Fairgrieve, *State Liability in Tort. A Comparative Law Study* (Oxford, Oxford University Press, 2003); *cf* also P Nacimiento, *Gemeinschaftsrechtliche und nationale Staatshaftung in Deutschland, Italien und Frankreich* (Baden-Baden, Nomos, 2006).

[35] For an interesting analysis of the EU public law liability in the UK, including a review of the effects of the ECtHR case-law, see M Varney and P Birkinshaw, 'Public Liability: European Influence and Domestic Change' in C Kombos (ed), *Studies in European Public Law: Thematic, National and Post-National Perspectives* (Athens–Thessaloniki, Sakkoulas Publications, 2010) 164ff.

[36] See eg, new state liability legislation described in the following contributions: A Bitans, 'Latvia' in H Koziol and BC Steininger (eds), *European Tort Law 2005* (Vienna, SpringerWienNewYork, 2006); J Lahe and I Kull, 'Estonia' in H Koziol and BC Steininger (eds), *European Tort Law 2006* (Vienna, SpringerWienNewYork, 2008) and AG Dias Pereira, 'Portugal' in H Koziol and BC Steininger (eds), *European Tort Law 2007* (Vienna, SpringerWienNewYork, 2008).

Another useful overview can be found in C von Bar (ed) *Principles of European Law: Non-Contractual Liability Arising out of Damage Caused to Another: v. 7 (European Civil Code Series)* (Oxford, Oxford University Press, 2009) 1011–19.

help to understand the pressures and developments at national level. However, it appears that so far there have been very few formally pressurising elements towards convergence of public liability systems.

C. Remarks in Relation to Public Liability in EU Law

Following the above examination of some features of national public liability systems in general we now make some observations on the two public liability systems established in EU law.

EU law-based public liability, in so far as Member State liability is concerned, has no explicit foundation in the treaties or legislative acts of the European Union. On reflection, for the operation of the system this does not appear a major problem. In Member States, even if some legislation exists on public liability, it does not cover all liability situations. Public liability is possible in many Member States without an express basis in legislation.[37]

For EU law-based liability, both for Member States and in particular for the Union, considerable case-law is available. An intuitive reaction would be to attempt to structure this case-law (or the two series of case-law) into a logical whole which would make sense and be as flawless as possible. Ossenbühl also considered this possibility when approaching German state liability law: to systematise the liability grounds which have been present in case-law. However, he abandons this approach right away. He rather starts from individual liability situations, and the scope of application which has 'grown around' that institution. This approach ensures that the link to the origin of liability is maintained.[38]

It seems clear from the ECJ case-law that the Court still attaches importance to the nature of the activity. It is true that in *Bergaderm* the dichotomy of legislative/administrative acts was finally abandoned and it is equally true that this division had led to almost acrobatic constructions (on the part of defendant EU institutions) to turn administrative measures into legislative in order to minimise the risk of damages liability.[39] What *Bergaderm* did was that it downgraded the question relating to the nature of the act of its decisive role in defining the applicable liability criteria. This did not mean that no importance whatsoever should be attached to the nature of the act. Therefore it is submitted here that the nature of the activity should remain to be taken into account as a kind of threshold issue before starting to assess the discretion available.[40] After the Lisbon Treaty

[37] It is of course possible to focus on the part covered by legislative provisions, see S Hakalehto-Wainio, *Valta ja vahinko* (n 20), examining liability under Finnish Damages Act.

[38] See Ossenbühl, *Staatshaftungsrecht* (n 20) 2–3.

[39] ECJ Case C-352/98 P *Bergaderm and Goupil v Commission* (appeal dismissed) [2000] ECR I-5291 [43] and [46].

[40] See eg, on discretion C Hilson, 'Liability of Member States in Damages: The Place of Discretion' (1997) *ICLQ* 941–47. The sectoral approach has also been applied in Germany, see F Ossenbühl, 'Anmerkungen zur Hoheitshaftung in Europarecht', in J Ipsen and B Stüer (eds), *Europa in Wandel. Festschrift für Hans-Werner Rengeling* (Cologne, Carl Heymanns Verlag, 2008) 376 ff.

it continues to be important whether the acts in question are legislative or administrative or judicial decisions.[41]

Another aspect is that we are dealing with case-law. It appears daring if not rash to attempt to construe perfect systems out of cases. The courts normally build up their case-law incrementally, little by little, and this is also what the ECJ clearly does.[42] But because the 'law' is represented and concretised in case-law in this sector, it appears justified to deal with that case-law extensively. This is also a choice to be made between an abstract and a concrete approach: here we have a concrete point of departure, by starting from cases and anchoring the analysis around them.

There are a number of important similarities between EU law-based liability of the Member States and of the European Union, but also certain differences. Harlow has noted that neither of these two are 'liability' principles, as 'in every European system fault still holds primacy in this respect', but they are 'compensation' principles which are intended to cover only exceptional cases.[43]

With regard to the functions of non-contractual liability of the Union, Hix has distinguished three basic functions.[44] He considers that the most important is the reparatory function (*Wiedergutmachungs- oder Ausgleichfunktion; Individualrechtsschutzfunktion*). In addition there is a preventive or (administrative) steering function (*Präventive, verhaltenssteurende Funktion*). Finally, non-contractual liability also legitimises the existence of the EU legal order as an independent order (*Legitimationsfunktion*).

When analysing Member State liability, compensation is undoubtedly an important issue, but it may not be the most important issue. *Francovich* (ECJ 1991)[45] and *Brasserie du Pêcheur* (ECJ 1996),[46] the former in particular, were based on the effectiveness of Community law in the Member States. Harlow in 1996 argued strongly that in this context liability is used first and foremost as a sanction. At the same time she asserts that what we have at issue here is 'conduct which cannot be deterred'.[47]

Moreover, in view of the refined detail of the national public liability rules described in the preceding section, EU law-based public liability both for the European Union itself and for the Member States appears much less developed and

[41] See G Di Federico, 'The Distinction between Legislative and Non-Legislative Acts in the Constitutional Treaty and its Possible Impact on Locus Standi and Non-Contractual Liability. Some Suggestions on the Necessary Adaptations Required by the Treaty Reform Process' in M Dony and S Rossi (eds), *Démocracie, cohérence et transparence. Vers une constitutionalisation de l'Union européenne?* (Brussels, Éditions de l'Université de Bruxelles, 2008) 30 ff and D Ritleng, 'De l'irresponsabilité extracontractuelle de la Communauté', in J-C Masclet and H Ruiz Fabri et al (eds), *L'Union européenne – Union de droit, union des droits. Mélanges en l'honneur du Professeur Philippe Manin* (Paris, Pedone, 2010) 930 ff.

[42] See U Everling, 'Reflections on the Reasoning in the Judgements of the Court of Justice of the European Communities', *Festskrift til Ole Due* (Köpenhamn, Gads Forlag, 1994).

[43] C Harlow, *State Liability: Tort Law and Beyond* (Oxford, Oxford University Press, 2004) 61.

[44] J-P Hix, 'Zur ausservertragliche Haftung der Gemeinschaft' in S Moreira de Sousa and W Heusel (eds), *Enforcing Community Law from Francovich to Köbler: Twelve Years of the State Liability Principle* (Cologne, Bundesanzeiger, 2004) 200.

[45] ECJ Joined Cases C-6/90 and C-9/90 *Francovich and Bonifaci* [1991] ECR I-5357.

[46] ECJ Joined Cases C-46/93 and C-48/93 *Brasserie du Pêcheur and Factortame* [1996] ECR I-1029.

[47] C Harlow, 'Francovich and the Problem of the Disobedient State' (1996) (3) *European Law Journal* 199–225, 204, 209.

narrower in coverage than that of national public liability laws, as will be shown later in this study.

In addition, it seems that the idea of convergence has to be understood in the context of public liability and its specificities; there can be no 'absolute' convergence, and one has to analyse convergence 'in like situations'. Therefore, the specifics of the systems should be kept in mind and the aim should be to establish some kind of 'relative convergence' between the two systems, not absolute symmetry, perfect harmony, or the like. Moreover, case-law is in a permanent state of refinement; it is developing constantly and in many directions. Any convergence is always subject to potential 'unravelling' or distinguishing in any future case.

III. OTHER PUBLIC LIABILITY SYSTEMS

A. Public Liability in the Agreement for the European Economic Area (EEA)

Rather surprisingly, the closest cousin to the EU public liability system is geographically very close and contains both the responsibility of the member states of an international treaty arrangement and the administrative bodies of that arrangement. The principle of state liability in the context of the Agreement on the European Economic Area (EEA) is not based on the provisions of the agreement itself:[48] rather, it has been created by the EFTA Court set up in the framework of that agreement.[49]

The EFTA Court has established EEA State liability through three judgments.[50] The foundations were laid down in *Sveinbjörnsdottir* (EFTA Court 1998),[51] and the doctrine has further been developed and applied in three subsequent cases, namely in *Karlsson* (EFTA Court 2002),[52] *Ngyuen* (EFTA Court 2008)[53] and *Kolbeinsson* (EFTA Court 2010).[54] Even if the importance of the similarities and the requirement of homogeneity between the EU and EEA system have been underlined,[55] some authors have pointed to the very different natures of the two systems, in view

[48] Agreement on the European Economic Area signed on 2 May 1992 and approved by Decision 94/1/EC, ECSC of the Council and the Commission of 13 December 1993 on the conclusion of the Agreement on the European Economic Area between the European Communities, their Member States and the Republic of Austria, the Republic of Finland, the Republic of Iceland, the Principality of Liechtenstein, the Kingdom of Norway and the Kingdom of Sweden [1994] OJ L1/1 (for an updated version see www.efta.int).

[49] Agreement between the EFTA States on the Establishment of a Surveillance Authority and a Court of Justice [1994] OJ L344/3 (for an updated version see www.efta.int).

[50] See C Baudenbacher, 'If Not EEA State Liability, Then What? Reflections Ten Years after the EFTA Court's Sveinbjörnsdóttir Ruling', in S Katuoka (ed) *Law in the Changing Europe: Liber Amicorum Pranas Kuris* (Vilnius, Mykolo Romerio Universitetas, 2008) 545ff and E Méndez-Pinedo, *EC and EEA Law. A Comparative Study of the Effectiveness of European Law* (Groeningen, Europa Law Publishing, 2009).

[51] EFTA Case E-9/97 *Sveinbjörnsdottir v Iceland* [1998] EFTA Court Reports 95.

[52] EFTA Case E-4/01 *Karl K. Karlsson v Iceland* [2002] EFTA Court Reports 240.

[53] EFTA Case E-8/07 *Celina Ngyuen* [2008] EFTA Court Reports 223.

[54] EFTA Case E-2/10 *Kolbeinsson v Iceland* [2010] EFTA Court Reports 234.

[55] L Sevón and M Johansson, 'The protection of the rights of individuals under the EEA Agreement' (1999) *European Law Review* 373–86.

of which the establishment of state liability in the EEA system by the EFTA Court would seem somewhat doubtful.[56]

The ECJ has been called on to rule on liability within the EEA framework in two cases. *Rechberger* (ECJ 1999) was an Austrian preliminary reference concerning the Package Travel Directive 90/314.[57] In *Andersson* (ECJ 1999), a Swedish court asked questions in relation to the Wage Guarantee Directive 80/987.[58] In both cases, part of the reference for a preliminary ruling related to the question of state liability under the EEA agreement, ie to events which had taken place after the entry into force of the EEA agreement on 1 January 1994, but before the accession of Austria and Sweden to the European Community on 1 January 1995. Therefore, in both cases the Court found that it is not competent to rule on questions relating to that period, when the states in question were still members of the European Free Trade Association (EFTA). The Court recalled, though, that it has jurisdiction in principle to give preliminary rulings concerning interpretation of the Agreement on the European Economic Area (EEA) when a question arises before one of the national courts, since the provisions of that Agreement form an integral part of the Community legal system.[59]

It seems unlikely that the ECJ would be in a position itself to pronounce on the existence or conditions for state liability in the EEA, because for the ECJ to be competent such a preliminary reference should come from a court of an EU Member State, but concern the liability of an EFTA Member State party to the EEA agreement. Such a reference would thus require that an EFTA Member State would be sued for state liability under the EEA agreement in an EU Member State court.[60]

As to liability of the EEA institutions, it is worth noting that non-contractual damages liability of the EFTA Surveillance Authority ('ESA') is foreseen in the agreement establishing the ESA.[61] The liability of the ESA could come into question in areas where it is competent, namely when it ensures application of the competition rules under the EEA Agreement (Article 5). Apparently no damages action has so far been brought against the ESA before the EFTA Court. Thus the question of convergence with the liability of EU institutions remains for the time being theoretical. If such action were ever brought, it would probably be inspired by the case-law on liability of EU institutions.

[56] M Eyjólfsson, 'Case comment Case E-9/97, Sveinbjörnsdottir v Iceland' (2000) *Common Market Law Review* 191–211.

[57] ECJ Case C-140/97 *Rechberger and others* [1999] ECR I-3499.

[58] ECJ Case C-321/97 *Andersson and Wåkerås-Andersson* [1999] ECR I-3551.

[59] See ECJ *Andersson and Wåkerås-Andersson* (n 58) [26]–[32] and ECJ *Rechberger and others* (n 57) [38]–[39]; in the latter paragraph the ECJ mentions the *Sveinbjörnsdottir* judgment of the EFTA Court, handed down some six months earlier.

[60] The first issue would thus be how to establish the competence of a EU Member State court.

[61] See Agreement between the EFTA States on the Establishment of a Surveillance Authority and a Court of Justice (n 49), Arts 39 and 46 para 2 and E Méndez-Pinedo, *EC and EEA Law* (n 50) 39.

B. Breaches of the European Convention of Human Rights (ECHR)

Breach of the rights guaranteed by the European Convention of Human Rights (ECHR) may also give rise to a certain type of monetary compensation under the rules of the Convention.[62] Most of the states parties to the Convention have adhered to a protocol in which they agree to pay 'just satisfaction' in cases where the convention organs, nowadays the European Court of Human Rights (ECtHR), find an infringement of the Convention. An award concerning 'just satisfaction' is not properly speaking damages liability, as that award is not commensurate with damage suffered.[63] Therefore, ECHR breaches do have a public/institutional component, but the remedy offered is not 'damages', but just satisfaction; it is also a highly specific form of remedy and not yet subject to case-law at EU level.[64]

In addition to this centralised compensation system, another aspect has increasingly been discussed by scholars, namely the intra-state effects of the ECHR and reparation in damages of breaches of Convention rights, that is to say damages awarded directly by the court of a Member State to the Convention, without the intervention of the ECtHR.[65] This is undeniably a subject where the liability of the state is in question. For the Member State's part, liability is based, as in the EU system, on an external legal source that the Member State courts are to apply.

A word should be said about the rights guaranteed by the ECHR. According to the case-law of the ECJ, the rights mentioned in the Convention reflect legal principles common to the Member States and are thus protected in EU law, too. A severe

[62] D Shelton, *Remedies in International Human Rights Law* (Oxford, Oxford University Press, 1999). See also Council of Europe, Recommendation No R (84) 15 of the Committee of Ministers to Member States relating to Public Liability [1984].

[63] See J-P Costa, 'The Provision of Compensation under Article 41 of the European Convention on Human Rights' in D Fairgrieve and M Andenas et al (eds), *Tort Liability of Public Authorities in Comparative Perspective* (London, BIICL, 2002).

[64] The question of liability of the EU for breaches of ECHR should be addressed upon accession to the ECHR, foreseen in the Lisbon Treaty. For collective liability of Member States for breaches by EU, see ECJ Case C-84/95 *Bosphorus v Minister for Transport, Energy and Communications and others* [1996] ECR I-3953 and ECtHR 2005 *Bosphorus Hava Yollari Turizm Ve Ticaret Anonim Sirketi v Ireland* (Case 45036/98) and A Potteau, 'A propos d'un pis-aller: la responsabilité des Etats membres pour l'incompatibilité du droit de l'Union avec la convention européenne des droits de l'homme' (2009) *Revue trimestrielle de droit européen* 697–716.

[65] See eg, for Finland, S Hakalehto-Wainio, 'Strasbourgista Suomeen – Ihmisoikeusloukkauksen korvaaminen Euroopan ihmisoikeustuomioistuimen käytännössä ja kansallisella tasolla [Von Strassburg nach Finnland – die Entschädigung für Verletzung eines Menschenrechtes in der Praxis des Europäischen Gerichtshofes für Menschenrechte und auf der nationalen Ebene]' (2010) *Defensor Legis* 747–63 and Hakalehto-Wainio, *Valta ja vahinko* (n 20) 126–34; for Sweden, H Andersson, 'Nationell EKMR-skadeståndsrätt – en argumentativ problemsinventeringsskiss' (2007) *Tidskrift utgiven av Juridiska Föreningen i Finland* 377–414 and BW Dufwa, 'Horizontal Effect of the European Convention: Swedish Case law' in A Colombi Ciacchi and C Godt et al (eds), *Haftungsrecht im dritten Millenium – Liability in the Third Millenium: Liber Amicorum Gert Brüggemeier* (Baden-Baden, Nomos, 2009), and for the specific situation of judicial liability, T Barkhuysen and ML van Emmerik, 'Accountability of the Judiciary on the National Level for Violations of the European Convention of Human Rights', in G Canivet and M Andenas et al (eds), *Independence, Accountability and the Judiciary* (London, BIICL, 2006).

infringement by an EU Member State (or by an EU institution) of the fundamental rights protected therein could also give rise to compensation under EU law.

The protection of rights guaranteed in the ECHR will gain even more in importance in the future, when the EU accedes to the ECHR in accordance with the Lisbon Treaty, and the complex liability issues would certainly merit a separate study.

C. Responsibility and Liability under International Law

The issues of (damages) responsibility of states or international organisations under public international law do present certain connective points with the subject matter of this study. However, this responsibility is based on international law and not on EU law. Therefore state responsibility under public international law is not at the heart of this study and will thus not be addressed further here.[66]

Private liability under international law should be mentioned in this context. Indeed, it is a question which can be distinguished from state responsibility under public international law.[67] This is an issue which has been left outside the scope of the International Law Commission's Articles on State Responsibility. Yet in certain specific fields, such as human rights law, or international humanitarian law this issue may arise.[68]

One question of state liability is whether and under which system a Member State could invoke the liability of another Member State for breaches of EU law. This has been analysed by Scholl. Her examples cover free movement of goods, competition law, health policy, environmental policy and institutional law.[69] While some of the examples cited seem plausible, it is difficult to see what court would finally be competent to rule on a damages action; it does not appear clear that the ECJ would be competent in the framework of Article 259 TFEU (infringement action by a Member State against another Member State).[70] Moreover, the political hurdles may be even bigger than the legal ones.

[66] See J Crawford, *The International Law Commission's Articles on State Responsibility. Introduction, Text and Commentaries* (Cambridge, 2002); E Paasivirta and PJ Kuijper, 'Does one size fit all? The European Community and the responsibility of international organizations', *Netherlands Yearbook of International Law Vol XXXVI – 2005* (Netherlands, 2007); M Lehto, *Indirect responsibility for terrorist acts: redefinition of the concept of terrorism beyond violent acts* (Leiden, Martinus Nijhoff, 2009) and J Crawford and A Pellet et al (eds), *The Law of International Responsibility* (Oxford, Oxford University Press, 2010).

[67] A Rosas, 'State responsibility and liability under civil liability regimes' in O Bring and S Mahmoudi (eds), *Current international law issues: Nordic perspectives: essays in honour of Jerzy Sztucki* (Stockholm, 1994).

[68] T Giegerich, 'Another Incoming Tide? Tort Liability in Public International Law' in A Colombi Ciacchi and C Godt et al (eds), *Haftungsrecht im dritten Millenium – Liability in the Third Millenium: Liber Amicorum Gert Brüggemeier* (Baden-Baden, Nomos, 2009).

[69] K Scholl, *Haftung zwischen den EG-Mitgliedstaaten bei Verletzung von Gemeinschaftsrecht. Begründung eines zwischenstaatlichen Schadensersatzanspruchs* (Munich, Beck, 2005) 214, 233.

[70] For an overview of some doctrinal proposals, see B Simma and D Pulkowski, 'Leges Speciales and Self-Contained Regimes' in J Crawford and A Pellet et al (eds), *The Law of International Responsibility* (Oxford, Oxford University Press, 2010) 152–55.

D. Public Liability in Canada and the United States

Crown liability (Canada) and governmental liability (United States) have been long-standing and popular themes.[71] It is interesting to see that some authors have taken up the issue of comparison of the US/EU public liability systems[72] and that some have, based on comparative aspects and pointing to elements similar in substance, suggested that certain elements of the US public liability system could be transplanted to EU public liability law.[73] Incidentally, these elements already exist in some Member State national public liability systems.

IV. PRIVATE LIABILITY FOR BREACHES OF EU LAW

At the same time as public liability for breaches of EU law was created by the ECJ, another form of EU law liability was on the agenda. This relates to damages liability of private persons (natural persons and companies) in damages for breach of EU law. This area thus also has rather close links with the subject of this study.[74]

Although this liability is based on EU law, it remains fundamentally different from EU public liability law. It has been gradually emerging in particular in the field of competition law following the opinion of Advocate General van Gerven in *Banks* (ECJ 1994) and the judgments in *Courage and Crehan* (ECJ 2001), *Manfredi* (ECJ 2006), *City Motors Groep* (ECJ 2007) and *Pfeiderer* (ECJ 2011).[75] It has also been actively promoted by the Commission through communications.[76] It is simi-

[71] For Canada in particular see Hogg and Monahan, *Liability of the Crown* (n 17), and for the United States, from a policy point of view, see eg, P Schuck, *Suing Government* (New Haven, Yale University Press, 1983).

[72] C Crawford Lichtenstein, 'Public Liability in U.S. Courts and *Brasserie du Pêcheur and Factortame* in the European Court' in D O'Keeffe (ed), *Judicial Review in European Union Law. Liber Amicorum in Honour of Lord Slynn of Hadley. Volume 1* (The Hague, Kluwer Law International, 2000) and JE Pfander, 'Member State Liability and Constitutional Change in the United States and Europe' (2003) (2) *American Journal of Comparative Law* 237–74.

[73] J Mabrito, 'The American and EC Approaches to Member State Liability and the Possibility of State Officer Liability in the EC' in P Eeckhout and T Tridimas (eds), *26 Yearbook of European Law 2007* (Oxford, Oxford University Press, 2008).

[74] See eg, W van Gerven, 'Courage v Crehan and the Way Ahead' in M Johansson and N Wahl et al (eds), *Liber Amicorum in Honour of Sven Norberg – A European for all seasons* (Brussels, Bruylant, 2006); T Eilmansberger, 'The Green Paper on Damages Actions for Breach of the EC Antitrust Rules and Beyond: Reflections on the Utility and Feasibility of Stimulating Private Enforcement through Legislative Action' (2007) *Common Market Law Review* 431–78; P Nebbia, 'Damages actions for the infringement of EC competition law: compensation or deterrence?' (2008) *European Law Review* 23–43; N Reich, 'Rights without duties? Reflections on the state of liability law in the multilevel governance system of the Community: Is there a need for a more coherent approach in European private law?' (2009) *Tidskrift utgiven av Juridiska Föreningen i Finland* 492.

[75] ECJ Case C-128/92 *Banks v British Coal* [1994] ECR I-1209; ECJ Case C-453/99 *Courage and Crehan* [2001] ECR I-6297; ECJ Joined Cases C-295/04 to C-298/04 *Manfredi v Lloyd Adriatico Assicurazioni* [2006] ECR I-6619, ECJ Case C-421/05 *City Motors Groep* [2007] ECR I-659 and ECJ Case C-360/09 *Pfeiderer* [2011] ECJ I-0000.

[76] COM(2005) 672. Green Paper – Damages actions for breach of the EC antitrust rules, 19.12.2005; COM(2008) 165. White Paper on Damages Actions for Breach of the EC antitrust rules, 2.4.2008 and SEC(2008) 404. Commission Staff Working Paper on Damages Actions for Breach of the EC antitrust rules. 2.4.2008.

lar to the object of this study in that it is also entirely based on case-law and requires a breach of EU law. However, it is not pursued against the state. Moreover, ECJ case-law in this area is less developed than the case-law concerning the liability of the Member States and the European Union for breaches of EU law. In fact, the nexus between the two key subject matters of this study is the public nature of the liability (money coming from the 'public purse'). Private liability does not have this public/institutional component.

It has been argued that albeit elements of private party liability for breaches of EU law are already present, there is yet not such a general principle and its creation by the ECJ would not be without controversy, in particular as regards the adequate normative justification required.[77] Be that as it may, in view of enhancing convergence, it is interesting to note that the transposition of the 'sufficiently serious breach' criterion to such a system has been already proposed.[78]

V. EUROPEAN CONVERGENCE OF PRIVATE LAW LIABILITY

Developments in private tort law can be seen as a part of wider developments towards common European private law and even a European civil code.[79] In particular, codification has been considered rather a problematic project by many, and it has been pointed out that behind any legal or technical harmonisation, such efforts immediately run into various fundamental underlying issues, such as social models.[80]

Yet over recent years, the 'private tort law' of the EU Member States has increasingly converged, although this is not to claim that it has been – or should be – in any way fully harmonised. Still, there are a number of signs of emerging convergence.

For analysis of developments in the three categories, the various means that contribute to convergence should be ordered conveniently. Markesinis has argued that

[77] D Leczykiewicz, 'Private Party Liability in EU Law: In Search of the General Regime', in C Barnard and O Odudu (eds), *Cambridge Yearbook of European Legal Studies. Vol 12, 2009-2010* (Oxford, Hart Publishing, 2010) 272ff.

[78] N Reich, 'Horizontal Liability in EC Law: Hybridization of Remedies for Compensation in case of Breaches of EC Rights' (2007) *Common Market Law Review* 705–42, 715.

[79] For these issues, which are not discussed here further, see eg, the Lando project and others, such as A Hartkamp and M Hesselink et al (eds), *Towards a European Civil Code. Third Fully Revised and Expanded Edition* (The Hague, Kluwer Law International, 2004); H Collins, *The European Civil Code: The Way Forward* (Cambridge, Cambridge University Press, 2008); O Lando and H Beale (eds), *Principles of European Contract Law. Parts I and II (Combined and Revised)* (The Hague, Kluwer Law International, 2000); T Wilhelmsson, 'Ole Landon kyydissä kohti eurooppalaista sopimusoikeutta' (2000) (3) *Defensor Legis* 440–51; L Sisula-Tulokas, 'To be or not to be – harmonisering av den europeiska avtalsrätten' (2001) *Tidskrift utgiven av Juridiska Föreningen i Finland* 708–20; E Tammi-Salminen, 'Kansainvälistyminen ja varallisuusoikeuden kansalliset opit' (2004) *Lakimies* 1340–54 and S Paasilehto, *Constellations – A New Approach to Legal Culture and European Integration of Private Law* (Helsinki, 2002). See also I Klauer, *Die Europäisierung des Privatrechts. Der EuGH als Zivilrichter* (Baden-Baden, Nomos, 1998).

[80] M Poiares Maduro, 'European Constitutionalism and Three Models of Social Europe' in M Hesselink (ed), *The Politics of a European Civil Code* (The Hague, Kluwer Law International, 2006).

there are five sources for unifying or harmonising pressures of law.[81] These are, here in reverse order of importance, the following: (1) academic work in the universities; (2) judges and practitioners; (3) international conventions; (4) EU directives and (5) the case-law of the Luxembourg courts. This order will be used in the following paragraphs.

A. Academic Work in the Universities, the Commissions, the Study Groups

Transnational approximation of national private liability laws in Europe has taken place in various forms. Issues of convergence have been presented in different forms of academic work. Issues of convergence of private liability law have been of interest to a certain number of researchers, including those working on comparative law. Several comparative textbooks have recently been published in this particular field. Some researchers such as Professors von Bar and van Gerven, have made, in various roles, a considerable contribution to convergence and its 'uncovering'.[82]

In addition to individual research, the role of different study groups has been important. The 'European Tort Law Group', now coordinated in Vienna in the European Centre of Tort and Insurance Law has drafted the *Principles of European Tort Law*.[83] The Group has also published a book series in which each volume addresses various questions of tort law at the European level.[84] The European Centre of Tort and Insurance Law also organises an annual seminar on tort law and has since 2001 published the proceedings in a yearbook called 'European Tort Law', which gives an interesting overview of national developments, including public liability.

The European Commission presented two Communications in 2001[85] and 2003,[86] which also resulted in enhanced activity in the field of approximation of

[81] BS Markesinis, 'Learning from Europe and Learning in Europe' in BS Markesinis (ed). *The Gradual Convergence: Foreign Ideas, Foreign Influences and English Law on the Eve of the 21st Century* (Oxford, Clarendon, 1994) 21.

[82] See eg, W van Gerven, 'Non-contractual Liability of Member States, Community Institutions and Individuals for Breaches of Community Law with a View to a Common Law for Europe' in W van Gerven and M Zuleeg (eds), *Remedies and Sanctions for the Enforcement of Community Law* (Cologne, Bundesanzeiger, 1996); C von Bar, *The Common European Law of Torts. Volume One* (Oxford, Clarendon, 1998); C von Bar, *The Common European Law of Torts. Volume Two* (Oxford, Clarendon, 2000); C Van Dam, *European Tort Law* (Oxford, Oxford University Press, 2006) and van Gerven et al, *Tort Law* (n 18). See also K Zweigert and H Kötz, *An Introduction to Comparative Law*, 3rd revised edn (Oxford, Clarendon, 1998) throughout.

[83] European Tort Law Group (ed), *Principles of European Tort Law: text and commentary* (Vienna, Springer, 2005).

[84] See eg, U Magnus (ed), *Unification of Tort Law: Damages* (The Hague, Kluwer Law International, 2000).

[85] COM(2001) 398 final. Communication from the Commission to the Council and the European Parliament on European Contract Law. Brussels, 11.07.2001.

[86] COM(2003) 68 final. Communication from the Commission to the European Parliament and the Council. A more coherent European Contract Law. An action plan. Brussels, 12.2.2003.

national liability laws. One of the very tangible results of these Communications was extensive comparative work on a 'Draft Common Frame of Reference' or 'Dcfr', which first came out in abridged[87] and then in extended form,[88] by Professor von Bar. There is also a specific extensive volume on 'Non-Contractual Liability Arising out of Damage Caused to Another' (2009).[89]

In addition to these Europe-wide projects, there are also projects with a more precise geographical scope, such as the works of Markesinis on German Tort law in English, which explain foreign private tort law systems.[90]

B. Judges and Practitioners

National judges and judgments not only resolve legal disputes but also bring to light concrete issues which need to be resolved. Van Gerven in an article in 1996 examined a series of damages cases under Dutch, English, French and German law (so-called 'cable cases' relating to damage in connection with electric cables) and concluded that albeit national tort rules at first sight present a wide diversity, there appears to be 'less variety at a second glance'.[91] The role of practitioners and advocates has been important in bringing alternative foreign solutions to the attention of judges.

C. International Conventions

International conventions in Europe, especially before the European Economic Community, were the principal way to harmonise legislation between states, including given aspects of tort law. This work was also done in specific sectors of tort law by the Council of Europe[92] and by the Hague Conference on Private International Law.[93] The effectiveness of that work has varied greatly, depending on the number of signatories, and the entry into force of each convention. In addition, more recently, the substance of many of such conventions has become part of Community or Union competences. Even if they have paved the way towards the more intense cooperation of today, nowadays, in relations between the Member

[87] C von Bar (ed), *Principles, Definitions and Model Rules of European Private Law: Draft Common Frame of Reference (Dcfr)*, outline edn (Oxford, Oxford University Press, 2008).

[88] C von Bar and E Clive et al (eds), *Principles, definitions and model rules of European private law: Draft Common Frame of Reference (DCFR) / prepared by the Study Group on a European Civil Code and the Research Group on EC Private Law (Acquis Group)* (Munich, Sellier European Law Publishers, 2009).

[89] C von Bar (ed), *Principles of European Law: Non-Contractual Liability Arising out of Damage Caused to Another: v. 7* (n 36).

[90] BS Markesinis and W Lorenz, et al, *The German Law of Obligations. Volume II. The Law of Torts: A Comparative Introduction*, 3rd edn with corrections and additions (Oxford, Clarendon, 1997).

[91] W van Gerven, 'Bridging the Unbridgeable: Community and National Tort Laws after Francovich and Brasserie' (1996) *ICLQ* 507–44, 508ff.

[92] For a list of conventions and their current status, see http://conventions.coe.int/

[93] For a list of conventions and their current status, see http://www.hcch.net

States, international conventions play a more limited role. However, in relation to the world outside the Union, conventions have maintained their importance. The Community has authorised the participation of its Member States to a convention in relation to third party liability in the field of nuclear energy,[94] a convention concerning damage resulting from oil spills from ships' bunkers[95] and to a convention concerning damage resulting from transport of dangerous substances by sea.[96] In addition, a number of proposals are pending.[97]

The effect of these conventions is that parts of the liability law of the Member States are harmonised through an international instrument implemented in the Community legal order by a Community act. However, all these instruments are characterised by a very limited sectoral approach, or are limited to one given area.

D. European Union Directives

One concrete way to bring about convergence in private law tort liability has been Community legislation. Albeit some instruments were adopted in the 1970s, it is in particular during the last decade that the legislator has been very active, following creation of new legal bases in the Treaty. These sectoral approaches are based on Community directives, adopted by the legislator, and subsequently interpreted and completed by the Court. Their common feature is that they do not provide for overarching harmonisation of any given area, but rather complete the rights laid down in the instrument. Overall, the harmonisation of national tort laws by the legislator has been punctual and has not purported to change the fundamental features of national liability systems.[98] The main instruments include the following:[99]

[94] Council Decision of 8 March 2004 authorising the Member States which are Contracting Parties to the Paris Convention of 29 July 1960 on Third Party Liability in the Field of Nuclear Energy to ratify, in the interest of the European Community, the Protocol amending that Convention, or to accede to it – Protocol to amend the Convention on Third Party Liability in the Field of Nuclear Energy of 29 July 1960, as amended by the Additional Protocol of 28 January 1964 and by the Protocol of 16 November 1982 (Council Decision 2004/294/EC) [2004] OJ L97/53.

[95] Council Decision of 19 September 2002 authorising the Member States, in the interest of the Community, to sign, ratify or accede to the International Convention on Civil Liability for Bunker Oil Pollution Damage, 2001 (the Bunkers Convention) (Council Decision 2002/762/EC) [2002] OJ L256/7.

[96] Council Decision of 18 November 2002 authorising the Member States, in the interest of the Community, to ratify or accede to the International Convention on Liability and Compensation for Damage in Connection with the Carriage of Hazardous and Noxious Substances by Sea, 1996 (the HNS Convention) (Council Decision 2002/971) [2002] OJ L337/55.

[97] COM(2010)686 Amended proposal for a Council Decision concerning the accession of the European Union to the Protocol of 2002 to the Athens Convention Relating to the Carriage of Passengers and their Luggage by Sea, 1974.

[98] For an interesting overall view of one aspect of harmonisation in this field (as regards the concept of fault) see M Lukas, 'Fault Liability', in H Koziol and R Schulze (eds), *Tort Law of the European Community* (Vienna, SpringerWienNewYork, 2008).

[99] *cf* WH van Boom, 'European tort law: an integrated or compartmentalized approach?' in A Vaquer (ed) *European private law beyond the Common Frame of Reference: essays in honour of Reinhard Zimmermann* (Groningen, Europa Law Publishing, 2008) 137–40.

First Motor Insurance Directive 72/166; Second Motor Insurance Directive 84/5; Third Motor Insurance Directive 90/232; Fourth Motor Insurance 2000/26 and Fifth Motor Insurance Directive 2005/14;[100]
Product Liability Directive 85/374;[101]
Package Travel Directive 90/314;[102]
Air Carrier Liability Regulation 2027/1997;[103]
Electric Signatures Directive 1999/93;[104]
Brussels I Regulation 44/2001[105] (recognition and enforcement of judgments in civil and commercial matters);
Air Passenger Assistance and Compensation Regulation; 261/2004[106]
Environmental Liability Directive 2004/35;[107]
Crime Victims Compensation Directive 2004/80;[108]
Unfair Business To Consumer Commercial Practices Directive 2005/29;[109]

[100] Council Directive 72/166/EEC of 24 April 1972 on the approximation of the laws of Member States relating to insurance against civil liability in respect of the use of motor vehicles, and to the enforcement of the obligation to insure against such liability (First Motor Insurance Directive) [1972] OJ L103/1, Second Council Directive 84/5/EEC of 30 December 1983 on the approximation of the laws of the Member States relating to insurance against civil liability in respect of the use of motor vehicles (Second Motor Insurance Directive) [1984] OJ L8/17, Third Council Directive 90/232/EEC of 14 May 1990 on the approximation of the laws of the Member States relating to insurance against civil liability in respect of the use of motor vehicles [1990] OJ L129/33, Directive 2000/26/EC of the European Parliament and of the Council of 16 May 2000 on the approximation of the laws of the Member States relating to insurance against civil liability in respect of the use of motor vehicles and amending Council Directives 73/239/EEC and 88/357/EEC (Fourth motor insurance Directive) [2000] OJ L181/65, Directive 2005/14/EC of the European Parliament and of the Council of 11 May 2005 amending Council Directives 72/166/EEC, 84/5/EEC, 88/357/EEC and 90/232/EEC and Directive 2000/26/EC of the European Parliament and of the Council relating to insurance against civil liability in respect of the use of motor vehicles (Fifth Motor Insurance Directive).

[101] Council Directive 85/374/EEC of 25 July 1985 on the approximation of the laws, regulations and administrative provisions of the Member States concerning liability for defective products [1985] OJ L210/29.

[102] Council Directive 90/314/EEC of 13 June 1990 on package travel, package holidays and package tours [1990] OJ L158/59.

[103] Council Regulation (EC) No 2027/97 of 9 October 1997 on air carrier liability in the event of accidents [1997] OJ L285/1.

[104] Directive 1999/93/EC of the European Parliament and of the Council of 13 December 1999 on a Community framework for electronic signatures [2000] OJ L13/12.

[105] Council Regulation (EC) No 44/2001 of 22 December 2000 on jurisdiction and the recognition and enforcement of judgments in civil and commercial matters [2001] OJ L12/1, corr. [2001] OJ L307/28; eg Art 5(4).

[106] Regulation (EC) No 261/2004 of the European Parliament and of the Council of 11 February 2004 establishing common rules on compensation and assistance to passengers in the event of denied boarding and of cancellation or long delay of flights, and repealing Regulation (EEC) No 295/91 [2004] OJ L46/1.

[107] Directive 2004/35/EC of the European Parliament and of the Council of 21 April 2004 on environmental liability with regard to the prevention and remedying of environmental damage [2004] OJ L143/56.

[108] Council Directive 2004/80/EC of 29 April 2004 relating to compensation to crime victims [2004] OJ L261/15.

[109] Directive 2005/29/EC of the European Parliament and of the Council of 11 May 2005 concerning unfair business-to-consumer commercial practices in the internal market and amending Council Directive 84/450/EEC, Directives 97/7/EC, 98/27/EC and 2002/65/EC of the European Parliament and of the Council and Regulation (EC) No 2006/2004 of the European Parliament and of the Council [2005] L149/22.

Regulation on rail passengers' rights and obligations 1371/2007;[110]
Rome II Regulation 864/2007[111]; and
Sea Carriers Liability Regulation 392/2009[112]

E. The Case-law of the ECJ

The role of the ECJ in the incremental creation of a common European private tort law should not be underestimated. Indeed, it seems that it has played an essential role. Questions of interpretation have mainly arrived at the Court through the preliminary rulings procedure from national courts, where the questions originally arose.[113]

In the ECJ case-law, one can distinguish two types of cases. The first category consists of cases where the ECJ is called upon directly to interpret a EU harmonisation instrument such as a directive as regards provisions concerning damages liability. This has been the case, for example, with the Product Liability Directive (eg, blood transfusions, defective vaccine),[114] for the Package Travel Directive (as to damage to be compensated under the Directive),[115] for the Motor Vehicle Insurance Directive (as to whether the compensation foreseen by the Directive can be refused in certain cases under national law)[116] and for the Air Passenger Assistance and Compensation Regulation (as to compensation for stranded passengers),[117] as well as for air carriers' liability[118] The second category includes cases where ECJ case-law affects the application of national tort law in a field not covered by a secondary EU law instrument. Such an effect is commonplace in the field of direct taxation, but examples in the field of tort law can also be found.[119]

[110] Regulation (EC) No 1371/2007 of the European Parliament and of the Council of 23 October 2007 on rail passengers' rights and obligations [2007] OJ L315/14.

[111] Regulation (EC) No 864/2007 of the European Parliament and of the Council of 11 July 2007 on the law applicable to non-contractual obligations (Rome II) [2007] OJ L199/40; see in particular chapter II on torts/delicts.

[112] Regulation (EC) No 392/2009 of the European Parliament and of the Council of 23 April 2009 on the liability of carriers of passengers by sea in the event of accidents [2009] L131/24.

[113] W van Gerven, 'The ECJ Case-Law as a Means of Unification of Private Law?' in A Hartkamp and M Hesselink et al (eds), *Towards a European Civil Code. Third Fully Revised and Expanded Edition* (The Hague, Kluwer Law International, 2004).

[114] For case-law see ECJ Case C-203/99 *Veedfald* [2001] ECR I-3569;, ECJ Case C-127/04 *O'Byrne* [2006] ECR I-1313; ECJ Case C-402/03 *Skov and Bilka* [2006] ECR I-199 and ECJ Case C-285/08 *Moteurs Leroy Somer* [2009] ECR I-4733.

[115] ECJ Case C-140/97 *Rechberger and others* [1999] ECR I-3499; ECJ Case C-168/00 *Leitner* [2002] ECR I-2631.

[116] ECJ Case C-63/01 *Evans* [2003] ECR I-14447; ECJ Case C-537/03 *Candolin and others* [2005] ECR I-5745 and the final judgment by the Supreme Court (Finland) Finland 2005 KKO:2005:145 and M Saarikoski, 'EY-oikeuden vaikutuksesta keskeiseen vahingonkorvaus- ja vakuutusoikeuteen – Esimerkkinä matkustajan myötävaikutus liikennevahinkoon' (2007) *Defensor Legis* 22–36.

[117] ECJ Case C-549/07 *Wallentin-Hermann* [2008] ECR I-11061 and ECJ Joined Cases C-402/07 and C-432/07 *Sturgeon and Others* [2009] ECR I-10923.

[118] ECJ Case C-301/08 *Bogiatzi* [2009] ECR I-10185 and ECJ Case C-63/09 *Walz* [2010] ECR I-0000 (judgment of 6 May 2010).

[119] See eg, ECJ Case C-470/03 *AGM-COS.MET* [2007] ECR I-2749, where the ruling by the ECJ triggered further discussion in Finland about the conditions to repair pure economic loss, see

VI. EUROPEAN CONVERGENCE OF ADMINISTRATIVE LAW

Another area of 'adjacent' convergence relates to developments which can be characterised as EU administrative law or European public law, and its convergence. This is an important and ever expanding area.[120] This follows naturally from the fact that public liability – that of the EU and of the Member States, be it in the field of EU law or national law – also covers administrative action. Thus development at the European level or national level as regards administrative law can be important for public liability, too. However, in comparison with the convergence of private law liability, convergence of administrative law appears to be more of an invisible sort.

Academic work in this area can be illustrated by books which attempt to uncover common features of European administrative law[121] or which detail in particular the development and current state of EU level administrative law, such as the works of Schwarze and Craig.[122] A logical extension of these themes are studies which analyse the effects of the ECJ case-law and the EU legislation on the administrative justice in the Member States.[123]

Co-operation between the supreme administrative jurisdictions of the Member States has led to creation of an association, and a website with multilingual national case-law updates and seminars.[124] The role of the European Ombudsman could be fitted into Markesinis' category of 'judges and practitioners'. Even if the Ombudsman examines instances of maladministration at the European institutions only, his findings and recommendations, which are made easily accessible through a website and often published in a number of languages, probably influence national administrations and the standard of action required from them.

L Sisula-Tulokas, 'Europeisering av vår skadeståndsrätt . . . que será, será' in H Lindfors and E Korkea-aho et al (eds), *Kovia aikoja: riitoja ja maksukyvyttömyyttä – Juhlakirja Risto Koulu 60 vuotta* (Helsinki, COMI & Edita, 2009) and L Sisula-Tulokas, 'Att ge och ta – ansvar för rena ekonomiska skador vid myndighetsutövning' (2010) *Tidskrift utgiven av Juridiska Föreningen i Finland* 291–321.

120 In this paragraph we will briefly analyse the convergence of administrative laws without the convergence of public law liability in Member States, as this has been analysed above in section II.

121 J Bell, 'Mechanisms for Cross-fertilisation of Administrative Law in Europe' in J Beatson and T Tridimas (eds), *New Directions in European Public Law* (Oxford, Hart Publishing, 1998) and P Beaumont and C Lyons et al (eds), *Convergence and Divergence in European Public Law* (Oxford, Hart Publishing, 2002).

122 See eg, J Schwarze, *European Administrative Law*, revised 1st edn (London, Sweet and Maxwell, 2006); P Craig, *EU Administrative law* (Oxford, Oxford University Press, 2006) and P Birkinshaw, *European Public Law* (London, Butterworths, 2003). In Finland Olli Mäenpää has carried out detailed research also in this area, see O Mäenpää, *Eurooppalainen hallinto-oikeus (3. painos)* (Helsinki, Talentum, 2011).

123 M Eliantonio, *Europeanisation of Administrative Justice. The Influence of the ECJ's Case Law in Italy, Germany and England* (Groeningen, Europa Law Publishing, 2008).

124 'Association of the Councils of State and Supreme Administrative Jurisdictions of the European Union', see www.juradmin.eu. The seminars have resulted in interesting publications on the practical issues the national jurisdictions have been confronted with when applying EU law, see eg, S Biernat and M Pilaszewicz-Kulikowska et al, *Consequences of Incompatibility with EC Law for Final Administrative Decisions and Final Judgments of Administrative Courts in the Member States* (Warsaw, Naczelny Sad Administracyjny, 2008).

The case-law of the Luxembourg courts has been important in expressing the requirements which EU law sets for national administrations. By the same token, it has been gradually creating a common framework for a common EU administrative law. European administrative law builds upon national administrative laws. It consists of two intertwined systems, namely of EU administrative law applied by EU institutions and of EU administrative law to be applied by Member State authorities.[125] For the development of these two, the case-law of the court has been important.[126]

Finally, it should be mentioned that the legislator has not (yet) expressly intended to globally harmonise European administrative law, albeit in certain sectors (such as agriculture or customs) the scope and depth of EU regulation has led to a certain degree of de facto harmonisation. In this instance it should be recalled however that the Treaty now provides a legal basis for a certain degree of harmonisation of administrative law, both at EU and national level.[127]

The contexts of convergence can be regrouped into three sectors, namely public law, private law and international law. These are summarised in Figure 3.1.

[125] For the latter, as regards Finland, see O Suviranta, *Virkamiehen ratkaisutoiminta ja Euroopan yhteisön oikeus [Das Entscheiden des Verwaltungsbeamten unter dem Aspekt des Europäischen Gemeinschaftsrechts]* (Vammala, 1996) 121–34 and as regards France, see J Sirinelli, *La transformation du droit administratif par le droit de l'Union européenne. Une contribution à l'étude du droit administratif européen* (Paris, LGDJ, 2011).

[126] Called in German '*Europäisches Eigenverwaltungsrecht*' and '*Gemeinschaftsverwaltungsrecht*', see T von Danwitz, *Europäisches Verwaltungsrecht* (Berlin Heidelberg, Springer, 2009) 8. The book makes an interesting parallel presentation of the two systems. In fact, the operation of the two systems very much recalls the operation of the two EU public liability systems.

A Danish dissertation provides a detailed assessment of the effects of EU law on Danish administrative law, including public liability in damages, see N Fenger, *Forvaltning & Faelleskab. Om EU-rettens betydning for den almindelige forvaltningsret: Konfrontation og frugtbar sameksistens* (Copenhagen, Jurist- og Økonomforbundets Forlag, 2004) 933ff.

[127] See Art 197 TFEU (Union level) and Art 298(2) TFEU (national level). A concise analysis of past developments and future perspectives is provided by C Ladenburger, 'Evolution oder Kodifikation eines allgemeinen Verwaltungsrechts in der EU' in H-H Trute and T Gross et al (eds), *Allgemeines Verwaltungsrecht – zur Tragfähigkeit eines Konzepts* (Tübingen, Mohr Siebeck, 2008) and C Harlow, 'Three Phases in the Evolution of EU Administrative Law' in P Craig and G de Búrca (eds), *The Evolution of EC Law*, 2nd edn (Oxford, Oxford University Press, 2011).

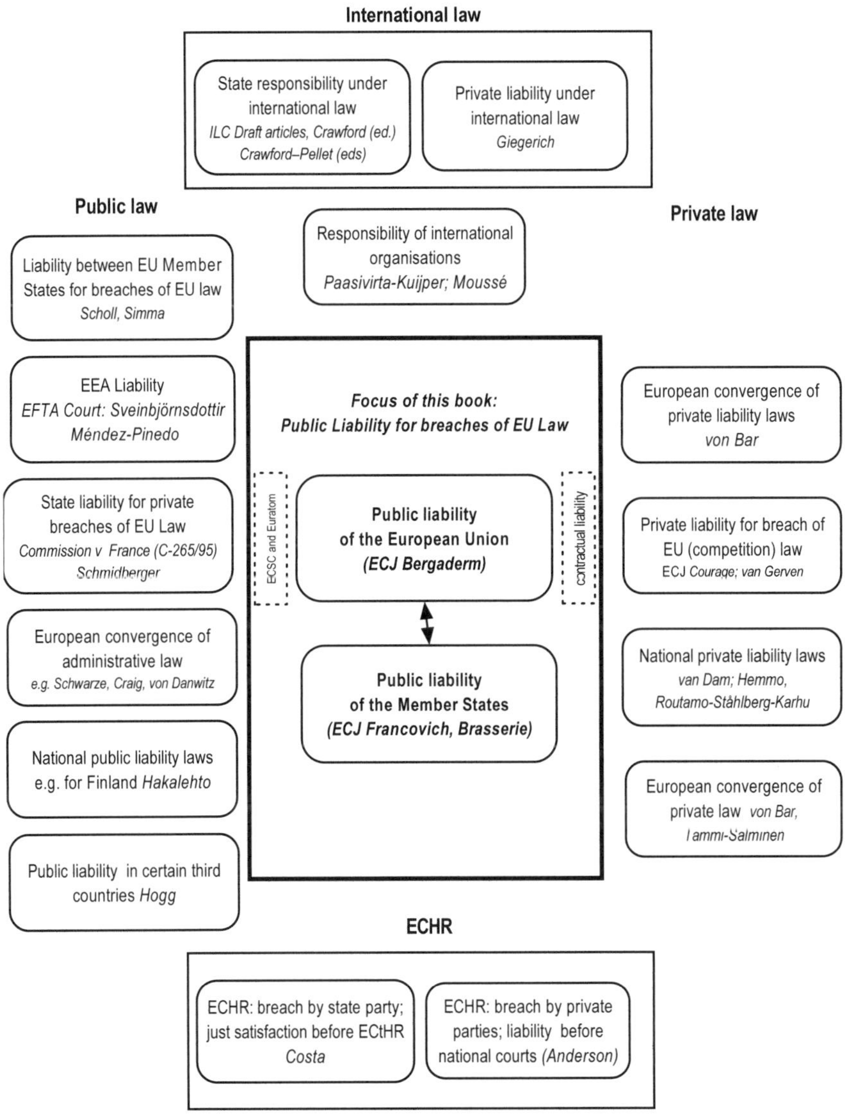

Legend: Names in italics refer to works and cases cited in bibliography.

Figure 3.1 Contexts of Convergence of Public Liability in EU Law as Regards Public Law, Private Law and International Law

4

Alignment of the Two Liability Systems

IN *BERGADERM* (ECJ 2000),[1] the Court of Justice put into practice the new conditions for non-contractual liability of the European Community.[2] The separate sets of conditions for liability resulting from legislative activities on the one hand (*Schöppenstedt* ECJ 1971; *Bayerische HNL* ECJ 1978)[3] and for liability resulting from administrative activities on the other hand (*Lütticke* ECJ 1971; *Adams* ECJ 1985)[4] were replaced by joint assessment criteria relating to the discretion available to the institution. The new conditions for Community's liability were already announced in *Brasserie du Pêcheur* (ECJ 1996)[5] where the Court declared that the conditions giving rise to liability of Member States or the Community for breaches of EC law should not, 'in the absence of particular justification', differ.

This chapter will briefly recall the development of case-law. Section I sets out the creation and conditions laid down in the original systems, while the following section II dwells on the currently applicable conditions. It will then assess the reasons and justification for alignment and shows that alignment has been essential for the new phase of Community liability and that mutual alignment has in principle been successfully implemented, save in one specific field (section III). In view of the Court's brief reasoning, we will seek help from developments in the opinions of the Advocates General. To conclude, section IV will assess the views according to which there would already be a fresh departure into different directions between the two liability systems and whether alignment was used by the Court only as a temporary justification.

[1] ECJ Case C-352/98 P *Bergaderm and Goupil v Commission* (appeal dismissed) [2000] ECR I-5291.

[2] This chapter discusses mainly developments preceding the Lisbon Treaty, so that references to the liability of the 'Community' are frequent.

[3] ECJ Case 5/71 *Zuckerfabrik Schöppenstedt v Council* (damages claim dismissed) [1971] ECR 975 [11] and ECJ Case 83/76 *Bayerische HNL and Others v Council and Commission* (damages action dismissed) [1978] ECR 1209 [4] and [5].

[4] ECJ Case 4/69 *Lütticke v Commission* (damages claim dismissed) [1971] ECR 325 [9] and ECJ Case 145/83 *Adams v Commission* (damages awarded) [1985] ECR 3539 [53].

[5] ECJ Joined Cases C-46/93 and C-48/93 *Brasserie du Pêcheur and Factortame* [1996] ECR I-1029.

I. THE LIABILITY SYSTEMS IN THEIR 'ORIGINAL' SETUP

A. Community Damages Liability: Conditions Laid Down in *Schöppenstedt* (ECJ 1971) and *Adams* (ECJ 1985)

The existence of liability in damages for the European Economic Community was expressly recognised in the original Treaty of Rome (1957) but it was left to the Court to establish conditions for liability in accordance with the general principles common to the laws of the Member States. Having established the three basic conditions for liability (illegal conduct by a Community institution, actual damage, and a causal connection between the two), the Court distinguished in its case-law between different types of illegal conduct. Thus in the case-law, different liability criteria were established for legislative action and administrative action of the Community.

The first category related to *legislative action*. In this sector the *Schöppenstedt* case (ECJ 1971) became the cornerstone.[6] According to that case-law, the Community was to incur liability only in cases of breach of a superior rule of law for the protection of individuals. In reality, this was a basic scenario which was applied very rarely, if at all. In practice, liability very often related to a specific variant of legislative action, namely to situations where the institution had *adopted a legislative measure in the exercise of a wide discretion*. In these cases it was further required that the breach be explicit, that is to say *manifest and serious*.[7] The illegality of Community action as such was a necessary condition for liability, but not in itself sufficient condition.[8] The fact that a Community measure was declared illegal or annulled was not enough to establish liability. A qualified breach was needed, a breach which was 'manifest and serious'.

In *Bayerische HNL* (ECJ 1978)[9] where the Court refined the 'Schöppenstedt criteria', it noted that it is necessary to take into consideration the principles in the legal systems of the Member States governing liability of public authorities for damage caused to individuals by legislative measures. It acknowledged that these principles vary considerably from one Member State to another, but held that the public authorities can only exceptionally and in special circumstances incur liability for legislative measures which are the result of choices of economic policy. According to the Court, the reason for this choice in the Member States was straightforward:

[6] ECJ *Zuckerfabrik Schöppenstedt* (n 3) [11].

[7] CFI Joined Cases T-481/93 and T-484/93 *Exporteurs in Levende Varkens and Others v Commission* (damages claim dismissed, no appeal) [1995] ECR II-2941 [81].

[8] ECJ Case C-282/90 *Vreugdenhil (No 2) v Commission* (damages action, dismissed) [1992] ECR I-1937 [19]: 'With regard to that argument, it should be stated that the mere fact that a legislative measure such as Article 13a of Regulation No 1687/76 is found to be invalid is insufficient by itself for the Community to incur non-contractual liability under the second paragraph of Article 215 of the EEC Treaty for damage caused to individuals. Such liability can only be incurred where a sufficiently serious breach of a superior rule of law for the protection of the individual has occurred (judgment in Bayerische HNL v Council and Commission, cited above, paragraph 4)'.

[9] ECJ *Bayerische HNL and Others* (n 3) [5].

the Court noted that the legislative authority cannot always be hindered in making its decisions by the prospect of applications for damages whenever it has occasion to adopt legislative measures in the public interest which may adversely affect the interests of individuals.

The second category established in the case-law related to damages action in respect of *administrative action*. Here the conditions were much less strict. For administrative action, any infringement of the law in principle constituted illegality which *could* give rise to liability on the part of the Community. The seminal case was probably *Adams* (ECJ 1985),[10] although it has been said that the case-law on liability based on administrative acts only started to develop from 1990 onwards.[11]

The very stringent conditions established for liability for a legislative act including choices of economic policy and the apparently much more lenient conditions for an administrative act naturally directed applicants to show that the act in question should be considered administrative. This brought about some rather surprising judgments.

In the first place, a Community act entitled 'decision' could well be characterised as a 'legislative' measure for the purposes of damages liability. The title of the measure was thus not conclusive. In *Schröder and Thamann* (CFI 1997), the CFI noted that '. . . the concept of legislative measure within the meaning of the case-law may apply to all the measures referred to by Article 189 and not only to regulations'. Therefore, '. . . the nature of a measure is not to be sought in its external form, but rather in whether or not the measure at issue is of general application'. The CFI further held that '. . . the contested decisions produce with regard to the applicants effects which are those of a measure of general application' and that, according to case-law,

> the legislative nature of a measure is not called in question by the fact that it is possible to determine more or less exactly the number or even the identity of the persons to whom it applies at any given time, as long as it is established that it applies to them by virtue of an objective legal or factual situation defined by the measure in question in relation to its purpose.[12]

Second, even if the qualification of the act remained administrative, the Court found in some cases that they were taken in a situation of wide discretion, where it was not easy to establish a breach.[13] An interesting example of an administrative decision for which wide discretion applied is *Candiotte* (CFI 1996).[14] In 1989,

[10] ECJ *Adams* (n 4) [53].

[11] MH Van Der Woude, 'Liability for Administrative Acts under Article 215(2) EC', in T Heukels and A McDonnell (eds), *The Action for Damages in Community Law* (The Hague, Kluwer Law International, 1997) 109.

[12] CFI Case T-390/94 *Schröder and Thamann v Commission* (no breach, appealed C-221/97 P) [1997] ECR II-501 [54]–[57]; upheld on appeal see ECJ Case C-221/97 P *Schröder and Thamann v Commission* (appeal dismissed) [1998] ECR I-8255.

[13] F Picod and L Coutron, 'La responsabilité de la Communauté européenne du fait de son activité administrative' in J-B Auby and J Dutheil de la Rochère (eds), *Droit administratif européen* (Brussels, Bruylant, 2007) 186–89.

[14] CFI Case T-108/94 *Candiotte v Council* (damages claim dismissed, no appeal) [1996] ECR II-87.

the Council had established a Committee tasked with selecting works of art to be acquired and installed in its new building in Brussels. Ms Candiotte was excluded at the second stage of the selection procedure. She claimed that the issue was here an illegal administrative act and thus the discretion of the institution, in the damages context, would be narrow by definition. The Court disagreed and found that the discretion was indeed wide (emphasis added):

> 30 The Court notes to begin with that the applicant, citing the decisions in Community staff cases relating to the composition of the selection board in competitions for the recruitment of officials, criticizes the Selection Committee for having failed to exercise effective control over the process of initial selection by the national working parties, in that it restricted itself to approving the lists drawn up by each national working party. The Court considers that those decisions cannot be applied in the present case. The selection of works of art to be placed in an office building and the recruitment of officials differ so much, as regards both subject-matter and purpose, that the Court cannot proceed by analogy and apply to artists' competitions the principles which govern the European civil service.
>
> 32 Firstly, as the Council rightly submits, the Selection Committee had a wide discretion with respect to the course of the competition, as shown in particular by the Council's decision of 12 June 1989 conferring on it the power to implement the procedure for selecting the works of art, and that discretion implied the possibility of adapting such a procedure to the circumstances. In cases such as this, where decisions have been taken on the basis of a *wide discretion*, review by the Community judicature must be limited to establishing that there was no manifest error in the assessment of the facts, no manifest breach of the rules governing the adoption of the decisions at issue, and no misuse of powers (see, for example, the judgments of the Court of Justice in Joined Cases 83/76, 94/76, 4/77, 15/77 and 40/77 HNL and Others v Council and Commission [1978] ECR 1209, paragraph 6, and in Case 188/85 Fediol v Commission [1988] ECR 4193, paragraph 6, and the judgment of the Court of First Instance in Joined Cases T-17/90, T-28/91 and T-17/92 Camara Alloisio and Others v Commission [1993] ECR II-841, paragraph 90).

The ruling establishing the existence of wide discretion would seem to make sense as regards the administrative nature of the task in question, namely selection of artwork. However, the curious thing in this case was that this finding was made years before the Court would say anything about the applicability of such criteria as regards administrative decisions. A similar statement can be found again in *Embassy Limousines* (CFI 1998) concerning tender procedures for the European Parliament.[15] The applicant was indeed awarded damages on the second claim, but the first claim was rejected: it clearly concerned an administrative decision, and the CFI took the view that where the Parliament had 'broad discretion' and that 'the applicant has put forward no evidence to show that the Parliament, in considering that none of the tenders received was totally satisfactory, has committed a grave and manifest error'.

[15] CFI Case T-203/96 *Embassy Limousines & Services v Parliament* (damages awarded, no appeal) [1998] ECR II-4239 [56] and [60].

B. Member State Damages Liability: Conditions Set in *Francovich* (ECJ 1991) and *Brasserie du Pêcheur* (ECJ 1996)

Pressure to amend the stringent criteria for Community liability acquired fresh impetus in *Francovich* (ECJ 1991)[16] when a second system of public liability in damages was introduced to the Community legal order. The finding of the Court that, where a Member State has breached its Community obligations by not transposing a directive in due time there is a right of reparation for the aggrieved party from the Member State, was fundamental in at least three respects. In the first place, it created a new remedy for individuals in the Member States. Secondly, it took the process of constitutionalisation of EU law one important step further. And thirdly, it re-ignited the discussion on the conditions for Community liability.

In *Francovich* the Court established criteria for Member State liability in the case of non-transposition of directives. The three conditions – that the result prescribed by the directive should entail the grant of rights to individuals; that it should be possible to identify the content of those rights on the basis of the provisions of the directive; and that there is a causal link between breach of the State's obligation and the loss and damage suffered by the injured parties – were markedly less stringent than those of the Community. Advocate General Mischo had noted this issue in his opinion, and had suggested alignment of the conditions, which the Court did not accept.[17] This was only done in 1996 in *Brasserie du Pêcheur*,[18] some five years later, where the right to reparation and the conditions thereof were defined more precisely and the remedy expressly generalised.

Indeed, in *Brasserie* (ECJ 1996), the Court ruled that, where a Member State infringes Community law, Community law confers a right to reparation where three conditions are met: (i) the rule of law infringed must be intended to confer rights on individuals; (ii) the breach must be sufficiently serious; and (iii) there must be a direct causal link between breach of the obligation resting on the State and the damage sustained by the injured parties.

However, for the purposes of Community liability, the key contribution of *Brasserie du Pêcheur* was the ruling that the criteria for the two liability systems should not, 'in the absence of particular justification', be different in like cases. It took several years before the ECJ was seized with a case where alignment could be put into practice. This was the appeal in the case of *Bergaderm*.

[16] ECJ Joined Cases C-6/90 and C-9/90 *Francovich and Bonifaci* [1991] ECR I-5357.

[17] ECJ Joined Cases C-6/90 and C-9/90 *Opinion of Advocate General Mischo – Francovich and Bonifaci* [1991] ECR I-5357 [71] and [72].

[18] ECJ *Brasserie du Pêcheur and Factortame* (n 5).

II. THE 'NEW' *BERGADERM* CONDITIONS

A. *Schöppenstedt* and its Criticism by Scholars

Rules regarding Community liability, as based on *Schöppenstedt* and *Bayerische HNL*, were subject to criticism. We may pick the following contributions from the end of the 1990's, ie before the alignment introduced in *Brasserie* and implemented in *Bergaderm* took place.

Judge Mancini, an eminent Member of the ECJ stated, in a speech given in 1993, that there were two areas in which 'the Court of Justice has let the individual down'. These two areas were damages liability of institutions and access to action for annulment.[19] The case-law was there to protect the institutions, not the individuals.

Ian Ward was of the same opinion. In 1996 he stated that 'Article 215 [now Article 340(2) TFEU] is effectively window-dressing. As ever, the interest that is protected is that of the institution itself, and not that of the European Citizen'.[20] For him, the requirement of breach of a superior provision could mean only another Treaty provision, and he found that only 'precious few' Treaty provisions were so explicit that they could be of any help. Furthermore, the fact that seriousness of breach required, as expressed in one case, 'conduct verging on the arbitrary', did not help either.

Francette Fines, whose dissertation on Community liability was published in 1990,[21] noted in 1997 that '[a]s cases succeed each other, the impression that the construction developed by the Court of Justice offers less and less protection for individuals seems to be confirmed'.[22] She observes that the test for liability is so restrictive that 'in practise the Community organs are quasi non liable and the protection of the victims is not guaranteed'. A second aspect was the exceedingly regressive case-law, where the *Vreugdenhil* damages case (ECJ 1992)[23] gives a brilliant illustration of the decrease of protection afforded to individuals.

In addition, some contributions contain fierce criticism with somewhat hidden legal methodology, but the policy message was clear: the system needed some rethinking.[24] Two issues in particular seemed problematic. In the first place, the sharp dichotomy as to choice of conditions on the basis of the nature of the act (legislative/administrative) was difficult to operate in practice. This dichotomy was not reflected in the hierarchy of Community law norms.[25] Second, after the estab-

[19] Republished in F Mancini, *Democracy and constitutionalism in the European Union: Collected Essays* (Oxford, Hart Publishing, 1999) 46–48.

[20] I Ward, *A Critical Introduction to European Law* (London, Butterworths, 1996) 64.

[21] F Fines, *Étude de la responsabilité extracontractuelle de la Communauté économique européenne* (Paris, LGDJ, 1990).

[22] F Fines, 'A General Analytical Perspective on Community Liability' in T Heukels and A McDonnell (eds), *The Action for Damages in Community Law* (The Hague, Kluwer Law International, 1997) 21–24.

[23] ECJ *Vreugdenhil (No 2)* (n 8) [19]–[21].

[24] C Stefanou and H Xanthaki, *A Legal and Political Interpretation of Article 215(2) [new Article 288(2)] of the Treaty of Rome. The Individual Strikes Back* (Aldershot, Ashgate, 2000).

[25] S Grossrieder Tissot, 'La responsabilité de la Communauté européenne du fait de l'activité normative de la Commission' (2001) *Revue trimestrielle de droit européen* 91–121.

lishment of Member State liability, the two regimes were markedly different and imbalanced: it appeared somewhat easier to establish Member State liability than that of the Community.

Moreover, the problems and restrictions arising out of the case-law relating to Community liability were exacerbated by the presence of the highly restrictive interpretation of the conditions in relation to an action for annulment under the Treaty. The way an individual had to be 'directly and individually' concerned by an act of general application in order to be able to contest its validity amounted to a real obstacle for legal protection within the Community regime. The strict limits to action for annulment were probably more debated than the strict limits to action for damages as such.[26]

The public liability system was established incrementally in ECJ case-law from the late 1960s and the full picture emerged gradually during the next 20 years or so with cases such as *Bayerische HNL* (ECJ 1978),[27] the *Isoglucose* cases (ECJ 1979)[28] and *Vreugdenhil (No 2)* (ECJ 1992).[29] As the cases followed each other, it became clear that even clearly illegal Community action would only very exceptionally lead to damages liability. At the same time, following the establishment of the CFI in 1988 and attribution of damages cases to the CFI at first instance, the ECJ was in fact put in the margins of development of damages case-law, and it was only to rule on these questions if a party appealed from the CFI to the ECJ, or by the 'back door', if the case related to Member State liability and came in as a preliminary ruling. In addition, influential members, such as Judge Mancini were publicly criticising the line taken by the Court. The time seemed ripe for a change.

B. *Bergaderm* (ECJ 2000)

The change came with *Bergaderm* (CFI 1998; ECJ 2000). *Bergarderm* was a damages action against the Commission. The facts of the case can be summarised as follows. An application for damages against the Commission was made by a company (and its chief executive) producing sun oil called Bergasol. The sun oil contained a substance (bergamot essence) on the effects of which there was no agreement between scientific experts, but there were studies which suggested a potentially carcinogenic effect when used in sun oil. The legal framework of the case was the Cosmetics

[26] Incidentally, both are mentioned by Mancini (n 19). Criticisms formulated against the strict conditions for action for annulment are aptly summarised in opinion of Advocate General Jacobs in ECJ Case C-50/00 P *Unión de Pequenos Agricultores* [2002] ECR I-6677. The Court disagreed with the Advocate General and maintained the strict rules.

[27] ECJ *Bayerische HNL* (n 3) [4] and [5].

[28] ECJ Joined Cases 103/77 and 145/77 *Royal Scholten Honig v Intervention Board for Agricultural products* [1978] ECR 2037; ECJ Joined Cases 116/77 and 124/77 *Amylum v Council and Commission* (damages claim dismissed) [1979] ECR 3497; ECJ Case 143/77 *Koninklijke Scholten-Honig v Council and Commission* (damages claim dismissed) [1979] ECR 3583.

[29] ECJ Case 22/88 *Vreugdenhil (No 1) and another v Minister van Landbouw en Visserij* (preliminary ruling) [1989] ECR 2049 [22] and ECJ *Vreugdenhil (No 2)* (n 8) [19]–[21].

Directive 76/768/EEC.[30] Following the appropriate comitology procedure and having heard a number of experts and the applicant, the Commission adopted the relevant directive on 10 July 1995 so that from July 1996 a maximum limit of 1 mg/kg was to be applied throughout the Community for 'psoralens' (which included Bergasol) and, as of 1 July 1997, any such product could no longer be sold or supplied to the final consumer. The company went bankrupt and sued the Community for damages.

The CFI, in its judgment in 1998,[31] placed the damages action in the framework of damages resulting from legislative measures. The CFI identified Article 10 of the Cosmetics Directive 76/768/EEC as the relevant provision and concluded that it was not infringed, and dismissed all the pleas and consequently the application itself.

The applicant appealed to the ECJ. Advocate General Fennelly, in his opinion of 27 January 2000, faithfully examined whether the measure was legislative or administrative, and concluded for the former. As there was no manifest breach, he proposed that the Court should reject the appeal.

The approach by the ECJ in its judgment on 4 July 2000 was different.[32] The Court first made a detailed reference to the *Brasserie du Pêcheur* case-law and underlined, as a novelty in the Community liability context, *discretion as the key element* (emphasis added):

> 43 As to the second condition, as regards both Community liability under Article 215 of the Treaty and Member State liability for breaches of Community law, the decisive test for finding that a breach of Community law is sufficiently serious is *whether the Member State* or *the Community institution concerned* manifestly and gravely disregarded the limits on its *discretion* (Brasserie du Pêcheur and Factortame, paragraph 55; and Joined Cases C-178/94, C-179/94, C-188/94, C-189/94, C-190/94 Dillenkofer and Others v Germany [1996] ECR I-4845, paragraph 25).

The ECJ revised its case-law and set aside the sharp dichotomy between administrative acts/legislative acts by ruling explicitly that discretion is the key issue (emphasis added):

> 46 In that regard, the Court finds that *the general or individual nature of a measure taken by an institution is not a decisive criterion* for identifying the limits of the discretion enjoyed by the institution in question.

As to the outcome, the ECJ found that the Commission had not breached the discretion available to it and dismissed the appeal by Bergaderm.

[30] Council Directive 76/768/EEC of 27 July 1976 on the approximation of the laws of the Member States relating to cosmetic products [1976] OJ L262/169.

[31] CFI Case T-199/96 *Bergaderm and Goupil v Commission* (damages claim dismissed, appealed C-352/98 P) [1998] ECR II-2805.

[32] ECJ *Bergaderm* (n 1).

C. Implementing *Bergaderm* and its Aftermath

Right after the ECJ judgment in *Bergaderm* in July 2000 it was probably not very clear what the bearing of the judgment was. The judgment is not very pedagogical and the opinion of the Advocate General, as it concentrates on the old doctrine, is of little help. It was only in subsequent cases that the new system was incrementally explained in more detail.[33] The CFI made a first reference to the new criteria just a couple of months later in *Fresh Marine* (CFI October 2000),[34] and applied them in more detail for example the following year in *Comafrica* (CFI 2001) and *Dieckmann* (CFI 2001).[35] At the ECJ, Advocate General Stix-Hackl analysed the new system in her opinion in the appeal in *Camar* (ECJ 2002), which was also the first case following *Bergaderm* where the ECJ itself applied the new criteria.[36] The current test which thus replaced the two tests (*Schöppenstedt/HNL* and *Lütticke/Adams*) is aptly summarised as follows in *CEVA and Pfizer*[37] (ECJ 2005) (emphasis added):

> 64 With regard to the second condition, the Court has stated that the *decisive test for determining whether a breach of Community law is sufficiently serious is whether the Community institution concerned manifestly and gravely disregarded the limits on its discretion* (Brasserie du Pêcheur and Factortame, paragraph 55; Bergaderm and Goupil v Commission, paragraph 43; Commission v Camar and Tico, paragraph 54; and Commission v Fresh Marine, paragraph 26).
>
> 65 Where that institution *has only a considerably reduced, or even no, discretion*, the mere infringement of Community law may be sufficient to establish the existence of a sufficiently serious breach (Bergaderm and Goupil v Commission, paragraph 44; Commission v Camar and Tico, paragraph 54; and Commission v Fresh Marine, paragraph 26).
>
> 66 The determining factor in deciding whether there has been such an infringement is therefore the discretion available to the institution concerned (Bergaderm and Goupil v Commission, paragraph 46; Commission v Camar and Tico, paragraph 55; and Commission v Fresh Marine, paragraph 27).

33 The same could be said about *Francovich* and the subsequent cases of *Brasserie du Pêcheur* etc. This appears to be a regular method used by the Court, as explained by a member of the Court: 'If the Court renders new principles on this basis [in new situations], it often decides in giving relatively general and narrowly motivated judgment, leaving interested lawyers to grope in the dark. But in this manner it reserves for itself the chance to re-examine, to more clearly define, to limit or even to correct the former judgment after the comments of critics or the intrusion of practical inconveniences'. See U Everling, 'On the Judge-Made Law of the European Community's Courts' in D O'Keeffe (ed), *Judicial Review in European Union Law. Liber Amicorum in Honour of Lord Slynn of Hadley. Volume 1* (The Hague, Kluwer Law International, 2000) 39, with further references.

34 CFI Case T-178/98 *Fresh Marine v Commission* (damages awarded, appealed C-472/00 P) [2000] ECR II-3331.

35 CFI Joined Cases T-198/95, T-171/96, T-230/97, T-174/98 and T-225/99 *Comafrica and Dole Fresh Fruit Europe v Commission* (no breach, no appeal) [2001] ECR II-1975 [136] and CFI Case T-155/99 *Dieckmann & Hansen v Commission* (damages claim dismissed, appealed C-492/01 P) [2001] ECR II-3143 [45].

36 ECJ Case C-312/00 P *Opinion of Advocate General Stix-Hackl – Commission v Camar and Tico* [2002] ECR I-11355.

37 ECJ Case C-198/03 P *Commission v CEVA and Pfizer* (CFI judgment set aside, damages action dismissed on appeal) [2005] ECR I-6357.

This is in essence the test that has been applied as regards breach since *Bergaderm* by the ECJ, CFI and CST.

D. What has *Bergaderm* Changed in Community Liability?

It should be noted from the outset that the conditions for Community liability had already been revised, amended and adjusted before. Therefore the fact that *Bergaderm* (ECJ 2000) did something to the criteria was not in itself any news. Even if the restrictive test was not changed before *Bergaderm*, the following revisions are worth mentioning:

In the first place, in *Mulder (No 1)* (ECJ 1992), the ECJ had already refined its view on the number of persons affected by illegal conduct. Indeed, one further condition had been that in order to be compensatable, the measure should have affected only a 'limited and clearly defined group of commercial operators'. This was to be inferred from the judgments in *Ireks-Arkady* (ECJ 1979), *Interquell* (ECJ 1979) and *Bayerische HNL* (ECJ 1978).[38] Advocate General van Gerven distinguished in *Mulder (No 1)* between a 'clearly defined group' and a 'limited group' (in terms of numbers) but the Court was silent on this point.[39] The outcome of the case shows that this issue was no longer a limitation. Second, further in *Mulder (No 1)*, the Court gave up the requirement of 'exceptional damage'.[40] Third, the infamous requirement that in order to be compensatable, action by a Community institution should have been 'verging on the arbitrary', mentioned in *Amylum* (ECJ 1979) and *Scholten-Honig* (ECJ 1979), was also revised. Originally in *Amylum* the Court had held that albeit the conduct of the institutions was illegal, it was not 'verging on the arbitrary' and therefore liability was not established.[41] However, some years later the ECJ had the opportunity to revert to this statement in *Stahlwerke Peine-Salzgitter* (ECJ 1993) and in practice declared that that condition should no longer be applied.[42]

[38] ECJ Case 238/78 *Ireks-Arkady v Council and Commission* (liability established) [1979] ECR 2955 [11] and ECJ Joined Cases 261 and 262/78 *Interquell Staerke-Chemie v Council and Commission* (liability established) [1979] ECR 3045 [15] and ECJ *Bayerische HNL* (n 3) [7]: 'In this connexion it is necessary to observe first that this measure affected very wide categories of traders, in other words all buyers of compound feeding-stuffs containing protein, so that its effects on individual undertakings were considerably lessened'.

[39] ECJ Joined Cases C-104/89 and C-37/90 *Opinion of Advocate General van Gerven – Mulder (No 1) and others v Council and Commission* [1992] ECR I-3061 [28].

[40] A Ward, *Judicial Review and the Rights of Private Parties in EU Law*, 2nd edn (Oxford, Oxford University Press, 2007) 392.

[41] ECJ *Amylum* (n 28) [19] (emphasis added): 'In fact, even though the fixing of the isoglucose production levy at five units of account per 100 kg of dry matter was vitiated by errors, it must nevertheless be pointed out that, having regard to the fact that an appropriate levy was fully justified, *these were not errors of such gravity that it may be said that the conduct of the defendant institutions in this respect was verging on the arbitrary* and was thus of such a kind as to involve the community in non-contractual liability'.

[42] ECJ Case C-220/91 P *Commission v Stahlwerke Peine-Salzgitter* (appeal dismissed) [1993] ECR I-2392 [51]: 'Furthermore, the concept of arbitrary conduct as mentioned only in the judgments in Joined Cases 116/77 and 124/77 Amylum v Council and Commission [1979] ECR 3497 and in Case

Two essential issues changed with *Bergaderm*. The most important in fact was that analysis in the judgment concentrates around the principal question, that is, discretion. It was the *'discretion test'* which replaced the dichotomy 'legislative acts – administrative acts' and the refined, differentiated tests for the two.

The second aspect, namely evolution from 'superior rule for the protection of the individual' to 'rule of law infringed must be intended to confer rights on individuals' is examined in more detail in chapter five, section II and chapter six, section II discussing rights. At this juncture it could already be noted that some authors assert that this change in Community liability, based on *Francovich*, made Community liability more difficult to establish.[43]

As regards the third condition (the causal nexus), it seems that it was not affected as well as the rest of the case-law relating to reparable damages and so on.

Overall, the change in *Bergaderm* (ECJ 2000) was indeed important, in particular in relation to the condition concerning discretion. Probably no single decisive factor was responsible for this, but rather it was the combined effect of several elements. The fact that the courts would from now on pay more attention to the discretion available to the actor in question seemed novel and promising, a kind of relaxation of the stringent criteria. These elements, combined with the earlier adjustments described above, seemed to enhance the possibility of establishing Community liability.

III. ARGUMENTS ADVANCED FOR CONVERGENCE OF THE TWO LIABILITY SYSTEMS

A. Scarce Justification for Convergence by the ECJ

Now what is interesting here is how alignment and the change in the law was justified and explained by the Court. It should once again be recalled that all the 'law' in this field is case-law and the change was thus not a change of legislation, but a reorientation of case-law.

The question of possible convergence of the two liability systems came into existence with the establishment of Member State liability in *Francovich* (1991).[44] *Bergaderm* (ECJ 2000) is usually cited as the first case where the new test for Community liability was put into practice. The judgment by the ECJ contains some three paragraphs where this new system is applied. The judgment does not give any explicit reasoning why the new test was justified. Reading the judgment can give

143/77 Koninklijke Scholten-Honig v Council and Commission [1979] ECR 3583, the latter of which is referred to by the Commission, does not provide a basis for holding that a finding of conduct verging on the arbitrary represents a necessary condition or formulation for the Community to be rendered liable within the framework of the EEC Treaty according to the abovementioned case-law of the Court of Justice'.

[43] Observation made by S Prechal, 'Member State liability and direct effect: what's the difference after all?' (2007) *European Business Law Review* 299–316.

[44] ECJ *Francovich and Bonifaci* (n 16).

the impression that what the Court is doing here is simply applying the crystal clear rules which had always been there.

On closer inspection it seems however that the decisive steps for transition were already taken during two preceding stages. *Brasserie du Pêcheur* (ECJ 1996),[45] in the first place, introduced the presumption that the conditions should be the same, without specifying what the conditions should be. Second, some paragraphs later it introduced discretion as the new criterion for both systems (emphasis added):

> 55 As to the second condition, *as regards both Community liability under Article 215 and Member State liability for breaches of Community law*, the decisive test for finding that a breach of Community law is sufficiently serious is whether the Member State or the Community institution concerned manifestly and gravely disregarded the limits on its discretion.

The same idea was repeated in *Dillenkofer* in October the same year (ECJ 1996).[46] The judgment, in relation to Member State liability, refers to the applicability of the same conditions in the two systems and incorporates a reference to case-law on Community liability which was not strictly necessary for that case:

> 25 On the one hand, a breach of Community law is sufficiently serious if a Community institution or a Member State, in the exercise of its rule-making powers, manifestly and gravely disregards the limits on those powers (see Joined Cases 83/76, 94/76, 4/77, 15/77 and 40/77 HNL and Others v Council and Commission [1978] ECR 1209, paragraph 6; Brasserie du Pêcheur and Factortame, paragraph 55; and British Telecommunications, paragraph 42). On the other hand, if, at the time when it committed the infringement, the Member State in question was not called upon to make any legislative choices and had only considerably reduced, or even no, discretion, the mere infringement of Community law may be sufficient to establish the existence of a sufficiently serious breach (see Hedley Lomas, paragraph 28).

The cited paragraph from *Bayerische HNL* (ECJ 1978)[47] in fact expressly refers to discretion. However, the issue *why* the criteria should be the same is not reasoned further.

On this point – alignment of conditions for liability – the ECJ in *Dillenkofer* (ECJ 1996)[48] followed the views presented by Member States in *Brasserie du Pêcheur.* The Member States that presented written observations in that case had suggested that the Court should use the same (restrictive) criteria as for Community liability. Indeed, the Court said that yes, the conditions must be the same, but no, we are not going to take over the extremely restrictive case-law as such. The Court simply defined a new set of criteria, taking inspiration from the existing case-law, but replacing the dichotomy by discretion and introducing a number of other elements.

[45] ECJ *Brasserie du Pêcheur and Factortame* (n 5).

[46] ECJ Joined Cases C-178/94, C-179/94, C-188/94, C-189/94 and C-190/94 *Dillenkofer and others v Bundesrepublik Deutschland* [1996] ECR I-4845.

[47] ECJ *Bayerische HNL* (n 3).

[48] ECJ *Dillenkofer* (n 46).

B. Further Elements in the Opinions of the Advocates General

While the reasoning of the Court for convergence of the two liability systems appears to be laconic and terse at some points, further clarification could be sought from the opinions of the Advocates General. The benefit of the opinions of the Advocates General is that they are often more detailed and sometimes even more coherent in reasoning when compared to judgments, as the text emanates from one single person and is not the compromise resulting from deliberations of the Court. Of course, the opinions do not replace judgments, but given the position and role of the Advocates General within the Court, the opinion may provide further elements for better understanding of the case. The opinions to be discussed below are from *Russo* (ECJ 1976), *Francovich* (ECJ 1991), *Hedley Lomas* (ECJ 1995), *Brasserie du Pêcheur* (ECJ 1995) and *Bergaderm* (ECJ 2000).[49]

At the time of *Russo* (ECJ 1976), the Community which had just in 1974 enlarged so that it comprised nine Member States, did have liability case-law concerning Community liability, but certainly not for Member State liability.[50] *Russo* was a preliminary reference from Italy concerning agriculture, common organisation of the market and unilateral action taken by Italy which had allegedly caused damage to a producer of durum wheat. The questions relating to damages liability of a Member State were new. Advocate General Reischl assessed the position of Community law in the Member States and the issue that the rule in question clearly conferred rights on individuals. However, this case still contained no explicit discussion on the liability of the Member States and its bearing. The Advocate General referred to the safeguarding of 'interests of individuals affected by any breach of provisions of Community law' and noted that 'when the other prerequisites under particular national law are present, a claim for damages may lie against the Member State which has not fulfilled its obligations under the Treaty'.[51] The Court took the same line and the judgment does not refer to possible liability of Member States.

We take *Francovich* (ECJ 1991) as the next step. The facts concerning non-transposition of the Wage Guarantee Directive 80/987 in Italy are well-known.[52] As mentioned above, in *Russo*, neither the Advocate General nor the Court discussed the pertinence of Community liability as regards possible Member State liability. Only in the summary of the facts in *Russo* is there a brief reference to the intervention of the Italian government on this issue.[53] What is then very interesting, when reading the report for the hearing of *Francovich*, is the position of the Commission. After assessing fulfilment of the conditions for direct effect of the directive, and con-

[49] See also *N Burrows and R Greaves*, The Advocate General and EC Law (Oxford, Oxford University Press, 2007) 215–62.

[50] ECJ Case 60/75 *Russo v AIMA* [1976] ECR 45.

[51] ECJ Case 60/75 *Opinion of Advocate General Reisch – Russo v AIMA* [1976] ECR 45, 62.

[52] The case comments on Francovich are all too numerous to be cited. For one highly analytical contemporary comment, see PP Craig, '*Francovich*, Remedies and the Scope of Damages Liability' (1993) *LQR* 595–621.

[53] ECJ *Russo v AIMA* (n 50) 53.

cluding in the negative, the Commission discusses the right to compensation and explains that what the Court did in *Russo* some 15 years earlier was that it had in fact just included in Member State liability certain limits already applied in Community liability: 'The Court thus transposed [in *Russo*] to the non-contractual liability of states for breaches of Community law a limit which it had already placed on then non-contractual liability of the institutions'.[54]

In *Francovich,* Advocate General Mischo discussed extensively Article 215(2) EEC [now Article 340(2) TFEU] case-law in his opinion and analysed the role of that case-law. He noted that the liability situations are often rather similar and that Article 215(2) EEC liability is *one* threshold which should lead to liability, but he carefully noted that liability should also be possible under national law where the conditions were less stringent.[55] However, when the ECJ established the principle of state liability in the *Francovich* judgment, the Court made no explicit or even implicit link with Article 215(2) EEC.[56] We learned from the judgment that such a principle was important in the Treaty.

When we approach the decisive year of 1996, two sets of opinions were issued before the seminal judgment in *Brasserie du Pêcheur* was handed down. Advocate General Tesauro gave his opinion in the case itself, but, already some months earlier, Advocate General Léger had given his opinion in *Hedley Lomas.* Despite the similarities, there are important differences between the two.

In the *Brasserie du Pêcheur* (ECJ 1996) proceedings, the Member States had referred to the liability criteria of the Community and asked the Court to transpose these – clearly restrictive criteria – to their liability, too. While Advocate General Tesauro initially stated that such a point of view did not seem 'completely baseless', he came to the conclusion that

> there is no reason for applying different criteria – naturally in like situations – depending on whether the infringement of Community law in question is attributable to a state or a Community institution. Conversely, different situations *can and must lead to different conclusions* as regards the criteria employed.

As to the touchstone of the system, he said that in the final analysis, 'what should be attained is a system of differentiated liability depending on whether or not the Community institutions (and the national authorities) have a *broad discretion*'.[57]

In *Hedley Lomas* (ECJ 1996), Advocate General Léger, on the other hand, came to the conclusion that conditions for Member State liability should not be copied from Community liability conditions, as this would make receiving damages impossible in practice. The touchstone should rather be discretion:[58]

[54] Report for the hearing, ECJ *Francovich and Bonifaci* (n 16) I-5366 [14ff]; see also Burrows and Greaves, *The Advocate General and EC Law* (n 49) 233.

[55] ECJ *Opinion of Advocate General Mischo – Francovich and Bonifaci* (n 17) [70ff].

[56] See in particular Craig (n 52) 605–08 and G Bebr, 'Case Comment Francovich' (1992) *Common Market Law Review* 557–84.

[57] ECJ Joined Cases C-46/93 and C-48/93 *Opinion of Advocate General Tesauro – Brasserie du Pêcheur and Factortame* [1996] ECR I-1029 [61], [67] and [68] (emphasis added).

[58] ECJ Case C-5/94 *Opinion of Advocate General Léger – Hedley Lomas* [1996] ECR I-2553 (footnotes omitted, emphasis added).

> 172 Thus, so far as the condition of breach of Community law is concerned, it is not State liability for breach of Community law which must be aligned with the liability provided for by Article 215 of the Treaty. *Such alignment would make it virtually impossible to raise the issue of the State's liability*, as the Court of Appeal's decision in Bourgoin v Ministry of Agriculture, Fisheries and Food, (181) itself based on the case-law of the Court of Justice on non-contractual liability, demonstrates. *I am suggesting the opposite.* As in the matter of State liability for breach of Community law, the conditions for enforcing liability against the Community for its legislative activity should, as far as the question of fault is concerned, *vary more according to the extent of the Community legislature's discretion.* Academic writers have long been advocating such a change in the conditions governing application of Article 215. '*It is not normal that the same liability rules should be applied to basic regulations of the Council and regulations adopted by the Commission pursuant to Council delegation. If the Council does not deserve to be placed in the situation of a democratically elected legislature, the same applies a fortiori to the Commission.* (182) [NB. The omitted footnote refers to R. Joliet: Les contentieux des Communautés européennes, 1981]

The Court in *Brasserie du Pêcheur* agreed with both Advocates General. Discretion became the touchstone, and the largely criticised liability conditions for Community liability were opened up, almost as obiter dicta. The approach, based on assessing the scope of discretion, was applied to Member State liability right away, from *Brasserie du Pêcheur* onwards.[59] The specific situation in relation to non-implemented directives was asserted in *Dillenkofer*.

With hindsight, what was probably somewhat surprising was that the new or restated criteria of 1996, based on breach of discretion, were not immediately applied, either before the CFI or before the ECJ. Those criteria were more beneficial to applicants when claiming damages from the Community but they were not invoked during the first years following *Brasserie du Pêcheur*. It would seem that there was no case where action was taken after 1996, until *Bergaderm*, where the applicants relied on the new, aligned criteria: it seems that all the applicants relied on the old, more restrictive criteria until *Bergaderm*, where it was taken up by the ECJ.[60]

In *Bergaderm* (ECJ 2000), the ECJ recalled in very brief terms the ruling in *Brasserie du Pêcheur* and transposed that to the case at hand, albeit the applicant had not referred to that case-law and that the Advocate General had not discussed this point at all.

After the judgment in *Bergaderm* was handed down, it can be said that the two regimes were now formally aligned. It appears that in the view of the ECJ the new system was applicable (at least) since 1996. This assumption is confirmed by the

[59] For an early appearance of discretion in the ECSC context, see ECJ Joined Cases C-363/88 and C-364/88 *Finsider and Falk v Commission* (damages claim dismissed) [1992] ECR I-359 [24] (emphasis added): '24 Thus, in order to appraise the nature of the fault required to render the Community liable, whether on the basis of Article 34 or of Article 40, neither of which, as has been stated, gives any details in that connection, it is appropriate to refer to the areas and conditions in which the Community institution acts. In that respect it is necessary to take into account in particular the complexity of the situations which the institution must regulate, the difficulties of applying the legislation and *the discretion available to the institution* under that legislation'.

[60] The first case where the applicant had referred to *Bergaderm* before the ECJ would seem to be *Camar and Tico* in 2002, see ECJ *Opinion of Advocate General Stix-Hackl – Commission v Camar and Tico* (n 36) [107] and [110].

ECJ judgment in *Commission v Camar and Tico* (ECJ 2002)[61] where a CFI judgment dating from 8 June 2000[62] (ie one month before *Bergaderm*) was set aside by the ECJ in 2002 as the CFI had not established discretion. That did not change much in the outcome for the applicant: the damages liability established by the CFI was still upheld. Advocate General *Stix-Hackl* was very hesitant as to whether this question should be examined at all.[63] She no longer had that problem with the appeal in *Fresh Marine* (ECJ 2003), as there the CFI had already referred to *Bergaderm*.[64]

To conclude, we may note that both Advocate General Mischo and Advocate General Tesauro supported the enhanced convergence of liability conditions. However, Advocate General Léger seemed to disagree on this, both for administrative liability, and in particular for judicial liability.

IV. NATURE OF CONVERGENCE OF THE TWO PUBLIC LIABILITY SYSTEMS

A. Striving for Convergence as a Fundamental Element of EU Law

We have examined above the way the two systems were gradually brought together under the common denominator of discretion. It seems justified to claim that convergent development of law is an essential element of Union action and EU law in general. Looking at the founding Treaties, it appears that striving for convergence is inherent and prevalent in the structure of the EU. The basic aim of the Treaties is to remove obstacles from free movement and harmonise and approximate national laws to attain this objective. The EU legislator can adopt instruments to attain convergence in a given field. The Commission may take legal action against a recalcitrant Member State in order to have its legislation declared in breach of commonly agreed objectives. Any national court can ask for preliminary rulings and the ECJ's replies are intended to safeguard uniform interpretation of converged legislation. In fact, the objective of attaining convergence in the Union system is so fundamental that exceptions to that rule have often been made explicitly. One such example is the legal basis for EU action in the field of culture, which expressly excludes harmonisation, and thus forced convergence.[65]

However, the view of the relationship between the European Union and Member State legal systems as a simple top-down road is not accurate. Indeed, EU law is not a 'one-way train towards integration'.[66] The 'second way' of analysing the relation-

[61] ECJ Case C-312/00 P *Commission v Camar and Tico* (damages upheld on appeal) [2002] ECR I-11355.

[62] CFI Joined Cases T-79/96, T-260/97 and T-117/98 *Camar and Tico v Commission and Council* (No 1; damages awarded, appealed C-312/00 P) [2000] ECR II-2193.

[63] ECJ *Opinion of Advocate General Stix-Hackl – Commission v Camar and Tico* (n 36) [135]–[142].

[64] ECJ Case C-472/00 P *Opinion of Advocate General Stix-Hackl – Commission v Fresh Marine* [2003] ECR I-7541.

[65] See eg, Art 167 TFEU on culture and *M Aziz*, The Impact of European Rights on National Legal Cultures (Oxford, Hart Publishing, 2004).

[66] P Beaumont and C Lyons et al (eds), *Convergence and Divergence in European Public Law* (Oxford, Hart Publishing, 2002), preface, v.

ship between the two systems is therefore 'feedback' from national systems to EU level and interaction between the two systems (cf. Figure 2.2). We can here take three examples of *'bottom-up' convergence.*

To start with a fairly recent example, Lyons (2002) argued on the basis of three Court cases and related opinions before the ECJ that the Court would rather carefully examine submissions based on the premise that if there is a certain common conception or principle in the Member States, then it should be a valid legal argument at EU level too.[67] She refers to *Netherlands v Council* (question whether public access to documents is a common principle in the Member States and whether on that basis it should be so at Community level too; ECJ 1996),[68] *Jippes* (same question re: principle of animal welfare; ECJ 2001)[69] and *Netherlands v Parliament and Council* (concept of *ordre public* in protection of biotechnology; ECJ 2001).[70] Her point is that convergence is not necessarily predicated on 'European Union institutional railroading of national values or culture or laws' but involves EU judicial space absorbing national influences and building upon them rather than diluting them, respecting national or local input.[71]

There are other types of example too. A well-known known transfer is that concerning the principle of protection of legitimate expectations. This principle started appearing in the 1960s and 1970s in ECJ case-law and gradually reached the status of a general principle of Community law. Oddly enough, on closer inspection this was a principle that only existed in Germany at the time. It was not possible to claim that it was truly something which was 'common' to the Member States when it came about as a 'general principle of Community law'.

Last but certainly not least: as mentioned above, national legal systems as a source of inspiration for Community law are mentioned in Article 340(2) TFEU and its predecessors laying down, albeit in somewhat vague terms, the conditions for Union liability in damages.

Therefore this type of *vertical convergence* (or even 'vertical unity') can have a beneficial influence on development of national law, but equally feedback from national systems can have important effects at Community level.

[67] C Lyons, 'Perspectives on Convergence Within the Theatre of European Integration' in P Beaumont and C Lyons et al (eds), *Convergence and Divergence in European Public Law* (Oxford, Hart Publishing, 2002), 88–95.

[68] ECJ Case C-58/94 *Netherlands v Council* [1996] ECR I-2169.

[69] ECJ Case C-189/01 *Jippes and others* [2001] ECR I-5689.

[70] ECJ Case C-377/98 *Netherlands v Parliament and Council* [2001] ECR I-7079.

[71] Lyons (n 67) 81. However, for the sake of clarity it should be added that the ECJ is not ready to accept just any argument whatsoever based on national law(s). There is ample case-law where the Court has stated that a given concept, for example, is an autonomous concept of Community law and its meaning cannot be inferred from national systems. See eg ECJ Case C-287/98 *Linster* [2000] ECR I-6917 [43]: 'The need for uniform application of Community law and the principle of equality require that the terms of a provision of Community law which makes no express reference to the law of the Member States for the purpose of determining its meaning and scope must normally be given an autonomous and uniform interpretation throughout the Community; that interpretation must take into account the context of the provision and the purpose of the legislation in question (Case 327/82 Ekro v Produktschap voor Vee en Vlees [1984] ECR 107, paragraph 11)'.

B. Maintaining Convergence

This vertical, two-way relationship between the two legal systems is followed, at least in certain areas, with a third relationship, this time horizontal. We are looking at development at EU level, between two areas of EU law.

As regards public liability we are in fact examining proposed convergence in a given area of law *within* the EU legal system and *not between* two legal systems. Indeed, to examine convergence, public liability in EU law appears to be a good candidate.[72]

Logically, if 'typical' convergence between the EU and national levels is clearly a two-way train and part of daily business, then surely convergence of public liability regimes at EU level is natural, or perhaps it could be qualified as a fundamental condition.

On the basis of the case-law, it seems that the Court has used the convergence argument to *create* convergence. It was used to streamline a Community liability system which had become overly restrictive. However, in order to *maintain* such convergence, one might be looking for mutual references between the two EU liability systems and the case-law developing that system. Oddly enough, these references are largely absent.[73] It seems that when the Community courts are assessing Community liability, the judgments refer only to previous case-law concerning Community liability. Conversely, when one reads case-law on Member State liability, references to *Brasserie du Pêcheur* are repeated, but seldom is any reference made to the ample case-law concerning Community liability. To be fair, one must say that with careful research some exceptions to this rule can be found, but they are not very numerous.[74]

What role, then, does the convergence argument play today? It was once used to justify restatement of liability conditions, but nowadays one could claim that it has only limited meaning. It seems that the convergence argument is fading or in

[72] For studies between legal systems examples can be found in respect of the harmonisation of contract law (European Civil Code and so-called Common Frame of Reference) and in respect of harmonisation of tort law (Principles of European Tort Law by European Tort Law Group).

[73] On the dialogue between the two courts, see M Fartunova, 'Le dialogue des juges. Les interactions entre le TPICE et la Cour' in P Mbongo and A Vauchez (eds), *Dans la fabrique du droit européen. Scènes, acteurs et publics de la Cour de justice des Communautés européennes* (Brussels, Bruylant, 2009).

[74] For such a reference in a case relating to Community liability, see CFI Case T-364/03 *Medici Grimm v Council* (damages claim dismissed, no appeal) [2006] ECR II-79 [81]: 'Furthermore, the protection of the rights which individuals derive from Community law cannot vary depending on whether a national authority or a Community authority is responsible for the damage (Bergaderm and Goupil v Commission, paragraph 41). It must therefore be recognised that, as with proceedings relating to the liability of Member States for infringement of Community law, in order to determine whether an infringement of Community law committed by a Community institution constitutes a sufficiently serious breach, the Community Court hearing a claim for compensation must take account of all the factors which characterise the situation put before it, and those factors include, in particular, the clarity and precision of the rule infringed, and whether any error of law was inexcusable or intentional (see, by analogy, Case C-424/97 Haim [2000] ECR I-5123, paragraph 43, and Case C-63/01 Evans [2003] ECR I-14447, paragraph 86)'.

practice playing a lesser role and even the departure of the case-law in two different directions has been invoked by certain scholars.

Was this the original intent of the Court, too? The statement establishing convergence as an aim in *Brasserie du Pêcheur* and *Bergaderm* seemed unequivocal. However, on closer inspection we note that for example Advocate General Léger already said in *Köbler* (ECJ 2003) that 'we cannot infer that the rules governing Member State liability and the rules in respect of the Community must develop in strict parallel', thereafter mentioning accession to the ECHR.[75]

C. Similarity – or Difference – Between Liability Situations?

As regards the situation today, in the post-Lisbon setting, we would now, in Figure 4.1 below, attempt to depict the two issues by two separate, but overlapping circles. The first circle depicts the first aspect of EU law-based liability, namely Union liability (Article 340(2) TFEU). The second circle represents the second aspect of EU law-based liability, the liability of the Member States (*Francovich* ECJ 1991; *Brasserie du Pêcheur* ECJ 1996). Both circles contain three horizontal zones, reflecting liability situations in the field of administrative, legislative and judicial issues. The overlapping area of the two circles in the middle contains liability situations which can be present in both systems. In fact, this overlapping area in the middle is surprisingly meagre.

It should be recalled that according to the Court, when situations are alike, then the conditions should be the same, unless there are good reasons to the contrary. So, when are situations alike? In this diagram, the areas where the situations are similar are depicted in the middle circle (Zone 'A&B', grey zone, in the middle). The requirement of similarity can be considered as fulfilled in cases where the national authority takes a decision regarding veterinary medicines (eg *Norbrook* ECJ 1998)[76] or where, conversely, the Commission prepares a decision in the field of medicinal products (eg *Synthon*, ECJ 2008),[77] both authorities are taking administrative decisions where the extent of discretion may be comparable. In such cases, logically, the conditions should be the same, when there are no particular reasons to the contrary.

Following the same logic, we may note that there are areas which are different. For example, as regards implementation of directives, this is only an obligation which exists for Member States (Zone 'B'). It is difficult to find a corresponding situation for EU liability. In the same vein, only the EU can be the defendant in staff cases (Zone 'A'), and we can only look in vain to find similar situations in the Member States. Therefore, following the Court's logic, there is no need to align such conditions with one another. It could be argued that, according to its own case-law, the Court is 'free' to set the liability conditions in such cases as it sees fit.

[75] ECJ Case C-224/01 *Opinion of Advocate General Léger – Köbler* [2003] ECR I-10239 [94].

[76] ECJ Case C-127/95 *Norbrook Laboratories* [1998] ECR I-1531.

[77] ECJ Case C-452/06 *Synthon* [2008] ECR I-7681.

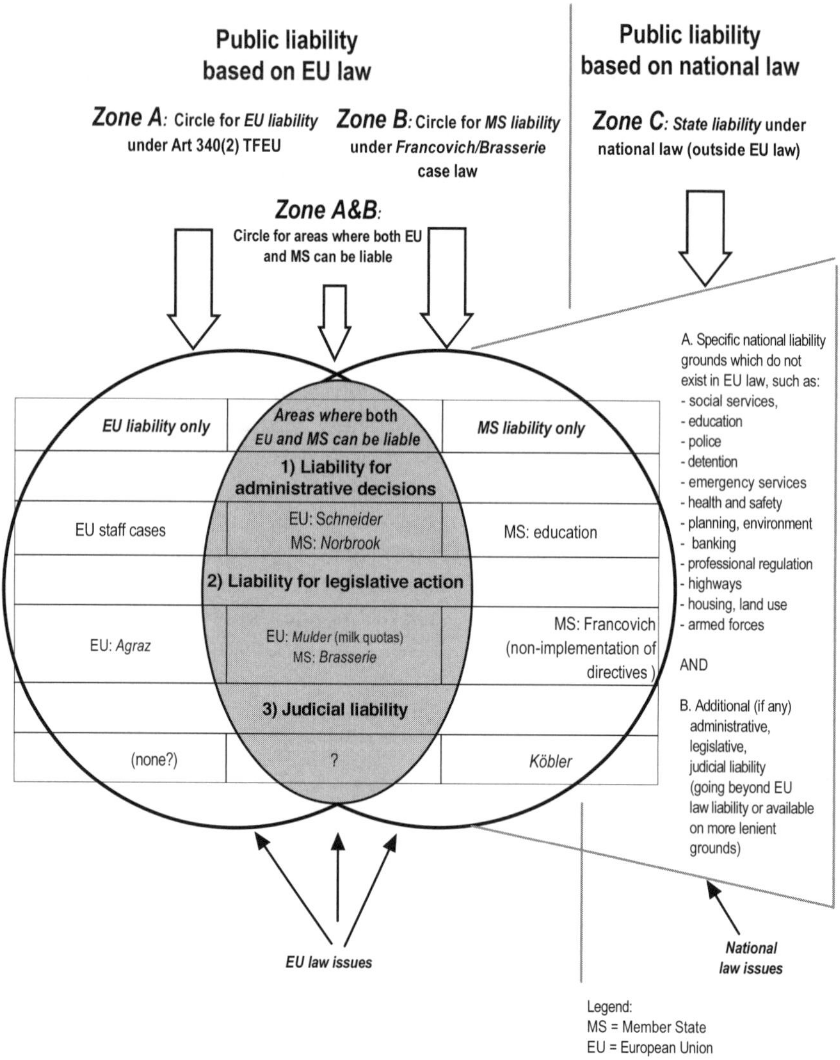

Figure 4.1 EU Law Liability and Non-EU Law Liability Sectors: 'the Two Circles and a Triangular Extension'

Finally, an additional aspect which should not be neglected is depicted in the right hand corner, namely the non-EU area of liability. This zone 'C' consists of national public liability rules of the Member States, outside EU law. This sector has a threefold role. First of all, it has functioned as a source of inspiration for both EU law based liability systems. Second, it is an essential element for the execution of Member State liability which always takes place in Member States. Third, and very interestingly, it will function as a receptor of influences from the EU system: convergent (or not) development between and within the two circles (zones 'A' and 'B') will inevitably have effects here, too.

D. Outlook

In this chapter we analysed how the law has developed for public liability law. We traced the way the change was brought about and attempted to find reasons why this was done. We concluded that the purpose underlying the change was probably to bring about more coherence and convergence to the Community legal system and liability conditions. This was justified by arguing a need for coherence. What we have attempted to show further was that this argument has been used rather scarcely ever since.

Whatever characterisation one finally attributes to the issue of convergence, we should note that the Court has, in this field, been fairly responsive to criticism. In this instance, the Court was able to do so. The criteria for Community liability was established by the Court itself, on the basis of principles common to the law of the Member States. The Court did not expressly state that these principles had already evolved over the years. The discretion available to the Court in this field becomes clear when revision of the liability criteria for the Community is juxtaposed with the criteria concerning conditions to introduce an action for annulment. Here, too, the case-law of the ECJ and the CFI had been criticized over the years. When the CFI attempted to interpret the criteria more openly in *Jégo-Quéré*,[78] the Court recalled on appeal that the wording of Article 230 EC as it then was did not allow such an interpretation and, consequently, the Treaty should be changed if such a change was to be brought about.[79]

This chapter has illustrated one aspect of ongoing developments in public liability for breaches of EU law. Yet the debate on alignment is not closed. One illustration is the fate of no-fault liability and the *FIAMM* case which has been before both the CFI and the ECJ. One of the questions of principle in that case is whether and under what conditions the Community may be held liable without fault (strict liability). For its part the CFI assessed the criteria for strict liability it had extracted from the case-law, but concluded that the conditions were not fulfilled (CFI 2005).[80]

[78] CFI Case T-177/01 *Jégo-Quéré v Commission* (appealed C-263/02 P) [2002] ECR II-2365.

[79] See ECJ *Unión de Pequenos Agricultores* (n 26) [44] and ECJ Case C-263/02 P *Commission v Jégo-Quéré* [2004] ECR I-3425 [36] (emphasis added): 'Although the condition that a natural or legal person can bring an action challenging a regulation only if he is concerned both directly and individually must be interpreted in the light of the principle of effective judicial protection by taking account of the various circumstances that may distinguish an applicant individually, *such an interpretation cannot have the effect of setting aside the condition in question, expressly laid down in the Treaty. The Community Courts would otherwise go beyond the jurisdiction conferred by the* Treaty'. Eventually, with the Lisbon Treaty, this article was amended and the criteria were somewhat opened up, *cf* Art 263 TFEU.

[80] CFI Case T-69/00 *FIAMM and FIAMM Technologies v Council and Commission* (dismissed, appealed C-120/06 P) [2005] ECR II-5393.

On appeal, however, the ECJ ruled that such a liability does not exist, at least not in the WTO context (ECJ 2008).[81] Be that as it may, and building on the core theme of this contribution, if the convergence argument were to be applied 'normally', and if there is no 'particular justification' for divergent conditions, such strict liability conditions – if they had been established – should then also have become applicable in the *Francovich/Brasserie du Pêcheur* context as regards breaches attributable to Member States. This form of liability would then have to be applied by the national courts for Member State liability.

[81] ECJ Joined Cases C-120/06 P and C-121/06 P *FIAMM and Fedon v Council and Commission* (appeal dismissed) [2008] ECR I-6513.

5

Liability of the European Union

THIS CHAPTER PRESENTS the elements to be analysed as regards the liability of the European Union. This and the following chapter will essentially follow the same structure. As an introduction a number of structural aspects of the liability of the European Union will be first set out (section I). The core of the chapter concentrates on the rights criterion (section II) and breach criterion (section III). Both of these sections will be based on extensive analysis of the case-law. The chapter concludes by a presentation of a selected number of successful damages cases.

I. STRUCTURAL ASPECTS

A. General Issues

The purpose of the Union's liability system seems to be twofold: even if it exists to ensure monetary compensation for breach of European Union law rights by Union institutions, the conditions for its application were at least originally designed so restrictively that it not only protects individuals but also Union institutions.

Save for three odd references at the Treaty level,[1] the source of law for Union liability is the case-law of the courts of the European Union.

Originally, all damages actions against the European Union were judged at first and final instance by the ECJ. Since establishment of the CFI in 1991, damages actions have been judged at first instance by the CFI, and now, after Lisbon, by the General Court.[2] Thus, since 1991, the CFI (GC) has been the main court to apply and define the criteria for damages liability of the Union. The ECJ has been involved only on appeal against the judgment of the CFI on a point of law.[3] It should be mentioned that following establishment of the Civil Service Tribunal in 2005, staff cases, including any damages aspect, are examined by that court at first instance.[4] An appeal lies against its judgments to the General Court.[5]

[1] See Arts 268 TFEU, 340(2) TFEU and Art 46 of the Statute of the Court of Justice of the European Union [ex Arts 235 and 288(2) EC, and ex-Art 46 of the Statute].

[2] On the competence of the General Court, see Art 256(1) TFEU, which also refers to Art 268 TFEU concerning damages actions against the Union.

[3] On appeals to the ECJ, see Art 56 of the Statute.

[4] See Annex I ('The European Union Civil Service Tribunal') to the Statute, Art 1.

[5] On appeals to the General Court, see Annex I to the Statute, Art 10. Very exceptionally, the first Advocate General may propose that a decision of the General Court be reviewed by the ECJ (Arts 256(2) and (3) TFEU and Arts 62, 62a and 62b of the Statute). For a case where the Court followed

As to the number of damages actions against the Union, between 1995 and 2010, some 10–20 new damages cases have been introduced each year before the CFI. This represents on average less than 4 per cent of cases.[6] Some of the variation in the number of the damages actions brought can be explained by a number of connected cases, introduced by different applicants on the same grounds.[7]

Table 5.1 Damages Actions Brought against the Communities before the CFI and GC (1995–2010)

Year	-95	-96	-97	-98	-99	-00	-01	-02	-03	-04	-05	-06	-07	-08	-09	-10
Damages actions brought	36	14	4	14	19	17	21	13	24	18	16	8	27	15	13	8
plus milk quota cases	(32)	(5)	(28)	(2)												
plus customs agents			(295)	(2)												
Total number of cases CFI/GC	244	220	624	238	384	398	345	411	466	536	469	432	522	629	568	636
Damages actions % of total cases (incl. milk quota/ customs agents)	14,8 %	6,4 %	0,6 %	5,9 %	4,9 %	4,3 %	6,1 %	3,2 %	5,2 %	3,4 %	3,4 %	1,9 %	5,2 %	2,4 %	2,3 %	1,3 %
	(27,9)	(8,6)	(52,4)	(7,5)												

Source: Annual Reports of the Court of Justice.

These figures can be contrasted with figures setting out the (published) judgments and orders of the CFI in damages cases. The number of judgments and orders by the CFI has varied between 3 and 15, the number of rulings establishing damages liability oscillating between 0 and 3, the typical value being 2.[8] The ECJ has given one or two important rulings each year in appellate cases.

The system of Union liability could be characterised as a closed system. Although the national legal systems have functioned as a source of inspiration, the rules have been designed by Union courts to function within the EU system. In the practical application of damages liability criteria, the EU courts do not refer to national law, even if the courts do not go so far as to say that the criteria for Union damages liability would be based on independent or autonomous concepts of European Union

such proposal, see ECJ Case C-197/09 RX-II *Review of the judgment in Case T-12/08P–M v EMEA* [2009] ECR (unpublished judgment of 17 December 2009) and for a case where it did not, see ECJ Case C-17/11 RX-II *Decision concerning review of the judgment in Case T-143/09 P Commission v Petrilli* (no review) [2011] ECR I-0000 (Decision of 8 February 2011).

[6] For a summary of cases between 1963 and 1989, see F Fines, *Étude de la responsabilité extracontractuelle de la Communauté économique européenne* (Paris, LGDJ, 1990) annex I, 425–49. Another overview is provided by C Stefanou and H Xanthaki, *A Legal and Political Interpretation of Article 215(2) [new Article 288(2)] of the Treaty of Rome. The Individual Strikes Back* (Aldershot, Ashgate, 2000).

[7] eg, the milk quota cases in 1995–98 and the customs agents cases in 1997 and 1998.

[8] The apparent difference between numbers of incoming cases and published judgments/orders can be explained by the fact that similar cases may be joined for the purposes of judgment/order, or that applications are withdrawn, or that applications are rejected by unpublished orders. For example, the figure for 2007 includes 18 damages actions which were brought by 18 cotton ginning undertakings. Of these 18 actions, 15 applications were withdrawn in 2008 (resulting in one order by the CFI) and three were dismissed in 2010 by one judgment, see GC Joined Cases T-252/07, T-271/07 and T-272/07 *Sungro v Council and Commission* (damages claim dismissed, no appeal) [2010] ECR II-55 [21], [24] and [25].

law. The Union courts have sole jurisdiction to rule on damages cases against the Union and no Member State court is competent to consider an action for damages against the Union.[9]

As to alternative remedies, those who have been damaged by Union action or inaction, can or indeed should use other means available to mitigate their loss. This can be done through an action for annulment[10] or by an action for inaction.[11] In national proceedings, where the national court makes a preliminary reference to the ECJ, the illegality of a Union measure can be invoked through a plea of illegality.[12]

B. Institutional Coverage: Legislative, Executive and Judicial Branches

From an organic point of view, the liability of the Union covers all Union institutions and bodies. By far the most damages actions are directed against the Commission and the Council, as they take most of the decisions or measures which may have adverse external effects.[13] Actions addressed in general against the Communities/ Union are admissible under certain conditions, but as a matter of practice damages actions are directed against the institution which is claimed to have caused the damage.[14] It should be noted that before the Lisbon Treaty, damages action against any resolution of the European Council was considered inadmissible.[15] Now the damages liability of the Union is also extended to the actions of the European Council, which has become an institution.[16]

Apart from the institutions, the Treaty expressly mentions the European Central Bank.[17] The position of the agencies has also been expressly clarified, as provisions relating to their liability were added to the basic acts.[18] It is now also clear that

[9] *cf* ECJ Case 5/68 *Sayag v Leduc (No 1)* (first preliminary ruling) [1968] ECR 395, 402.

[10] Under Art 263 TFEU (ex-Art 230 EC).

[11] Under Art 265 TFEU (ex-Art 232 EC).

[12] *cf* ECJ Case 120/86 *Mulder* [1988] ECR 2321 [28] and ECJ Case 170/86 *Von Deetzen v Hauptzollamt Hamburg-Jonas* [1988] ECR 2355 [17], which led to the milk quota damages cases.

[13] As regards the various activities by each institution which may lead to liability, see A Czaja, *Die Außervertragliche Haftung der EG für ihre Organe* (Baden Baden, Nomos, 1996) 71–191.

[14] As to damages cases addressed against the Community, instead one of its institutions directly, see ECJ Case 106/81 *Kind v EEC* (damages claim dismissed) [1982] ECR 2885 and ECJ Case 59/83 *Biovilac v EEC* (damages claim dismissed) [1984] ECR 4057 [25].

[15] See CFI Case T-346/03 *Krikorian and others v European Parliament and others* (dismissed, appealed C-18/04 P) ECR II-6037 and ECJ Case C-18/04 P *Krikorian and others* (appeal dismissed) [2004] ECR (unpublished order of 29 October 2004).

[16] See Art 13(1) TEU.

[17] CFI Joined Cases T-3/00 and T-337/04 *Pitsiorlas v Council and ECB* (damages claim dismissed, appealed C-84/08 P) [2007] ECR II-4779 and ECJ Case C-84/08 P *Pitsiorlas v Council and ECB* (appeal dismissed, lodged out of time) [2008] ECR I-104*, Summ.pub. (order of 3 July 2008).

[18] As to 'classic' agencies, see eg, Art 19(2) ('Liability') of Regulation (EC) No 1920/2006 of the European Parliament and of the Council of 12 December 2006 on the European Monitoring Centre for Drugs and Drug Addiction (recast) [2006] OJ L376/1

In substance, a similar provision is applied for executive agencies, see eg Council Regulation (EC) No 58/2003 of 19 December 2002 laying down the statute for executive agencies to be entrusted with certain tasks in the management of Community programmes [2003] OJ L11/1, Art 21 'Liability'.

However, the agencies created under the EU II pillar (CFSP) are subject to different arrangements.

damages actions may be brought against the Ombudsman for his activities as regards alleged instances of maladministration.[19] The European Investment Bank is also covered.[20]

On the other hand, damages actions against acts of primary law (founding Treaties, amending Treaties and Treaties of Accession) are inadmissible.[21] Furthermore, damages actions against measures by bodies which are not part of the institutions are also inadmissible (eg actions directed against measures adopted by the political groups of the European Parliament): they are not acts of the institutions.

Before the Lisbon Treaty, damages actions for activities under the EU Treaty (second and third pillar) against the European Union were not admissible either. In *Segi* (CFI 2004), the CFI found that it did not have jurisdiction to hear an action for damages seeking compensation for any damage which may have been caused by a common position based on Article 34 EU, since, according to Article 46 EU, no judicial remedy for compensation is available in the context of Title VI of the EU Treaty.[22] The Court confirmed this on appeal (ECJ 2007).[23] As this last Article has been abrogated, a new case in post-Lisbon setting would be analysed on that basis.[24]

However, when measures relating to Common Foreign and Security Policy (II pillar) were implemented through Union instruments (I pillar), damages actions against implementing Community measures have been considered admissible (*Sison* CFI 2007).[25] Following the Lisbon Treaty, Article 275 TFEU now contains a specific provision on this question.[26]

There has been no doubt that the liability of the Community can be engaged as a result of administrative or legislative action. The special feature of the system is

[19] See ECJ Case C-234/02 P *Médiateur (Ombudsman) v Lamberts* (appeal dismissed) [2004] ECR I-2803, CFI Case T-412/05 *M v Ombudsman* (damages awarded €10000, no appeal) [2008] ECR II-197*, Summ.pub. (judgment of 24 September 2008).

[20] CFI Case T-140/97 *Hautem v BEI (No 1)* (damages awarded, appealed C-449/99 P) [1999] ECR II-897; ECJ Case C-449/99 P *BEI v Hautem (No 1)* (appeal dismissed; damages upheld) [2001] ECR I-6733; CFI Case T-336/06 *2K-Teint and others v Commission and EIB* (damages claim inadmissible, no appeal) [2008] ECR II-52*, Summ.pub. (order of 10 April 2008).

[21] CFI Case T-113/96 *Dubois et Fils v Council and Commission* (damages claim dismissed, appealed C-95/98 P) [1998] ECR II-125; ECJ Case C-95/98 P *Dubois et Fils v Council and Commission* (appeal dismissed) [1999] ECR I-4835 (alleged damage resulting from Single European Act).

[22] CFI Case T-338/02 *Segi and Others v Council* (dismissed, appealed C-355/04 P) [2004] ECR II-1647.

[23] ECJ Case C-355/04 P *Segi* (appeal dismissed) [2007] ECR I-1657 [33ff].

[24] *cf* also G Lysén, *EU Framework decisions: Who is liable to pay compensation for the violation of the rights of the individual. A public international law approach* (Uppsala, Iustus, 2006).

[25] As regards damages action in the context of restrictive measures against certain persons and entities with a view to combating terrorism, where a second pillar measure is implemented in the first pillar, see CFI Case T-47/03 *Sison v Council* (liability conditions fulfilled, annulment sufficient compensation, no appeal) [2007] ECR II-73*, Summ.pub. (judgment of 11 July 2007) [228]–[51].

[26] Art 275 TFEU: 'The Court of Justice of the European Union shall not have jurisdiction with respect to the provisions relating to the common foreign and security policy nor with respect to acts adopted on the basis of those provisions.

However, the Court shall have jurisdiction to monitor compliance with Article 40 of the Treaty on European Union and to rule on proceedings, brought in accordance with the conditions laid down in the fourth paragraph of Article 263 of this Treaty, reviewing the legality of decisions providing for restrictive measures against natural or legal persons adopted by the Council on the basis of Chapter 2 of Title V of the Treaty on European Union'.

that the whole issue of liability did not start developing from administrative issues, but from legislative ones (eg *Schöppenstedt*, ECJ 1971).[27] The question was rather: under what circumstances should the liability of the Community be engaged for its legislative action. Thus the development of Community liability started from an area which, for example in Finland, was out of the question for any state liability.[28] It is true that issues relating to administrative activities and related liability arose very early (eg *Lütticke*, ECJ 1971)[29], but that branch of liability was not developed much further, as cases were lacking. Liability for administrative acts remained somewhat 'underdeveloped', as situations giving rise to damages actions were considered by the applicants as legislative or, ultimately, at least qualified as such by the Court.

The third branch is judicial activity. Nothing in the Treaty expressly excludes the Union from making good any damage which the Union courts themselves may cause when exercising judicial activity.[30] In 1996, the Court stated that Member States should be held liable for breaches of EU law, independently of whether the damage was caused by the executive, the judiciary or the legislative. Indeed, only some years later was the existence of such liability confirmed vis-à-vis the Supreme Court of Austria (*Köbler*; ECJ 2003), and reconfirmed in a later case regarding Italy (*Traghetti*; ECJ 2006).[31] Following *Brasserie du Pêcheur* (ECJ 1996), it is clear that the Union courts are not categorically excluded from liability for judicial activities.[32] However, such damages liability has not been pronounced to date and it seems that any of the courts of the union has never been sued for judicial liability.[33] It may still take quite some time before we may read of a finding by the General Court that the ECJ has 'manifestly and gravely' breached the limits of its discretion when exercising its judicial activities. It seems that the rights guaranteed by the

[27] ECJ Case 5/71 *Zuckerfabrik Schöppenstedt v Council* (damages claim dismissed) [1971] ECR 975 [11].

[28] H Kulla, 'The Responsibility of the State as Legislator' in T Modeen (ed), *Finnish National Reports to the XVTH Congress of the International Academy of Comparative Law (Bristol, July 26 – August 1, 1998)* (Helsinki, 1998) 207.

[29] ECJ Case 4/69 *Lütticke v Commission* (damages claim dismissed) [1971] ECR 325 [9].

[30] The Court of Justice can undoubtedly be liable in damages for its activities in other than judicial functions, eg in personnel cases, or for public procurement issues. *cf* eg CFI Case T-256/02 *I v Court of Justice* (damages claim dismissed, no appeal) [2004] ECR FP-I-A-289, II-1307.

[31] ECJ Case C-224/01 *Köbler* [2003] ECR I-10239; ECJ Case C-173/03 *Traghetti del Mediterraneo* [2006] ECR I-5177.

[32] See eg, by J-G Huglo, 'Fasc. 371 – Cour de justice – Responsabilité extracontractuelle – Conditions de fonde du recours en indemnité – Décision de la Cour (à jour au 28 avril 2004)' *Jurisclasseur Europe Traité*, 2004) [5].

[33] See ECJ Case 20/88 *Roquette frères v Commission* (damages claim dismissed) ECR 1553 [19] and [20]. A reduction of a fine was awarded by the ECJ for the excessive length of proceedings, including before the CFI, see ECJ Case C-185/95 P *Baustahlgewebe v Commission* (reasonable satisfaction for excessive duration of proceedings – €50000 in fine reduction) [1998] ECR I-8417. In ECJ Case C-385/07 P *Der Grüne Punkt – Duales System Deutschland v Commission* (appeal dismissed) [2009] ECR I-6155, the Court noted expressly that 'the failure on the part of the Court of First Instance to adjudicate within a reasonable time can give rise to a claim for damages brought against the [Union]' ([193]).

ECHR could be the most likely candidate for this type of case,[34] especially after the EU accedes to it.[35]

C. Sectors of Liability: Examples

The management structures of the Union and European Union Law are directly linked to the issue of what areas the Union may be sued in for damages. Implementation or administration of European Union law is in many areas and in many cases entrusted to the Member States. Damages actions against the European Union have been chiefly lodged in fields of direct administration of EU law, such as agriculture, fisheries, public procurement of the institutions, and competition decisions.

An important category is areas directly administered by Union institutions. Here the main area is agriculture. Common agricultural policy is administered directly at Union level through market organisations, and their alleged or established malfunctioning has led to many damages actions. Amendments to the Union milk quota system in 1984 were carried out in a way which did not take into account certain types of producers who were thus treated in a discriminatory way. Once the illegality of the Union measure was established by the ECJ, the CFI was flooded with damages actions. A number of damages cases were settled on the basis of a statutory compensation scheme laid down in a regulation, but a number of cases were still maintained.[36] Similar long-standing litigation areas have arisen on issues relating to banana regimes, for example.[37]

[34] See eg a scenario presented as regards the 'commissaire de gouvernement' and Advocate General, in W van Gerven, 'Judicial Convergence of Laws and Minds in European Tort law and Related Matters in A Colombi Ciacchi and C Godt, et al (eds), *Haftungsrecht im dritten Millenium – Liability in the Third Millenium: Liber Amicorum Gert Brüggemeier* (Baden-Baden, Nomos, 2009) 35ff.

[35] When the Union accedes to the ECHR, the Strasbourg court would potentially be competent to find an infringement of the ECHR by a Union institution. For the courts of the states parties to the ECHR, such a finding is often related to the exceedingly long duration of the proceedings. However, the possible 'just satisfaction' following such finding would not be compensation for damage under Art 340(2) TFEU.

[36] A concise account of the milk quota damages is given by E Sharpston, 'Milk Lakes, SLOMs and Legitimate Expectations', in D O'Keeffe (ed) *Judicial Review in European Union Law. Liber Amicorum in Honour of Lord Slynn of Hadley. Volume 1* (The Hague, Kluwer Law International, 2000).

[37] CFI Case T-571/93 *Lefebvre and others v Commission* (damages claim dismissed, no appeal) [1995] ECR II-2379; CFI Case T-521/93 *Atlanta and others v Communauté européenne* (damages claim dismissed, appealed C-104/97 P) [1996] ECR II-1707; ECJ Case C-104/97 P *Atlanta v European Community* (appeal dismissed) [1999] ECR I-6983, CFI Joined Cases T-79/96, T-260/97 and T-117/98 *Camar and Tico v Commission and Council (No 1)* (damages awarded, appealed C-312/00 P) [2000] ECR II-2193; CFI Case T-2/99 *T Port v Council* (no breach, no appeal) [2001] ECR II-2093; CFI Joined Cases T-198/95, T-171/96, T-230/97, T-174/98 and T-225/99 *Comafrica and Dole Fresh Fruit Europe v Commission* (no breach, no appeal) [2001] ECR II-1975; CFI Case T-30/99 *Bocchi Food Trade International v Commission* (damages claim dismissed, no appeal) [2001] ECR II-943; CFI Case T-52/99 *T. Port v Commission* (damages claim dismissed, appealed C-213/01 P) [2001] ECR II-981; CFI Case T-18/99 *Cordis v Commission* (damages claim dismissed, no appeal) [2001] ECR II-913; ECJ Case C-312/00 P *Commission v Camar and Tico* (damages upheld on appeal) [2002] ECR I-11355; CFI Case T-99/98 *Hameico Stuttgart and others v Council and Commission* (damages claim dismissed, no appeal) [2003] ECR II-2195; CFI Case T-57/00 *Banan-Kompaniet and Skandinaviska Bananimporten v Commission and Council* (not sufficiently serious, no appeal) [2003] ECR II-607; CFI Case T-56/00 *Dole Fresh Fruit International v Commission and Council*

One area which has generated a certain amount of case-law is external trade relations, and another is litigation in relation to anti-dumping duties imposed on economic operators.

Competition law, in the broad sense and including anti-trust, merger and state aids proceedings, has also been a source of rather extensive litigation. Yet another which merits mention is decisions relating to Union funds, in particular in relation to public procurement procedures.[38]

D. Applicants

When staff cases are excluded, the typical applicant in a damages action against the Community (Union) has been an economic operator involved in the agricultural sector. Most often applicants are legal persons, with the notable exception of the milk quota cases where most of the applicants were individuals.[39] Where individuals sue Union institutions for damages, they are often Union officials or persons in close relation with the institution.[40]

E. Procedural Questions

It should be noted at the outset that each and every damages case against the Community judged by the CFI (and the ECJ) does not contain an assessment of each of the criteria for damages liability.

(not sufficiently serious, no appeal) [2003] ECR II-577; ECJ Case C-213/01 P *T. Port v Commission* (appeal dismissed) [2003] ECR I-2319; CFI Joined Cases T-64/01 and T-65/01 *Afrikanische Frucht-Compagnie v Council* (damages claim dismissed, no appeal) [2004] ECR II-521, CFI Case T-303/00 *Beamglow v European Parliament, Council and Commission* (damages claim dismissed, no appeal) [2005] ECR II-5459; CFI Case T-260/97 *Camar v Council and Commission (No 2)* (assessment of loss; damages awarded €5m, no appeal) [2005] ECR II-2741, CFI Case T-139/01 *Comafrica and Dole Fresh Fruit Europe v Commission* (damages claim dismissed, no appeal) [2005] ECR II-409; CFI Joined Cases T-457/04 and T-223/05 *Camar v Commission* (inadmissible, no appeal) [2008] ECR II-215*, Summ.pub. (judgment 15 October 2008).

[38] The areas of Union liability will be explored in more detail in s II and s III below when discussing the case-law.

[39] For milk quota cases, see eg ECJ Joined Cases C-104/89 and C-37/90 *Mulder (No 1) and others v Council and Commission* (liability established) [1992] ECR I-3061; CFI Case T-50/93 *Haas v Council and Commission* (removed from register) [1994] ECR (unpublished order of 31 August 1994); CFI Joined Cases T-195/94 and T-202/94 *Quiller and Heusmann v Council and Commission* (damages awarded, no appeal) [1997] ECR II-2247; CFI Case T-222/97 *Steffens v Council and Commission* (damages claim dismissed, no appeal) [1998] ECR II-4175; ECJ Joined Cases C-162/01P and C-163/01P *Bouma and Beusmans v Council and Commission* (appeal dismissed) [2004] ECR I-4509; CFI Case T-373/94 *Werners v Council and Commission* (damages claim dismissed, no appeal) [2006] ECR II-4631, CFI Joined Cases T-8/95 and T-9/95 *Pelle and Konrad v Conseil et Commission* (damages awarded, no appeal) [2007] ECR II-4117; CFI Case T-94/98 *Alferink and others v Commission* (damages claim dismissed, no appeal) [2008] ECR II-1125.

[40] ECJ Joined Cases 169/83 and 136/84 *Leussink-Brummelhuis v Commission* (liability established) [1986] ECR 2801; CST Case F-10/06 *André v Commission* (damages awarded; appealed T-69/07 P) [2006] ECR FP-I-A-1-183, II-A-1-755; CFI Case T-144/02 *Eagle and others v Commission* (damages awarded between £91000 and £291000, no appeal) [2007] ECR III-2721; ECJ Case C-348/06 P *Commission v Girardot* (appeal dismissed) [2008] ECR I-833.

In fact, the Community courts readily stop examining the case if they find that one of the liability conditions is not fulfilled. According to the case-law, the cumulative nature of those conditions means that, if any one of them is not satisfied, the action for damages must be dismissed in its entirety and it is unnecessary to consider the other conditions for non-contractual liability.[41] Thus for example in *Pitsiorlas* (CFI 2007; ECJ 2008),[42] when the existence of damage could not be established and when the same applied to direct causal link, it was not necessary to address the question of a rule of law granting rights to individuals.[43] The Courts have been criticised for this practice as being 'unpedagogical'.[44] In practice this approach means that many damages cases against the Community/Union only contain useful assessment of one of the criteria, but not of all the criteria. Therefore albeit CFI/GC damages judgments as regards Community are numerous, they are often 'patchy'. There is also a procedural explanation to this: the CFI does not have to make a complete legal analysis for the national court, but it can dismiss the case in a more straightforward manner.[45] In contrast, in preliminary references pertaining to Member State liability a more comprehensive assessment is often given by the ECJ, provided that it has been requested by the national court.

Another important difference is that since the establishment of the CFI the liability of the EU has been part of the competences of the CFI. Indeed, for the purposes of this study it should be noted that after *Bergaderm* (ECJ 2000) only a limited number of appeal cases have been brought to the ECJ in which it has been put in a position to develop further or review the convergent criteria the ECJ set in that judgment. In all the other cases the final assessment has been made by the CFI, ie a different court that assesses Member State liability.

What is more, as regards Union liability, in cases where the original CFI judgment has been appealed, a second assessment is offered by the ECJ, either concurring with and upholding the CFI, or, perhaps even more interesting, dissenting and overruling the CFI.[46]

Compared to Member State liability, what can be said from the outset is that for Community/Union liability much more case-law is available relating to manifest breach of EU law, so that assessment and the approach to breach can be more nuanced.

[41] See to this effect eg GC *Sungro v Council and Commission* (n 8) [36]; ECJ Case *T. Port v Commission* ECR [30]; ECJ Case C-257/98 P *Lucaccioni v Commission* (appeal dismissed) [1999] ECR I-5251 [14] and [63].

[42] CFI *Pitsiorlas v Council and ECB* (n 17); ECJ *Pitsiorlas v Council and ECB* (n 17).

[43] The same approach was also present in CFI *Alferink and others v Commission* (n 39) [60].

[44] F Picod and L Coutron, 'La responsabilité de la Communauté européenne du fait de son activité administrative' in J-B Auby and J Dutheil de la Rochère (eds), *Droit administratif européen* (Brussels, Bruylant, 2007).

[45] However, sometimes the CFI proceeds to a full analysis, as if preparing for a possible appeal against its judgment. If the CFI did not do that, the ECJ would not necessarily have all the elements to appreciate the case and to give a final judgment; it would then have to return the case to the CFI for fuller analysis.

[46] The same aspect is present in personnel cases dealing with damages claims in the relation between the CST and the CFI.

II. GRANTING OF RIGHTS TO INDIVIDUALS : LIABILITY OF THE EUROPEAN UNION AND EU LAW RIGHTS BREACH OF WHICH MAY GIVE RISE TO LIABILITY

A. Introduction

Three preliminary observations should be made.[47] First, regarding the difference between liability of the Union and liability of the Member States in so far as rights are concerned, the main issue is the role of direct effect and related questions. Most of the discussion for Member State liability as regards the rights condition relates one way or the other to the question of direct effect, either as an alternative remedy in the Member State or as regards its relation to granting of rights (eg, vertical direct effect, consequences of absence of horizontal direct effect of directives). Due to this difference in approach, the case-law cannot be classified the same way.

Second, it is important to notice that contrary to Member State liability, the liability rights condition for liability of the European Union (Community) has been substantially modified with *Bergaderm* (ECJ 2000). The original *Schöppenstedt* condition (ECJ 1971) concerning 'a superior rule of law intended for the protection of the individual' was replaced in *Bergaderm* (ECJ 2000) with a 'rule of law granting rights to individuals'.[48]

Third, and this is partly linked to the preceding paragraph, the sources of rights have been different. Until *Bergaderm* (ECJ 2000), the sources of rights which had qualified as 'superior rules of law intended for the protection of the individual' were mainly, if not solely, legal principles. Even today the bulk of the case-law is still based on assessment of breach of legal principles, albeit claims based on breach of legislation are already appearing more and more frequently. In the future, the way may well lead towards more concrete norms, including the rights set out in the EU Charter of Fundamental Rights.[49]

B. Types of EU Law Rights Invoked in Liability Case-law Concerning the European Community

Three groups of cases can be distinguished when analysing the Courts' case-law on Community liability and cases concerning the question of granting rights to individuals (or a superior rule of law for the protection of the individual).

The first, and smallest, group consists of cases where breach of a rule of law granting rights to individuals is established and all the other conditions for liability are fulfilled. The first group is thus the fully successful cases, where the Community has

[47] The questions underlying this section have been discussed in ch 2, s V above.

[48] A Ward, *Judicial Review and the Rights of Private Parties in EU Law*, 2nd edn (Oxford, Oxford University Press, 2007) 54–58.

[49] Charter of Fundamental Rights of the European Union, proclaimed in Nice on 7 December 2000 and as adapted at Strasbourg on 12 December 2007 [2007] OJ C303/1.

been held liable. For the period after *Bergaderm* (2000–2010), there are altogether some 10 cases,[50] one every year.

The second group includes cases where the court has established infringement of rights but one of the other two conditions for liability has not been fulfilled, ie the Community has finally been held not liable.

The third residual category then includes all the damages actions examined by the courts, independently of whether breach of an individual right has been established. These cases are more difficult to qualify as regards the rights invoked: in some cases it appears that the right invoked (which was thus not necessarily examined by the court) looks reasonably potential to be granting rights to individuals, whereas in some other cases that is clearly not so. As to the case-law before *Bergaderm*, it has been set out above that the condition of 'granting rights to the individual' appears to be less stringent than the *Schöppenstedt* condition of 'superior rule of law for the protection of the individual'. Thus the pre-*Bergaderm* cases where an infringement of the 'rights' condition has been found, are generally good law even today. However, the fact that the 'rights' condition has not been fulfilled in pre-*Bergaderm* case-law does not necessarily mean that that would be the case even post-*Bergaderm*.

It should be noted that in the cases presented below damages have not always been awarded, but it appears from the judgments that in these cases the court has apparently considered the rules of law presented below as *potentially* 'granting rights to individuals', in contrast to the rules in the next section where that qualification has been ruled out. The following analysis attempts to cover at least all the cases in which damages have been awarded. We will place particular emphasis on post-*Bergaderm* case-law, where available, since for pre-*Bergaderm* case-law the old, tighter condition of breach of a superior rule of law for the protection of individuals applied. As a result of fields of direct Community administration and the centre of gravity for economic interest, most litigation has occurred in fields related to agriculture: milk quotas, bananas, maize grits, starch and cotton.

i. Legitimate Expectations

In terms of Community damages liability, the principle of which breach has led to the most numerous damages liability cases is protection of legitimate expectations. For traders, the principle of protection of legitimate expectations is a kind of test of the prudent trader. According to that principle, any trader in regard to whom an institution has given rise to justified hopes may rely on the principle of protection of legitimate expectations. The limitation is that if a prudent and discriminating trader could have foreseen adoption of a Community measure likely to affect his interests, he cannot plead that principle if the measure is adopted.[51]

[50] Excluding staff cases and milk quota cases.

[51] CFI Case T-489/93 *Unifruit Hellas v Commission* (dismissed, appealed C-51/95 P) [1994] ECR II-1201 [51], see ECJ Case C-51/95 P *Unifruit Hellas v Commission* (appeal dismissed) [1997] ECR I-727 (order).

The leading cases on breach of the principle of legitimate expectations are the milk quota cases. The Court established breach of principle in two preliminary rulings. In *Mulder* and *Deetzen* (ECJ 1988) the Court established that total and continuous exclusion of certain categories of milk producers from resuming the marketing of milk at the end of a five-year voluntary exclusion period was not an occurrence which those producers could have foreseen when they entered into an undertaking, for a limited period, not to deliver milk. The Court noted that there was nothing in the provisions of the relevant Regulation[52] or in its preamble to show that the non-marketing undertaking entered into under that Regulation might, upon its expiry, entail a bar to resumption of the activity in question. Therefore, such an effect frustrated those producers' legitimate expectation that the effects of the system to which they had rendered themselves subject would be limited.[53]

In subsequent years, a huge number of damages actions were introduced. In the leading case of *Mulder II* (ECJ 1992) one of the issues for the Court to decide was whether the infringement was sufficiently serious. The Court found so for one of the heads, but for the other the Court did not consider it sufficiently serious.[54] In one of the follow-up cases, namely in *Quiller and Heusmann* (CFI 1997), the Court noted that the legislator had failed to take into account a clearly defined category of economic operators and the consequences thereof were entirely unforeseeable and the risks were not within the bounds of normal risks inherent in the economic activity in question.[55]

However, the first case where breach of legitimate expectations led to establishing damages liability was *CNTA* No 1 (ECJ 1975),[56] which related to the monetary compensatory amounts applicable to colza and rape seeds, and to the oils obtained from those seeds. The question was whether a given trader (that had undertaken transactions following receipt of an export licence fixing the amount of the refund in advance) could legitimately expect that no unforeseeable alteration should occur which could have the effect of causing him inevitable loss, by re-exposing him to exchange risk. The ECJ answered in the affirmative and ruled that the Community should be liable if, in the absence of an overriding matter of public interest, the Commission abolished with immediate effect and without warning the application of compensatory amounts in a specific sector without adopting transitional

[52] Council Regulation (EEC) No 1078/77 of 17 May 1977 introducing a system of premiums for the non-marketing of milk and milk products and for the conversion of dairy herds [1977] OJ L131/1.

[53] ECJ *Mulder* (n 12) [26] and [27]; ECJ *Von Deetzen v Hauptzollamt Hamburg-Jonas* (n 12) [17].

[54] ECJ *Mulder (No 1) and others v Council and Commission* (n 39) [17]. One of the particular features of the milk quota litigation is that the Council established a statutory reparation scheme, through which a number of cases were settled. For those cases where the parties did not agree on damages liability, the litigation continued, eg ECJ Joined Cases C-104/89 and C-37/90 *Mulder (No 2) and others v Council and Commission* (quantum) [2000] ECR I-203, most notably for the quantum of damages.

[55] CFI *Quiller and Heusmann v Council and Commission* (n 39), see [66]–[69] and [75].

[56] ECJ Case 74/74 *CNTA v Commission (No 1)* (interlocutory; liability established) [1975] ECR 533 [42] and [43].

measures which would at least permit traders to avoid the loss which would have been suffered in the performance of export contracts.[57]

In *Embassy Limousines* (CFI 1988),[58] the Parliament had infringed the principle of legitimate expectations in the framework of a public tendering procedure concerning passenger transport with chauffeur-driven vehicles. The CFI found that the breach in the procedure consisted of the fact that the Parliament, first, had induced a legitimate expectation on the part of the applicant by encouraging it to take a risk which went beyond that normally run by tenderers in a tendering procedure and, secondly, that the Parliament had failed to inform the applicant of an important change in the conduct of the tendering procedure.

Sofrimport (ECJ 1990) concerned import of Chilean dessert apples.[59] While the merchandise was in transit from Chile to the European Community, the Commission adopted protective measures in the fruit and vegetable sector concerning imports from non-member countries without taking any account whatsoever of the position of traders whose goods were in transit to the Community. The ECJ ruled that such a measure, which was taken without invoking any overriding public interest, disregarded the legitimate expectation created by Article 3(3) of Regulation No 2707/72. Consequently, it gave rise to non-contractual liability on the part of the Community.

Even if breach of legitimate expectations has been a successful basis in some cases, in many judgments the claimed breach thereof has not been established.

The case of *Dieckmann & Hansen* (CFI 2001) concerned a German company which had imported caviar for the last 130 years.[60] It imported fresh caviar in large units, packaged it in smaller portions and sold these on to its customers inside and outside the Community. The applicant purchased its caviar mainly from the sole producer of caviar in Kazakhstan. In early March 1999, the applicant concluded a contract for imports of some 10 tons of caviar from Kazakhstan, while some weeks later the Commission adopted a decision banning imports from that country. The applicant company ceased its activity and was wound up. The Court noted that under the relevant legislation the Commission had a wide discretion to evaluate the production situation in the country in question. Consequently, said the Court, any trader in whom an institution has aroused justified expectations can in principle rely on that principle, but traders cannot have a legitimate expectation that an existing situation which is capable of being altered by the Community institutions in the exercise of their discretionary power will be maintained. Therefore, in the case at hand, the Commission's broad discretion in the matter empowered it to alter, so

[57] In the second CNTA ruling it turned out that that applicant was finally unable to show damage, despite the positive ruling of principle, see ECJ Case 74/74 *CNTA v Commission (No 2)* (no loss suffered) [1976] ECR 797 [17].

[58] CFI Case T-203/96 *Embassy Limousines & Services v Parliament* (damages awarded, no appeal) [1998] ECR II-4239 [86].

[59] ECJ Case 152/88 *Sofrimport v Commission* (damages awarded) [1990] ECR I-2477 [26]–[29].

[60] CFI Case T-155/99 *Dieckmann & Hansen v Commission* (damages claim dismissed, appealed C-492/01 P) [2001] ECR II-3143 [77] and ECJ Case C-492/01 P *Dieckmann & Hansen v Commission* (appeal dismissed) [2003] ECR (unpublished order of 6 February 2003).

far as necessary, the existing situation, so that the applicant could not reasonably harbour a legitimate expectation that that situation would be maintained.

In *Emesa Sugar* (CFI 2001), which was about sugar imports from overseas countries and territories in the framework of Decision 97/803/EC, the CFI noted that even if the protection of legitimate expectations is one of the fundamental principles of the Community, traders cannot have a legitimate expectation that an existing situation which is capable of being altered by the Community institutions in the exercise of their discretion will be maintained.[61]

Finally, *Biret* (CFI 2002) related to the prohibition of certain substances with hormonal action and the GATT.[62] In particular, with reference to the effect of talks in progress within the framework of GATT between 1991 and 1994, the Court recalled that in the absence of specific assurances given by the administration, no one may claim breach of the principle of the protection of legitimate expectations. The applicant was not even claiming that it had received such assurances from the Community authorities regarding the outcome of talks.

ii. Principle of Non-discrimination (Equality)

The principle of non-discrimination, or the principle of equality, has also played a key role in damages liability and its infringement has led to damages liability. To start with, in *Dumortier (No 1)* (ECJ 1979) the Court held that the Community incurred liability because it abolished refunds for maize grits by Regulation No 665/75 and those for broken rice by Regulation No 668/75 and yet retained them for maize starch, thus infringing the principle that there should be equal treatment.[63] The Court found that the principle of equality, embodied in particular in the second subparagraph of Article 40 (3) of the EEC Treaty, had been breached. That principle, which prohibits discrimination in the common organisation of the agricultural markets, occupies a particularly important place among the rules of Community law intended to protect the interests of the individual.

The CFI has confirmed in post-Bergaderm case-law that breach of the principle of non-discrimination qualifies as a rule granting rights to individuals. Thus in *Dole Fresh Fruit International* (CFI 2003),[64] the Court noted that breach of the principle of non-discrimination had already been pre-established in an earlier annulment action against the Council.[65] The CFI, citing *Bergaderm* (ECJ 2000), confirmed that this rule gave rights to individuals. However, it found that the breach was not sufficiently serious and thus dismissed the damages action.

[61] CFI Case T-43/98 *Emesa Sugar v Council* (damages claim dismissed, no appeal) [2001] ECR II-3519 [87].

[62] CFI Case T-174/00 *Biret International v Council* (no breach, appealed C-92/03 P) [2002] ECR II-17 and ECJ Case C-93/02 P *Biret International v Council* (appeal dismissed) [2003] ECR I-10497.

[63] ECJ Joined Cases 64 and 113/76, 167 and 239/78, 27, 28 and 45/79 *Dumortier and others v Council (No 1) (liability established)* [1979] ECR 3091 [13]; see also ECJ Joined Cases 241/78, 242/78 and 245/78 to 250/78 *DGV v Council and Commission* (liability established) [1979] ECR 3017 [13] and ECJ Case 256/81 *Pauls Agriculture v Council and Commission* (damage, quantum) [1983] ECR 1707 [8]–[17].

[64] CFI *Dole Fresh Fruit International v Commission and Council* (n 37) [72] and [73].

[65] ECJ Case C-122/95 *Germany v Council* [1998] ECR I-973.

Furthermore in *Dolianova* (CFI 2004), the CFI found that the Commission had breached the principle of non-discrimination and that the breach was sufficiently serious.[66] However, on appeal the ECJ ruled that the action was out of time and dismissed it as inadmissible (ECJ 2008).[67] The action was brought by certain Italian wine producers in view of a payment by the Commission of aid allegedly owed to them under Regulation No 2499/82 laying down provisions concerning preventive distillation.

iii. Prohibition of Unjust Enrichment

In *Dolianova* (CFI 2004), cited above, the CFI also confirmed that the prohibition of unjust enrichment is a general principle of Community law that grants rights to individuals.[68] The CFI awarded damages, but as stated above, the whole action was finally considered inadmissible by the ECJ.[69]

iv. Protection of Personal Data

The principle of protection of personal data was infringed in *Nikolaou* (CFI 2007) and damages were awarded.[70] The case concerned an inquiry by the European Anti-Fraud Office (OLAF) relating to Ms Nikolaou, a Member of the Court of Auditors. The Court found that in the framework of the inquiry the Commission, of which the OLAF is an independent part, had infringed, among others, certain articles of the OLAF Investigations Regulation and the Data Protection Regulation of the Community institutions, as regards a leak of an ongoing enquiry concerning Ms. Nikolaou.[71]

v. Duty of Care

In the post-Bergaderm setting, the CFI has confirmed for example in *MyTravel* (CFI 2008) that the duty of diligence, together with some other rules, grants rights for individuals.[72] This case related to liability of the Community, based on

[66] CFI Case T-166/98 *Cantina sociale di Dolianova and Others v Commission* (liability established; appealed C-51/05 P) [2004] ECR II-3991 [176].

[67] ECJ Case C-51/05 P *Commission v Cantina sociale di Dolianova and Others* (CFI judgment set aside; damages action dismissed as inadmissible) [2008] ECR I-5341.

[68] CFI *Cantina sociale di Dolianova and Others v Commission* (n 66) [160] and [162].

[69] On this question in general see R Williams, *Unjust Enrichment and Public Law. A Comparative Study of England, France and the EU* (Oxford, Hart Publishing, 2010) 207ff.

[70] CFI Case T-259/03 *Nikolaou v Commission* (damages awarded €3000, no appeal) [2007] ECR II-99*, Summ.pub. (judgment of 12 September 2007).

[71] Regulation (EC) No 1073/1999 of the European Parliament and of the Council of 25 May 1999 concerning investigations conducted by the European Anti-Fraud Office (OLAF) [1999] OJ L136/1, Art 8(3) and Regulation (EC) No 45/2001 of the European Parliament and of the Council of 18 December 2000 on the protection of individuals with regard to the processing of personal data by the Community institutions and bodies and on the free movement of such data [2001] OJ L8/1, Arts 2, 3, 4(1) and 5(a) and (e); see [200]–[216], [230]–[233] of the judgment.

[72] CFI Case T-212/03 *MyTravel v Commission* (damages action; dismissed, no appeal) [2008] ECR II-1967 [49], [50] and [132].

a Commission decision declaring a concentration of two companies (Airtours and FirstChoice) incompatible with the common market, which decision was eventually annulled by the CFI. In the subsequent damages action, as regards the question concerning a rule of law intended to confer rights on individuals, the CFI noted that the duty of diligence is breached if, as in this case, there is a finding of an irregularity which in comparable circumstances would not have been committed by a normally prudent and diligent administration. Institutional conduct of this kind constitutes a kind of illegality that involves Community liability. The CFI noted in particular that the case-law clearly recognises the protective nature of the duty of diligence in relation to individuals which imposes on the competent institution the obligation to examine carefully and impartially all the relevant elements of the individual case, relating to the principle of sound administration.

On that basis the CFI confirmed that Article 2(3) of Regulation No 4064/89, read in conjunction with Article 2(1) and (2) and with Article 8(2) and (3) of the Regulation, and taken together with the duty of diligence, lays down rules the purpose of which is to confer rights on undertakings which are concerned by a decision which prohibits a concentration being put into effect. However, even if in this case the existence of a breach had been established in a preceding action for annulment, the breach was not considered to be sufficiently serious, and the application was thus dismissed.

Reference can be made to two further cases where damages were awarded. *Fresh Marine* (CFI 2000) concerned anti-dumping duties for Norwegian salmon. The applicant claimed damages for breach of the duty of diligence and good administration. The Court does not say explicitly what were the principles breached, but apparently accepts these as granting rights to individuals, as it accepted the damages claim.[73]

Furthermore, in *Cobrecaf* (CFI 1995) damages were awarded in relation to lack of care by the Commission.[74] The case related to Community financial assistance for the construction of fishing vessels under Regulation (EEC) N° 4028/86. The applicants had applied for Community financial aid to construct two tuna fishing vessels, but it turned out that that due to a drafting error within the Commission, a certain amount was excluded from the eligible expense. Even if the error was eventually noted, it was not corrected in due time. Therefore, in those circumstances, the Commission committed an administrative fault of a kind for which it incurs non-contractual liability in failing, within a reasonable time, to rectify the error which it accepts that it made. The fact that it took 15 months to rectify a manifest error shows obvious lack of care on its part.[75]

[73] CFI Case T-178/98 *Fresh Marine v Commission* (damages awarded, appealed C-472/00 P) [2000] ECR II-3331 [63] and ECJ Case C-472/00 P *Commission v Fresh Marine* (damages upheld to NOK 431000) [2003] ECR I-7541.

[74] CFI Case T-514/93 *Cobrecaf and others v Commission* (damages awarded, no appeal) [1995] ECR II-621.

[75] ECJ Joined Cases C-363/88 and C-364/88 *Finsider and Falk v Commission* (damages claim dismissed) [1992] ECR I-359 [22].

Finally, in *Nölle* (CFI 1995),[76] the CFI ruled that the principle of care had not been breached and dismissed the action. The case related to a definitive anti-dumping duty on imports of brushes originating in the People's Republic of China.

vi. Protection of Confidentiality of Information

Adams (ECJ 1985) led to damages for infringement of the principle of protection of confidentiality of information, referred to in Article 214 EEC (now Article 339 TFEU).[77] The applicant had in 1973 divulged to the Commissioner for competition a number of anti-competitive practices engaged in by his employer Hoffmann-La Roche & Co. He had requested that his name be not disclosed in this context. However, the Commission did not respect that request and the applicant was to bear a number of extremely uncomfortable consequences. He sued the Commission for damages.

On the duty of confidentiality, the Court pointed out that Article 214 of the EEC Treaty laid down an obligation, in particular for the members and the servants of the institutions of the Community, 'not to disclose information of the kind covered by the obligation of professional secrecy, in particular information about undertakings, their business relations or their cost components'. The wording ('in particular') shows that the principle in question is a general one which also applies to information supplied by natural persons, especially if transmitted voluntarily with a request for confidentiality. An institution which accepts such information is bound to comply with such a condition. The Court found that the duty of confidentiality had been infringed, and awarded damages. The right breached was thus one founded on the Treaty.

vii. Protection of Intellectual Property Rights

In *Systran* (GC 2010, under appeal) the applicant claimed that the Commission had infringed the applicants' intellectual property rights by altering, without their permission, the machine translation software the applicants had developed. The General Court considered that the action by Commission amounted to breach of the general principles common to the laws of the Member States applicable to protection for copyright and know-how, and while all the other conditions were fulfilled, awarded damages. The case has been appealed to the ECJ.[78]

viii. Principle of Proportionality

The role of the principle of proportionality as a general and basic principle of Community law is today well-established. It can be characterised as an expression

[76] CFI Case T-167/94 *Nölle v Council and Commission* (damages claim dismissed, no appeal) [1995] ECR II-2589 [76].

[77] ECJ Case 145/83 *Adams v Commission* (damages awarded) [1985] ECR 3539.

[78] GC Case T-19/07 *Systran and Systran Luxembourg v Commission* (damages awarded €12m; appealed C-103/11 P, pending) [2010] ECR II-0000 (judgment of 16 December 2010) [200ff].

of the idea that the lawfulness of prohibition of an economic activity is subject to the condition that the prohibitory measures are appropriate and necessary in order to achieve the objectives legitimately pursued by the legislation in question. If a choice exists between several appropriate measures, recourse must be had to the least onerous, and the disadvantages caused must not be disproportionate to the aims pursued.[79] Although the courts have considered that it can qualify as a rule of law for the protection of the individual,[80] it has not been very successfully invoked in the damages context. Actions based on the claim that the principle of proportionality had been breached were dismissed, for example, in *Emesa Sugar* (CFI 2001),[81] in *Unifruit Hellas* (CFI 1994),[82] *Zuckerfabrik Bedburg* (ECJ 1994)[83] and *Werhahn Hansamuehle* (ECJ 1973)[84] and *Arcelor* (GC 2010).[85]

ix. Procedural Rights – Rights of Defence in Merger Proceedings

The question of the role of rights of defence in merger proceedings was addressed by the CFI in *Schneider* (CFI 2007).[86] The damages action followed a successful annulment action in relation to the procedure for examining the compatibility of a concentration with the common market.

The CFI put first forward some general considerations on the qualification of the rights in this context. It did not rule out that manifest and serious defects affecting the economic analysis underlying competition policy decisions may constitute sufficiently serious breaches of a rule of law to cause the Community to incur non-contractual liability. It further noted that certain principles and certain rules which must be observed in any competitive analysis are indeed rules intended to confer rights on individuals, but that not all norms, whether of primary or secondary law or deriving from case-law, which the Commission must observe in its economic assessments can automatically be held to be rules of that kind.

The CFI then went on to consider the breach of procedural rights and guarantees invoked in the framework of Merger Regulation 4064/89.[87] It recalled that before adopting a decision finding that a concentration is incompatible with the common market, the Commission is required, under Article 18(1) of the Regulation, to give the notifying undertakings an opportunity, on several occasions, of making known

[79] eg ECJ Case C-331/88 *Fedesa* [1990] ECR I-4023 [13].

[80] eg CFI *Unifruit Hellas v Commission* (n 51) [42].

[81] CFI *Emesa Sugar v Council* (n 61).

[82] CFI *Unifruit Hellas v Commission* (n 51), appealed ECJ *Unifruit Hellas v Commission* (n 51).

[83] ECJ Case 281/84 *Zuckerfabrik Bedburg v Council and Commission* (damages claim dismissed) [1987] ECR 49 [40].

[84] ECJ Joined Cases 63/72 to 63 to 69/72 *Werhahn Hansamuehle and others v Council* (damages claim dismissed) [1973] ECR 1229 [16]–[28].

[85] GC Case T-16/04 *Arcelor v Parliament and Council* (damages claim dismissed; no appeal) [2010] ECR II-0000 (judgment of 2 March 2010) [153]–[160].

[86] CFI Case T-351/03 *Schneider Electric v Commission* (damages action; liability established, appealed C-440/07 P) [2007] ECR II-2237 [129], [130], [145], [146]–[151].

[87] Council Regulation (EEC) No 4064/89/EEC of 21 December 1989 on the control of concentrations between undertakings [1989] OJ L395/1, corr. [1990] OJ L257/13.

their views on the objections against them. Furthermore, any incompatibility decisions could only be based on objections on which the undertakings concerned have been able to submit their observations.

The CFI then underlined the importance of the statement of objections. This is specifically intended to enable the undertakings concerned to react to the concerns expressed by the regulatory institution, first by giving their views on the matter and, second, by considering whether to propose to the Commission measures intended to correct the negative impact of the notified concentration. It is an essential part of the respect of rights of defence in procedures concerning control of concentrations between undertakings.

The CFI also took into account both the importance of the financial interests involved and the industrial implications of a concentration having a Community dimension and of the considerable scope of the investigatory powers available to the Commission to regulate competition in the common market.

In view of these findings the CFI confirmed that Schneider was alleging breach of a rule intended to confer rights on individuals. The CFI found that all the liability conditions had been fulfilled and ordered the Commission to pay very substantial damages, the exact amount of which was to be agreed between the parties. The Commission appealed to the ECJ, which in turn reduced the damages payable to a fraction of that ordered by the CFI (see ECJ 2009 and 2010),[88] but the appeal case did not concern this criterion.

x. *Procedural Rights – Rights of Defence in Asset Freezing Cases*

Following the terrorist attacks in New York in September 2001, the international community, led by the United Nations, stepped up the fight against terrorism. One of the instruments in this field was the freezing of assets of certain persons who were considered to have links with terrorism. In the European Union, United Nations Security Council resolutions were put into practice through second and first pillar instruments.[89] In *Sison* (CFI 2007) the Court was asked to examine the inclusion of Mr Sison in the so-called EU terrorism list, established in Council Regulation (EC) No 2580/2001, as amended.[90] The CFI annulled the listing owing to procedural errors (breach of rights of defence). As to the damages claim, the CFI considered that the rights breached did confer rights on individuals for the purposes of damages liability, and that the breach was even sufficiently serious.[91]

[88] ECJ Case C-440/07 P *Commission v Schneider Electric (No 1 extent of liability)* (liability reduced on appeal to less than €2m) [2009] ECR I-6413 and ECJ Case C-440/07 P *Commission v Schneider (No 2 quantum)* (damages awarded €50000) [2010] ECR I-0000.

[89] Arts 15 and 34 of TEU, and Arts 60 and 201 EC, respectively.

[90] CFI *Sison v Council* (n 25) and Council Regulation (EC) No 2580/2001 of 27 December 2001 on specific restrictive measures directed against certain persons and entities with a view to combating terrorism [2001] OJ L344/70.

[91] The claim for damages was finally treated as follows [240]–[241]: 'In the circumstances of this case, the Court considers that the breach of the applicant's rights of the defence is sufficiently serious for the Community to incur liability. . . . Nevertheless, the fundamental principle that the rights of the defence must be observed being essentially a procedural guarantee (Case C-344/05 P Commission v De

xi. Principle of Sound Administration and its 'Dual Character'

Problems relating to the criterion concerning granting of rights to individuals are well reflected in the case-law concerning the principle of sound administration, breaches of which have even been found to lead to damages liability. The case-law on that principle, which is also enshrined in Article 41 of the Charter of Fundamental Rights,[92] does not seem to be fully coherent.

a) Breach Established

Two cases can be mentioned where breach of the principle of sound administration has in fact led to damages liability.

In *AFCon* (CFI 2005) the main applicant was a consultancy company specialising in agricultural projects in countries whose economies are in transition.[93] It had participated in a tendering procedure organised by the Commission for a project financed by the Tacis programme, regarding agricultural extension services in South Russia. The applicant claimed damages for irregularities in the tendering procedure, which were due to a finding of a conflict of interest and its subsequent treatment. The conflict existed between a member of the evaluation committee and one of the tenderers. The Court addressed this as follows (emphasis added):

> 75 After the discovery of a conflict of interests between a member of the evaluation committee and one of the tenderers, the Commission must act with due diligence and on the basis of all the relevant information when formulating and adopting its decision on the outcome of the procedure for the award of the tender at issue. That obligation derives in particular from the principles of sound administration and equal treatment (see, by analogy, Case T-231/97 *New Europe Consulting and Brown* v *Commission* [1999] ECR II-2403, paragraph 41). The Commission is required to ensure at each stage of a tendering procedure equal treatment and, thereby, equality of opportunity for all the tenderers (see, to that effect, Case C-496/99 P *Commission* v *CAS Succhi di Frutta* [2004] ECR I-3801, paragraph 108, and Case T-145/98 *ADT Projekt* v *Commission* [2000] ECR II-387, paragraph 164).
>
> . . .
>
> 90 It follows from the foregoing that the Commission, in failing to investigate the relations between Mr A and the GFA consortium, made a manifest error of assessment. In infringing the *principle of sound administration* in that way, the Commission also violated the principle of equal treatment as between tenderers, which requires it to examine each tender impartially and objectively in the light of the requirements and general principles

Bry [2006] ECR I-10915, paragraph 39), the Court considers that, in the circumstances, annulment of the contested act will constitute adequate compensation for the damage caused by that breach (see, to that effect, Joined Cases T-120/01 and T-300/01 De Nicola v BEI [2004] ECR-SC I-A-365 and II-1671, paragraphs 140 to 142, and the case-law cited)'.

[92] [2007] OJ C303/1.

[93] CFI Case T-160/03 *AFCon Management Consultants and others v Commission* (damages €48000, no appeal) [2005] ECR II-981.

governing the tendering procedure, in order to ensure that all the tenderers are afforded the same opportunities

The CFI awarded €48000 in damages. The judgment was not appealed.

In *Agraz* (CFI 2005), some one hundred companies of Spanish, Italian, Greek, French and Portuguese origin operating in the processed tomato products sector, claimed damages from the Commission in relation to fixing production aid for processed tomato products.[94] After extensive litigation, they were finally awarded damages (see below).

For the purposes of this section the essential point is that the applicants in *Agraz* claimed damages for breach of the principle of sound administration. In their view and taking into account the rules concerning common organisation of the markets in processed fruit and vegetable products, the Commission had calculated aid on the wrong basis for the 2000/01 marketing year, as it had not obtained the necessary information from the Chinese authorities.

The CFI examined possible breach of the principles of care and of sound administration. It started by noting that the Commission enjoys a discretion when required, by virtue of the principles of duty of care and of sound administration, to gather the factual elements necessary for the exercise of its discretion. There was consistent case-law according to which, where a Community institution has a wide discretion, observance of the procedural guarantees conferred by the Community legal order is of even more fundamental importance. Those guarantees include, in particular, the obligation for the competent institution to examine carefully and impartially all the relevant elements of the individual case. This was also required so that the Community courts were able to verify whether the elements of fact and of law on which the exercise of the discretion depends were present.

The obligation to act diligently, which flowed from the basic regulation, implied, in particular, the duty to assemble all the essential factual elements provided for in Article 4(2) of that Regulation [1519/2000] which were capable of having a significant impact on the outcome of the decision-making procedure, in order to allow the Commission to exercise its discretion to the full and in a proper manner.

In this case, the cost of the raw material originating in China was one of the essential elements which the Commission was required to take into account in calculating the amount of production aid, as China was considered at the time to be one of the major third countries competing with Community production. Now what the Commission did wrong, and which amounted to breach of the principles of care and of sound administration, was that it acted too passively. It sent to the Chinese delegation to the European Union a single letter, dated 4 February 2000, requesting the necessary information. When no answer to that letter was received, it took no further steps to obtain the information during the period to July 2000. However, it was missing some essential information and did not undertake even the minimum effort to be expected of a diligent institution to acquire the information

[94] CFI Case T-285/03 *Agraz and others v Commission (No 1)* (damage not certain, dismissed, appealed C-243/05 P) [2005] ECR II-1063 [49]–[54].

required that was indispensable for the lawfulness of the exercise of the discretion in fixing the aid in question. The CFI thus concluded that the Commission's failure to act after sending the letter of 4 February 2000 constituted a sufficiently serious breach, within the meaning of the case-law, of the principles of care and of sound administration. As for the other liability conditions, however, the CFI held that the damage was not certain and rejected the application.

Agraz is also an interesting case in the sense that the ECJ (2006), for once, disagreed with the CFI for the benefit of the applicant: more often than not, the (rare) damages rulings by the CFI have been overturned on appeal. In this case, however, the ECJ held that the CFI had wrongly held that damage was not certain, and referred the case back to the CFI.[95] During the second round the CFI (2008) finally awarded damages, defined as an additional percentage (15.54 per cent) in relation to the original aid.[96]

b) No Breach

There are cases where damages liability has been rejected as the principle of sound administration was not breached.

The damages action in *Pharos* (CFI 1998) was brought by a company specialising in the biotechnology and pharmaceuticals industry.[97] In 1994 it created a veterinary product called 'Smoltine' which was designed to help salmon make the transition from fresh water to sea water. The pharmacologically active substance in Smoltine is somatosalm, a substance belonging to the somatotropin family. On 17 October 1994 Pharos applied for the inclusion of somatosalm in Annex II to Regulation No 2377/90.[98] The procedure for setting maximum residue limits became too slow according to the applicant, as the Adaptation Committee failed to deliver an opinion and thus it was not possible to respect the deadline for proposing measures to the Council. In the damages action the applicant claimed inter alia breach of the principle of sound administration on the part of the Commission.[99]

The issue basically turned on the relation of the principle of sound administration to consulting the Committee for Veterinary Medicinal Products (CVMP). Had the Commission breached the principle when it did not consult the CVMP earlier?

The CFI noted that the Commission did not initially ask the CVMP for further information because it did not foresee that the representatives of the Member States would object to the inclusion of somatosalm in Annex II because of the moratorium on Bovine Somatotropin (BST). According to the CFI this was acceptable:

[95] ECJ Case C-243/05 P *Agraz v Commission* (referred back to CFI) [2006] ECR I-10833.

[96] CFI Case T-285/03 *Agraz and others v Commission (No 2)* (damages awarded with interest, no appeal) [2008] ECR II-285*, Summ.pub. (judgment of 26 November 2008).

[97] CFI Case T-105/96 *Pharos v Commission* (damages claim dismissed, appealed C-151/98 P) [1998] ECR II-285 and ECJ Case C-151/98 P *Pharos v Commission* (appeal dismissed) [1999] ECR I-5441.

[98] Council Regulation (EEC) No 2377/90 of 26 June 1990 laying down a Community procedure for the establishment of maximum residue limits of veterinary medicinal products in foodstuffs of animal origin [1990] OJ L224/1.

[99] NB The Court discussed it as a superior rule of law for the protection of the individual ([63]).

the Commission was entitled to take the view initially that inclusion of somatosalm would not meet with any serious opposition, since the moratorium on BST related only to BST and not to other somatotrophins.

When, later in the procedure, the circumstances changed and it became apparent that the representatives of the Member States were establishing a link between the moratorium and somatosalm, the Commission requested a further opinion from the CVMP following a reasonable period of reflection. This being the case, the Commission's reasoning and the steps which it took in no way disclosed any mismanagement of the matter on its part. Therefore, the CFI concluded that the Commission did not commit a breach of the principle of proper administration such as to give rise to Community liability.

In *Area Cova* (CFI 2001), the applicants contested measures taken in the field of fisheries.[100] With a view to conservation of marine resources, the Community had agreed in the framework of the Convention on Future Multilateral Cooperation in the North-West Atlantic Fisheries a catch quota for the Community fishing fleet as regards Greenland Halibut. The applicants brought an action for annulment of the relevant Community Regulation and a request to declare inapplicable another regulation setting the Community quota. In addition to a request for a declaration that the bilateral fisheries agreement between the Community and the Canadian Government is inapplicable in so far as it refers to establishment of a Community quota for catches of Greenland halibut, they also claimed damages.

The CFI was asked to assess the role of the principle of sound administration in this context. The Court referred to *Bergaderm* and assessed the role of the principle of sound administration and noted that 'the applicants have not pleaded the infringement of a rule of law intended to confer rights upon individuals'. The possible illegality they complained of consisted only in infringement of the principle of sound administration. Therefore the first condition for triggering Community liability had not been established.

This finding may sound somewhat surprising in the light of the case-law cited above. It may be clarified by a later case. In *Tillack* (CFI 2006), the applicant was a journalist employed by the German magazine Stern.[101] He was the author of two articles published in Stern in early 2002, in which he described financial irregularities within the European institutions. The articles were based inter alia on a memorandum of August 2001 by Mr van Buitenen, an official of the Commission of the European Communities, in which he notified the existence of possible irregularities in a number of the Commission's services, and the results of the investigation by the European Anti-Fraud Office (OLAF).

Following the articles, OLAF organised an enquiry into publication of confidential information, as bribery and breach of professional secrecy were suspected. The enquiry resulted in a communication to the national judicial authorities of

[100] CFI Case T-196/99 *Area Cova and others v Commission and Council* (no infringement, no appeal) [2001] ECR II-3597 [43] and [44].

[101] CFI Case T-194/03 *Tillack v Commission* (no causal link, no appeal) [2006] ECR II-3995 [127].

information relating to situations liable to lead to criminal proceedings and search of the home and office of the journalist.

Mr Tillack brought an action for annulment of the act by which OLAF forwarded information to the German and Belgian judicial authorities concerning suspicions of breach of professional secrecy and bribery. In addition, he claimed damages in compensation for non-material injury as a result of forwarding that information and of the publication of press releases by OLAF. As regards breach of the principle of sound administration, which was the only principle alleged to have been breached in this context, the CFI noted again that this does not, in itself, confer rights upon individuals,

> except where it constitutes the expression of specific rights such as the right to have affairs handled impartially, fairly and within a reasonable time, the right to be heard, the right to have access to files, or the obligation to give reasons for decisions, for the purposes of Article 41 of the Charter

which was not the case here.

In this case, the CFI thus added clarification to *Area Cova* and confirmed the limitations on the scope of application of the principle of sound administration as a basis for a damages action against the Community. The principle of sound administration would therefore not seem to be operational in the damages context without additional procedural or other rights completing it.

One final remark should be made. It is interesting that in the same Article 41 of the Charter where the right to good administration is discussed, there is third paragraph which states that

> [e]very person has the right to have the Union make good any damage caused by its institutions or by its servants in the performance of their duties, in accordance with the general principles common to the laws of the Member States.

This could seem like a somewhat superfluous repetition of a treaty provision. Yet, in the dynamic structure of the Union this combination in the Charter may become one argument when developing the doctrine as regards breaches of principles of good administration as a liability ground.[102]

xii. Other Rights Examined by the EU Courts Where Damages Have Been Awarded

Citymo (CFI 2007)[103] concerned Community liability to compensate for damage sustained by the applicant as a result of a Commission decision to terminate pre-contract negotiations undertaken with a view to concluding a lease agreement.

[102] *cf* O Mäenpää, 'Hyvä hallinto oikeutena ja yleisenä oikeusperiaatteena' in H Kaila and E Pirjatanniemi, et al (eds), *Yksilön oikeusasema Euroopan unionissa – Individens rättsställning inom Europeiska Unionen: Juhlakirja Allan Rosas – Festskrift Allan Rosas* (Turku/Åbo, 2008) 471. A detailed analysis of the principle is provided by J Reichel, *God förvaltning i EU och i Sverige* (Stockholm, Jure, 2006).

[103] CFI Case T-271/04 *Citymo v Commission* (damages awarded €20000, no appeal) [2007] ECR II-1375 [127], [131], [132], [133], [136], [137], [138], [155] and [156].

The CFI first examined the claim relating to the principle of good faith and the rules against abuse of rights. This concerned the Commission's right not to contract, while for more than two months it was continuing negotiations which it knew were bound to fail. The CFI found that in view of the length of that period, the Commission clearly delayed informing the other party to the negotiations of its decision to abandon the procurement. The Commission thus continued the pre-contract negotiations which it knew were bound to fail and deprived the applicant of the opportunity to seek another tenant for the building. In the context of a property procurement negotiated with the applicant alone, concerning a building which was not available because of pre-contract negotiations, the Commission's conduct breached the principle of good faith and amounted to an abuse of its right not to contract.

Second, as regards alleged breach of the principle of protection of legitimate expectations, the CFI recalled that the right to rely on the principle of protection of legitimate expectations extends to any individual in a situation where the Community authorities, by giving precise assurances, have caused that individual to entertain legitimate expectations. Such assurances, in whatever form they are given, are precise, unconditional and consistent information from authorised and reliable sources. However, a person may only plead breach of the principle if he has been given such precise assurances. In addition, the case-law shows that assurances which do not take account of the relevant provisions cannot give rise to a legitimate expectation on the part of the person concerned, even if it is proved that they were given. This principle thus gave rights to individuals.

The CFI found that in this case the Commission had infringed the principle of protection of legitimate expectations in a sufficiently serious manner by breaking off pre-contract negotiations after encouraging the applicant to fit out the building so as to be able to let it as discussed in the negotiations.

In conclusion, the CFI held that (1) in breaking off the pre-contract negotiations, the Commission's conduct was unlawful and capable of giving rise to non-contractual liability on the Commission's part by allowing pre-contract negotiations, which it knew were bound to fail, to continue, and (2) by breaking off the pre-contract negotiations after encouraging the applicant to carry out the fitting-out work necessary for letting the building from 1 November 2003. The remainder of the applicant's submission was dismissed as unfounded. The CFI awarded €20000 in damages and there was no appeal.

In *Camós Grau* (CFI 2006), an official sued the Commission for damages arising from an investigation by the European Anti-Fraud Office (OLAF) into the management and funding of the Institute for European-Latin American Relations (IRELA).[104] The applicant alleged a potential conflict of interest on the part of an investigator.

[104] CFI Case T-309/03 *Camós Grau v Commission* (damages awarded €10000, no appeal) [2006] ECR II-1173.

The Court held that the requirement of impartiality, to which the institutions are subject in carrying out investigative tasks of the kind entrusted to OLAF, is intended, as well as ensuring respect for the public interest, to protect the persons concerned and confers on them a right as individuals to see that the corresponding guarantees are complied with. Therefore the applicant was alleging infringement of a rule intended to confer rights on individuals. As all the other conditions for damages liability were fulfilled, a sum of €10000 was awarded for non-material damages.

In *M* (CFI 2008) a damages action was brought by a Commission official against the European Ombudsman.[105] The case related to a complaint to the Commission questioning the conduct of a Member State as to its duties under Community law. The Commission decided not to pursue infringement proceedings and this decision in turn was questioned by the complainant before the European Ombudsman. The applicant criticised the handling of the complainant mainly because the applicant was named in the decision of the European Ombudsman of 18 July 2002 concerning a suspected instance of maladministration.

The applicant sued the Ombudsman for infringement of the right to respect for private life, and of the principles of proportionality and the right to be heard. The CFI agreed that the fact that the Ombudsman had in his decision mentioned the applicant by name was in effect a breach of these rights which granted rights to individuals. The CFI ordered the European Ombudsman to pay Mr M compensation of €10000.[106]

One of the questions in the damages action in *Artegodan* (GC 2010, under appeal) was whether Directive 65/65 and in particular its Article 11 granted rights to individuals. That provision relates to the obligation for the authorities to maintain a marketing authorisation granted in respect of a medicine, unless the conditions laid down in that article for withdrawal are fulfilled. The Court concluded that this article grants rights to the holder of the marketing authorisation.[107]

C. No Rights for Individuals (or no Superior Rules of Law for Protection of the Individual)

One interesting question is to find out what rules have *not* constituted 'superior rules of law for the protection of the individual' or 'granting rights to individuals', ie with respect to what rules the damages liability test failed on this criterion. The following lines can be noted from the case-law.[108]

[105] CFI *M v Ombudsman* (n 19).

[106] For a damages action where the naming of a company in a report by the Court of Auditors did not lead to a damages award, see CFI Case T-277/97 *Ismeri Europa Srl v Court of Auditors* (no breach, dismissed, appealed C-315/99 P) [1999] ECR II-1825 and ECJ Case C-315/99 P *Ismeri Europa v Court of Auditors* (appeal dismissed) [2001] ECR I-5281.

[107] GC *Artegodan v Commission* (dismissed, appealed C-221/10P) [2010] ECR II-0000 [92]–[94] and Council Directive 65/65/EEC on the approximation of provisions laid down by law, regulation or administrative action relating to medicinal products [1965–1966] English Spec Ed OJ/20, as amended.

[108] F Picod and L Coutron, 'La responsabilité de la Communauté européenne du fait de son activité administrative') (n 44) 196, with case-law and citations.

Breach of duty to give reasons. Applicants have frequently argued that the inadequacy of reasoning in a regulatory measure – which in itself could indeed lead to its annulment under an action for annulment – could result in Community liability. The courts have systematically rejected this, for example in *Kind* (ECJ 1982).[109] In the 'old' case-law the Court does not explain why this is so, but it appears that in so far as regulatory measures of general application are concerned, that principle or duty does not intend to confer rights on individuals.[110] *Eurocoton* (ECJ 2003) related to failure by the Council to adopt a proposal for a regulation imposing definitive anti-dumping duties.[111] The applicants lost their action for annulment before the CFI, but finally got the decision annulled on appeal before the ECJ. They further claimed that damages were due in view of the breach of duty to state reasons. The ECJ recalled that it had consistently held that any inadequacy in the statement of reasons for a legislative measure is not sufficient to cause the Community to incur liability. It further noted that although proceedings in respect of anti-dumping duties are similar in several respects to an administrative procedure, an inadequate statement of reasons for an act bringing such proceedings to an end is also not of itself sufficient to cause the Community to incur liability. Thus, any deficiencies in the statement of reasons as regards anti-dumping duties do not refer to rights granted to individuals.

The action for damages in *Emesa Sugar* (CFI 2001) concerned the association arrangements for overseas countries and territories (OCTs) and Decision 97/803/EC[112] as regards sugar imports to the Community.[113]

The CFI first noted that in accordance with the case-law, breach of duty to give reasons was not sufficient for the Community to incur non-contractual liability. Secondly it then noted that as regards the plea alleging infringement of Article 240 of the OCT Decision in that the Council was no longer, by virtue of that provision, competent *ratione temporis* to adopt the contested decision, it was hard to imagine that that provision could constitute a rule of law which conferred rights on individuals. Thirdly, and in contrast, it recalled that the principle of proportionality referred to in the second plea and the principle of protection of legitimate expectations referred to in the fourth plea, constituted rules of law conferring rights on individuals.

[109] ECJ *Kind v EEC* (n 14) [14]: '. . . any inadequacy in the statement of the reasons upon which a measure contained in a Regulation is based is not sufficient to make the Community liable'. See also CFI *Nölle v Council and Commission* (n 76) [57], CFI Case T-390/94 *Schröder and Thamann v Commission* (no breach, appealed C-221/97 P) [1997] ECR II-501 [66] and CFI Case T-362/05 *Nuova Agricast v Commission* (dismissed, appealed C-67/09 P) [2008] ECR II-297*, Summ.pub. (judgment of 2 December 2008) [89] and [90].

[110] As regards individual decisions the situation may be different. One could imagine an individual decision affecting the rights of the person in question. If such a decision were contested, the Court might rule that the annulment of the contested act – which is sometimes considered to be sufficient reparation – would not be so in that case.

[111] ECJ Case C-76/01 P *Eurocoton and Others v Council* (appeal on damages dismissed) [2003] ECR I-10091.

[112] Council Decision of 24 November 1997 amending at mid-term, Decision 91/482/EEC on the association of overseas countries and territories with the European Economic Community (97/803/EC) [1997] OJ L329/50.

[113] CFI *Emesa Sugar v Council* (n 61).

Failure to observe the balance between the institutions. As 'the aim of the system of the division of powers between the various Community institutions is to ensure that the balance between the institutions provided for in the Treaty is maintained, and not to protect individuals' it seems logical that non-respect for this balance cannot cause Community liability.[114] On closer inspection, this scenario is interesting. Take a situation where an institution adopts a provision which it is not competent to adopt. Adoption of the measure causes damage. Instinctively the reaction would be to say that such damage should be compensated. However, under the Community rule in force at the time, and even under the current post-*Bergaderm* EU rules, recovering damages is not possible. It is submitted that the criteria on this point may need reconsidering in specific circumstances or exceptional cases.

Provisions on division of compentences between the Union and the Member States. In *Artegodan*, the illegality of a Commission decision had already been established in an earlier action for annulment (CFI 2002, ECJ 2003).[115] The applicant brought an action for damages, claiming inter alia that because the Commission was incompetent to adopt the acts in question, the applicant should be granted damages. The acts in question were three Commission decisions withdrawing marketing authorisations, initially issued by the competent national authorities, for medicinal products containing amphetamine-like anorectic agents. The General Court started its examination from the question whether the issue of incompetence could be construed as a rule of law granting rights to individuals. The Court ruled that the infringed provisions of Directive 75/319 did not grant rights to individuals but merely established division of competencies between the Commission and its Member States. Therefore the fact that the Commission had acted ultra vires did not open a right to damages (GC 2010, under appeal).[116]

WTO Agreements. Of the various areas where tensions between EU rules and international rules have become tangible in the damages context, the *primus inter pares* is undoubtedly the World Trade Organisation, its rules and their effects on Community banana imports. According to the *locus classicus* of the Court,

> having regard to their nature and structure, [all the agreements and memoranda contained in Annexes 1 to 4 of the WTO Agreement] are not in principle among the rules in the light of which the Court is to review the legality of measures adopted by the Community institutions.[117]

[114] ECJ Case C-282/90 *Vreugdenhil (No 2) v Commission* (damages action, dismissed) [1992] ECR I-1937 [19]–[21]. This is also a notable case in the sense that Art 13a of Commission Regulation No 1687/76 had been declared invalid in a preliminary ruling, namely ECJ Case 22/88 *Vreugdenhil (No 1) and another v Minister van Landbouw en Visserij* (preliminary ruling) [1989] ECR 2049 [26].

[115] CFI Joined Cases T-74/00, T-76/00, T-83/00 to T-85/00, T-132/00, T-137/00 and T-141/00 *Artegodan and others v Commission* (annulment action, decision annulled, appealed C-39/03 P) [2002] ECR II-4945 and ECJ Case C-39/03 P *Commission v Artegodan and others* (appeal dismissed) [2003] ECR I-7885.

[116] GC *Artegodan v Commission* (n 107) [71]–[78].

[117] ECJ Case C-149/96 *Portugal v Council* [1999] ECR I-8395 [17].

It follows that 'as the WTO rules are not in principle intended to confer rights on individuals, the Community cannot incur non-contractual liability as a result of infringement of them'.[118]

WTO DSB 'determinations'. WTO rules are not intended for the protection of the individual or to grant rights to individuals. *FIAMM* (CFI 2005)[119] concerned recommendations and rulings of the WTO Dispute Settlement Body (WTO DSB) and its 'determination' that the Community regime governing the import of bananas was incompatible with WTO rules. In that case, the United States of America had imposed retaliatory measures – authorised by the WTO – in the form of increased customs duty levied on imports of certain products from various Member States, including batteries produced by the applicant. The principal claim advanced by the applicants before the CFI was that the Community had incurred non-contractual liability by reason of the unlawful conduct of its institutions. It was the failure of the Council and the Commission to adopt amendments to the Community regime governing the import of bananas such as to bring it into conformity with the obligations entered into by the Community under WTO agreements within the time limit laid down by the DSB that infringed the *pacta sunt servanda* principle, the principles of protection of legitimate expectations and of legal certainty, their rights to property and pursuit of an economic activity and, finally, the principle of proper administration. The CFI found as follows (emphasis added):

> 110 However, the principle pacta sunt servanda cannot be asserted against the defendants in the present case since, in accordance with settled case-law, *the WTO agreements are not in principle, given their nature and structure, among the rules in the light of which the Community courts review the legality of action by the Community institutions* ([judgment in Case C-149/96] Portugal v Council [[1999] ECR I-8395], paragraph 47; order in Case C-307/99 OGT Fruchthandelsgesellschaft [2001] ECR I-3159, paragraph 24; and judgments in Joined Cases C-27/00 and C-122/00 Omega Air and Others [2002] ECR I-2569, paragraph 93, Case C-76/00 P Petrotub and Republica v Council [2003] ECR I-79, paragraph 53, and Case C-93/02 P Biret International v Council [2003] ECR I-10497, paragraph 52).

FIAMM appealed but the ECJ found that the CFI had ruled correctly on this point (ECJ 2008).[120] The ECJ ruled that the CFI had rightly decided that, notwithstanding the expiry of the period allowed for implementing a DSB decision, the Community courts could not, in the circumstances of the case in point, review the legality of the conduct of the Community institutions in the light of WTO rules. The ECJ further recalled that this interpretation was in line with the ruling it had given in respect of the provisions of the GATT 1994. The question of damages liability for breach of

[118] CFI *T. Port v Commission* (n 37).

[119] CFI Case T-69/00 *FIAMM and FIAMM Technologies v Council and Commission* (dismissed, appealed C-120/06 P) [2005] ECR II-5393.

[120] ECJ Joined Cases C-120/06 P and C-121/06 P *FIAMM and Fedon v Council and Commission* (appeal dismissed) [2008] ECR I-6513 [132] and [133].

WTO rules has intrigued many researchers over the years and FIAMM will certainly not be the end of that discussion.[121]

Principle of relative stability and respect for traditional fisheries rights. These two principles and their breach have been invoked in a number of damages actions relating to fisheries. Two cases will be examined here. The first is *Area Cova* (CFI 2001).[122] This case, explained above, concerned the Convention on Future Multilateral Cooperation in the North-West Atlantic and Greenland halibut. The applicants claimed that they had suffered recoverable loss due to the catch quota allocated to the Community fleet. The loss was due to (1) acceptance by the Commission and the Council of a total allowable catch for 1995 of 27000 tonnes of Greenland halibut in the Regulatory Area defined in the Convention and (2) conclusion of a bilateral agreement between the Community and Canada and the adoption of Council Regulation (EC) No 1761/95.

Here the CFI noted, however, that the principle of relative stability concerns only relations between Member States and that principle cannot confer individual rights upon private parties. Rights based on respect for traditional fisheries rights could in any case endure only to the benefit of states, to the exclusion of individual vessel owners, so that this principle provides no further rights to individuals for damages purposes, either.

In *Cofradía de pescadores 'San Pedro' de Bermeo* (CFI 2005) the CFI was asked to rule in a case relating to fishing quota exchanges between Member States.[123] Part of the fishing quota for anchovy allocated to Portugal was transferred to France and the applicants requested annulment of the provisions authorising that transfer, which meant a reduction, for Spain, of effective fishing possibilities. The Court addressed the question relating to the concept of a rule of law conferring rights on individuals. It confirmed that the principle of relative stability, even together with Article 161(1)(f) of the Act of Accession, is not intended to confer rights on individuals for the purposes of a damages action.

The judgment of the CFI is exceptional when analysing the condition of grant of rights and shows the level of detail where the court may have to go to resolve the issue of whether a provision grants rights or not. It is also noteworthy for the point that there is an express rejection of the argument put forward by the Council on the basis of the old case and relating to the 'higher ranking rule of law'. The case was

[121] See for example four German dissertations on the WTO-related liability: K Höher, *Die Haftung der Europäischen Gemeinschaft für Verstöße gegen das WTO-Recht: eine Untersuchung am Beispiel des WTO-Bananenstreitverfahrens* (Baden-Baden, Nomos, 2006); S Held, *Die Haftung der EG für die Verletzung von WTO-Recht* (Tübingen, Mohr Siebeck, 2006); A Steinbach, *Die Haftung der EG und ihrer Mitgliedsstaaten für WTO-Rechtsverletzungen aus rechtswissenschaftlicher und ökonomischer Perspektive* (Berlin, Duncker & Humblot, 2009) and A Thies, *The Liability of the European Community for Conduct in the Context of International Trade Disputes* (Munich, 2009). All of them discuss the situation before the ECJ judgment in *FIAMM*, and show the amplitude of the discussion on this point. See also A Thies, 'The Impact of General Principles of EC Law on its Liability Regime Towards Retaliation Victims after FIAMM' (2009) *European Law Review* 889–913.

[122] CFI *Area Cova and others v Commission and Council* (n 100) [149]–[154].

[123] CFI Case T-415/03 *Cofradía de pescadores 'San Pedro' de Bermeo and others v Council* (damages claim dismissed, appealed C-6/06 P) [2005] ECR II-4355.

appealed, but the ECJ (2007) found that the appeal was in part unfounded and in part inadmissible.[124]

D. Interim Conclusion

The case-law governing liability of the Union as regards the criterion 'granting of rights to individuals' is in its current state concentrated on assessment of possible breach of legal principles. The fact that the criteria have been opened up in *Bergaderm* can be seen in recent successful damages actions. The level of detail of the case-law also shows a number of situations where no rights are granted to individuals.

III. SUFFICIENTLY SERIOUS BREACH: LIABILITY OF THE EUROPEAN UNION AND ASSESSMENT OF SERIOUSNESS OF BREACH IN CASE-LAW

A. Assessing Breach for Liability of the European Union: from Dichotomy to a Sliding Scale

As to the condition concerning 'breach' for European Union liability, it is important to recall that a considerable part of the case-law (until *Bergaderm* ECJ 2000) relates to the old conditions, which defined the degree of breach required in relation to the nature of the act.[125] Here a distinction was drawn between administrative acts on the one hand and legislative acts with wide discretion on the other. It was for this criterion that the decisive change took place. Before *Bergaderm/Brasserie*, the standard to be applied was defined according to the *nature* of the act causing damage. After *Bergaderm/Brasserie*, the key element is the *discretion available* to the institution adopting the act causing damage.

Therefore, following the 'revirement' in *Bergaderm*, the question whether the measure taken by Union institutions was of a general or individual nature has been reduced in importance. It is no longer *a decisive criterion* for identifying the limits of discretion enjoyed by the institution in question.[126] In *Camar and Tico* (ECJ 2002) the ECJ found that the CFI had erred in law while it 'held that the Commission's liability could arise from the mere illegality of the Decision on 17 July 1997, without taking account of the discretion which the Commission enjoyed in the adoption of that measure'.[127] In subsequent cases, the CFI has generally taken care to qualify the discretion available, when discussing liability.[128]

[124] ECJ Case C-6/06 P *Cofradía de pescadores 'San Pedro' de Bermeo and others v Council* (appeal dismissed) [2007] ECR I-164*, Summ.pub. (judgment of 22 November 2007).

[125] The questions underlying this section have been discussed in ch 2, s VI above.

[126] ECJ Case C-352/98 P *Bergaderm and Goupil v Commission* (appeal dismissed) [2000] ECR I-5291 [46].

[127] ECJ *Commission v Camar and Tico* (n 37).

[128] CFI *M v Ombudsman* (n 19).

B. First Limb: Existence of a Breach of EU Rule of Law

i. Mechanisms to Establish Breach

As noted above, there are numerous ways to establish a breach by the Union with a view to a damages action.[129] Apart from a damages action itself, in many cases such an action has been preceded by annulment action (successful or not) or alternatively a plea of illegality under the preliminary ruling procedure. Neither of these steps is formally required for admissibility of a damages action, but it can facilitate a damages action.[130]

In the line of case-law which has led to the most numerous compensation awards so far, the milk quota cases, the basic finding of illegality of Community action was established through the preliminary rulings procedure. This was the case of *Mulder* (ECJ 1988).[131] A similar finding of illegality was made in *Zuckerfabrik Jülich* (ECJ 2008) in a preliminary ruling relating to production quotas and levies for sugar.[132]

In several other cases, the illegality of the measure, or even the annulment of a contested measure, has been confirmed by the EU courts (by the CFI for direct actions, in most cases). Of the more recent examples we can mention *Dole* (CFI 2003).[133] In that case the illegality of the measure had been established in a successful earlier action for annulment introduced by Germany, so that the issue in the damages case was sufficient seriousness of breach.[134] The action establishing the breach does not have to be introduced by the applicant.

Even a pre-established breach may have to be nuanced in the damages liability context, as was the case in *Mulder (No 1)* (ECJ 1990). The existence of breach led the Court to conclude that sufficiently serious breach existed on some issues, whereas on the others, where the breach had equally been established, it was not sufficiently serious for damages purposes.[135]

[129] See ch 2, s VI.B (Table 2.3) above.

[130] A damages action is a remedy independent of the annulment of the measure. On this question in general see E Cujo, 'L'autonomie du recours en indemnité par rapport au recours en annulation – évolutions jurisprudentielles' (1999) *Revue du Marché Commun et de l'Union Européenne* 414–20.

[131] See ECJ *Mulder* (n 12) [25], where the Court ruled that Council Regulation (EEC) No 857/84 of 31 March 1984, as supplemented by Commission Regulation (EEC) No 1371/84 of 16 May 1984, is invalid in so far as it does not provide for the allocation of a reference quantity to producers who, pursuant to an undertaking entered into under Council Regulation (EEC) No 1078/77 of 17 May 1977, did not deliver milk during the reference year adopted by the Member State concerned. See also, on the same day, ECJ *Von Deetzen v Hauptzollamt Hamburg-Jonas* (n 12) [17].

[132] ECJ Joined Cases C-5/06 and C-23/06 to C-36/06 *Zuckerfabrik Jülich and others* [2008] ECR I-3231.

[133] CFI *Dole Fresh Fruit International v Commission and Council* (n 37) [72]. 'In the present case, the existence of a breach of a rule of law must be considered to be established because in Germany v Council, the Court of Justice annulled the first indent of Artic1e (1) of Council Decision 94/800 to the extent that the Council thereby approved the Framework Agreement, in so far as the latter exempts Category B operators from the export licence system for which it provides and, in T. Port, the Court declared invalid Article 3(2) of Regulation No 478/95'.

[134] For further discussion on this type of situations (including two merger cases *Airtours* and *Schneider*), see below.

[135] ECJ *Mulder (No 1) and others v Council and Commission* (n 39).

ii. No Breach

In the damages context there are of course numerous cases where no breach whatsoever of EU law by a Community institution was found. This was the outcome for example in *Danzer* (CFI 2006), where two managers of Austrian companies claimed compensation from the Council in respect of damage allegedly suffered due to the obligation to disclose certain information in the annual accounts of the companies, by virtue of two Council directives on company law.[136] The CFI examined the claims and noted that there were no doubts about the legality of the measures. In the absence of any breach, the damages claims presented were dismissed.[137]

The *FIAMM* case before the CFI (2005) and the subsequent appeal before the ECJ (2008) were remarkable in several respects. The origin of the lengthy litigation was bananas. After considerable litigation the WTO Dispute Settlement Body had found that the EU regime governing the import of certain bananas was incompatible with WTO rules. In this context the United States imposed retaliatory measures in the form of increased customs duty levied on imports of certain products – not bananas – from various Member States of the European Union. The applicants suffered damage from these measures. The activities of the applicants relate inter alia to stationary batteries used mainly in the telecommunications field which were among the products subject to increased customs duty from 19 April 1999 to 30 June 2001.

The CFI found however that there was no breach of a rule of law on which individuals could rely (CFI 2005).[138] The crux of the matter was the existence of no-fault liability, which the CFI accepted as a matter of principle, but found that the conditions had not been fulfilled in this case. FIAMM appealed to the ECJ. In its judgment, the ECJ made an important ruling as to the current non-existence of no-fault liability, but at the end of the day the damages claim was dismissed, in the absence of a breach of a EU rule of law (ECJ 2008).[139]

C. Second Limb: the Threshold of 'Sufficiently Serious Breach' and the Scope of Discretion

If breach of EU law is established, the courts will proceed to assess the seriousness of the breach. For Community liability, the concept of discretion has taken a more prominent place after *Brasserie du Pêcheur* and *Bergaderm*. Yet there have been

[136] The damage resulted, according to the applicants, from the obligation to disclose certain information in the annual accounts of the companies of which they are managers under Art 2(1)(f) of First Council Directive 68/151/EEC of 9 March 1968 on coordination of safeguards which, for the protection of the interests of members and others, are required by Member States of certain companies with a view to making such safeguards equivalent throughout the Community, and Art 47 of Fourth Council Directive 78/660/EEC of 25 July 1978 on the annual accounts of certain types of companies.

[137] CFI Case T-47/02 *Danzer and Danzer v Council* (damages claim dismissed, no appeal) [2006] ECR II-1779.

[138] CFI *FIAMM and FIAMM Technologies v Council and Commission* (n 119).

[139] ECJ *FIAMM and Fedon v Council and Commission* (n 120).

some hesitations in its use. What makes *Ceva and Pfizer* a particularly interesting case is that the action led to opposite results before the CFI (2003)[140] and before the ECJ (2005).[141] The essential divergence was about discretion and its establishment.

The applicants in the case were pharmaceutical companies each of which marketed a veterinary medicinal product containing the active ingredient progesterone. The case stemmed from Commission delay in classifying the list of substances for which a maximum residue limit need not be set. This list is to be drawn up pursuant to Community legislation on veterinary medicinal products. In 1993 CEVA applied to the Commission to establish a maximum residue limit ('MRL') for progesterone in cattle and horses. Certain substances[142] are to be listed in Annex I where MRLs have been established and in Annex II where following an evaluation it appears that it is not necessary for the protection of public health to establish a MRL. During the procedure before the Commission, during which the relevant expert committee was consulted several times, the Commission did not finally take a decision on the application made in 1993. The applicants sued the Commission for damages. The CFI (2003) concluded that the Commission's inaction between 1 January 2000 and 25 July 2001 was such as to render the Community liable.[143]

The Commission appealed the judgment and the ECJ (2005) took a different view.[144] The ECJ noted in the first place that the CFI did not at any point in the judgment under appeal explain in detail the discretion which the Commission enjoys in establishing MRLs, even if the scope of that discretion had been the subject of discussion between the parties (with the applicants at the time arguing that the Commission had no discretion and the Commission, on the contrary, arguing that it had broad discretion). In the absence of such analysis, the CFI should have set out adequately the reasons or circumstances which might exceptionally have explained why such an analysis would serve no purpose, but it did not do so.

Therefore the ECJ held that the CFI had erred in law in holding in paragraph 103 of the judgment under appeal, without having established the scope of the discretion enjoyed by the Commission, that the Commission's inaction between 1 January 2000 and 25 July 2001 constituted a clear and serious breach of Community law giving rise to liability on the part of the Community and annulled the judgment of the CFI.

The ECJ went on to analyse the facts of the case itself. The ECJ assessed the progesterone file and found that the Commission 'must be given a discretion which is sufficient to allow it to determine, on a fully informed basis, the measures that are necessary and appropriate for the protection of public health'. The ECJ's conclusion was that in the light of all elements of the file, the Commission, 'in not

[140] CFI Joined Cases T-344/00 and T-345/00 *CEVA and Pharmacia Enterprises v Commission* (damages awarded; appealed C-198/03 P) [2003] ECR II-229.

[141] ECJ Case C-198/03 P *Commission v CEVA and Pfizer* (CFI judgment set aside, damages action dismissed on appeal) [2005] ECR I-6357.

[142] Namely 'pharmacologically active substances used in veterinary medicines for food-producing animals'.

[143] CFI *CEVA and Pharmacia Enterprises v Commission* (n 140).

[144] ECJ *Commission v CEVA and Pfizer* (n 141) [67]–[69], [80].

submitting a draft regulation prior to 25 July 2001' did not breach Community law in a sufficiently serious way as to give rise to liability on the part of the Community.

Although in *Ceva and Pfizer* the ECJ strongly condemned the non-establishment of discretion by the CFI, it does not appear to have done so in other appeals it has been dealing with ever since. Therefore, it seems that on the basis of the current case-law, establishment of discretion needs to be express, at least when a dispute exists between the parties, otherwise it can be implied. This is also supported by the finding in the Member State liability context where 'pure' discretion plays much of a lesser role.

In this context, the judgment in *Artegodan* is of special interest (GC 2010, under appeal). In this case the Court first established the discretion. It noted that in general the Commission has wide discretion as regards measures relating to public health. However, in this specific case the Commission had no discretion whether to withdraw a marketing authorisation or not, as those conditions were laid down in detail in the relevant directive. Yet absence of discretion did not automatically lead to sufficiently serious breach. The Court examined the various legal and factual specificities of the case and considered the breach excusable, and did not establish liability.[145]

D. Wide Discretion

i. Wide Discretion, no Breach: Area Cova

In *Area Cova* (CFI 2001), the applicants and three associations of fishing vessel owners had already brought an action for annulment, which had been rejected.[146] In the ensuing damages cases, they claimed compensation for two issues, namely (1) for the fact that the Commission and the Council had accepted a total allowable catch for 1995 of 27000 tonnes of Greenland halibut in the Regulatory Area defined in the relevant fisheries convention and (2) for conclusion of a bilateral agreement between the Community and Canada and the amendment to a Council Regulation laying down certain conservation and management measures for fishery resources in the Regulatory Area as defined in the relevant fisheries convention.

The applicants invoked breach of the principles of legitimate expectations and sound administration. The CFI referred to *Bergaderm* and found that the Commission and Council had acted in an area where they had wide discretion. As regards conformity of the result of negotiations with the scientific data (fixing the total allowable catches to 27000 tonnes), the Court reasoned in the following terms. It first noted that the scientific advisory board had found that the stock of Greenland halibut had considerably diminished, that a catch quota exceeding 40000 tonnes would not be adequate to restrain fishing and that the latter, in 1995, had to be substantially reduced in order to halt the tendency of the biomass to

[145] GC *Artegodan v Commission* (n 107) [97], [104] and [110].

[146] CFI *Area Cova and others v Commission and Council* (n 100).

diminish. Thus 40000 tonnes did not constitute the optimum proposed solution but rather the smallest reduction tolerable, namely the threshold from which fishing had started to be reduced. Therefore fixing a total allowable catch of 27000 tonnes was not in clear contradiction with the opinion of the scientific advisory board. On that basis the CFI concluded that the Commission did not obviously and seriously disregard the limits on its wide discretion. The action was dismissed and the judgment was not appealed.

ii. Wide Discretion, no Breach: Dieckmann

The year following *Bergaderm*, the CFI made a remarkable pedagogical exercise in *Dieckmann & Hansen* (CFI 2001), when it set out the preliminary remarks for assessment of cases and the issue of discretion.[147] The case related to an amendment to Decision 97/296/EC drawing up a list of third countries from which the import of fishery products is authorised for human consumption, to exclude from that list Kazakhstan from which the applicant had been importing caviar for over 100 years. The CFI noted that for the assessment of breach, the rules developed by the ECJ require that, inter alia, the complexity of the situations to be regulated, difficulties in the application or interpretation of the texts and, more particularly, the margin of discretion available to the author of the act in question must be taken into account.[148] It then continued with an extraordinary series of cross-references to both liability systems (emphasis added):

> 42 The Court of Justice has held that, where the Community institutions enjoy a *wide discretion* in implementing their policies, the condition relating to unlawful conduct on the part of the institution is met if it is established that the rule of law infringed is intended to confer rights on individuals and the breach is sufficiently serious (see, to that effect, Factortame, cited above, paragraphs 44, 47 and 51, and Bergaderm and Goupil, cited above, paragraph 42).
>
> 43 As to the requirement that the breach be sufficiently serious, the Court has held that the decisive test for that is whether the Community *institution manifestly and gravely disregarded the limits on its discretion* (Factortame, cited above, paragraph 55, Joined Cases C-178/94, C-179/94, C-188/94, C-189/94 and C-190/94 Dillenkofer and Others [1996] ECR I-4845, paragraph 25, and Bergaderm and Goupil, cited above, paragraph 43).
>
> 44 Nevertheless, where the institution has only a limited discretion, or even none at all, the mere infringement of Community law may be sufficient to establish the existence of a sufficiently serious breach (see, to that effect, Case C-5/94 Hedley Lomas [1996] ECR I-2553, paragraph 28, and Bergaderm and Goupil, cited above, paragraph 44).
>
> 45 The Court has held, in that regard, that whether a measure taken by an institution is general or individual is not decisive for determining the limits of the discretion enjoyed by the institution (Bergaderm and Goupil, cited above, paragraph 46).

[147] CFI *Dieckmann & Hansen v Commission* (n 60) [42]–[46], [55] and [56].

[148] It referred simultaneously to ECJ Joined Cases C-46/93 and C-48/93 *Brasserie du Pêcheur and Factortame* [1996] ECR I-1029 [43] (a cross-reference to Member State liability) and to ECJ *Bergaderm and Goupil v Commission* (n 126) [40] (reference to Community liability).

> 46 In those circumstances, *examination of Community liability must*, in the present case, *centre on determining the extent of the discretion enjoyed by the Commission when it adopted the contested decision without there being any need to decide whether the decision was a legislative or an administrative one.*

The CFI noted that the Commission's discretion in this particular case was wide as it was adopting a decision to remove a country from the list of third countries from which the import of fishery products is authorised. Following a detailed examination, the CFI came to the conclusion that the Commission had not breached the limits of its discretion: the applicant had not established that the Commission overstepped the bounds of its discretion in the present case. Thus there was no sufficiently serious breach of Community law, and the application for damages was dismissed. The judgment was appealed, but the appeal was equally dismissed.[149]

iii. Wide Discretion, Breach: Agraz

The applicants in *Agraz* (CFI 2005)[150] were producers of processed tomato products from Spain, France, Greece, Italy and Portugal. In fixing the minimum price and the amount of production aid for processed tomato products for the 2000/01 marketing year, the Commission had, by letter of 4 February 2000, requested the Chinese authorities to provide it as quickly as possible with certain information. That letter remained unanswered and the decision of the Commission was taken on an inadequate basis. The applicants claimed however that the Commission was under a duty to find out and take into account the situation in China. The basic regulation for aid required the Commission namely to take into account, when fixing the aid, the 'main producing and exporting third countries' (Article 4(1)) and the 'major [or main] competing third countries' (Article 4(2) and (5)). The applicants argued that the Commission had here breached the basic regulation and Article 33 EC (now Article 39 TFEU) relating to the objectives of common agricultural policy, as well as the principles of duty of care and of sound administration.

The CFI assessed first the discretion and found that it was rather wide in this particular area:

> 42 It should be borne in mind, first of all, that it is settled case-law that the Community legislature enjoys a considerable power of discretion in circumstances where it is necessary to evaluate a complex economic situation, as is the case as far as the common agricultural and fisheries policies are concerned. Its discretion is not limited solely to the nature and scope of the measures to be taken but also, to some extent, to the finding of basic facts. Accordingly, where it is called upon to ascertain whether the alleged breach of a rule of law is sufficiently serious, the Court must confine itself to examining whether the institution accused of that breach has made a manifest error in the exercise of its discretion or misused its powers or whether the authority in question has clearly exceeded the bounds of its discretion (see, to that effect, Case 113/88 Leukhardt [1989] ECR 1991, paragraph 20; Case C-4/96 NIFPO and Northern Ireland Fishermen's Federation [1998] ECR I-681,

[149] ECJ *Dieckmann & Hansen v Commission* (n 60).

[150] CFI *Agraz and others v Commission (No 1)* (n 94).

paragraphs 41 and 42; Case C-179/95 Spain v Council [1999] ECR I-6475, paragraph 29; Case C-120/99 Italy v Council [2001] ECR I-7997, paragraph 44; and Case T-13/99 Pfizer Animal Health v Council [2002] ECR II-3305, paragraphs 166 and 168).

Even if the discretion was wide under the basic regulation in fixing the aid, that discretion did not cover the presence of facts and figures corresponding to the criteria which the Commission is obliged to take into account, such as prices of raw material in major third countries within the meaning of Article 4(2)(a) of the basic regulation.

While the Court found that the discretion was wide, it noted that in such a situation respect for procedural guarantees is even more important (emphasis added):

> 49 The Commission enjoys a discretion, while being required, by virtue of the principles of a duty of care and of sound administration, to gather the factual elements necessary for the exercise of its discretion. According to a consistent line of decisions, *where a Community institution has a wide discretion, observance of the procedural guarantees conferred by the Community legal order is of even more fundamental importance.* Those guarantees include, in particular, the obligation for the competent institution to examine carefully and impartially all the relevant elements of the individual case. Only in that way is the Community judicature able to ascertain whether the elements of fact and of law on which the exercise of the discretion depends were present.

Despite the wide discretion, the Court found that there was a sufficiently serious breach of the principles of care and of sound administration. The Court also found that the Commission had infringed the basic regulation.

Having established sufficient seriousness of breach, the CFI then assessed whether the damage for which compensation is sought must be actual and certain. As on this point the CFI found that the damage calculated by the applicants was not certain, it finally dismissed the action for damages.

However, the applicants appealed on this issue to the ECJ, which found that the CFI had erred in law on this point and referred the case back to the CFI.[151] The CFI took up the case again, and ordered damages to be paid, while a number of issues had already been settled amicably between the parties.[152]

E. Narrow Discretion

i. *No Discretion, but Breach Still not Sufficiently Serious:* Medici

Medici is a damages case in the context of anti-dumping proceedings concerning imports of leather handbags originating in the People's Republic of China (CFI 2006).[153] It is interesting in particular as regards discretion: the CFI found that the Council had no discretion (at all), but still there was no breach, because the

[151] ECJ *Agraz v Commission* (n 95).

[152] CFI *Agraz and others v Commission (No 2)* (n 96), see eg, [43] and [44].

[153] CFI Case T-364/03 *Medici Grimm v Council* (damages claim dismissed, no appeal) [2006] ECR II-79 [81].

ituation was so complex. It was necessary to take account of the complexity of the situation to be regulated, the difficulties in application or interpretation of the legislation, the clarity and precision of the rule infringed, and whether the error of law made was inexcusable or intentional.

Medici is also a case involving a 'convergent cross-reference' to Member State liability and the reference moreover goes in two ways: to ECJ case-law, and not only to the case-law on liability of the Community, but also to a different liability system, namely to Member State liability.

ii. Narrow Discretion, Breach: Fresh Marine

Fresh Marine (CFI 2000) is one of the first cases in which the CFI applied the new *Bergaderm* criteria (ECJ 2000).[154] Fresh Marine is a Norwegian company specialising in the sale of farmed Atlantic salmon. Having received complaints, the Commission announced in August 1996 the initiation of an anti-dumping and an anti-subsidy proceeding concerning imports of farmed Atlantic salmon originating in Norway. Following that investigation it found that it was necessary to impose definitive anti-dumping and countervailing measures in order to eliminate the harmful effects of dumped imports and the subsidies complained of. It imposed provisional anti-dumping and countervailing duties, which were later repealed. Yet the applicant brought an action for damages.

The CFI made several interesting findings which merit citation at some length (emphasis added):

> 38 *The nature – be it legislative or administrative – of a measure* for which a Community institution is criticised *has no bearing on the admissibility of an action for damages.* In the context of such an action, that factor is relevant exclusively to assessment of the substance of the case, where what is at issue is the definition of the test of what degree of fault is required when examining the non-contractual liability of the Community (see, in particular Case C-152/88 Sofrimport v Commission [1990] ECR I-2477, paragraph 25; Nölle v Council and Commission, cited in paragraph 35 above, paragraphs 51 and 52, and Case T-199/96 Laboratoires Pharmaceutiques Bergaderm and Goupil v Commission [1998] ECR II-2805, paragraphs 48 to 51, confirmed by the Court of Justice in Case C-352/98 P Bergaderm and Goupil v Commission [2000] ECR I-5291).
>
> 39 It is not therefore necessary to enquire at this stage into the nature of the Commission's measure allegedly giving rise to the damage claimed by the applicant and the Court concludes that the nature of that act, whatever it may be, cannot in any event be a bar to the admissibility of the present action for damages.
>
> ...
>
> 61 In conclusion, mere infringement of Community law will be sufficient, in the present case, to lead to the non-contractual liability of the Community (see Bergaderm and Goupil v Commission, cited in paragraph 38 above, paragraph 44). In particular, a finding of an error which, in analogous circumstances, *an administrative authority exercising*

[154] CFI *Fresh Marine v Commission* (n 73).

ordinary care and diligence would not have committed will support the conclusion that the conduct of the Community institution was unlawful in such a way as to render the Community liable under Article 215 of the Treaty.

62 It is therefore necessary to examine whether the Commission, when monitoring compliance by the applicant with its undertaking on the basis of the October 1997 report, committed an error which an administrative authority exercising ordinary care and diligence would not have committed in the same circumstances.

...

82 It must therefore be held that, when analysing the October 1997 report, the *Commission committed an error* which would not have been committed in similar circumstances by an administrative authority exercising ordinary care and diligence.

The CFI established a sufficiently serious breach and awarded damages. The Commission appealed the judgment to the ECJ. The appeal was dismissed and the damages were upheld for a total amount of NOK 431 000 (ECJ 2003).[155] The ECJ noted that there was a legislative act but the Commission had only little, or no, discretion. The ECJ first recalled, with cross references to the two systems, the three conditions of liability, and then went on as follows (emphasis added).[156]

26 As regards the second condition, the decisive test for finding that a breach of Community law is sufficiently serious is whether the Community institution concerned manifestly and gravely disregarded the limits on its discretion. Where that institution has only considerably reduced, or even no, discretion, the mere infringement of Community law may be sufficient to establish the existence of a sufficiently serious breach (see, inter alia, Bergaderm and Goupil, paragraphs 43 and 44, and Commission v Camar and Tico, paragraph 54).

27 Therefore, the determining factor in deciding whether there has been such an infringement is not the general or individual nature of the act in question but the discretion available to the institution concerned (see, to that effect, Bergaderm and Goupil, paragraph 46, and Commission v Camar and Tico, paragraph 55).

28 Since the provisional anti-dumping and countervailing duties were imposed on the basis of Article 8(10) of Regulation No 384/96 and Article 13(10) of Regulation No 2026/97 respectively, *the limits to which the Commission's discretion was subject in this case must be determined.*

29 The provisions referred to in the preceding paragraph, while granting the Commission *the power to impose provisional anti-dumping and countervailing duties, require at the same time that there be reason to believe that the undertaking has been breached* and that the decision imposing such duties be *taken on the basis of the best information available.*

30 In the present case, *the Commission*, when adopting Regulation No 2529/97, which imposed provisional duties on Fresh Marine's imports, *relied solely on the analysis of a report* which, as the Court of First Instance found at paragraphs 79 and 80 of the contested

[155] ECJ *Commission v Fresh Marine* (n 73).

[156] ECJ *Brasserie du Pêcheur and Factortame* (n 148) [51]; ECJ *Bergaderm and Goupil v Commission* (n 126) [41] and [42]; ECJ *Commission v Camar and Tico* (n 37) [53].

judgment, gave reason to believe that that company had complied with its undertaking not to make sales on the Community market below a minimum average price, but *which the Commission had amended on its own initiative, without taking the precaution of asking Fresh Marine what impact its unilateral action might have on the reliability of the information* which Fresh Marine had provided to it.

31 It follows that *the Commission clearly did not comply with its obligation to impose provisional duties only where there is reason to believe that the undertaking has been breached.* In the circumstances of the present case, such conduct must be *regarded as a sufficiently serious breach* of a rule of Community law satisfying one of the conditions for the incurring of non-contractual liability by the Community (see, inter alia, Bergaderm and Goupil, paragraphs 42 to 44, and Commission v Camar and Tico, paragraphs 53 and 54).

The finding concerning breach by the Commission was maintained by the ECJ and the damages liability upheld.

iii. Reduced Discretion, Not Sufficiently Serious: Holcim

The damages action in *Holcim* (CFI 2005) related to Commission Decision 94/815/EC, where the Commission had established the existence of a large-scale cartel in the cement market and fixed fines for a number of companies. In the subsequent action for annulment, the fines imposed on Holcim were annulled (CFI 2000; ECJ 2004).[157] As Holcim had furnished a bank guarantee for the duration of the proceedings, it attempted to recover the charges for this guarantee as compensation and filed a damages action against the Commission. In its judgment the CFI did not define the discretion, but yet dismissed the action.[158] On appeal, the ECJ (2007) did not find any illegalities in the CFI decision, and dismissed the appeal.[159]

iv. Narrow Discretion, Breach: Airtours [*later* MyTravel], Schneider

In 2002, the CFI handed down two judgments in which a Commission Decision declaring a concentration to be incompatible with the common market and the EEA Agreement, taken on the basis of Merger Regulation (EEC) No 4064/89, were annulled.[160] Both successful annulment actions, *Airtours* [later *MyTravel*] (CFI 2002)[161] and *Schneider* (CFI 2002),[162] were followed by damages actions. The

[157] CFI Joined Cases T-25/95, T-26/95, T-30/95 to T-32/95, T-34/95 to T-39/95, T-42/95 to T-46/95, T-48/95, T-50/95 to T-65/95, T-68/95 to T-71/95, T-87/95, T-88/95, T-103/95 and T-104/95 *Cimenteries CBR and Others v Commission* (appealed C-204/00 P) [2000] ECR II-491 and ECJ Joined Cases C-204/00 P, C-205/00 P, C-211/00 P, C-213/00 P, C-217/00 P and C-219/00 P *Aalborg Portland and others v Commission* (CFI judgment partly set aside) [2004] ECR I-123.

[158] CFI Case T-28/03 *Holcim (Deutschland) v Commission* (dismissed, appealed C-282/05 P) [2005] ECR II-1357.

[159] ECJ Case C-282/05 P *Holcim (Deutschland) v Commission* (appeal dismissed) [2007] ECR I-2941.

[160] [1989] OJ L395/1, corr. [1990] OJ L257/13.

[161] CFI Case T-342/99 *Airtours v Commission* (annulment action; annulled, no appeal) [2002] ECR II-2585.

[162] CFI Case T-310/01 *Schneider Electric v Commission* (annulment action; annulled, no appeal) [2002] ECR II-4071.

damages action in *Airtours* [later *MyTravel*] was rejected by the CFI in 2008, and there was no appeal.[163] In *Schneider*, the damages action resulted before the CFI in a finding of liability (2006),[164] which finding was however considerably limited by the ECJ (2009) on an appeal by the Commission.[165]

The interesting issue from the damages point of view and as regards sufficiently serious breach in particular was that in both cases the existence of certain breaches had already been pre-established in successful annulment actions.[166] The breach or breaches that led to the annulments had to be of a certain seriousness; any petty breach would not have led to such a result.

In the *Airtours* [later *MyTravel*] damages action (CFI 2008), in the preliminary considerations of the CFI regarding the conditions in which non-contractual liability may arise, the CFI recorded an important point on which the parties agreed. That is, the parties recognised that

> the concept of a sufficiently serious breach does not comprise all errors or mistakes which, even if of some gravity, are not incompatible with the normal conduct of an institution responsible for overseeing the application of competition rules, which are complex, delicate and subject to a considerable degree of discretion.

This was important for the CFI, because it noted that to accept that the position was otherwise, by equating, without further analysis, the annulment established in *Airtours v Commission* with a sufficiently serious breach within the meaning of *Bergaderm*,

> would risk compromising the capacity of the Commission fully to function as regulator of competition, a task entrusted to it by the EC Treaty, as a result of the inhibiting effect that the risk of having to bear the losses alleged by the undertakings concerned might have on the control of concentrations.

Moreover, the CFI ruling contains a lucid passage on the fine difference between breach and sufficiently serious breach (emphasis added):

> 43 Because of the need to have regard to such an effect, which is contrary to the general Community interest, a failure to fulfil a legal obligation, which, regrettable though it may be, can be explained by the objective constraints to which the institution and its officials are subject in the control of concentrations, cannot be held to constitute a breach of Community law which is sufficiently serious to give rise to the non-contractual liability of the Community. Conversely, *the right to compensation for damage resulting from the conduct of the institution becomes available where such conduct takes the form of action manifestly contrary to the rule of law and seriously detrimental to the interests of persons*

[163] CFI *MyTravel v Commission (damages action)* (n 72).

[164] CFI *Schneider Electric v Commission (damages action)* (n 86).

[165] ECJ Case *Commission v Schneider Electric (No 1 extent of liability)* (n 88).

[166] NB. In the Airtours annulment action, the third plea, which related to the lawfulness of the Commission's assessment of the effects of the Airtours/First Choice concentration on competition in the common market, was declared to be well founded. As this was sufficient for the annulment, the CFI did not examine the fourth plea concerning the lawfulness of the Commission's assessment of the commitments submitted during the administrative procedure. This plea was first examined in the damages case, see CFI *MyTravel v Commission (damages action)* (n 72) [11].

> *outside the institution and cannot be justified or accounted for by the particular constraints to which the staff of the institution, operating normally, are objectively subject.*

While the CFI admitted that it cannot be ruled out that 'manifest and grave defects affecting the economic analysis' which underlie a Commission decision declaring a concentration incompatible with the common market could exist, it recalled that the situation can be complex:

> 81 However, for such a finding to be made, it is necessary to bear in mind that the economic analyses necessary for the characterisation in competition law, of a given situation or transaction involve generally, as regards both the facts and the reasoning based on the recital of the facts, complex and difficult intellectual exercises, which may inadvertently contain some inadequacies, such as approximations, inconsistencies, or indeed certain omissions. That applies all the more in the control of concentrations, in view in particular of the time constraints to which the institution is subject.

The Court further examined the 'other errors' established in the *Airtours* [later *MyTravel*] annulment case and found that the Commission had not committed a sufficiently serious infringement of a rule of law intended to confer rights on individuals within the meaning of the case-law in analysing the Airtours/First Choice concentration in the light of the criteria relating to creation of a collective dominant position.

In addition, the CFI analysed the potentially unlawful conduct that would have occurred at the stage of the analysis of the commitments made by the applicant:

> 131 Without it being necessary to state a view on whether it was possible in the time available for the Commission to examine the amended commitments submitted on 15 September 1999, it follows from the above that it is apparent that those commitments did not respond clearly to the objections raised at that stage as regards the compatibility of the concentration with competition on the common market. The Commission's conduct did not therefore result in the applicant being deprived of all possibility of having the concentration declared compatible with the common market. The Commission accordingly did not infringe its duty of diligence in that regard.

The CFI thus concluded that in this regard the Commission did not commit a breach of a rule of law intended to confer rights on individuals that was sufficiently serious to give rise to Community liability. Therefore the action for damages was dismissed, and as stated above, there was no appeal.

The other important case was *Schneider*. Schneider Electric SA ('Schneider') and Legrand SA ('Legrand') are French companies engaged in electrical distribution and electrical equipment respectively. The aim was that Schneider would acquire control of Legrand in its entirety by means of a public exchange offer. The Commission found that the envisaged merger was incompatible with the common market. This decision was challenged by Schneider and eventually annulled by the CFI (2002).[167] There was no appeal against this judgment.

[167] CFI *Schneider Electric v Commission (annulment action)* (n 162).

A damages action was subsequently brought against the Commission before the CFI. The damages claimed were at an unprecedented level: they were above €1.6 billion. In assessing the damages claim, the CFI first identified where the illegality to be assessed was to be found (emphasis added):

> 139 *The only defect* in the incompatibility decision which, according to the Schneider I judgment, is liable to have deprived the applicant of an opportunity to secure a decision allowing it to proceed with the transaction is therefore to be found in the *discrepancy identified between the statement of objections of 3 August 2001 and the incompatibility decision itself*, regarding the objection concerning the buttressing of the positions of the parties to the transaction. It is therefore *the nature and gravity of that sole defect in the incompatibility decision that must be assessed* in determining whether the threshold for Community liability was overstepped by that decision.

According to the CFI the infringement in question was very serious (emphasis added):

> 152 In this case, a manifest and serious breach of Article 18(1) and (3) of the regulation *stems from the fact of the Commission's drafting a statement of objections in such a way that*, as is apparent from the Schneider I judgment, *the applicant could not ascertain that, if it did not submit corrective measures conducive to reducing or eliminating the support between its positions and those of Legrand in the French sectoral markets, it had no chance of securing a declaration that the transaction was compatible with the common market.*

Justifications advanced by the Commission did not convince the CFI and it summed up the situation in two consecutive paragraphs, the second one introducing all of a sudden the concept of fault (emphasis added):

> 156 It follows that the breach of Schneider's rights of defence is to be regarded in this case as a manifest and serious disregard by the Commission of the limits to which it is subject and, as such, constitutes a sufficiently serious breach of a rule of law intended to confer rights on individuals.
>
> 157 *The breach* of Schneider's rights of defence *therefore constitutes a fault on the part of the Commission* such as to cause the Community to incur non-contractual liability, provided that it is established in addition that there was real and certain damage and a sufficiently direct causal link between that damage and the sufficiently serious breach of Community law constituting a fault.

As all other conditions were fulfilled, the CFI established a potentially very substantial damages liability indicating how it should be calculated and asked the parties to come back with a proposal for quantum.[168]

The parties did not come back with a proposal for quantum, as the Commission introduced an appeal before the ECJ. In a way, the truly essential question after establishment of sufficiently serious breach (and the fact that the rule of law breached intended to create rights for individuals) was the existence of damage and the causal link. These were some of the issues invoked in the Commission appeal. Advocate General Ruiz-Jarabo Colomer considered in his opinion (2009) that the

[168] All the other breaches invoked by the applicant were dismissed.

main part of the damages awarded by the CFI was not actually suffered by the applicant (emphasis added):[169]

> 153. In short, since Schneider had assumed both risks of its own and, contractually, those of Wendel-KKR, the Court of First Instance's award of compensation for the reduced price that the former company had to concede to the latter while waiting for conclusion of the pending proceedings, would provide companies choosing to follow the route provided by Article 7(3) of the regulation with a guarantee or insurance against additional costs of all kinds which might arise in the event of an infringement, even if the infringement is of procedural rules which have no direct effect on the economic substance of the merger.
>
> 154. For all the above reasons, I consider that the ground of appeal should be upheld and *the judgment under appeal should be set aside in so far as it awarded Schneider compensation for damage resulting from the reduction in the sale price for Legrand which it had to offer Wendel-KKR as payment for the deferral of the sale until 10 December 2002.*

Furthermore, the Advocate General found that the required causal link was broken:

> 177. In the circumstances described, assuming that Schneider still wished to complete the merger with Legrand, (77) it would have been more logical to withdraw from the sale, relying on that clause, in order to minimise the damage claimed, because the sum of EUR 180 million cannot be compared to the compensation of almost EUR 1 700 million which is being claimed. An action to establish the non-contractual liability of the Community to the extent of the sum referred to in the cancellation clause would have been more reasonable and more in line with the course of events.
>
> 178. It is therefore my view that, by selling without being legally obliged to do so and by failing to act with due diligence, *Schneider broke the chain of causation* and I therefore propose that, in the alternative, the fifth ground of appeal be upheld.

The judgment of the ECJ (2009) followed the main lines of this reasoning and the damages liability of the Commission was finally reduced to €50000.[170]

v. Discretion in Staff Cases: Petrilli

Petrilli was a staff case where the applicant contested Commission's decision to refuse to renew her contract as a member of the contract staff. The refusal was based on a decision concerning the maximum duration of contracts for non-permanent staff in the Commission services.

The CST (2009) found the refusal illegal, annulled the decision and awarded damages. In establishing the liability, the Civil Service Tribunal did not examine the Commission's discretion or how serious the breach was.[171] The Commission appealed to the General Court, pointing to these issues which it considered to be errors in law. The General Court (2010), however, dismissed the appeal. The

[169] ECJ Case C-440/07 P *Opinion of Advocate General Ruiz-Jarabo Colomer – Commission v Schneider Electric* [2009] ECR I-6413.

[170] ECJ *Commission v Schneider Electric (No 1 extent of liability)* (n 88), and ECJ *Commission v Schneider (No 2 quantum)* (n 88).

[171] CST Case F-98/07 *Petrilli v Commission* (damages awarded, appealed T-143/09 P) [2009] ECR (judgment of 29 January 2009) [68]–[70].

General Court held that the Commission had a special duty, when acting as an employer, to make good any damage caused by its illegal action. Thus no assessment of discretion nor seriousness of the breach was required.[172] The ECJ (2011) became exceptionally involved through the re-examination procedure, as the First Advocate General proposed the Court to re-examine the case. The Court, however, ruled that 'examination of the judgment of the General Court in *Commission* v *Petrilli* has not revealed that there is a serious risk of the unity or consistency of European Union law being affected' and decided not to proceed to re-examination. The Court noted that 'it is now solely for the Civil Service Tribunal and the General Court of the European Union to develop the case-law in matters relating to the civil service'.[173] It remains to be seen how the damages liability will develop in future in staff cases, but at least there seems to be no indication that the *Petrilli* case-law, if confirmed, would be applicable outside the damages cases initiated by the staff.[174]

F. Interim Conclusion

The different types of breach cases are located on a sliding scale in the figure below. At the very left end appear cases concerning liability of the Union which are either outside the scope of application of EU law or where there was no breach. At the right-hand side at the far end appear the 'absolutely' serious breaches of EU law by the Union.

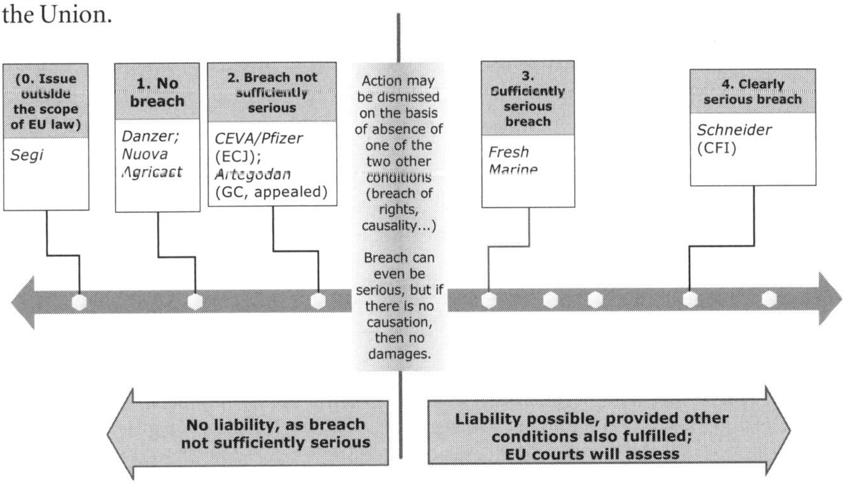

Figure 5.1 Degree of Breach in Case-law as Regards Breaches by the European Union

[172] GC Case T-143/09 P *Commission v Petrilli* (appeal dismissed) [2010] ECR II-0000 (judgment of 16 December 2010) [46].

[173] ECJ *Decision concerning review of the judgment in Case T-143/09 P Commission v Petrilli* (n 5) [4] and [5].

[174] *Petrilli* seems to depart from CFI's recent own case-law, see CFI Case T-57/99 *Nardone v Commission* (damages awarded €66000, no appeal) [2008] ECR (unpublished judgment of 10 December 2008), where the CFI underlined the need for convergence of the criteria and the examined whether there was a sufficiently serious breach [164], [168] and [173].

What probably is most interesting here is the relationship between *Schneider* (ECJ) on the one hand and *CEVA/Pfizer* (CFI, ECJ), *Artegodan* (GC, under appeal) and *MyTravel* (CFI) on the other. All of these cases included a successful action for annulment. In other words, in all of them a Commission decision was annulled as illegal. Yet only in *Schneider* did the applicant manage to qualify the breach as sufficiently serious for damages purposes. In *CEVA/Pfizer* and *Artegodan* the courts attached particular importance to the issue of human health. The fact that the breach was held excusable is probably linked to the specificities of the substance of the cases.

IV. SUCCESSFUL CASES

One matter of some interest is that in how many cases have all conditions of liability been established and damages finally awarded. It seems that there are some 20 cases, when staff cases are excluded, where damages have been awarded against the Union by the CFI or ECJ.[175] Most notably damages have been awarded in the so-called milk quota cases, maize grits cases and in one competition case where the Commission wrongfully prohibited a merger.

Amongst the successful damages claims are interesting cases where assessment of the two courts has been different, ie where the outcome of the damages ruling has changed between the CFI and ECJ. In some cases the applicant was unsuccessful before the CFI, but successful before the ECJ[176] – or the other way round.[177]

As to the types of damages caused by the Union, action or inaction by Union institutions rarely leads to liability as regards physical injury to persons, although this is not unheard of.[178] The typical form of damage is pure economic loss, which

[175] eg CFI *Schneider Electric v Commission* (n 86) and ECJ *Commission v Schneider Electric (No 1 extent of liability)* (n 88); ECJ *Commission v Schneider (No 2 quantum)* (n 88); CFI *Agraz and others v Commission (No 2)* (n 96); CFI *M v Ombudsman* (n 19); CFI Case T-48/05 *Franchet and Byk v Commission* (damages awarded €56000, no appeal) [2008] ECR II-1585; CFI *Nikolaou v Commission* (n 70); CFI *Citymo v Commission* (n 103); CFI *Camós Grau v Commission* (n 104); CFI *Camar v Council and Commission* (n 37); CFI *AFCon Management Consultants and others v Commission* (n 93); ECJ *Commission v Fresh Marine* (n 73); ECJ *Mulder (No 2) and others v Council and Commission* (n 54); CFI Case T-231/97 *New Europe Consulting and Brown v Commission* (damages awarded, no appeal) [1999] ECR II-2403; CFI *Embassy Limousines & Services v Parliament* (n 58); CFI *Cobrecaf and others v Commission* (n 74); ECJ Case C-308/87 *Grifoni (No 2)* (quantum of damages) [1994] ECR I-341; ECJ *Sofrimport v Commission* (n 59) [29]; ECJ *Pauls Agriculture v Council and Commission* (n 63), ECJ Joined Cases 256, 257, 265 and 267/80 and 51/81 and 282/82 *Birra Wührer and others v Council and Commission (No 2)* (liability established) [1984] ECR 3693; ECJ *Adams v Commission* (n 77); ECJ Joined Cases 64 and 113/76, 167 and 239/78, 27, 28 and 45/79 *Dumortier and others v Council (No 2; quantum)* [1982] ECR 1733; ECJ Case 238/78 *Ireks-Arkady v Council and Commission* (liability established) [1979] ECR 2955 [11]; ECJ *DGV v Council and Commission* (n 63); ECJ *CNTA v Commission (No 2)* (n 57) [13].

[176] CFI *Agraz and others v Commission (No 1)* (n 94) and ECJ *Agraz v Commission*, (n 95); CFI *Agraz and others v Commission (No 2)* (n 96).

[177] CFI *Cantina sociale di Dolianova and Others v Commission* (n 66) and ECJ *Commission v Cantina sociale di Dolianova and Others* (n 67). The applicant was successful in GC *Systran and Systran Luxembourg v Commission* (n 78), but an appeal introduced by the Commission is pending.

[178] See eg, ECJ Case C-308/87 *Grifoni (No 1)* (liability established) [1990] ECR I-1203 [18] and ECJ *Grifoni (No 2)* (n 175) (under Euratom Treaty); CFI Case T-138/03 *E.R. et al v Council and Commission*

can be immediate financial loss, consequential economic loss, or even non-financial loss. The heads of damage also differ somewhat from the heads of damage in actions against Member States. Damage for which compensation is sought must be actual and certain.[179] Moreover, it should also be recalled that there is often a difference between the heads of damage requested and heads of damage ordered by the court.[180]

Apart from individual damages action, as a rather exceptional remedy in a very exceptional situation the Community has once resorted to a compensation scheme. A considerable number of milk producers received damages under compensation schemes set up after the *Mulder* judgments.[181]

Some damages actions against the Union may, despite their outcome, merit citation in view of their particular creativity. Any person who has been engaged in writing a doctoral dissertation must feel some sympathy in reading *Pitsiorlas v Council and ECB* (CFI 2007).[182] Mr Pitsiorlas had asked from the Council and the European Central Bank access to certain documents, which he needed for his doctoral thesis. The institutions refused access. The applicant sued the institutions in order to annul the refusals and for damages to compensate the allegedly illegal action. The applicant couched one part of the damages claim in the following terms:

(no causal link, appealed C-100/07 P) [2006] ECR II-4923 and ECJ Case C-100/07 P *E.R. et al v Council and Commission* (appeal dismissed) [2007] ECR I-136*, Summ.pub. (order of 4 October 2007) (damage allegedly suffered by the applicants as a consequence of the infection and subsequent death of members of their families who developed a new variant of Creutzfeldt-Jakob disease linked to the appearance and spread within Europe of bovine spongiform encephalopathy ('mad cow disease'), for which the Council and the Commission were allegedly liable).

[179] ECJ Joined Cases 256, 257, 265 and 267/80 and 51/81 and 282/82 *Birra Wührer and others v Council and Commission (No 1)* (commencement) [1982] ECR 85 [9]; CFI Case T-478/93 *Wafer Zoo v Commission* (damages claim dismissed, no appeal) [1995] ECR II-1479 [49].

[180] As to heads of damages in general *cf* eg ECJ *Mulder (No 2) and others v Council and Commission* (n 54); ECJ Case C-470/03 *AGM-COS.MET* [2007] ECR I-2749 and CFI *Schneider Electric v Commission (damages action)* (n 86).

[181] The schemes were set up by three regulations, namely Council Regulation (EEC) No 2187/93 of 22 July 1993 providing for an offer of compensation to certain producers of milk and milk products temporarily prevented from carrying on their trade [1993] OJ L196/6; Commission Regulation (EEC) No 2376/93 of 27 August 1993 establishing the form for applications for compensation under Council Regulation (EEC) No 2187/93 for certain producers of milk and milk products [1993] OJ L218/11 and Commission Regulation (EEC) No 2648/93 of 28 September 1993 laying down detailed rules for the application of Council Regulation (EEC) No 2187/93 providing for an offer of compensation to certain producers of milk or milk products temporarily prevented from carrying on their trade [1993] OJ L234/1.

See also COM (1995) 150. Communication from the Commission on Compensation for Certain Producers of Milk and Milk Products Temporarily Prevented from Carrying On Their Trade ('Slom' Producers) – Implementation of Council Regulation (EEC) Nr 2187/93 and COM (1998) 287. Communication from the Commission on compensation for certain producers of milk products temporarily prevented from carrying on their trade (SLOM producers) – follow-up to the implementation of Council Regulation (EEC) n° 2187/93 COM (1998) 287. On this series of case-law, see Sharpston, 'Milk Lakes, SLOMs and Legitimate Expectations' (n 36).

[182] CFI *Pitsiorlas v Council and ECB* (n 17).

> 296 As regards the condition relating to the existence of damage, the applicant states, first, that the refusal of the two Community 'institutions' to grant him access to the document requested disrupted his timetable for writing his thesis and is still preventing him to this day – three years and four months after the expiry of the deadline set for handing in his thesis (31 March 2001) – from finishing it and submitting it to the Thessaloniki Faculty of Law. It is a logical result of that situation that the applicant has suffered material damage in the form of loss of revenue which he would have received by reasonably and appropriately using the doctorate which he would have obtained, in this case by securing a legal position within an international institution or body such as the ECB or the International Monetary Fund (IMF).

The applicant estimated that the various heads of damages consisted inter alia of the following:

> 303 The applicant claims, second, that the delay of approximately three and a half years in finishing his thesis caused him very serious non-material damage consisting in:
>
> – a significant prolongation of his anxieties concerning the completion of his thesis;
> – the delay to his career and financial advancement;
> – the impossibility of applying for job opportunities in Greece and, in particular, abroad, for which a doctorate was necessary;
> – the postponement of a career in an academic environment which requires a doctorate, the resulting uncertainty and the worsening of his situation, in view also of his age;
> – the need to update his thesis repeatedly as a result of constant developments in the EMU and the resulting loss of time and fatigue;
> – the psychological pressure suffered to this day concerning the completion of his thesis, the negative and ironic comments made about him and which continue to be made, and the obligation to have to give an explanation every time he his asked when his thesis will be completed;
> – the loss of time and energy brought about by the proceedings before the Court of First Instance and the Court of Justice;
> – the psychological strain caused by the length of the proceedings, the outcome of which is fundamental for his future.
>
> 304 The applicant claims that, in those circumstances, he should be awarded the sum of EUR 90 000 by way of compensation for the non-material damage which he has suffered.

The CFI's analysis of this claim focused, correctly, it is submitted, on the causal link:

> 314 The applicant claims that the material and non-material damage springs directly from the refusal by the Council and the ECB to grant access to the documents constituting the Basle/Nyborg Agreement.
>
> 315 First, as regards the material damage, categorised as loss of opportunity or loss of potential earnings, that damage consists, in the applicant's view, in the loss of the income that he would have earned through reasonable and appropriate use of the doctorate which he would already have obtained, in his case through securing a legal position with an international institution or body such as the ECB or the IMF.
>
> 316 It is, however, apparent from the applicant's written submissions that the alleged loss of opportunity and potential earnings are themselves the consequence of an initial

event, namely the failure to complete the thesis before the submission date and the subsequent failure to qualify for a doctorate in law.

317 That initial event cannot be considered to be the direct cause of the alleged loss of opportunity or loss of potential earnings, in so far as the applicant does not establish that possession of a doctorate was a necessary precondition for obtaining a position with one of the bodies to which he refers.

318 Nor does the failure to complete and submit the thesis before the deadline of 31 March 2001 appear to be the direct consequence of the contested decisions refusing access, which were brought to the applicant's knowledge in August and November 1999 whereas, by his own admission, his research was already at an advanced stage in the summer of 1999. That situation can be considered only as having been brought about by the applicant himself, who – besides challenging the refusals – should have been vigilant as to the progress of his thesis so that he could submit and defend it within the period allowed for that purpose, albeit in the belief that his research was incomplete.

Thus the application for damages brought by Mr Pitsiorlas was dismissed by the CFI. Eventually the applicant lodged an appeal before the ECJ, but unfortunately it was lodged late, so the ECJ did not have the opportunity to analyse the well-foundedness and legality of the ruling by the CFI.[183]

Overall, the proportionate number of successful cases for damages actions against the Community/Union may seem very low. Closer examination of the case-law shows that many damages actions are rejected as inadmissible or manifestly unfounded. This can look surprising, but in actual fact it seems to be in line with the trends before the CFI.[184] It seems that many unsuccessful cases are introduced by recurrent applicants, or that they are included as a last complementary heading in an action for annulment, without serious attempt to establish the liability criteria. Some cases are apparently brought even without any basic knowledge of the liability conditions, or the procedural requirements. It appears that the damages action is sometimes used as some kind of 'final option' against the Union, or even the Member States.[185]

[183] ECJ *Pitsiorlas v Council and ECB* (n 17).

[184] Indeed, '. . . an intelligent and informed observer from Mars would justifiably regard it as surprising that as many as one-third of all the ordinary direct actions filed in the Court of First Instance of the EC are dismissed, for one reason or another, as inadmissible. And this is so, despite the fact that all applicants are required to be represented by a lawyer'. Judge Nicholas Forwood, in Foreword (p vii) to A Ward, *Judicial Review and the Rights of Private Parties in EU Law* (n 48).

[185] Direct damages actions against Member States before the EU Courts are inadmissible, see CFI Case T-141/09 *Molter v Germany* (dismissed, appeal C-361/09P) [2009] ECR (unpublished order of 12 August 2009) and CFI Case T-354/09 *Goldman Management v Commission and Bulgaria* (dismissed, appealed C-507/09 P) [2009] ECR (unpublished order of 19 November 2009) and ECJ Case C-507/09 P *Goldman Management v Commission and Bulgaria* (appeal dismissed) [2010] ECR (unpublished order of 6 May 2010).

6

Liability of the Member States

THIS CHAPTER PRESENTS the elements to be analysed as regards the liability of the Member States. The chapter will set out the aspects to be examined following in essence the same structure as the preceding one to facilitate the comparison. First, as an introduction a certain number of structural aspects of the liability of Member States will be set out (section I). Thereafter the presentation concentrates on the rights criterion (section II), but in contrast to the preceding chapter, a framework based on the Hohfeldian analysis is used to facilitate the analysis. It is followed by an assessment of the breach criterion (section III). Both sections will be based on extensive analysis of the case-law. The chapter concludes by a presentation of a selected number of successful damages cases.

I. STRUCTURAL ASPECTS

A. General Issues

When discussing Member State liability for breaches of EU law, the focus is on the effects of European Union law in national legal systems. In a way, this is the normal way EU law operates. For most 'clients' or addressees of European Union law, it always appears as intertwined with the national legal system. EU law operates in conjunction with national law. When looked at from the national level, 'pure' EU law, applied at EU level without the influence of national law, is a kind of distant rarity.

The position of European Union law within national legal systems is defined by European Union law itself. In this respect, Member State liability forms the fourth branch of the constitutional principles governing the position of EU law in the Member States. The three principles preceding it are primacy of EU law,[1] interpretation in conformity with EU law[2] and inapplicability of conflicting national rules.[3]

[1] Based on ECJ Case 6/64 *Costa v ENEL* [1964] ECR 585, 594.

[2] ECJ Case C-106/89 *Marleasing v Comercial Internacional de Alimentación* [1990] ECR I-4135 [8]; ECJ Case C-262/97 *Engelbrecht* [2000] ECR I-7321 [39] and ECJ Case C-60/02 *X* [2004] ECR I-651 [59]–[60]; ECJ Case C-555/07 *Kücükdeveci* [2010] ECR I-0000 (judgment of 19 January 2010).

[3] An insightful analysis of these classic principles is offered by B de Witte, 'Direct Effect, Primacy and the Nature of Legal Order' in P Craig and G de Búrca (eds), *The Evolution of EC Law*, 2nd edn (Oxford, Oxford University Press, 2011).

The key reasoning for the establishment of Member State liability has been the need to ensure the effectiveness of Community rules and protection of the rights granted to individuals, as established in *Francovich* (ECJ 1991).[4] Member State liability was also advocated as a remedy for a situation discovered some years earlier, namely the fact that Member States were not implementing Community law properly.[5]

Member State liability for breaches of EU law is based on pure case-law; the key source of law is the case-law of the courts of the European Union.[6]

Damages actions against a Member State are always initiated in a court of a Member State. These cases only arrive in the Luxembourg courts through the preliminary ruling procedure under Article 267 TFEU and currently preliminary rulings are solely adjudicated by the Court of Justice.[7] It is always the national court which takes the final decision.

In contrast to the liability of the Union, the total number of cases for Member State responsibility judged by the ECJ is considerably lower. Since *Francovich* (1991), to the end of 2010 there have been altogether some 40 cases where Member State liability has been addressed by the ECJ, of which some 15 before *Bergaderm* (2000) and some 25 thereafter.

As Member State liability cases are in the last resort decided by national courts, their global number is very difficult to trace. They are handled by a number of different courts in different Member States. An additional complication is that cases are normally available only in the national language. There is no centralised source of information on national cases, their outcomes or damages awarded. The best second-hand sources are studies[8] or reports.[9]

[4] ECJ Joined Cases C-6/90 and C-9/90 *Francovich and Bonifaci* [1991] ECR I-5357 [33]: 'The full effectiveness of Community rules would be impaired and the protection of the rights which they grant would be weakened if individuals were unable to obtain redress when their rights are infringed by a breach of Community law for which a Member State can be held responsible'.

[5] On this 'enforcement deficit' see a contemporary analysis by F Snyder, 'The Effectiveness of European Community Law: Institutions, Processes, Tools and Techniques' (1993) *MLR* 19–54.

[6] However, at the Inter-Governmental Conference of 1996 that resulted in the Treaty of Amsterdam (1997), the United Kingdom proposed an explicit (and limitative) Treaty provision on that state liability. That idea was not adopted, and apparently it has not been considered seriously in subsequent IGCs.

[7] In accordance with Art 256(3) TFEU, by amending the Statute, the General Court may be given jurisdiction to hear and determine preliminary rulings in specific areas.

[8] It is possible to trace some national cases through various studies, which can be comparative in nature or concentrate just on the situation of one Member State. For comparative studies see eg, G Vandersanden and M Dony (eds), *La responsabilité des États membres en cas de violation du droit communautaire. Études de droit communautaire et de droit national comparé* (Brussels, Bruylant, 1997) and M-PF Granger, 'National applications of *Francovich* and the construction of a European administrative *ius commune*' (2007) *European Law Review* 157–92.

[9] In addition, worth mentioning are the Commission's *Annual Report on the Application of Community Law*, which contains an annex, compiled by the Research and Documentation Department of the Court of Justice. This annex addresses two or three actual questions of Community law developments in the Member States. One of the issues over the recent years has been national case-law on damages liability of Member States for breaches of Community law. XXIVth Report on monitoring the application of Community law COM(2007) 398 – Annex VI: Application of EU law by national authorities. In the report published for 2006 the second question was formulated as follows: 'Y a-t-il eu des décisions intéressantes faisant application de la jurisprudence de la Cour en matière de responsabilité de l'État pour violation du droit communautaire?' For the report of the following year, this question was no longer included, see

When compared to the liability of the Union, the liability of Member States is an open system in two respects. In the first place, the Member State liability system in EU law is incomplete; it always operates in conjunction with national law, in particular national administrative and procedural law. Secondly, alternative remedies available are defined in national law.

If the conditions for liability are fulfilled, the Member State must make reparation for the consequences of loss and damage caused on the basis of the rules of national law on liability, provided that the conditions for reparation of loss and damage laid down by national law are not less favourable than those relating to similar domestic claims (principle of equivalence) and are not so framed as to make it, in practice, impossible or excessively difficult to obtain reparation (principle of effectiveness).[10] In *Transportes Urbanos* (ECJ 2010), a reference from the Spanish Tribunal Supremo, the Court was asked for a ruling on compatibility of a national rule under which actions for damages against the state, alleging a breach of EU law by national legislation (which had already been established in an action under Article 226 EC [now Article 258 TFEU]) could only succeed if the applicant has already exhausted all domestic remedies to challenge the validity of the harmful administrative measure, when such a rule is not applicable to an action for damages against the state alleging breach of the Constitution by national legislation which has been established by the competent court. The Court ruled that such a rule is precluded by EU law, basing its analysis on the principle of equivalence.[11]

One example of integration with national law is the applicability of national limitation periods for damages actions against Member States based on EU law. For example in *Danske Slagterier* (ECJ 2009) the Court confirmed that the three-year prescription period applicable for similar national damages actions in Germany was compatible with the requirements of EU law.[12]

B. Institutional Coverage: Legislative, Executive and Judicial Branches

It is worth noting that in Member States no public bodies or sectors are exempt from liability when they apply European Union law. The Court affirmed in *Brasserie du Pêcheur and Factortame* (ECJ 1996) that a state is viewed as a single entity in international law.[13] Therefore, also for the purposes of the EU legal order, it does not matter whether the breach which gave rise to damage is attributable to the legislature,

25th Annual Report on Monitoring the Application of Community law [COM(2008) 777] – Annex VI: Application of EU Law by National Authorities.

A useful source has also been the Francovich follow-up web site, founded by Professor Gerrit Betlem, see http://www.eel.nl, now hosted at www.asser.nl.

[10] ECJ Case C-224/01 *Köbler* [2003] ECR I-10239 [58]; ECJ Case C-524/04 *Test Claimants in the Thin Cap Group Litigation* [2007] ECR I-2107 [123] and ECJ Case C-118/08 *Transportes Urbanos y Servicios Generales* [2010] ECR I-0000 (judgment of 26 January 2010) [31].

[11] ECJ *Transportes Urbanos y Servicios Generales* (n 10) [33] and [48].

[12] ECJ Case C-445/06 *Danske Slagterier* [2009] ECR I-2119.

[13] ECJ Joined Cases C-46/93 and C-48/93 *Brasserie du Pêcheur and Factortame* [1996] ECR I-1029 [34].

the judiciary, or the executive. In the EU legal order all state authorities, including the legislature, are bound to comply with the rules laid down by European Union law, which directly governs the situation of individuals.

Even if this has been accepted for the administration,[14] or for the legislator,[15] the question of liability on the basis of national court action has been far more controversial. As a matter of European Union law, this issue now seems settled after the judgments in *Köbler* and *Traghetti*[16] concerning judicial liability.[17] State liability does not cover private activity outside the public sphere, nor does it involve the individual liability of national civil servants, unless their action is attributable to the state.[18]

C. Sectors of Liability: Examples

Potential sectors where Member States may be sued for liability in damages for breach of European Union law are in the first place limited to sectors where the Member State implements and applies EU law in its territory. Moreover, the core areas for liability are those where potential damage can be readily quantified in money terms. The sectors will be presented through examples in more detail later on,[19] but at this stage it can be noted that questions relating to the four areas of free movement have been central: there is ample case-law on free movement of goods, freedom of establishment and free movement of capital.

Of the other sectors, the Wage Guarantee Directive 80/987 has very often been invoked. In addition, provisions intended to protect consumers, or laying down administrative systems for the functioning of the internal market (pharmaceutical products, veterinary medical products, or Machines Directive) have also been the basis of a damages action. The ECJ ruled between 2006 and 2008 on four preliminary rulings originating from the same UK court[20] and relating to freedom of establishment, free movement of capital and corporation tax. These *Test Claimants* cases were connected to taxation of dividends, amongst others. Indeed, in three cases out of four the ECJ found a sufficiently serious infringement of EU law giving

[14] For Member State liability for administrative decision see eg, ECJ Case C-5/94 *Hedley Lomas* [1996] ECR I-2553 or ECJ Case C-452/06 *Synthon* [2008] ECR I-7681.

[15] For Member State liability for legislation see eg, ECJ *Brasserie du Pêcheur and Factortame* (n 13) or ECJ Case C-150/99 *Stockholm Lindöpark* [2001] ECR I-493.

[16] For Member State liability for judicial acts see ECJ *Köbler* (n 10) and ECJ Case C-173/03 *Traghetti del Mediterraneo* [2006] ECR I-5177. Previously on this question see eg, H Toner, 'Thinking the Unthinkable? State Liability for Judicial Acts after *Factortame III*' *17 Yearbook of European Law 1997* (Oxford, Clarendon, 1999).

[17] See below s III.G.

[18] ECJ Case C-470/03 *AGM-COS.MET* [2007] ECR I-2749 [66]. Private liability for breaches of EU law (*Courage* doctrine) was briefly discussed in ch 3, s IV.

[19] The sectors of Member State liability will be explored in more detail in ss II and III of this ch 6.

[20] High Court of Justice of England and Wales, Chancery Division (United Kingdom).

rise to damages liability.[21] Other issues relating to direct and indirect taxation have also been taken up in the damages context.[22]

D. Applicants

Somewhat contrary to intuitive expectations, individuals have been applicants in a fairly large number of damages actions against Member States in preliminary rulings introduced before the ECJ. Individuals, as workers, consumers, travellers, pensioners, or just as 'natural persons', have been claiming damages for breach of their EU law rights in many cases before the ECJ.[23] [24] Naturally, economic operators (eg, companies, trade associations) have also been applicants in cases relating to Member State liability.[25] In *DEB* (ECJ 2010) the Court was called to assess the access to justice of a company which did not have the means to pursue a damages action against a Member State for breach of EU law.[26]

[21] ECJ Case C-446/04 *Test Claimants in the FII Group Litigation* [2006] ECR I-11753; ECJ Case C-374/04 *Test Claimants in Class IV of the ACT Group Litigation* [2006] ECR I-11673; ECJ *Test Claimants in the Thin Cap Group Litigation* (n 10) and ECJ Case C-201/05 *Test Claimants in the CFC and Dividend Group Litigation* [2008] ECR I-2875. These cases will be examined in more detail below.

[22] ECJ Joined Cases C-283/94, C-291/94 and C-292/94 *Denkavit Internationaal and others v Bundesamt für Finanzen* [1996] ECR I-5063 (Directive 90/435); ECJ Case C-319/96 *Brinkmann Tabakfabriken v Skatteministeriet (No 1)* [1998] ECR I-5255 (Taxes other than turnover tax which affect the consumption of manufactured tobacco Directive 79/32); ECJ *Stockholm Lindöpark* (n 15) (VAT) and ECJ Case C-470/04 *N* [2006] ECR I-7409 (Freedom of establishment – Article 43 EC – Direct taxation).

[23] On preliminary references relating to claims for state liability by private persons, see eg, ECJ *Francovich and Bonifaci* (n 4), ECJ Joined Cases C-178/94, C-179/94, C-188/94, C-189/94 and C-190/94 *Dillenkofer and others v Bundesrepublik Deutschland* [1996] ECR I-4845; ECJ Joined Cases C-94/95 and C-95/95 *Bonifaci and others and Berto and others v INPS* [1997] ECR I-3969; ECJ Case C-373/95 *Maso and others v INPS and Repubblica italiana* [1997] ECR I-405; ECJ Case C-261/95 *Palmisani v INPS* [1997] ECR I-4025; ECJ Case C-140/97 *Rechberger and others* [1999] ECR I-3499; ECJ Case C-302/97 *Konle* [1999] ECR I-3099; ECJ Case C-321/97 *Andersson and Wåkerås-Andersson* [1999] ECR I-3551; ECJ Case C-131/97 *Carbonari and others* [1999] ECR I-1103; ECJ Case C-424/97 *Haim* [2000] ECR I-5123; ECJ Case C-118/00 *Larsy (No 2)* [2001] ECR I-5063; ECJ *Köbler* (n 10); ECJ Case C-160/01 *Mau* [2003] ECR I-4791; ECJ Case C-63/01 *Evans* [2003] ECR I-14447; ECJ Case C-222/02 *Paul and others* [2004] ECR I-9425; ECJ *N* (n 22); ECJ Case C-300/04 *Eman and Sevinger* [2006] ECR I-8055; ECJ Case C-278/05 *Robins and others* [2007] ECR I-1053.

[24] Harlow has noted that there is no reason to speak about 'squad of citizen policemen', though. See C Harlow, 'Francovich and the Problem of the Disobedient State' (1996) (3) *European Law Journal* 199–225, 204.

[25] On preliminary references relating to claims for state liability by legal persons, see eg, ECJ *Brasserie du Pêcheur and Factortame* (n 13); ECJ *Hedley Lomas* (n 14); ECJ Case C-302/94 *British Telecommunications (No 2)* [1996] ECR I-6417; ECJ Case C-127/95 *Norbrook Laboratories* [1998] ECR I-1531; ECJ *Brinkmann Tabakfabriken (No 1)* (n 22); ECJ Case C-111/97 *EvoBus Austria* [1998] ECR I-5411; ECJ Case C-397/98 *Metallgesellschaft and others* [2001] ECR I-1727; ECJ *Stockholm Lindöpark* (n 15); ECJ Case C-511/03 *Ten Kate Holding Musselkanaal e.a.* [2005] ECR I-8979; ECJ *Traghetti del Mediterraneo* (n 16); ECJ *Test Claimants in the FII Group Litigation* (n 21); ECJ *Test Claimants in Class IV of the ACT Group Litigation* (n 21); ECJ *Test Claimants in the Thin Cap Group Litigation* (n 10); ECJ *Test Claimants in the CFC and Dividend Group Litigation* (n 21); ECJ *AGM-COS.MET* (n 18); ECJ *Synthon* (n 14); ECJ *Danske Slagterier* (n 12) and ECJ C-527/07 *Generics (UK)* [2009] ECR I-5259.

[26] ECJ Case C-279/09 *DEB* [2010] ECR I-0000 [59]–[62].

II. GRANTING OF RIGHTS TO INDIVIDUALS: LIABILITY OF THE MEMBER STATES AND EU LAW RIGHTS BREACH OF WHICH MAY GIVE RISE TO LIABILITY

A. Relationship Between Granting Individual Rights in the Damages Context and Direct Effect

The first condition laid down in the case-law for liability of Member States is identification of a rule of law granting rights to individuals.[27] There are two keys to understanding the case-law relating to the intention to confer rights on individuals in the context of liability of Member States.[28]

The *first key* is to note that as regards the intention to confer rights at least two groups of case-law can be distinguished.[29]

The *first group* consists of cases where the right conferred on individuals and the obligation breached are the *same*. This was for example the situation in *Brasserie/Factortame* (ECJ 1996). The source of rights for the applicant in *Brasserie du Pêcheur* was free movement of goods (Article 30 of the EC Treaty) and the obligation breached by the German authorities was the same. In similar vein, the individual right and obligation breached were the same in *AGM* (ECJ 2007).[30] Article 4 of the Machines Directive 98/37 granted rights to economic operators as regards placing on the market machinery and safety components complying with the Directive, and it was equally a breach of this provision by Finland which was established in this case.

The *second group* includes cases where the right conferred and the obligation breached are *different*. A prominent example is of course *Francovich* itself: the right conferred on individuals was the wage guarantee under Article 7 of the Directive, whereas the obligation the Member State breached was the duty to implement the Directive, ie Article 11(1) of the Directive viz Article 189 of the EC Treaty. Another example can be offered by *Köbler*.[31] Here the right conferred on an individual flowed from Article 48 of the Treaty and Article 7(1) of Regulation 1612/68, but Mr Köbler was unable to obtain those rights, as the national court acted in breach of Article 234 EC concerning the duty to make and maintain a reference for a preliminary ruling.

[27] The questions underlying this section have been discussed in ch 2, s V above.

[28] On rights in the EU context in general see eg, N Reich, '"System der subjektiven öffentlichen Rechte" in the Union: A European Constitution for Citizens of Bits and Pieces', *Collected Courses of the Academy of European Law. Volume VI, Book I (1995). European Community law* (The Hague, Kluwer Law International, 1998) and JM Prinssen and A Schrauwen (eds), *Direct Effect – Rethinking a Classic of EC Legal Doctrine* (Groningen, Europa Law Publishing, 2002).

[29] This point was made by M Dougan, 'The Intention to Confer Rights under the Francovich Case Law: Still Waters Run Deep'. UKAEL Seminar 'Damages Claims in EU Law', London, 22 February 2008 (unpublished presentation).

[30] ECJ *AGM-COS.MET* (n 18) [79], where the rights conferred to individuals and the rule of law breached were both to be found in Art 4(1) of Directive 98/37/EC of the European Parliament and of the Council of 22 June 1998 on the approximation of the laws of the Member States relating to machinery [1998] OJ L207/1.

[31] ECJ *Köbler* (n 10); see [102] on rights conferred to individuals (Arts 48 of the Treaty and 7(1) of Regulation 1612/68) and [117]/[118]for the rule of law breached (Art 234 of the Treaty).

Although in this section the focus is on this distinction as regards grant of rights, ie the first criterion of damages liability, this distinction is also important for the second criterion, namely when assessing sufficient seriousness of breach.

The *second key* to the rights discourse for Member State liability is to understand its relation to the concept of direct effect. It has been noted that the principle of direct effect and the principle of Member State liability are different in character and have different functions in the system of judicial protection, but the common ground for both is the notion of 'rights'.[32] It has also been highlighted that conferral of rights can occur without direct effect and that direct effect can occur without conferral of rights.[33]

To begin with analysis of the relationship between 'granting of rights' in the damages context and the concept of 'direct effect', it should be recalled that according to the case-law of the Court, the direct effect of an infringed provision does not prevent a damages action,[34] but rather, a rule of law with direct effect normally satisfies the condition of grant of rights to individuals for damages purposes.[35] However, the absence of direct effect of a provision does not necessarily mean that it cannot create rights for individuals.[36]

These indications do not necessarily make understanding the system much easier. On the basis of the case-law it is clear that rights capable of giving rise to damages liability can formally be based at least on the founding Treaties (eg *Brasserie du Pêcheur*) and legislation (*Francovich*). The rights breached can either be directly effective (*Brasserie du Pêcheur*) or they may lack this element (*Francovich*). What is equally important is that such rights can be positive, that is, purported to ensure a positive action from a Member State (*Francovich*), but they can also be negative rights, ie meaning that they forbid a Member State from doing something (*Brasserie du Pêcheur*).

It seems that a helpful way forward for a better understanding of the rights criterion in EU public liability law is to recall briefly the salient features of development of 'rights' case-law outside the damages context. This development has mainly taken place in relation to EU law in Member States. A rather common, yet still helpful approach is to present development of the case-law through different periods.[37]

[32] S Prechal, 'Member State liability and direct effect: what's the difference after all?' (2007) *European Business Law Review* 299–316, 303.

[33] A Maunu, 'Direktiivien oikeusvaikutukset kansallisissa tuomioistuimissa: oireet, diagnoosi ja hoitokeinot', in H Kaila and E Pirjatanniemi et al (eds), *Yksilön oikeusasema Euroopan unionissa – Individens rättsställning inom Europeiska Unionen: Juhlakirja Allan Rosas – Festskrift Allan Rosas* (Turku/Åbo, 2008) 617ff.

[34] *Brasserie du Pêcheur and Factortame* (n 13) [18] and [22].

[35] See eg, ECJ *Danske Slagterier* (n 12) [22].

[36] ECJ *Francovich and Bonifaci* (n 4).

[37] The following is based primarily on T Eilmansberger, 'The Relationship between Rights and Remedies in EC Law: In Search of the Missing Link' (2004) *Common Market Law Review* 1199–246. For an earlier analysis, see T Ojanen, 'The Changing Concept of Direct Effect of European Law' (2000) *European Review of Public Law* 1253–70, 1257ff. A very comprehensive view is offered by M Dougan, 'The Vicissitudes of Life at the Coalface: Remedies and Procedures for Enforcing Union Law before the National Courts' in P Craig and G de Búrca (eds), *The Evolution of EC Law*, 2nd edn (Oxford, Oxford University Press, 2011).

Individual rights deriving from Community law were 'found' or created in the context of direct applicability in *van Gend en Loos* (ECJ 1962).[38] Eilmansberger notes that creation of subjective rights in this judgment 'was a bit of an accident'.[39] The next step was establishment of an inherent linkage between individual rights and direct applicability. That came about as a 'by-product' of direct applicability.

The case-law following *van Gend en Loos* shed more light on the direct applicability of various primary and secondary Community law rules, but, again according to Eilmansberger, the case-law did not really clarify the exact content and meaning of 'individual rights' resulting from directly applicable community law norms.[40] An important element to note was that persons protected through 'individual rights' were not limited *rationae personae*; the case-law was thus 'generous'.

More protection for 'naked' individual rights was offered at a later stage. It is often said that individual rights as acknowledged by the ECJ remained vulnerable in the absence of adequate protection and the absence of suitable remedies at national level. There is a certain line of case-law, referred to as 'second generation case-law', where protection of individual rights was enhanced through further elaboration of the concepts of direct effect, direct applicability and supremacy of Community law. The cases cited in this context are *Simmenthal* (ECJ 1978),[41] *Factortame I* (ECJ 1990),[42] *Johnston* (ECJ 1986),[43] *Peterbroeck* (ECJ 1995)[44] and *Kühne* (ECJ 2004).[45] However, Eilmansberger is of the opinion that in so far as identification of the substance of any individual rights is concerned, these cases have not been very helpful. Their essence is rather consolidation of the concept of 'invocability', ie the idea that direct effect and supremacy of EC law are secured by ensuring that they can be invoked in Member States.

The 'real second generation' of the case-law was made concrete, according to Eilmansberger, in the series of cases relating to restitution of charges levied contrary to EC law on the one hand and with cases establishing damages liability for breach of Community law on the other. The system is completed with the case-law relating to pre-emptive remedies to be provided to individuals to prevent breach of Community law ('primary remedies to prevent possible or impending

[38] The origin of the 'granting rights doctrine' for both 'direct effect/direct applicability' and Member State liability is to be found in 'negative rights': the seminal case of *van Gend en Loos* (ECJ, 1963) was about negative right; see ECJ Case 26/62 *Van Gend en Loos* [1963] ECR 1, 13: 'The wording of Article 12 contains a clear and unconditional prohibition which is not a positive but a negative obligation. This obligation, moreover, is not qualified by any reservation on the part of states which would make its implementation conditional upon a positive legislative measure enacted under national law. The very nature of this prohibition makes it ideally adapted to produce direct effects in the legal relationship between Member States and their subjects'. The same applies for the rights in *Brasserie du Pêcheur*, too.

[39] Eilmansberger, 'The Relationship between Rights and Remedies in EC Law' (n 37) 1202.

[40] Eilmansberger, 'The Relationship between Rights and Remedies in EC Law' (n 37) 1204.

[41] ECJ Case 106/77 *Amministrazione delle finanze dello Stato v Simmenthal* [1978] ECR 629 [24].

[42] ECJ Case C-213/89 *Factortame and others* [1990] ECR I-2433 [21].

[43] ECJ Case 222/84 *Johnston v Chief Constable of the Royal Ulster Constabulary* [1986] ECR 1651 [57].

[44] ECJ Case C-312/93 *Peterbroeck, Van Campenhout & Cie v Belgian State* [1995] ECR I-4599.

[45] ECJ Case C-453/00 *Kühne & Heitz* [2004] ECR I-837.

infractions').[46] One possible way of categorising rules of law intended to confer rights on individuals is the following:[47]

- a provision which gives a right to individuals which the national courts must protect, so that it has direct effect;[48]
- a provision which creates an advantage which could be defined as a vested right;[49]
- a provision which is designed for the protection of the interests of individuals;[50] or
- a provision which entails the grant of rights to individuals, the content of those rights being sufficiently identifiable.[51]

Another way of approaching this question is proposed by Dougan, who has elaborated two models, namely the 'primacy model' and the 'trigger model'. His primacy model is based on the supremacy of Community law as an approach to settling all disputes before national courts, while the trigger model sees supremacy as a normal remedy which is administered by national courts when resolving disputes involving Community law.[52] He has examined the relationship between right (non-effective right in particular) and damages claim, and explains it as follows (emphasis added):[53]

> The 'trigger' model can, in fact, offer an alternative explanation for the *Francovich* case law. *Francovich transforms* the non-directly effective Community expectation of a particular substantive benefit (say, to guaranteed payment of outstanding wages when one's employer becomes insolvent), into the directly effective Community right to reparation against the Member State responsible for failing to deliver a legal framework capable of fulfilling that expectation (because the Member State failed to implement the relevant directive correctly or on time).

In other words, something which could have been claimed on the basis of the Directive becomes an enforceable (and different) right after expiration of the transposition deadline. Dougan takes the view that following the rulings in *Pfeiffer*[54] and *Berlusconi*,[55] the Court has apparently rejected the approach he describes as the 'primacy model'.[56]

A pedagogical and almost surprisingly lucid passage in *Savas* (ECJ 2000) illustrates in one single case several aspects of Community law rights, albeit it was not a

[46] Eilmansberger, 'The Relationship between Rights and Remedies in EC Law' (n 37) 1227, 1228.

[47] *cf* CFI Case T-415/03 *Cofradía de pescadores 'San Pedro' de Bermeo and others v Council* (damages claim dismissed, appealed C-6/06 P) [2005] ECR II-4355 [86].

[48] ECJ *Brasserie du Pêcheur and Factortame* (n 13) [54].

[49] CFI Case T-113/96 *Dubois et Fils v Council and Commission* (damages claim dismissed, appealed C-95/98 P) [1998] ECR II-125 [63]–[65].

[50] ECJ Case 83/76 *Bayerische HNL and Others v Council and Commission* (damages action dismissed) [1978] ECR 1209 [5].

[51] ECJ *Dillenkofer and others v Bundesrepublik Deutschland* (n 23) [22].

[52] M Dougan, 'When worlds collide! Competing visions of the relationship between direct effect and supremacy' (2007) *Common Market Law Review* 931–63, 932–34.

[53] Dougan, 'When worlds collide!' (n 52) 944–45.

[54] ECJ Joined Cases C-397/01–C-403/01 *Pfeiffer* [2004] ECR I-8835.

[55] ECJ Joined Cases C-387/02, C-391/02 and C-403/02 *Berlusconi et al* [2005] ECR I-3565.

[56] Dougan, 'When worlds collide!' (n 52) 953.

damages case.[57] The case concerned Mr Savas, a Turkish national, and a decision by the UK authorities refusing to grant him leave to remain in the United Kingdom and an order for his deportation from the territory of that Member State. The central issue of the case was the interpretation of Article 41(1) of the Additional Protocol to the EEC-Turkey Association agreement. That article introduced a standstill clause as regards new restrictions on freedom of establishment and freedom to provide services.[58]

The Court, after a detailed analysis of the Agreement and all the relevant provisions, came to the following conclusions, which set out neatly some of the various roles that one single provision can play in the rights context. The Court ruled, first, that Article 41(1) of the Additional Protocol *has 'direct effect'* in Member States. However, and this is the second finding of the Court, that provision '*is not in itself capable of conferring* upon a Turkish *national a right of establishment* and, as a corollary, a right of residence in the Member State in whose territory he has remained and carried on business activities as a self-employed person in breach of the domestic immigration law.' The third dimension was that the provision however did prohibit '*the introduction of new national restrictions* on freedom of establishment and right of residence of Turkish nationals as from the date on which that protocol entered into force in the host Member State.' Therefore, although the provision did have 'direct effect', it did not confer a positive (directly invocable) right of establishment for the applicant, but it did at any rate create a negative (indirect) right so that no new restrictions could be imposed.

B. Hohfeldian Framework for Analysing Rights in EU Law

Purely on the basis of the case-law one can observe that, indeed, Community law rights appear to be different in different cases. To better apprehend these situations, some analytical framework is needed. In a way, one starting point for my research was for some time the idea by Dougan concerning the transformation of a non-effective EU law right to an enforceable right.[59]

Bengoetxea and Jääskinen have proposed an updated framework for rights analysis. Their model builds upon the Hohfeldian rights analysis by Hilson and Downes, completes it and furnishes references to newer case-law.[60] In this model the Hohfeldian entitlements and burdens are transposed in a comprehensive manner to the EU legal system:[61]

[57] ECJ Case C-37/98 *Savas* [2000] ECR I-2927.

[58] Article 41(1) of the Additional Protocol reads as follows: 'The Contracting Parties shall refrain from introducing between themselves any new restrictions on the freedom of establishment and the freedom to provide services'.

[59] Dougan, 'The Intention to Confer Rights' under the Francovich Case Law' (n 29).

[60] See C Hilson and T Downes, 'Making Sense of Rights: Community Rights in E.C. Law' (1999) *European Law Review* 121–38 and T Ojanen, *The European Way. The Structure of National Court Obligation under EC Law* (Saarijärvi, 1998) 160–64.

[61] See J Bengoetxea and N Jääskinen, 'Rights and Diverse Effects in EC law: a Hohfeldian Approach to the Doctrine of Direct Effect of Directives' in R Banakar (ed), *Rights in Context: Law and Justice in Late*

> The purpose of the Hohfeldian reconstruction of the notion of direct effect as it has been expressed in the jurisprudence of the ECJ is to demonstrate that in the situations of direct effect the membership obligations of Member States, which are Hohfeldian burdens, are transformed into Hohfeldian entitlements of individuals.

Accordingly, a Community right, based on direct effect of EU law, can thus be a 'claim right', or a 'liberty', 'power' or 'immunity', where the corresponding position of a Member State is a 'duty', 'no-right', 'liability' or 'disability'.[62] In Table 6.1 below, the Hohfeldian entitlements and burdens are applied to EU law 'rights'.

It seems that this approach could usefully be transposed in EU public law liability to take the thinking one step further. The rights invoked in EU institutional liability and Member State liability differ in their nature. Thus the Hohfeldian framework would not seem to bring much added value in institutional EU liability (that is why it was not presented in the previous chapter), while it seems rather helpful when analysing the different obligations and corresponding individual rights as regards Member States.

Table 6.1 Entitlements and Burdens by Hohfeld, as Applied to EU Law 'Rights'

Hohfeldian relation for individual	**[1] Right (Claim-Right)**	**[2] Liberty**	**[3] Power**	**[4] Immunity**
Example in case-law	CORRELATIVE OF THE ORIGINAL PROVISION 2) *Wells*: Mrs Wells can claim that environmental impact assessment (EIA) is carried out, although the directive provides no rights to individuals	CORRELATIVE OF THE ORIGINAL PROVISION 2) *van Gend en Loos*: liberty not to pay higher customs duty 4) *Becker*: liberty not to act in the way required by national law, as it is based on a No-Right	CORRELATIVE OF THE ORIGINAL PROVISION 2) *Kraaijeveld*: 'Right to call for a judicial review' Secondary level power against Member State	CORRELATIVE OF THE ORIGINAL PROVISION 2) *CIA Security*: invocabilité d'exclusion Immunity from a sales ban which results from a technical requirement which has not been notified

Modern Society (Farnham, Ashgate, 2010); the Hohfeldian analysis in this article builds on an earlier article by N Jääskinen, 'EU ja Hohfeld' in H Kanninen and H Koskinen et al (eds), *Puhuri käy. Muuttuva suomalainen ja eurooppalainen valtiosääntömme. Heikki Karapuu 30.12.1944 – 15.6.2006* (Helsinki, Edita, 2009) 297.

[62] See WN Hohfeld, *Fundamental Legal Conceptions as applied in judicial reasoning and other legal essays* (New Haven, Yale University Press (digital version at www.archive.org), 1920) 36.

Table 6.1 (*cont.*):

Hohfeldian relation for Member State/EU institution	[5] **Duty**	[6] **No-Right**	[7] **Liability**	[8] **Disability**
Example in case-law	ORIGINAL PROVISION 1) *Wells*: Duty to Member State to carry out an EIA	ORIGINAL PROVISION 1) *van Gend en Loos*: standstill obligation to Member States in EEC Treaty 3) *Becker*: duty to Member State in directive to exempt certain transactions	ORIGINAL PROVISION 1) *Kraaijeveld*: Member State may have to carry out an EIA (not imposed directly by Community law)	ORIGINAL PROVISION 1) *CIA Security*: Non-notified technical provisions cannot be used to ban sales of imported items

Legend: names in italics refer to cases discussed in the text.

An appropriate starting point for analysis of direct effect is a right as a Hohfeldian '*liberty*' of an individual [2].

The relationship *Liberty [2] – No-Right [6]* can be explained as the possibility to object to application of an obligation based on national law. The classic example is *van Gend en Loos* (ECJ, 1963):[63] in Hohfeldian terms, the applicant invoked a 'liberty' that it was not obliged to pay the higher customs duty required by national law. That 'liberty' was not written down in the Treaty as a 'liberty' for the individual, but as a 'no-right' to Member States ('The Member States shall not'). Therefore, to explain the nature of the right in *van Gend en Loos*, it could be said that the Hohfeldian 'no-right' of the Member State was transformed (or corresponded to) a Hohfeldian 'liberty' of an individual. Another example is *Becker* (ECJ 1982).[64] Ms Becker was invoking an exception based on a Community VAT directive that had not yet been implemented in Germany. The directive did not provide that 'individuals shall not pay VAT on'. Rather, it provided what transactions were to be exempt from VAT. Thus, the directive imposed a 'no-right' on Member States, which resulted in a 'liberty' to Ms Becker.

The relationship *Right [1] – Duty [5]* can be somewhat simpler. There are innumerable EU law provisions that directly confer a classic 'right' on somebody: these might be a right to an agricultural subsidy, or a right to access to documents held by EU institutions. This is also often a way in which fundamental rights are formulated.[65] The more complicated part is now transformation of a 'duty' of a Member

[63] ECJ *Van Gend en Loos* (n 38) 12.
[64] ECJ Case 8/81 *Becker* [1982] ECR 53 [33].
[65] For example, according to Art 2(1) of the Charter, everybody has the right to life.

State to a 'right' of an individual. On the basis of the Environmental Impact Assessment Directive ('EIA Directive') in *Wells*, it was clear that the Member State had a duty to carry out an assessment.[66] But when the Directive was not correctly transposed into national law, the Court construed the individual 'right' from the Member State 'duty'. A bare reading of the Directive mentions nothing about individual rights at all.

The relationship *Power [3] – Liability [7]* is then slightly more complex. An example could be found again from the EIA Directive, now in the case of *Kraaijeveld*.[67] The EIA was compulsory in cases listed in Annex I of the Directive, while it was optional and left to the discretion of the national legislator in cases referred to in Annex II. According to the choices of the Dutch legislator, certain dykes were left out of the scope of the EIA. The question now was whether this legislative choice could be contested on the basis of another provision of the Directive which limited the scope of discretion of Member States. The Court replied in the affirmative. Thus an individual who could not claim a 'right' on the basis of the Directive was yet able to invoke the question of legality. 'Liability' of the Member State corresponded to a 'power' for control of legality for individuals.

The relationship *Immunity [4] – Disability [8]* is the fourth aspect. The way how rights are created 'through the back door' can be exemplified by *CIA Security International* (ECJ 1996).[68] Directive 83/189[69] requires that Member States must notify new technical standards to the Commission. The Court ruled that absence of notification made a new Belgian technical standard inapplicable (unopposable) towards private parties. There was again no mention in the Directive 83/189 of any rights that it was to confer on individuals. These had to be construed from Member State obligations.

In conclusion, it seems that the Hohfeldian system could indeed be used for a more analytical assessment of the different types of rights involved in the damages context, too. The problem, however, would seem to be that this Hohfeldian framework, although it seems to bring some added value as regards EU law in Member

[66] ECJ Case C-201/02 *Wells* [2004] ECR I-723; *cf* A Maunu, 'Direktiivin yksityisiä velvoittava vaikutus täsmentyy yhteisöjen tuomioistuimen Delena Wells –ratkaisussa (EYTI C-201/02)' (2004) *Defensor Legis* 302.

[67] See ECJ Case C-72/95 *Kraaijeveld and others* [1996] ECR I-5403, summary [3] according to which 'Article 4(2) of Directive 85/337 on the assessment of the effects of certain public and private projects on the environment provides that projects of the classes listed in Annex II are to be made subject to an assessment where Member States consider that their characteristics so require and that to that end Member States may specify the types of projects subject to an assessment or establish the criteria and/or thresholds necessary to determine which projects are to be subject to an assessment. That provision, together with point 10(e) of Annex II, which refers to canalization and flood-relief works, must be interpreted as meaning that where, in connection with dyke work which requires an assessment, a Member State establishes those criteria or thresholds in such a way that, in practice, all such projects are exempted in advance from the requirement of an impact assessment, it exceeds the limits of its discretion under Arts 2(1) and 4(2) of the directive unless all the projects excluded could, when viewed as a whole, be regarded as unlikely to have significant effects on the environment'.

[68] ECJ Case C-194/94 *CIA Security International v Signalson and Securitel* [1996] ECR I-2201.

[69] Council Directive 83/189/EEC of 28 March 1983 laying down a procedure for the provision of information in the field of technical standards and regulations [1983] OJ L109/8.

States, does not do so for liability of the EU, which is mainly based on breach of principles and in which the various obligations imposed operate within the EU legal system only.

C. Implementing Hohfeld in *Francovich*: Rights Invoked in Member State Liability Cases in a Hohfeldian Setting

Having circumscribed a framework for analysis, we will next assess the case-law on rights in Member State liability to see how rights granted to individuals have been construed in the case-law. In a pure damages context the Court has only considered a relatively small number of EU law provisions so far. These provisions have primarily been those relating to the four freedoms and they have had a component that had to be quantifiable in monetary terms. The classification of the case-law below is based on the four Hohfeldian relations explained above and in Figure 6.1.

i. The Relationship Liberty [2] – No-Right [6]

This relationship was explained above as a possibility to object to application of an obligation based on national law. Classic examples in the damages context are Treaty provisions forbidding Member States from doing something, in particular in relation to the four freedoms. First, as regards free movement of goods, the interdiction prohibiting quantitative restrictions on imports and all measures having equivalent effect laid down now in Article 34 TFEU[70] gave the correlative liberty to economic operators, for example in *Brasserie du Pêcheur* (ECJ 1996) and *Danske Slagterier* (ECJ 2009).[71] *Idem* for Article 35 TFEU[72] as regards the interdiction prohibiting quantitative restriction on exports and all measures having equivalent effect, as explained in *Hedley Lomas* (1996).[73] The interdiction of restrictions on free movement of capital ('no-right') gave rise to a corresponding 'liberty', and thus to rights in the damages context in *Test Claimants in the FII Group Litigation* (ECJ 2006).[74]

[70] Ex-art 30 of the EC Treaty and Art 28 EC.

[71] See eg, ECJ *Brasserie du Pêcheur and Factortame* (n 13) [23]: 'In this case, it is undisputed that the Community provisions at issue, namely Art 30 of the Treaty in Case C-46/93 and Art 52 in Case C-48/93, have direct effect in the sense that they confer on individuals rights upon which they are entitled to rely directly before the national courts. Breach of such provisions may give rise to reparation'. See also ECJ *Danske Slagterier* (n 12) [22].

[72] Ex-art 34 of the EC Treaty and Art 29 EC.

[73] ECJ *Hedley Lomas* (n 14) [27]: 'As regards the first condition, as is clear from the answer given to the first question, the United Kingdom's refusal to issue an export licence to Hedley Lomas constituted a quantitative restriction on exports contrary to Article 34 of the Treaty which could not be justified under Article 36. Whilst Article 34 imposes a prohibition on Member States, it also creates rights for individuals which the national courts must protect (judgment in Case 83/78 Pigs Marketing Board v Redmond [1978] ECR 2347, paragraphs 66 and 67)'.

[74] ECJ *Test Claimants in the FII Group Litigation* (n 21) [211]: 'In the main proceedings, the first condition is plainly satisfied as regards Articles 43 EC and 56 EC. Those provisions confer rights on individuals (see, respectively, Brasserie du Pêcheur and Factortame, paragraphs 23 and 54, and Joined

The provisions of the Sixth VAT Directive 77/388[75] were considered in *Stockholm Lindöpark* (ECJ 2001).[76] The ECJ noted that the provisions of the Directive precluded national legislation from allowing a general exemption from value added tax for certain services. Therefore the applicant in the main proceedings could invoke the 'duty' of the Member State to grant it VAT status ('claim-right'), and in its absence, a right qualifying for damages purposes was founded.

As regards the Machines Directive 98/34,[77] the Court found in *AGM* (ECJ 2007)[78] that Article 4(1) of the Directive is intended to confer on individuals operating in the market rights which they can enforce against Member States. Article 4(1) stipulates that 'Member States shall not prohibit, restrict or impede the placing on the market and putting into service in their territory of machinery and safety components which comply with this Directive'. Therefore, the position of the Member States was to be qualified as a 'no-right', corresponding to a 'liberty' for economic operators.

For the Community Human Medicines Code 2001/83,[79] the Court ruled in *Synthon* (ECJ 2008)[80] that its Article 28 (now Article 34 TFEU) precluded a Member State to which an application is made for mutual recognition of a marketing authorisation of a medicinal product for human use granted by another Member State [under the abridged procedure provided for in Article 10(1)(a)(iii) of that directive] from refusing that application on the ground that the medicinal product in question is not essentially similar to the reference product.

ii. The Relationship Right [1] – Duty [5]

This is the situation of pure and direct EU law-based rights, to be found in many EU law provisions that directly confer a classic right on somebody. Freedom of establishment is couched in these terms in the Treaty. In fact, in Hohfeldian terms, Article 52 of the EC Treaty[81] is a good example. In its original text, it lays down a 'duty' for Member States to abolish restrictions on freedom of establishment in the course of a transitional period (paragraph 1) and at the same time sets out the contents of 'claim-rights' of nationals in the other Member States (paragraph 2).[82] This

Cases C-163/94, C-165/94 and C-250/94 Sanz de Lera and Others [1995] ECR I 4821, paragraph 43)'. Note that Art 43 EC, as applicable after the amendment (Art 49 TFEU), also belongs here; see also ECJ *Test Claimants in the CFC and Dividend Group Litigation* (n 21) [120].

[75] Sixth Council Directive (77/388/EEC) of 17 May 1977 on the harmonisation of the laws of the Member States relating to turnover taxes – Common system of value added tax: uniform basis of assessment [1977] OJ L145/1.

[76] ECJ *Stockholm Lindöpark* (n 15).

[77] (n 30).

[78] ECJ *AGM-COS.MET* (n 18).

[79] Directive 2001/83/EC of the European Parliament and of the Council of 6 November 2001 on the Community code relating to medicinal products for human use [2001] OJ L311/67.

[80] ECJ *Synthon* (n 14).

[81] Later Art 43 EC and now Art 49 TFEU.

[82] What makes this article even more interesting is that in its current form in Art 49 TFEU, after the amendment of the wording, it has in fact moved to the 'liberty'–'no-right' category, as the 'duty' of the Member States to abolish the restrictions has been modified to a 'no-right' through interdiction.

provision has been addressed in *Factortame* (ECJ 1996),[83] in *Haim* (ECJ 2000)[84] and in *N* (ECJ 2006).[85]

As to secondary legislation, an example of Member State duties can be found in the Consumer Credit Directive 87/102[86] analysed in *El Corte Ingles* (ECJ 1996).[87] The Court was called on to interpret Article 11(2) of the Directive. That article foresees the conditions under which a Member State must ensure that the consumer can pursue remedies against the grantor of credit.[88] That duty for Member States contained a corresponding 'claim-right' for consumers in the case of non-transposition.

In the same vein, 'duties' for Member States and corresponding 'claim-rights' were established in the Wage Guarantee Directive 80/987.[89] This directive in particular has given rise to considerable litigation in the damages context; see for example the cases of *Francovich* (ECJ 1991); *Wagner Miret* (ECJ 1993); *Bonifaci and Berto*

[83] ECJ *Brasserie du Pêcheur and Factortame* (n 13) [23]: 'In this case, it is undisputed that the Community provisions at issue, namely Article 30 of the Treaty in Case C-46/93 and Article 52 in Case C-48/93, have direct effect in the sense that they confer on individuals rights upon which they are entitled to rely directly before the national courts. Breach of such provisions may give rise to reparation'.

[84] ECJ *Haim* (n 23) [15]: 'The Court added, however, that it is not permissible under Article 52 of the Treaty for the competent authorities of a Member State to refuse appointment as a dental practitioner under a social security scheme to a national of another Member State'.

[85] ECJ *N* (n 22) [35]: 'In this case, analogously with what the Court has already found in relation to a similar system (de Lasteyrie du Saillant, paragraph 46), a taxpayer wishing to transfer his residence outside Netherlands territory, in exercise of the rights guaranteed to him by Article 43 EC, was subjected at the time of the facts to disadvantageous treatment in comparison with a person who maintained his residence in the Netherlands. That taxpayer became liable, simply by reason of such a transfer, to tax on income which had not yet been realised and which he therefore did not have, whereas, if he had remained in the Netherlands, increases in value would have become taxable only when, and to the extent that, they were actually realised. That difference in treatment was likely to discourage the person concerned from transferring his residence outside the Netherlands'.

[86] Council Directive 87/102/EEC of 22 December 1986 for the approximation of the laws, regulations and administrative provisions of the Member States concerning consumer credit [1987] OJ L42/48.

[87] ECJ Case C-192/94 *El Corte Inglés v Blázquez Rivero* [1996] ECR I-1281.

[88] Para 6 of the judgment cites the directive as follows: 'The national court took the view that Article 11(2) of the directive enabled the consumer to bring an action against the finance company. Article 11(2) provides as follows:

> "Where:
>
> (a) in order to buy goods or obtain services the consumer enters into a credit agreement with a person other than the supplier of them; and
> (b) the grantor of the credit and the supplier of the goods or services have a pre-existing agreement whereunder credit is made available exclusively by that grantor of credit to customers of that supplier for the acquisition of goods or services from that supplier; and
> (c) the consumer referred to in subparagraph (a) obtains his credit pursuant to that pre-existing agreement; and
> (d) the goods or services covered by the credit agreement are not supplied, or are supplied only in part, or are not in conformity with the contract for supply of them; and
> (e) the consumer has pursued his remedies against the supplier but has failed to obtain the satisfaction to which he is entitled,

the consumer shall have the right to pursue remedies against the grantor of credit. Member States shall determine to what extent and under what conditions these remedies shall be exercisable"'.

[89] Council Directive 80/987/EEC of 20 October 1980 on the approximation of the laws of the Member States relating to the protection of employees in the event of the insolvency of the employer [1980] OJ L283/23.

(ECJ 1997); *Palmisani* (ECJ 1997); *Maso* (ECJ 1997); *Mau* (ECJ 2003) and *Robins* (ECJ 2007).[90]

In the field of consumer policy, the Court considered the provisions of the Home Contracts Directive 85/577[91] in *Faccini Dori* (ECJ 1994).[92] It found that the duties of Member States were clearly laid down in the Directive, in which the provisions of Article 1(1) and (2) and Article 5 were unconditional and sufficiently precise as regards determination of the persons for whose benefit they were adopted and the minimum period within which notice of cancellation must be given. Even if Articles 4 and 5 of the Directive allowed Member States some latitude regarding consumer protection in certain cases, that latitude did not make it impossible to determine minimum rights which must on any view be provided to consumers. The 'duty' of the Member States was thus defined, and a corresponding 'right' was created.

The Package Travel Directive 90/314[93] was discussed in *Dillenkofer* (ECJ 1996) and *Rechberger* (ECJ 1999).[94] In both cases the Court considered the role of Article 7 of the Directive concerning guarantees. In *Dillenkofer* the Court ruled that the result prescribed by Article 7 of the Directive, which provides that the organiser and/or retailer party to the contract is to provide sufficient evidence of security for the refund of money paid over by the consumer and for his repatriation, entails the grant to package travellers of rights guaranteeing a refund of money paid over and their repatriation in the event of the organiser's insolvency and that the content of those rights is sufficiently identifiable. Moreover, in *Rechberger* the Court found that the limitations to this protection were manifestly incompatible with the provisions of the Directive.

iii. The Relationship Power [3] – Liability [7]

As noted above, this relationship is slightly more complex. An example was cited above from the EIA Directive in *Kraaijeveld.*[95]

It seems that in the damages context this relation can be exemplified by *Köbler* (ECJ 2003).[96] A Member State (in this case a national court) had competence to do something (to ask for a preliminary ruling), but it was an obligation subject to interpretation in the light of the particular circumstances of the case. However, if that liability was breached, it entailed a 'power' to individuals. Thus the 'liability'

[90] ECJ *Francovich and Bonifaci* (n 4); ECJ Case C-334/92 *Wagner Miret v Fondo de garantía salarial* [1993] ECR I-6911; ECJ *Bonifaci and others and Berto and others v INPS* (n 23); ECJ *Palmisani v INPS,* (n 23); ECJ *Maso and others v INPS and Repubblica italiana* (n 23); ECJ *Robins and others* (n 23); ECJ *Mau* (n 23).

[91] Council Directive 85/577/EEC of 20 December 1985 to protect the consumer in respect of contracts negotiated away from business premises [1985] OJ L372/31.

[92] ECJ Case C-91/92 *Faccini Dori v Recreb* [1994] ECR I-3325.

[93] Council Directive 90/314/EEC of 13 June 1990 on package travel, package holidays and package tours [1990] OJ L158/59.

[94] ECJ *Dillenkofer and others v Bundesrepublik Deutschland* (n 23) and ECJ *Rechberger and others* (n 23).

[95] See ECJ *Kraaijeveld and others* (n 67), summary [3].

[96] ECJ *Köbler* (n 10).

under Article 234 EC (now Article 267 TFEU) to ask for and maintain a request for a preliminary ruling, when breached, led to a 'power' enhancing applicability of Article 48 of the EC Treaty (now Article 45 TFEU). In the judgment the Court addresses Hohfeldian 'liability' as follows (emphasis added):

> 117 Accordingly, since the Verwaltungsgerichtshof amended its interpretation of national law by classifying the measure provided for in Article 50a of the GG as a loyalty bonus after the judgment in *Schöning-Kougebetopoulou* had been sent to it and since the Court had not yet had the opportunity of expressing a view on whether the obstacle to freedom of movement for workers constituted by a loyalty bonus could be justified, the Verwaltungsgerichtshof ought to have maintained its request for a preliminary ruling.
>
> 118 That court was not entitled to take the view that resolution of the point of law at issue was clear from the settled case-law of the Court or left no room for any reasonable doubt (Case 283/81 *CILFIT and Others* [1982] ECR 3415, paragraphs 14 and 16). *It was therefore obliged under the third paragraph of Article 177 of the Treaty to maintain its request for a preliminary ruling.*
>
> 119 Moreover, as is clear from the reply to the third question, a measure such as the special length-of-service increment provided for in Article 50a of the GG, even if it may be classified as a loyalty bonus, entails an obstacle to freedom of movement for workers contrary to Community law. *Accordingly, the Verwaltungsgerichtshof infringed Community law by its judgment of 24 June 1998.*

Accordingly, the corresponding 'power' of the individual was described in the following terms:

> 102 The rules of Community law whose infringement is at issue in the main proceedings are, as is apparent from the reply to the third question, Articles 48 of the Treaty and 7(1) of Regulation No 1612/68. Those provisions specify the consequences resulting from the fundamental principle of freedom of movement for workers within the Community by way of the prohibition of any discrimination based on nationality as between the workers of the Member States, in particular as to remuneration.

iv. The Relationship Immunity [4] – Disability [8]

The fourth relationship where rights are created 'through the back door' was exemplified above by *CIA Security International* (ECJ 1996).[97] However, in the damages context it is difficult to find a corresponding situation where damages liability has been considered.

D. Other Sources

i. External Relations

As regards agreements to which the European Union [Community] is a party, it should be recalled that the Court has rarely accepted them as a source for indi-

[97] ECJ *CIA Security International v Signalson and Securitel* (n 68).

vidual rights. For the WTO agreement, this was confirmed in *Portugal v Council* (ECJ 1999).[98]

In *Kondova* (ECJ 2001) the claimant invoked an international agreement (Association Agreement between the Communities and Bulgaria) binding on the Community as a source of individual rights in the damages context.[99] The basic question was whether Article 45 of the Association Agreement confers rights of establishment upon a Bulgarian national who, under national immigration law, is treated as having entered the territory of that Member State illegally. However, the Court put the question of interpretation in a wider context. It found that the right of establishment was not absolute, but could be subjected to conditions.[100] Therefore, the right in question had not been infringed, and the Court did not have to address the damages question. Even if there appear to be no further preliminary rulings with underlying damages actions, there are cases where rights are invoked in a context where a monetary remedy may become applicable.[101]

ii. Additional Legal Sources

As regards Member State liability, the role of principles or fundamental rights as a source of infringed rights seems so far very limited. However, in *Eman and Sevinger* (ECJ 2006),[102] which concerned the right to vote in the elections of the European Parliament, the Court found that the principle of equal treatment had been infringed. It noted first that there is nothing in Community law which precludes Member States from defining the conditions of the right to vote and to stand as a candidate in elections to the European Parliament by reference to the criterion of residence in the territory in which the elections are held. However, it underlined at the same time that the principle of equal treatment prevents any such criteria from being chosen which would result in different treatment of nationals who are in comparable situations, unless that difference in treatment can be objectively justified.

In fact, it is rather difficult to find ECJ case-law regarding damages actions for breach of principles granting rights to individuals. It seems that an interesting issue is creation of legally protected positions which result from the joint effects of several legal instruments or norms. In such cases, principles can play an important complementary role.

[98] ECJ Case C-149/96 *Portugal v Council* [1999] ECR I-8395 [47]: 'It follows from all those considerations that, having regard to their nature and structure, the WTO agreements are not in principle among the rules in the light of which the Court is to review the legality of measures adopted by the Community institutions'.

[99] ECJ Case C-235/99 *Kondova* [2001] ECR I-6427.

[100] Para 91: 'The right of establishment, as defined by Article 45(1) of the Association Agreement, means that rights of entry and residence, as corollaries of the right of establishment, are conferred on Bulgarian nationals wishing to pursue activities of an industrial or commercial character, activities of craftsmen, or activities of the professions in a Member State. However, it follows from Article 59(1) of that Agreement that those rights of entry and residence are not absolute privileges, inasmuch as their exercise may, in some circumstances, be limited by the rules of the host Member State governing the entry, stay and establishment of Bulgarian nationals'.

[101] See eg, ECJ Case C-242/06 *Sahin* [2009] ECR I-8465.

[102] ECJ *Eman and Sevinger* (n 23) [61].

iii. No Rights Granted to Individuals

An equally important question is *for whom* are rights intended by the relevant Community rule of law. For example, Directive 85/577 on door-to-door sales seeks to protect only the consumer, but not an undertaking as a buyer.[103] The importance of this criterion is underlined by *Francovich No 2* (ECJ 1995)[104] where it turned out that the person after whom the budding new principle was named was not in fact himself protected by Wage Guarantee Directive 80/987.

E. Specific Issues

Arguably, indications of a more refined approach to the question of granting rights can be found in some more recent cases, namely *Paul* (ECJ 2004)[105] and *Danske Slagterier* (ECJ 2009).[106] In these cases, the questions put by national courts to the ECJ have been more refined and they have enabled the Court to make a more detailed assessment of the situation than just to declare that a provision has already had, or will from now on have, direct effect. The Court has been induced to delve more explicitly into the rights discussion and that issue has been made more explicit by the preceding opinions of the Advocates General.

In some ways, the judgment in *Paul* (ECJ 2004) goes to the heart of conferral of rights. It also provides a very good example of how procedural settings can influence the outcome.

The Community rules at issue were Directive 94/19 on deposit-guarantee schemes and certain other banking directives.[107] The Directive required Member States to set up deposit guarantee schemes and required that any deposits should be guaranteed to up to €20000 for each depositor. The Directive was not transposed in time in Germany. A German bank went bankrupt and its clients sued the state in damages. The national court had already awarded damages up to €20000 in view of the breach of Community law by the Member State. However, for any damages beyond €20000 the action had been dismissed and the main issue then became whether that Directive or any other directive, taken alone or together, granted depositors rights that had required the banking supervisory authorities to take measures. The existence of such an obligation would have enabled the appli-

[103] [1985] OJ L372/31.

[104] ECJ Case C-479/93 *Francovich v Italy (No 2)* [1995] ECR I-3843.

[105] ECJ *Paul and others* (n 23).

[106] ECJ *Danske Slagterier* (n 12).

[107] See Directive 94/19/EC of the European Parliament and of the Council of 30 May 1994 on deposit-guarantee schemes [1994] OJ L135/5 and provisions of First Council Directive 77/780/EEC of 12 December 1977 on the coordination of the laws, regulations and administrative provisions relating to the taking up and pursuit of the business of credit institutions [1977] L322/30, of Council Directive 89/299/EEC of 17 April 1989 on the own funds of credit institutions [1989] OJ L124/16 and of Second Council Directive 89/646/EEC of 15 December 1989 on the coordination of laws, regulations and administrative provisions relating to the taking up and pursuit of the business of credit institutions and amending Directive 77/780 [1989] L386/1.

cants to receive further compensation for damages. Advocate General Stix-Hackl found that none of the banking directives conferred such rights on individuals, and the Court followed that finding in substance. It appears that it was in *Paul* that the Court was confronted with a case where a rule of law invoked in the damages liability context did not confer rights on (any) individuals. This was one of the first times where the damages liability test faltered on this condition. The ruling has been widely criticised in doctrine.[108]

The potential effects of *Paul* may be illustrated by another damages case, namely *AGM* (ECJ 2007).[109] It is recalled that in this case the ECJ ruled that the purpose of Article 4 of the Machines Directive 98/37[110] was to protect producers. A different scenario can be imagined. A product marked with the CE mark is involved in an accident and there is some damage, as the protection required by the Directive had not been put in place. The person suffering the damage could sue the state in damages and claim that the state should have taken appropriate action to withdraw the CE marking which had erroneously shown that the product was in conformity with the Directive. In *AGM*, the Court was careful to underline the *duty of Member States* to respect the procedures laid down in the Directive. Could the person now claim that the applicable provisions of the Directive confer on him rights directly, as the applicant in *AGM* did? From the outset, this would seem plausible. However, *Paul* may point to a different result. In *Paul* the Court analysed the relevant directives and concluded that their primary purpose is only minimum harmonisation for a single licensing system for the banking sector, and that moreover they did not *expressly* grant any rights to individual depositors:[111]

> the harmonisation under Directives 77/780, 89/299 and 89/646, since it is based on Article 57(2) of the Treaty, is restricted to that which is essential, necessary and sufficient to secure the mutual recognition of authorisations and of prudential supervision systems, making possible the granting of a single licence recognised throughout the Community and the application of the principle of home Member State prudential supervision.

Accordingly, could it still be argued that Machines Directive 98/37 is primarily only aimed at granting rights to producers, not for the safety of consumers, as there is no express provision granting any right to safe products to the general public?

A rather different setting is offered by *Danske Slagterier* (ECJ 2009) which was a preliminary reference submitted by the German Federal Court of Justice (BGH).[112] The case had been brought by an industry association of Danish slaughterhouses and pig farmers. They claimed that over many years Germany had wrongly

[108] See eg, J-H Binder, 'Cutting Back State Liability for Regulatory Negligence: The ECJ's decision in *Paul and Others v. Germany*' (2005) *Banking and Insurance Law Review* 133–49 and M Tison, 'Do not attack the watchdog! Banking supervisor's liability after *Peter Paul*' (2005) *Common Market Law Review* 639–75.

[109] ECJ *AGM-COS.MET* (n 18).

[110] (n 30).

[111] ECJ *Paul and others* (n 23) [42].

[112] ECJ *Danske Slagterier* (n 12).

applied the relevant Treaty provisions and legislation for imports of pig meat from Denmark, which had then caused the applicants damage by considerably reducing their possibilities to sell pig meat in Germany.

The German government had appealed this ruling, and the appeal court posed a number of questions to the ECJ. One of the questions was whether there in fact was a rule of law granting rights to individuals.[113] The applicants thought so and referred to the directives in question and the Treaty provisions; their views were in essence shared by the Commission and the Czech government. In contrast, several governments argued that no rights were granted.

The views of Advocate General Trstenjak and the Court diverged on this point. The Advocate General found that no rights were granted, while the Court said that rights were granted by the relevant instruments. The Advocate General cited earlier case-law on directives and stated the following (emphasis added):[114]

> The directives interpreted by the Court in the abovementioned judgments [references omitted] are characterised by the fact that they *confer either private law rights on employees or consumers in the form of a right to compensation* **or** *public law rights on individuals vis-à-vis the authorities to a specific benefit defined in the directive.* There, as the Court correctly held, both the persons to whom the right is granted and the content of the right may be identified with sufficient clarity from the wording and the spirit and purpose of the provisions concerned. However, as follows from an interpretation of the relevant Community provisions, comparable features are absent in the present case.

The Advocate General thus concluded that the provisions in question do not place the producers and distributors of pig meat in a position that could give rise to a claim seeking to establish state liability.

However, the Court took a different approach.[115] The Court recalled first that Article 28 EC (now Article 34 TFEU) has direct effect in the sense that it confers on individuals rights upon which they are entitled to rely directly before the national courts and that breach of that provision may give rise to reparation. It then analysed the contents of the directives and found that they were in fact implementing and rendering more precise the contents of the Treaty article. In addition, as the two directives had harmonised the field exhaustively, the only acceptable grounds to justify obstacles to free movement were to be founded on the directive. Therefore the Court concluded that individuals who have been harmed by incorrect transposition and application of Directives 64/433 and 89/662 may rely on the right to free movement of goods in order to be able to render the state liable for breach of Community law.

The diverging views of the Advocate General and the Court make interesting reading. It seems that this case may illustrate a trend where analysis as to the grant

[113] ie whether Art 5(1)(o) and Art 6(1)(b)(iii) of Directive 64/433 as re-enacted by Council Directive 91/497, in conjunction with Art 5(1), Art 7 and Art 8 of Council Directive 89/662, grant producers and distributors of pigmeat 'subjective' rights [or individual rights].

[114] ECJ Case C-445/06 *Opinion of Advocate General Trstenjak – Danske Slagterier* [2009] ECR I-2119 [64].

[115] ECJ *Danske Slagterier* (n 12) [22]–[26].

of rights is getting down to detail: assessment of the binary question whether there was direct effect or not is replaced with a more nuanced analysis.

In this context, one further case should be mentioned. It is not directly a damages case in itself, although there was an earlier damages action.[116] The issue in *Brinkmann No 2* (ECJ 2000)[117] was whether one article of the Tobacco Taxation Directive 92/80 did grant rights to individuals so as to enable them to avoid application to them of one part of the tax formula laid down in that directive. The Court replied in the negative with the following formulation (emphasis added):

> 2. Article 3(1) of Directive 92/80 on the approximation of taxes on manufactured tobacco other than cigarettes *does not confer on persons chargeable to a tax* on cigars or cigarillos, which is calculated ad valorem without being able to be below a minimum amount, *the right to rely on it before a national court in order to avoid the application to them* solely of the element of the tax formula relating to the levying of the minimum specific duty and, consequently, to have solely an ad valorem tax levied.

This position was reasoned as follows (emphasis added):

> Although taxable persons can rely on Article 3(1) of the Directive which allows Member States a certain discretion by leaving them the choice between three different tax formulae in order to avoid the application to them of a tax formula which goes beyond the discretion left to the national legislature, *that provision does not confer on them the right to rely on it before a national court in order to avoid the application to them solely of the minimum levy.* First, it is not the minimum specific duty taken separately, but the whole tax formula which goes beyond the discretion and, second, to consider that taxable persons may rely on Article 3(1) of the Directive in order to avoid solely the application of the minimum specific duty presupposes that that provision gives rise to the right for them to be taxed according to the ad valorem formula. However, that formula is only one of the options provided by the Directive, and the Directive cannot be interpreted as requiring the national court to take the place of the national legislature on which alone it is incumbent to choose the tax formula which it deems appropriate, within the framework defined in the abovementioned article.
>
> However, the national court, where it applies provisions of national law adopted either before or after a directive, *must interpret them, as far as possible, in the light of the wording and the purpose of the Directive.*

It thus seems that the Court took the view that the provision did not grant the specific right the applicants had claimed, and that in general the provision in question did not have direct effect. Despite these two factors, the national court had a duty to interpret the national provisions in conformity with the provisions of the Directive.

F. Interim Conclusion

In a nutshell, the type of provision which qualifies for an EU rule of law granting rights to individuals would seem to call for a rather wide interpretation. 'Rights'

[116] ECJ *Brinkmann Tabakfabriken v Skatteministeriet (No 1)* (n 22).

[117] ECJ Case C-365/98 *Brinkmann (No 2)* [2000] ECR I-4619, see [31], [33], [36]–[39], [41] and operative part 2.

qualifying for damages vary considerably: they can be basically any of the four types presented in the Hohfeldian setting above. The rights do not have to be 'legally enforceable'. In fact, even if the presence of direct effect may help in establishing the granting of rights, the existence of direct effect may not be sufficient to ascertain that individual rights are granted to the person in question. The finding of direct effect in the damages context can be an essential, yet not adequate finding. Thus one could claim that while the concept of granting of rights in the damages context is not quite as confusing as the concept of direct effect, it may come very close.

One side remark: have rights been evacuated from directives after *Francovich* (ECJ 1991)? It is interesting to note that since *Francovich* there has apparently been damages case-law only on two directives adopted after *Francovich* (Machines Directive and the Human Medicines Code, both of which in actual fact date from before; as the new texts are consolidated versions of the old ones).[118] In other words, since Member State damages liability was established in 1991, the Community legislator has adopted only two directives which granted direct rights to individuals and have been considered in the damages context in Community courts. It is difficult to say whether all this is just a coincidence, but it cannot be excluded that the legislator (principally the Member States) had intended to act so as not to create new secondary law instruments leading potentially to damages liability.

III. SUFFICIENTLY SERIOUS BREACH: LIABILITY OF THE MEMBER STATES AND ASSESSMENT OF SERIOUSNESS OF BREACH IN CASE-LAW

A. First Limb: Existence of a Breach of EU Rule of Law

This Section examines the issue of breach in the light of the case-law on Member State liability.[119] In the same way as for liability of the EU, for the liability of Member States the assessment of the breach consists of two limbs.

The first limb is that a breach of an EU rule of law is committed by public authorities of a Member State. Naturally, if there is *no breach*, it is not necessary to pursue the examination as regards damages.

For example, in *British Telecommunications (No 2)* (ECJ 1996),[120] the Court analysed whether transposition of the two Telecommunications Directives 90/387[121] and 92/44[122] had been done in the UK within the limits set by Community law. As this was the case, there was no breach, so that examination of damages liability was not pursued by the ECJ.

[118] ECJ *AGM-COS.MET* (n 18), concerning Machines Directive and ECJ *Synthon*, (n 14), concerning Human Medicines Code ([43]).

[119] The questions underlying this section have been discussed in ch 2, s VI above.

[120] ECJ *British Telecommunications (No 2)* (n 25).

[121] Council Directive 90/387/EEC of 28 June 1990 on the establishment of the internal market for telecommunications services through the implementation of open network provision [1990] OJ L192/1.

[122] Council Directive 92/44/EEC of 5 June 1992 on the application of open network provision to leased lines [1992] OJ L165/27.

In the same vein, in *Kondova* (ECJ 2001) the issue related to interpretation and application of the EEC–Bulgaria Association Agreement. An English court had asked questions about the proper interpretation of the agreement and the obligations it imposed on Member States. It also asked one question in relation to possible damages liability. As the ECJ concluded that, on its interpretation, there was no breach, it did not explore issues relating to damages liability.[123]

In *Schmidberger* (ECJ 2003), no breach was finally established.[124] The case before the national court arose from permission implicitly granted by the Austrian authorities to an environmental group to organise a demonstration on the Brenner motorway, the effect of which was to close completely that motorway to traffic for some 30 hours. The six questions for a preliminary ruling related to the interpretation of Articles 30, 34 and 36 of the EC Treaty read together with Article 5 of the EC Treaty.[125] The Court noted that the national authorities had wide discretion, and in view of that discretion, they were entitled to find that the legitimate objective pursued by the demonstration could not have been reached through a measure that would have restricted intra-community trade less.

A similar result was reached in one of the Test Claimants cases originating from the United Kingdom. In *Test Claimants in Class IV of the ACT Group Litigation* (ECJ 2006) the reference for a preliminary ruling concerned interpretation of certain Treaty articles on freedom of establishment and on free movement of capital.[126] The reference was made in proceedings between groups of companies and the UK Tax authorities (Commissioners of Inland Revenue) relating to refusal by the latter to grant a tax credit to non-resident companies in those groups for dividends paid to them by resident companies. The Court analysed the issues and concluded that there was no breach of Community law.[127] However, in some other Test Claimants cases, there was a breach of Community law and thus the question of liability was discussed in more detail (see below).

In *Generics* (ECJ 2009), the reference for preliminary ruling concerned the interpretation of Article 10 of the Community Human Medicines Code 2001/83 and the refusal of the national licensing authority to grant a marketing authorisation for

[123] ECJ *Kondova* (n 99).

[124] ECJ Case C-112/00 *Schmidberger* [2003] ECR I-5659 [93].

[125] Now Arts 34, 35 and 36 TFEU, and Art 4(3) TEU, respectively.

[126] ECJ *Test Claimants in Class IV of the ACT Group Litigation* (n 21). The provisions concerned were Arts 43 EC, 56 EC, 57 EC and 58 EC [now Arts 49, 63, 64 and 65 TFEU].

[127] *Test Claimants Class IV* (n 21), dispositive: '1. Articles 43 EC and 56 EC do not prevent a Member State, on a distribution of dividends by a company resident in that State, from granting companies receiving those dividends which are also resident in that State a tax credit equal to the fraction of the corporation tax paid on the distributed profits by the company making the distribution, when it does not grant such a tax credit to companies receiving such dividends which are resident in another Member State and are not subject to tax on dividends in the first State.

2. Articles 43 EC and 56 EC do not preclude a situation in which a Member State does not extend the entitlement to a tax credit provided for in a double taxation convention concluded with another Member State for companies resident in the second State which receive dividends from a company resident in the first State to companies resident in a third Member State with which it has concluded a double taxation convention which does not provide for such an entitlement for companies resident in that third State'.

the generic medicinal product containing galantamine.[128] The second question of the national court concerned precisely the assessment criteria for the seriousness of the breach. However, as the ECJ found that there was no breach, it did not reply to the second question.

It should also be noted that there is damages case-law in situations where the existence of the infringement had already been established by the national court or by the ECJ in infringement proceedings,[129] or that the compatibility of the national situation with EU law had been called into question through an interpretation of EU law given by the ECJ in a preliminary ruling. Such an example is the case of *Danske Slagterier* (ECJ 2009), where the issues before the ECJ related to more specific questions, including limitation periods.[130]

B. Second Limb: the Threshold of a 'Sufficiently Serious Breach'

The second limb is that the breach must be sufficiently serious. Even if breach of an EU law rule by a Member State has been identified, such a breach would not, in itself, fulfil the second condition. The breach must be 'sufficiently serious'; ie there must have been 'manifest and grave disregard of the limits of powers' by the Member State.[131]

The Court distinguishes between two main categories when examining whether a breach is sufficiently serious, namely whether the Member State authority enjoyed *wide or limited discretion*, as explained succinctly in *Haim* (ECJ 2000) in light of the case-law (emphasis added):[132]

> As regards, more particularly, the second of those conditions, the Court has held that a breach of Community law is sufficiently serious where a Member State, in the exercise of its legislative powers, has manifestly and gravely disregarded the limits on its powers (see *Brasserie du Pêcheur and Factortame*, paragraph 55; British Telecommunications, paragraph 42; and *Dillenkofer and Others*, paragraph 25) and that where, at the time when it committed the infringement, the Member State in question had only considerably reduced, or even no, discretion, the mere infringement of Community law may be sufficient to establish the existence of a sufficiently serious breach (see *Hedley Lomas*, paragraph 28; and *Norbrook Laboratories*, paragraph 109).

[128] ECJ *Generics (UK)* (n 25) [38] and [2001] OJ L311/67, as amended.

[129] See eg, ECJ *Transportes Urbanos y Servicios Generales* (n 10) [9]. The incompatibility of the limitations on the right to deduct VAT laid down in Spanish law were held to be incompatible with the Sixth VAT Directive in ECJ Case C-204/03 *Commission v Spain* [2005] ECR I-8389.

[130] ECJ *Danske Slagterier* (n 12).

[131] In this context, it has been noted that this expression and the expressions used in German and Italian texts only loosely correspond with the French expression 'violation suffisamment caractérisée', which suggests that the breach must be, to some degree, patent or obvious. See D Edward and W Robinson, 'Is there a Place for Private Law Principles in Community Law?' in T Heukels and A McDonnell (eds), *The Action for Damages in Community Law* (The Hague, Kluwer Law International, 1997). See also D Simon, 'The Sanction of Member States' Serious Violations of Community Law' in D O'Keeffe (ed), *Judicial Review in European Union Law. Liber Amicorum in Honour of Lord Slynn of Hadley. Volume 1* (The Hague, Kluwer Law International, 2000).

[132] ECJ *Haim* (n 23) [38] and [40].

In the same judgment the Court stated that the existence and scope of discretion are determined by reference to Community law and not by reference to national law. Therefore, the discretion that may be conferred by national law on the official or the authority responsible for the breach of Community law is not relevant in this respect.

C. Breach, but Not 'Sufficiently Serious' or 'Excusable'

There are cases where the Member State in question has breached EU law, but the breach has not been qualified as 'sufficiently serious'. For example, In *British Telecommunications* (No 1, ECJ 1996),[133] concerning proper implementation of the Public Procurement Directive (excluded sectors) 90/531/EEC[134] in the United Kingdom, the Court assessed the wording of Article 8(1) of the Directive, which contained an exclusion from the scope of the Directive.[135] It noted that the provision

> is imprecisely worded and was reasonably capable of bearing, as well as the construction applied to it by the Court in this judgment, the interpretation given to it by the United Kingdom in good faith and on the basis of arguments which are not entirely devoid of substance.

The Court also mentioned that the interpretation was not manifestly contrary to the wording of the Directive or to the objective pursued, and that the same interpretation was shared by other Member States. There was furthermore no case-law to guide the Member States, while the Court also attached some importance to the fact that the Commission had not taken up this issue. In view of all these elements, the transposition of Article 8(1) of the Directive in the UK was not correct as such, but it did not amount to sufficiently serious breach.

In *Denkavit* (ECJ 1996),[136] with respect to implementation of the Parents/Subsidiaries Taxation Directive 90/435/EEC[137] in Germany, the issue was whether incorrect transposition of the Directive would give parent companies a right to compensation for loss of interest incurred through postponement of distribution of a subsidiary's profits until completion of the minimum holding period laid down by Article 3(2) of the Directive. The Court pointed out that the German government's interpretation of the rule in question[138] had been adopted by almost all the

[133] ECJ Case C-392/93 *British Telecommunications (No 1)* [1996] ECR I-1631.

[134] Council Directive 90/531/EEC of 17 September 1990 on the procurement procedures of entities operating in the water, energy, transport and telecommunications sectors [1990] OJ L297/1.

[135] Art 8(1) reads as follows: '1. This directive shall not apply to contracts which contracting entities ... award for purchases intended exclusively to enable them to provide one or more telecommunications services where other entities are free to offer the same services in the same geographical area and under substantially the same conditions'.

[136] ECJ *Denkavit Internationaal and others v Bundesamt für Finanzen* (n 22) [41], [51], [52] and [53].

[137] Council Directive 90/435/EEC of 23 July 1990 on the common system of taxation applicable in the case of parent companies and subsidiaries of different Member States [1990] OJ L225/6.

[138] ie the condition that the holding period must have been completed by the time when the tax advantage is granted.

other Member States which exercised the option to derogate. Member States had discussed the matter within the Council, after which they had adopted this view. The Court noted two further issues, namely that Article 1(2) of the Directive refers expressly to prevention of abuse and that, as this was the first case to concern the Directive, there was no case-law from the Court to provide any indication as to how the provision at issue was to be interpreted. In these circumstances, the fact that a Member State took the view that it was entitled to require that the minimum holding period should have been completed at the time when profits are distributed could not be regarded as a sufficiently serious breach.

Robins (ECJ 2007)[139] concerned, once again, the Wage Guarantee Directive 80/987/EEC.[140] The reference by an English court was made in the course of proceedings between, on the one hand, Ms Robins and 835 other members of two private occupational pension schemes and, on the other hand, the Secretary of State for Work and Pensions (responsible for employment and pension matters in the UK), regarding reduction of their entitlement to old-age benefits following the insolvency of their employer. The issue was whether Article 8 of the Directive[141] was correctly transposed into national law as regards supplementary company or inter-company pension schemes with respect to old-age benefits and protection of rights conferring immediate entitlement.

The Court recalled that the first thing the national court would have to take into account here was the clarity and precision of Article 8 of the Directive with regard to the level of protection required. It noted that during the preliminary rulings procedure none of the parties (the parties to the main proceedings, the Member States submitting observations, or the Commission) had been able to suggest with precision the minimum degree of protection that in their view is required by the Directive, if it should be considered that the latter does not impose a full guarantee. Earlier in the judgment the Court had already ruled that neither Article 8 of the Directive nor any other provision therein contained anything that makes it possible to establish with any precision the minimum level required in order to protect entitlement to benefits.

The Court pointed out further that the national court could also take into consideration a Commission report concerning transposition of the Directive, in which the Commission had concluded, albeit with careful wording, that the rules adopted by the United Kingdom appeared to meet the requirements of Article 8. The Court concurred with the Advocate General in suggesting that this assessment may have reinforced the view of the Member State concerned with regard to transposition of the Directive into domestic law.

[139] ECJ *Robins and others* (n 23).

[140] [1980] OJ L283/23.

[141] According to Art 8 of Council Directive 80/987/EEC, 'Member States shall ensure that the necessary measures are taken to protect the interests of employees and of persons having already left the employer's undertaking or business at the date of the onset of the employer's insolvency in respect of rights conferring on them immediate or prospective entitlement to old-age benefits, including survivors' benefits, under supplementary company or inter-company pension schemes outside the national statutory social security schemes'.

Having explained all these elements, the Court recalled the classic formula that *if* Article 8 of the Directive has not been properly transposed into domestic law (which was thus for the national court to assess), the liability of the Member State concerned is contingent on a finding of manifest and grave disregard by that state of the limits set on its discretion. The ECJ here left the final analysis to the national court, but gave the national court rather clear indications pointing to the direction that if there was a breach, it would not at least be of manifest character.

D. Wide Discretion of National Legislator or Administrative Authority

The first category to be analysed are cases where the Member State in question has had wide discretion, but yet exceeded the limits thereof. In this section the situation will be analysed in respect of the exercise of legislative/administrative powers. *Locus classicus* can be found in *Brasserie du Pêcheur and Factortame* (ECJ 1996), where the Court first established that both the German legislator (in *Brasserie*) and the UK legislator (in *Factortame*) had wide discretion.[142] The ECJ then analysed whether the German legislature exceeded the limits of wide discretion (emphasis added):

> 59 In Case C-46/93 a distinction should be drawn between the question of the German legislature's having maintained in force provisions of the Biersteuergesetz concerning the purity of beer prohibiting the marketing under the designation 'Bier' of beers imported from other Member States which were lawfully produced in conformity with different rules, and the question of the retention of the provisions of that same law prohibiting the import of beers containing additives. As regards the provisions of the German legislation relating to the designation of the product marketed, *it would be difficult to regard the breach of Article 30 by that legislation as an excusable error,* since the incompatibility of such rules with Article 30 was manifest in the light of earlier decisions of the Court, in particular Case 120/78 Rewe-Zentral [1979] ECR 649 ('Cassis de Dijon') and Case 193/80 Commission v Italy [1981] ECR 3019 ('vinegar'). In contrast, having regard to the relevant case-law, the criteria available to the national legislature to determine whether the prohibition of the use of additives was contrary to Community law were significantly less conclusive until the Court's judgement of 12 March 1987 in Commission v. Germany, cited above, in which the Court held that prohibition to be incompatible with Article 30.

In the same judgment, as regards the reference in *Factortame* (ECJ 1996), the Court analysed the situation in the United Kingdom. It established that the direction was wide, and then proceeded to analyse whether the limits of that discretion had been breached as follows (emphasis added):

> 61 The decision of the United Kingdom legislature to introduce in the Merchant Shipping Act 1988 provisions relating to the *conditions for the registration of fishing vessels* has to be assessed differently in the case of the provisions making registration subject to a nationality condition, which constitute *direct discrimination manifestly contrary to Community law,* and in the case of the provisions laying down residence and domicile conditions for vessel owners and operators.

[142] ECJ *Brasserie du Pêcheur and Factortame* (n 13) [48] and [49].

> 62 The latter conditions are *prima facie incompatible* with Article 52 of the Treaty in particular, but the United Kingdom sought to justify them in terms of the objectives of the common fisheries policy. In the judgment in Factortame II, cited above, the Court rejected that justification.
>
> 63 In order to determine whether the breach of Article 52 thus committed by the United Kingdom was sufficiently serious, *the national court might take into account*, inter alia, the legal disputes relating to particular features of the common fisheries policy, the attitude of the Commission, which made its position known to the United Kingdom in good time, and the assessments as to the state of certainty of Community law made by the national courts in the interim proceedings brought by individuals affected by the Merchant Shipping Act.
>
> 64 Lastly, consideration should be given to the assertion made by Rawlings (Trawling) Ltd, the 37th claimant in Case C-48/93, that the *United Kingdom failed to adopt immediately the measures needed to comply with the Order of the President of the Court* of 10 October 1989 in Commission v United Kingdom, cited above, and that this needlessly increased the loss it sustained. If this allegation – which was certainly contested by the United Kingdom at the hearing – should prove correct, it should be regarded by the national court as constituting in itself a manifest and, therefore, sufficiently serious breach of Community law.

Thus, in *Brasserie du Pêcheur and Factortame*, the guidance provided by the Court to the two national courts as to interpretation of the condition relating to breach is very detailed. Yet there seem to be no clear-cut conditions under which one could simply conclude that the Member State in question has breached its *wide margin* of discretion. The analysis in the cases cited above shows that the Court uses – and encourages national courts to use – a global approach to analyse all the facts of the case. These cases also show that in order to qualify for sufficiently serious breach, a certain degree of obviousness must be present in the breach.

E. Narrow Discretion of National Administrative Authority or National Legislator

i. Narrow Discretion of National Administrative Authority

The second category of cases consists of situations where at the time when it committed the infringement, the Member State had only considerably reduced, or even no, discretion. In these cases, mere infringement of EU law may be sufficient.

First, in so far as the *administrative authorities* of the Member States are concerned, a case in point is *Hedley Lomas* (ECJ 1996).[143] Here the Court ruled that when the United Kingdom Ministry of Agriculture, Fisheries and Foods systematically refused to issue licences for the export to Spain of live animals, it acted in breach of Council Directive 74/577/EEC.[144] The discretion of the United Kingdom

[143] ECJ *Hedley Lomas* (n 14) [28], [29].

[144] Council Directive 74/577/EEC of 18 November 1974 on stunning of animals before slaughter [1974] OJ L316/10.

was limited, and it was in no position to justify its actions afterwards. The United Kingdom could not produce proof of non-compliance with the Directive by the Spanish slaughterhouse to which the animals for which the export licence was sought were destined.

Norbrook Laboratories (ECJ 1997)[145] concerned Directives 81/851 and 81/852 relating to veterinary medicinal products.[146] The competent national authority included in a marketing authorisation some conditions which went beyond the conditions imposed by the Directives, thus breaching EU law. Here, however, the Court did not itself rule on the question whether the breach was sufficiently serious, but left it for the national court to determine whether this was the case.

Another case relating to medicinal products, this time for human use, was *Synthon* (ECJ 2008).[147] Synthon is a Dutch company operating in the pharmaceutical sector. It had a dispute with the UK Licensing Authority which had refused an application for mutual recognition of a marketing authorisation of a medicinal product already licensed in one Member State. The legal issue was interpretation of Article 28 of Directive 2001/83/EC,[148] the Community Human Medicines Code, which establishes a procedure for mutual recognition of marketing authorisations for medicinal products. The Court found first that this Article

> precludes a Member State to which an application is made for mutual recognition of a marketing authorisation of a medicinal product for human use granted by another Member State under the abridged procedure . . . from refusing that application on the ground that the medicinal product in question is not essentially similar to the reference product,

even when the authorisation has been given under the abridged procedure (para 33). In this respect, the Directive 'clearly and precisely precludes any possibility for the Member State to refuse an application for mutual recognition without having first undertaken the procedure provided for in that provision'. Therefore, 'a breach of Article 28 of that directive, such as that committed by the Licensing Authority in the main proceedings, is enough to establish a sufficiently serious breach of Community law'.[149]

Now, going beyond formal administrative acts, in *AGM* (ECJ 2007), cited above, the Court assessed a breach of EU law allegedly committed by factual conduct of

[145] ECJ *Norbrook Laboratories* (n 25) [64].

[146] Council Directive 81/851/EEC of 28 September 1981 on the approximation of the laws of the Member States relating to veterinary medicinal products [1981] OJ L317/1 and Council Directive 81/852/EEC of 28 September 1981 on the approximation of the laws of the Member States relating to analytical, pharmaco-toxicological and clinical standards and protocols in respect of the testing of veterinary medicinal products [1981] OJ L317/16.

[147] ECJ *Synthon* (n 14).

[148] [2001] OJ L311/67. Art 28 lays down detailed conditions for the application of the principle according to which a marketing authorisation for a medicinal product shall be recognised by the other Member States.

[149] Paras 42 and 43. It is noteworthy that the UK and the Commission had advanced that the 'concept of an essentially similar medicinal product is complex' and had only been clarified by the Court in recent case-law; see [43]–[45].

a Member State official.[150] The Court found that the provision in question of the Machines Directive[151] gave Member States no discretion. Therefore a mere infringement was enough to establish a sufficiently serious breach.[152]

In *Larsy* (ECJ 2001)[153] the discretion available to the national administrative authority was reduced by an earlier preliminary ruling. The case concerned Council Regulation No 1408/71 on the application of social security schemes to certain persons[154] and addressed in particular the refusal by the authorities to apply an earlier ECJ ruling in a similar case. Mr Larsy, a Belgian national established in Belgium near the French border, was a self-employed nursery gardener in Belgium and France. Mr Larsy applied to Belgian social security institution Inasti[155] for a retirement pension as a self-employed worker. The provisions in question had already been interpreted in an earlier case, brought by Mr Larsy's brother, who was in a similar situation. As a result of that judgment by the ECJ the margin of discretion of the national authorities was completely reduced. As the competent national authority had no substantive choice, by refusing the application by Mr Larsy it failed to draw all the consequences from the previous *Larsy* judgment.[156]

ii. National Legislator

Even the *national legislator* may find its discretion is limited. The Austrian case of *Rechberger* (ECJ 1999)[157] concerned Package Travel Directive 90/314[158] and the consequences stemming from the fact that Article 7 of that Directive was not correctly implemented. This Article imposed a certain date from which the rights prescribed in the Directive were to be applicable. However, the Austrian legislator chose a later date. This prevented the plaintiffs, who had bought package travel in principle covered by the Directive, from obtaining reimbursement of money paid to a travel organiser who became insolvent. One of the questions of the

[150] ECJ *AGM-COS.MET* (n 18) [82].

[151] Art 4(1) of the Machines Directive 98/37 (n 30).

[152] In this case the Court gave very detailed guidance to the national Court, when it established that the breached norm gave rights to individuals ([79]), that the breach took place under narrow discretion and was thus automatically sufficiently serious ([82]) and even that there appeared to be, 'subject however to verification by the national court', a causal link between the breach of the obligation of the state and the damage suffered by the injured parties ([84]). The only thing left to the national court was to establish whether the action by the official in question was attributable to the state. For this, the Court gave further detailed guidance ([58]). The case was reportedly settled out of court in Autumn 2008, see *Helsingin Sanomat* 12.1.2009.

[153] ECJ *Larsy (No 2)* (n 23).

[154] Regulation (EEC) No 1408/71 of the Council of 14 June 1971 on the application of social security schemes to employed persons, to self-employed persons and to members of their families moving within the Community, as amended and updated by Council Regulation (EEC) No 2001/83 of 2 June 1983 (OJ L230/6), as amended by Council Regulation (EEC) No 1248/92 of 30 April 1992 [1992] OJ L136/7.

[155] 'Institut national d'assurances sociales pour travailleurs indépendants'.

[156] With respect to the misapplication by Inasti of Art 95a of Regulation No 1408/71, the Court also found an infringement, with regard to the clarity and precision of that provision (see [46]–[49] of the judgment).

[157] ECJ *Rechberger and others* (n 23).

[158] [1990] OJ L158/59.

national court was whether defective transposition of Article 7 of the Directive constitutes a sufficiently serious breach which would give rise to a right to reparation where, as is the case here, all the other provisions of the Directive have been implemented.

The Court pointed out that amongst the factors to be taken into account in assessment of seriousness of breach is the clarity and precision of the rule breached.[159] It found that there was nothing in the Directive to permit Member States to limit the application of Article 7 to trips taken on a date later than the time limit prescribed for transposition of the Directive. Therefore the Member State in question here *enjoyed no margin of discretion* as to the entry into force, in its own law, of the provisions of Article 7. That being so, the limitation of protection prescribed by Article 7 to trips with a departure date of 1 May 1995 or later was manifestly incompatible with the obligations under the Directive and thus constitutes a sufficiently serious breach of Community law. Even the fact that the Member State has implemented all the other provisions of the Directive did not alter that finding.

Another example of the limited discretion of the legislator is *Stockholm Lindöpark* (ECJ 1999),[160] relating to the incorrect transposition of the Sixth VAT Directive in Sweden upon its accession to the European Union. Lindöpark was a development company running a golf course for the exclusive use of businesses. The company golf activity run by Lindöpark was exempt from VAT and the firm was therefore not entitled to deduct input VAT incurred on goods and services used for the purposes of that activity. This legislation remained in force until 1 January 1997. The Court found first

> that the provisions of Article 17(1) and (2) of the Sixth Directive, read together with those of Articles 2, 6(1) and 13B(b), are sufficiently clear, precise and unconditional for an individual to rely on them as against a Member State before a national court.

The Court then went on to analyse the question with respect to the exercise of the legislative powers of the Member State. It pointed out first that the general exemption enacted by the Swedish legislature has no basis in the Sixth Directive and therefore became clearly incompatible with the Directive as from the date of Swedish accession to the EU. It also noted that the wording of the Directive was clear: Sweden was not in a position to make any legislative choices and had only a considerably reduced, or even no, discretion. Thus a mere infringement of Community law may be sufficient to establish the existence of a sufficiently serious breach. In addition the Court took into account that the national legislation at issue was repealed with effect from 1 January 1997, two years after Sweden's accession. For the Court this indicated that the Swedish legislature had become aware that it was incompatible with Community law. The Swedish government finally argued that if there was a breach, it would be excusable, as there was no case-law and no infringement proceedings against Sweden. The Court rejected this argumentation.

[159] ECJ *British Telecommunications (No 1)* (n 133) [42].

[160] ECJ *Stockholm Lindöpark* (n 15) [40] and [41].

Case *N* (ECJ 2006),[161] a request for a preliminary ruling from the Gerechtshof te Arnhem, was about free movement of persons and direct taxation. Following assessment of questions concerning interpretation of the relevant EU law provisions the Court further analysed the question of damages liability. It referred to *Hedley Lomas* and the passage concerning the situation where the Member State in question had only considerably reduced, or even no, discretion. It stated that the rules had been in force and directly applicable well before the facts in the main proceedings, but noted also that only its more recent case-law had brought 'final' clarity to the issue.

Eman and Sevinger (ECJ 2006) concerned a right of a fundamental nature, namely the right to vote in the European elections, granted to citizens of the Union.[162] The Court noted that Dutch legislation differentiating the treatment of the applicants, Netherlands citizens residents of Aruba,[163] was not justified and thus in breach of EU law. As to the question by the national courts on the remedies, the ECJ mentioned only briefly the possibility of Member State liability in damages.[164]

F. Establishing Discretion – or Defining the Branch of State Responsible?

Brasserie du Pêcheur (ECJ 1996) announced a departure from the original legislative/administrative dichotomy and led to the introduction of criteria relating to discretion into Community/Union liability. In *Brasserie du Pêcheur*, the discretion (and the fact that it was wide) was pointed out together with the branch of state in question (the legislator).[165]

It could be recalled in this context that for *Community liability*, *Bergaderm* (ECJ 2000) clearly put the emphasis on discretion and finally in *CEVA and Pfizer* (ECJ 2005) a judgment of the CFI was annulled by the ECJ, as the CFI had not established the scope of discretion.[166] Now, as regards *Member State liability*, it seems that the case-law is more ambiguous. The ECJ seems to use two tests interchangeably, either by asking 'What was the scope of discretion enjoyed' or 'What was the branch of state in question'. The flagship of the '*discretion approach*' is *Haim* (ECJ 2000),[167]

[161] ECJ *N* (n 22) [66].

[162] ECJ *Eman and Sevinger* (n 23) [61] and [69].

[163] Aruba is listed in Annex II to the EC Treaty concerning 'Overseas Counties and Territories to which the provisions of Part Four of the Treaty apply', *cf* Art 299(3) EC.

[164] From the outset, it can be difficult to define what should be the quantum of damages awarded for non-material loss. The fact that the rule breached can be considered to be of a fundamental nature would probably have to be taken into account in that assessment. However, the preliminary question to be answered before that is whether the breach was sufficiently serious or not.

[165] ECJ *Brasserie du Pêcheur and Factortame* (n 13) [48] and [49].

[166] ECJ Case C-198/03 P *Commission v CEVA and Pfizer* (CFI judgment set aside, damages action dismissed on appeal) [2005] ECR I-6357 [69] (emphasis added): 'It must for those reasons be concluded that the Court of First Instance erred in law in holding in paragraph 103 of the judgment under appeal, *without having established the scope of the discretion enjoyed by the Commission*, that the Commission's inaction between 1 January 2000 and 25 July 2001 constituted a clear and serious breach of Community law giving rise to liability on the part of the Community"

[167] ECJ *Haim* (n 23).

whereas the '*branch of state approach*' (legislative, administrative or judicial) is present for example in one of the *Test Claimants* cases, namely that of the *Controlled Foreign Companies/Dividend Group Litigation* (ECJ 2008).[168] There appears to be a discrepancy here between Member State liability and EU liability. It is not clear why the Court (the ECJ, that is) does not systematically analyse discretion, but rather anchors its assessment primarily, or at least very often, to the branch of state. One pragmatic explanation could be that the branch of state approach is more suitable for the preliminary reference procedure.

G. Breach by a National Court – Liability Applies, under Specific Conditions

While the national courts of last instance are included among the state actors whose activity may render Member States liable, the ECJ has attempted to take the special position of the courts into account in its case-law. It is clear from the case-law that as regards the activities of the legislative and administrative bodies, the approach used by the ECJ to sufficient seriousness of breach has revolved with similar criteria and in similar terms. The courts, however, are in a category of their own. Even if a national court was to found to have breached EU law (the conditions are more stringent), the grounds to excuse its action are wider and liability will not easily arise. This was the outcome of *Köbler* (ECJ 2003).[169] There is no immunity for national courts, as explained in more detail in *Traghetti* (ECJ 2006),[170] but they are subject to a liability system where the threshold for establishing liability is higher. This form of liability has probably been the most controversial and has given rise to lively discussion.

Indeed, the Austrian reference in *Köbler* was the occasion for the ECJ to lay down a detailed approach for damages liability for sufficiently serious breaches of EU law committed by courts of final instance. The case concerned equal treatment as regards remuneration of university professors and indirect discrimination in view of a length-of-service increment. The Court established that there was a breach, and then examined the seriousness of the breach in the following terms (emphasis added):

> 120 It must therefore be examined whether that infringement of Community law is manifest in character having regard in particular to the factors to be taken into consideration for that purpose as indicated in paragraphs 55 and 56 above.
>
> 121 In the first place, the infringement of Community rules at issue in the reply to the third question cannot in itself be so characterised.
>
> 122 Community law *does not expressly cover the point* whether a measure for rewarding an employee's loyalty to his employer, such as a loyalty bonus, which entails an obstacle to freedom of movement for workers, can be justified and thus be in conformity with

[168] ECJ *Test Claimants in the CFC and Dividend Group Litigation* (n 21).
[169] ECJ *Köbler* (n 10).
[170] ECJ *Traghetti del Mediterraneo* (n 16).

> Community law. *No reply* was to be found to that question *in the Court's case*-law. *Nor,* moreover, *was that reply obvious.*
>
> 123 In the second place, the fact that the national court in question ought to have maintained its request for a preliminary ruling, as has been established at paragraph 118 hereof, is not of such a nature as to invalidate that conclusion. In the present case the Verwaltungsgerichtshof had decided to withdraw the request for a preliminary ruling, on the view that the reply to the question of Community law to be resolved had already been given in the judgment in Schöning-Kougebetopoulou, cited above. Thus, it was owing to its *incorrect reading of that judgment* that the Verwaltungsgerichtshof no longer considered it necessary to refer that question of interpretation to the Court.
>
> 124 In those circumstances and in the light of the circumstances of the case, the infringement found at paragraph 119 hereof *cannot be regarded as being manifest in nature* and thus as sufficiently serious.
>
> 125 It should be added that that reply is without prejudice to the obligations arising for the Member State concerned from the Court's reply to the third question referred.
>
> 126 The reply to the fourth and fifth questions must therefore be that an infringement of Community law, such as that stemming in the circumstances of the main proceedings from the judgment of the Verwaltungsgerichtshof of 24 June 1998, *does not have the requisite manifest character* for liability under Community law to be incurred by a Member State for a decision of one of its courts adjudicating at last instance.

The reasoning of the ECJ in *Köbler* can probably be clarified in the light of the opinion of Advocate General Léger which the Court largely followed (emphasis added):[171]

> 138 In these circumstances, as the Court's case-law stands at present, I am of the opinion that it is not necessary to determine whether, in the exercise of the judicial function, the State has a broad discretion or not. On the other hand, it is important to determine whether the factors adopted by the Court in order to evaluate whether there is a sufficiently serious breach of Community law, for which the legislature or the administrative authorities are responsible, can be totally or partially transposed to the case of a breach for which a supreme court is responsible.
>
> 139 In my opinion, the decisive factor is whether the error of law at issue is excusable or inexcusable. That characterisation can depend either on the clarity and precision of the legal rule infringed, or on the existence or the state of the Court's case- law on the matter. A number of examples can be given to that effect
>
> 140 Accordingly, the State can be rendered liable, for example, where a supreme court gives a decision contrary to provisions of Community law although their meaning and scope are clear. That would be the case where the wording of the provisions in question was clear and precise in every respect and unambiguous, so that it ultimately leaves no room for interpretation, but only straightforward application.

As a question of principle the Court laid down in *Brasserie du Pêcheur* three sets of elements on the basis of which the competent court should be able to assess whether

[171] ECJ Case C-224/01 *Opinion of Advocate General Léger – Köbler* [2003] ECR I-10239.

a breach is sufficiently serious. It has been correctly underlined that the Court gave particular emphasis to the special nature of the judicial function.[172]

The Italian preliminary reference in *Traghetti* (ECJ 2006) was also about long-standing damages litigation in national courts. In that litigation, the key issue was whether national legislation that excluded state liability, in a general manner, as regards courts of final instance, where the infringement resulted from an interpretation of provisions of law or an assessment of fact or evidence by that court, was acceptable. As expected, the Court found that such a rule is precluded by Community law, as it would in practice render the principle of state liability meaningless. In *Traghetti* the Court further re-endorsed the conditions for judicial liability laid down in *Köbler*. The additional point made was that in the field of state aid, the limitations laid down in Italian law were particularly harmful.[173]

Scherr's dissertation provides an excellent overview of the problems of reception regarding *Köbler*.[174] She has analysed all 27 Member States by dividing them into four representative groups. Group I – 'total exclusion of state liability for judicial breaches under domestic law – consists of the United Kingdom, Ireland, The Netherlands, Bulgaria, Greece and Malta. Group II – 'restricted scope of state liability for judicial breaches according to the source and/or the nature of the judicial act causing the breach – is formed by Austria, Estonia, Germany, Italy, Romania, Slovenia and Sweden. Group III – described as 'restricted form of state liability under domestic law limited by the degree of fault in a judicial act – comprises Austria, Denmark, Finland, France, Germany, Hungary, Italy, Portugal, Spain and Sweden. Finally, Group IV – 'procedural obstacles to a comprehensive recognition of the principle of state liability for judicial breaches – is made up of Belgium, Cyprus, Czech Republic, Lithuania, Luxembourg, Poland and Slovakia.

From the vast diversity of the approaches she concludes that there is no common theoretical matrix for state liability for judicial breaches in Europe. The doctrine of judicial liability exposes Member States to numerous conceptual and procedural challenges, thus making it very difficult to operate in practice.

One could argue that the Court in *Köbler* was thinking of giving a reminder to national courts, and in *Traghetti* to legislators setting limitation rules for judicial liability as regards their responsibilities in applying EU law. *Köbler* highlighted and acknowledged the somewhat hidden issue that national courts, too, may well misinterpret and even infringe EU law. It seems that until recently the Commission has been rather reluctant to sue Member States for suspected breaches of EU law by national courts. Yet in *Commission v Italy* the ECJ, sitting as a full court, accepted the Commission's application that Italy had infringed its Treaty obligations through

[172] J Salminen, 'Euroopan yhteisöjen tuomioistuimen tuomio asiassa C-224/01, Gerhard Köbler vastaan Itävallan tasavalta – Lisiä oppiin unionin jäsenvaltion vahingonkorvausvastuusta yhteisön oikeuden rikkomisesta?' (2004) *Lakimies* 1125–35, 1133.

[173] ECJ *Traghetti del Mediterraneo* (n 16) [41].

[174] See KM Scherr, *The Principle of State Liability for Judicial Breaches. The case Gerhard Köbler v. Austria under European Community Law and from a comparative national law perspective* (Florence, European University Institute, 2008) 418–19.

administrative and court practices including of the Corte Suprema di Cassatione (ECJ 2003).[175]

Commission v Spain (ECJ 2009)[176] may shed some more light on Court's thinking. The Commission claimed in that case that Spain was infringing the VAT Directive. Spain defended the interpretation applied and said it could not change it, because the interpretation had its origins in the case-law of Supreme Court. When assessing the situation the Court recalled that in *Commission v Italy* it had contrasted two situations. On the one hand, if the alleged failure to fulfil obligations consisted of 'isolated or numerically insignificant judicial decisions in the context of case-law taking a different direction', or 'a construction disowned by the national Supreme Court', it could not be taken into account. On the other hand, if the case-law reproached presented as 'a widely-held judicial construction which has not been disowned by the Supreme Court, but rather confirmed by it', the assessment would be different.[177] As the situation analysed belonged rather to the second category, the Court established the infringement. Finally the constitutional importance of judicial liability was underlined in *Opinion 1/09* (ECJ 2011), where the full Court ruled that the creation of Patent Court was not in conformity with EU law as its decision could not be the subject of infringement proceedings nor could it give rise to any financial liability on the part of one or more Member State.[178] As the application of the principle is now fairly well established for Member States, it remains to be seen in what kind of setting the first damages cases for judicial liability of the European Union will appear.

H. Breach Clearly or 'Automatically' Sufficiently Serious

Failure to implement directives, which was the case in *Francovich, Wagner Miret, Faccini Dori* and *El Corte Ingles,* was initially probably the most flagrant case of state liability. Perhaps currently it is no longer the most typical or frequent case, but it still is the case where sufficiently serious breach is easiest to demonstrate – only a calendar is needed as proof– and it remains one of the breaches most readily sanctioned by the ECJ.

After *Brasserie,* it was highlighted that where a Member State fails to take measures necessary to achieve the result prescribed by a directive, a mere infringement of EU law may be sufficient to establish sufficiently serious breach.[179] The conditions of liability in this 'classic' situation were clarified to a certain extent in *Dillenkofer* (ECJ 1996):

[175] ECJ Case C-129/00 *Commission v Italy* [2003] ECR I-14637 [41].

[176] ECJ Case C-154/08 *Commission v Spain* [2009] ECR I-187*, Summ.pub. (judgment of 12 November 2009) [125].

[177] See ECJ *Commission v Italy* (n 175) [32].

[178] ECJ Opinion 1/09 *Draft Agreement on the creation of a European and Community Patent Court* [2011] ECR I-0000 (Opinion of 8 March 2011) [86].

[179] ECJ *Hedley Lomas* (n 14) [28] and ECJ *Dillenkofer and others v Bundesrepublik Deutschland* (n 23) [25].

> 27 Consequently, such a breach gives rise to a right to reparation on the part of individuals if the result prescribed by the directive entails the grant of rights to them, the content of those rights is identifiable on the basis of the provisions of the directive and a causal link exists between the breach of the State's obligation and the loss and damage suffered by the injured parties: no other conditions need be taken into consideration.

Hence, even after *Brasserie,* the criteria for damages liability in case of failure to implement a directive remain faithful to the original ruling in *Francovich.* Fulfilment of the second criterion is thus easier to establish, but the scope of use of this test is limited to those cases only where rights can be identified solely on the basis of the directive.

Finally, it should be recalled that in some instances the breach should be qualified as sufficiently serious *per se.* In *Brasserie* (para 57) the Court ruled that a breach of Community law is clearly sufficiently serious if it has persisted despite a judgment finding the infringement in question to be established, or a preliminary ruling or settled case-law of the Court on the matter from which it is clear that the conduct in question constituted an infringement. In these instances, there is, in principle, not even a limited discretion, but in actual fact, no discretion at all.

The specific feature in the Belgian case of *Larsy* (ECJ 2001), cited above, was that the legal issue had already been clarified by the ECJ.[180] The Court found very little justification for a case where a national social security institution did not apply the Court's earlier case-law[181] as regards Social Security Regulation 1408/71,[182] in the light of the earlier judgment of the Court concerning the brother of the applicant.

I. Excursion: The *Test Claimants* Cases

One way to illustrate the challenges for national judges concerning assessment of breach is the Test Claimants cases, which were four separate preliminary references from the High Court of Justice (England and Wales) and which all concerned various taxation-related issues against the Commissioners of Inland Revenue (the then tax authority in the United Kingdom). In two of the cases, the ECJ gave an interpretation of EU law which pointed to incompatibility of national law; in one case there was partial incompatibility and in one case no incompatibility was found. They also perfectly illustrate the potential legal and factual complexity of damages cases.

The first case, '*ACT group litigation case*' (ECJ 2006), was about national proceedings where the Inland Revenue refused to grant to a group of companies a tax credit to non-resident companies in those groups for dividends paid to them by resident companies.[183] The ECJ found that there was no infringement of EU law rules.

[180] ECJ *Larsy (No 2)* (n 23).
[181] ECJ Case C-31/92 *Larsy* (No 1) [1993] ECR I-4543.
[182] [1992] OJ L136/7.
[183] ECJ *Test Claimants in Class IV of the ACT Group Litigation* (n 21).

The second case, '*FII Group Litigation Case*' (ECJ 2006), related to the same national legislation as the first case, namely the UK's regime of Advance Corporation Tax ('ACT') in force between 1973 and 1999.[184] The first case concerned the tax treatment of dividends paid by UK-resident companies to corporate shareholders resident in other Member States, but this second case was about the tax treatment of dividends received by UK-resident corporate shareholders from companies resident in other Member States and third countries. Although the Court ruled that the applicable provisions, Articles 43 and 56 EC, did not preclude certain types of national legislation, it also found several types of situation where the applicable national rules were contrary to these provisions. On these points therefore the key issue became whether the infringement was sufficiently serious. The Court first recalled the criteria set out in *Brasserie*[185] and then gave the following guidance (empasis added):

> 215 In the present case, *in order to determine whether a breach* of Article 43 EC committed by the Member State concerned *was sufficiently serious*, the national court must take into account the fact that, in a field such as direct taxation, the *consequences arising from the freedoms of movement guaranteed by the Treaty have been only gradually made clear, in particular by the principles identified by the Court* since delivering judgment in Case 270/83 Commission v France. Moreover, as regards the taxation of dividends received by resident companies from non-resident companies, *it was only in Verkooijen, Lenz and Manninen that the Court had the opportunity to clarify the requirements* arising from the freedoms of movement, in particular as regards the free movement of capital.
>
> 216 Apart from cases to which Directive 90/435 applied, *Community law gave no precise definition of the duty of a Member State* to ensure that, as regards mechanisms for the prevention or mitigation of the imposition of a series of charges to tax or economic double taxation, dividends paid to residents by resident companies and those paid by non-resident companies were treated in the same way. It follows that, until delivery of the judgments in Verkooijen, Lenz and Manninen, the issue raised by the order for reference in the present case had not yet been addressed as such in the case-law of the Court.
>
> 217 It is in the light of those considerations that the national court should assess the matters referred to in paragraph 213 of this judgment, *in particular the clarity and precision of the rules infringed and whether any errors of law were excusable or inexcusable.*

The Court acknowledged here that interpretation of the relevant Treaty provisions had not always been evident and that the 'consequences arising from the freedoms of movement guaranteed by the Treaty' became only gradually clear, save for cases covered by the provisions of the relevant directive.[186]

The third judgment, in the '*Thin Cap Group case*' (ECJ 2007), concerned compatibility with the EC Treaty free movement provisions of the UK's so-called 'thin capitalisation' ('thin cap') rules, by which the UK restricts the deductibility of interest payments made by UK subsidiaries to non-resident parent or intermediate group

[184] ECJ *Test Claimants in the FII Group Litigation* (n 21).

[185] ECJ *Brasserie du Pêcheur and Factortame* (n 13) [56] and [57].

[186] *cf* this to ECJ *Brasserie du Pêcheur and Factortame* (n 13), where the interpretation of the relevant provision had already been clear for some time.

companies.[187] The Court found that the difference in treatment between resident subsidiaries, based on the place where their parent company has its seat, constitutes a restriction on freedom of establishment. As to seriousness of breach, the Court followed the same pattern as in the *FII Group Litigation* Case, cited above, by noting that the particular issue at stake here had been clarified in a judgment of 2002.

In the last case, '*Controlled Foreign Companies/Dividend Group*' (ECJ 2008), the national proceedings were between several groups of international companies and the Commissioners of Inland Revenue concerning the taxation of resident companies on profits made by, and dividends received from, non-resident subsidiary companies. Here an infringement was found on several points, but for seriousness of breach the Court recalled its earlier case-law in the *Test Claimants* series on the fact that interpretation of the relevant provisions had only gradually become clear.[188]

The *Test Claimants* cases illustrate a specific, partly new category of litigation, where a series of cases are submitted to the ECJ with very precise questions so as to find out whether the fundamental features of a given part of national application of EU rules are compatible with EU law. The outcome directly affects a wide category of persons, in contrast to cases where the effects of the interpretation are more of an individual nature (eg *AGM*, ECJ 2007).[189] This type of litigation would seem to have three pre-conditions. First, on the part of the applicants, it requires readiness, economic means and time available to litigate and challenge the compatibility of the national provisions before national courts. Secondly, it can be facilitated or hindered by national procedural rules (eg possibility of a class action or not). Third, its availability is contingent upon the readiness of national jurisdictions to refer the case to the ECJ.

J. Interim Conclusion

Following presentation of the relevant case-law above, it would appear helpful to locate the different types of cases on a sliding scale, in function of the degree of breach. In Figure 6.1 below, at the very left end appear cases which are either outside the scope of application of EU law or where there was no breach. At the right hand side at the far end there appear the 'absolutely' serious breaches of EU law.

To illustrate the two ends of the vector ('0. Issue outside the scope of EU law' – '4. Clearly serious breach') two examples can be cited. At one end (on the left, that is), are situations outside the scope of the Treaties where there can be no breach of EU law. An extreme example might be a Euratom case *Commission v UK* (ECJ

[187] ECJ *Test Claimants in the Thin Cap Group Litigation* (n 10) [61].

[188] In this case the ECJ asked from the national Court whether it wanted to maintain the reference for preliminary ruling, as the reply could already be 'clearly deduced from the existing case-law'. The national court wished to maintain the reference. It still took some 132 paragraphs for the ECJ to set out this result 'clearly deduced from the existing case-law'.

[189] ECJ *AGM-COS.MET* (n 18).

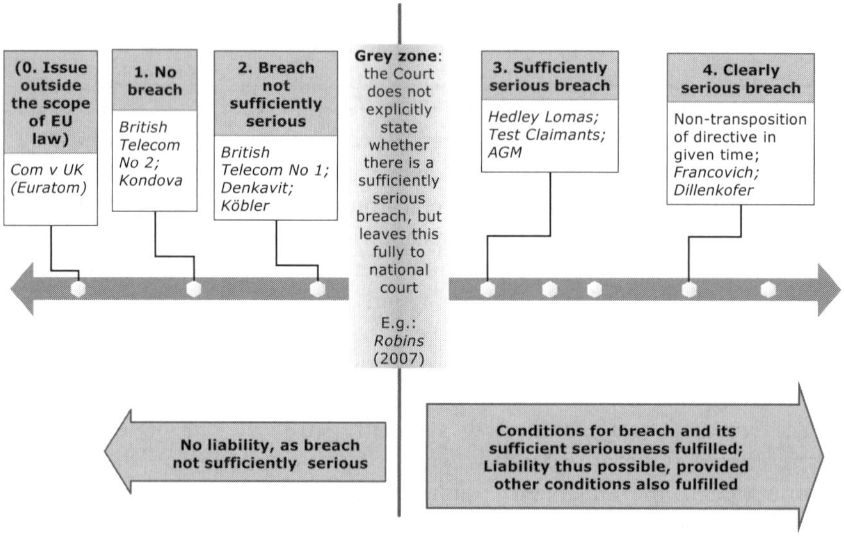

Figure 6.1 Degree of Breach in Case-law as Regards Breaches by Member States

2006), where the Commission sued a Member State for breach of EC Treaty obligations, as it had not transposed a waste directive as regards military use of nuclear power.[190] The Court did not take a position on whether there was a breach of the objectives of the directive, because it ruled that the whole question is outside the scope of application of the Euratom Treaty (and any other Union treaty, for that matter). Therefore no breach of EU law was even possible.

The other end (on the right side) might be the '*Francovich*' situation or a situation where the Commission has already successfully sued a Member State for infringement of its Treaty obligations and the Court found a breach of EU law or cited a preliminary ruling (*Larsy* ECJ 2001).[191] If there is a further judgment under Article 267 TFEU, that fact does not change the appreciation as regards Member State liability, but may show the persistence of the breach. What is noteworthy is that discretion is often mentioned but not discussed in more detail in Member State liability. So for this purpose it is useful to examine the case-law concerning liability of the Union, presented in chapter five above. It should again be recalled that the criteria and their application is a matter for the national court. The question is whether, in a situation where the criteria still remain somewhat abstract and despite the number of cases there is rather little guidance, the system works properly. Finally, it seems that the Luxembourg court shows more understanding and tolerance for judicial breaches. Of course, in such a case, the 'obligations' and 'rights' are different, and, according to the ECJ's own words, the conditions must vary according to the situation.

[190] ECJ Case C-65/04 *Commission v United Kingdom* [2006] ECR I-2239.
[191] ECJ *Larsy (No 2)* (n 23).

IV. APPLICATION IN PRACTICE AND SUCCESSFUL DAMAGES CASES

When attempting to find out which damages cases against Member States for breaches of EU law have succeeded, one must take into account two aspects. Firstly, it should be verified in which cases the ECJ has established (with greater or lesser clarity) that the damages conditions have been, in its view, fulfilled. Secondly, and more importantly, one should check in what national cases the competent national court has established damages liability, whether damages have in reality been awarded and whether the damages award has become final.

Problems relating in particular to the second issue have been highlighted above. Therefore, as mere examples, the following cases could be mentioned, which have also at national level led to damages, either by judgment or by settlement.[192] The other half of *Brasserie du Pêcheur*, namely the case relating to Spanish fishermen, *Factortame* (ECJ 1996), led finally to a considerable damages award. The House of Lords in 1999 confirmed the breach and corresponding liability of the United Kingdom. According to the applicants' counsel, the damages awarded were £55m plus costs.[193] In a Finnish reference for preliminary ruling *AGM*, from Tampereen käräjäoikeus, the ECJ gave detailed guidance in 2007 on liability conditions and the compatibility of national law. The national case, once the preliminary ruling was handed down, was finally settled for a secret amount in 2008; the original claim was apparently more than €1m.[194] *Dillenkofer* resulted in considerable damages claims against Germany: reportedly some 9000 individual claimants asked for an aggregate compensation of 20m DM. It is remarkable that the final amounts paid were somewhat over 11 m DM (over €5m).[195] Some interesting cases, such as *Test Claimants in the FII Group Litigation* (ECJ 2006)[196] or *Danske Slagterier* (ECJ 2009)[197] are still pending before the national courts.

[192] Granger, 'National applications of *Francovich* and the construction of a European administrative *ius commune*' (n 8). For an assessment of damages actions against Sweden see J Engström, *The Europeanisation of Remedies and Procedures through Judge-Made Law. Can a Trojan Horse Achieve Effectiveness?* (Florence, European University Institute, 2009) 487–514.

[193] ECJ *Brasserie du Pêcheur and Factortame* (n 13); House of Lords Factortame IV – R v *Secretary of State for Transport, Ex Parte Factortame Ltd and Others* [1999] UKHL 44; [2000] 1 AC 524; [1999] 4 All ER 906; [1999] 3 WLR 1062 (28 October 1999); see D Vaughan, '*Factortame* and After: A Fishy Story' (2005) *European Business Law Review* 511–17.

[194] See ECJ Case C-470/03 *Opinion of Advocate General Kokott – AGM-COS.MET* [2007] ECR I-2749 [45]; ECJ *AGM-COS.MET* (n 18), and Finland, Tampere District Court (settled and withdrawn); *Helsingin Sanomat* 12.1.2009.

[195] T Krümmel and RM D'Sa, 'Implementation by German Courts of the Jurisprudence of the European Court of Justice on State Liability for Breach of Community Law as Developed in Francovich and subsequent cases' (2009) *European Business Law Review* 273–86, 278.

[196] ECJ *Test Claimants in the FII Group Litigation* (n 21) and UK High Court 2008 *Test Claimants In the FII Group Litigation v HM Revenue & Customs* [2008] EWHC 2893 (Ch) (27 November 2008).

[197] ECJ *Danske Slagterier* (n 12). The case was sent back from the Bundesgerichtshof to the court below, once the preliminary ruling was handed down. Bundesgerichtshof (Federal Supereme Court). Urteil des III. Zivilsenats vom 4.6.2009 – III ZR 144/05 (*Danske Slagterier*). The national court below had already awarded certain damages before the preliminary reference was made.

In all of these cases the national finding of liability was preceded by a request for preliminary ruling to the ECJ as regards fulfilment or interpretation of the conditions for state liability. Such a reference is not necessary, as the Court has repeatedly pointed out. Two cases can be mentioned where liability has been established without preliminary reference. In the first, *Sté Arizona Tobacco Products et SA Philip Morris* (1992), the French Conseil d'État ruled that the national price-fixing system for tobacco imported from other Member States was contrary to the relevant Community directive. A damages award of 230000 FF was made.[198] The second case, this time from Spain, led to a very substantial award. In *Canal Satélite Digital* (2003),[199] the Tribunal Supremo awarded over €26m in compensation for national legislation which had been adopted in infringement of Community law provisions and restricting the rights of the applicant operator of digital satellite television services. Here, though, it is noteworthy that the *Tribunal Supremo* had put a preliminary question to the ECJ, but that reference was only made in relation to interpretation of the relevant substantive provisions, ie to find out whether there was an infringement of Community law or not. The request did not contain questions relating to damages liability.[200]

Of course, not all applicants have been successful. The most blatant defeat was probably experienced by *Brasserie du Pêcheur* itself. The namesake of the new era of public liability for breaches of EU law was well-celebrated in spring 1996, when the ECJ handed down its remarkable judgment. Only half a year later when the Bundesgerichtshof applied the criteria to the facts, it established that the infringement was not sufficiently serious, so that no damages were finally awarded.[201]

What this brief overview of national applications still shows, though, is that damages liability for breaches of EU law has been applied in practice in Member State courts, and that even very substantial damages awards have been made – when all the conditions for liability have been fulfilled according to the national court. State liability is no theoretical liability.

[198] C.E., Ass., 28 February 1992, *Sté Arizona Tobacco Products et SA Philip Morris France*, n° 87753. Reported in English in A Oppenheimer (ed), *The Relationship between European Community law and national law: the cases. Volume 1* (Cambridge, Cambridge University Press 1994) 357–84; for a detailed assessment see C Broyelle, *La responsabilité de l'Etat du fait des lois* (Paris, LGDJ, 2003) 257ff.

[199] Tribunal Supremo (Spanish Supreme Court), Administrative Law Chamber, judgment of 12 June 2003, Canal Satélite Digital (Case 46/1999). See F Castillo de la Torre, 'Tribunal Supremo (Spanish Supreme Court), Administrative Law Chamber, judgment of 12 June 2003, Canal Satélite Digital (Case 46/1999)' (2004) *Common Market Law Review* 1717–34.

[200] ECJ Case C-390/99 *Canal Satélite Digital* [2002] ECR I-607.

[201] Bundesgerichtshof (Federal Supereme Court). Urteil vom 24.10.1996 (III ZR 127/91) – Bras*serie du Pêcheur*. Reported in English in [1997] 1 Common Market Law Reports 971 and A Oppenheimer (ed), *The Relationship between European Community law and national law: the cases. Volume 2* (Cambridge, Cambridge University Press 2003) 588–96.

7

Conclusions

THIS CONCLUDING CHAPTER will first set out the comparison of the two systems in a table form (section I). It will then examine the convergence of the criteria in the two systems. The criteria were presented separately as regards rights[1] and as regards breach[2] in each system. In this chapter the convergence is set out for the rights criterion (section II) and the breach (section III). In addition, a more general appreciation of convergence is presented, how it was created and how it could develop in the future (section IV). The book concludes with an outlook beyond convergence (section V).

I. MAIN ASPECTS OF THE TWO LIABILITY SYSTEMS

The aim of this study was to assess convergence of the two public liability systems of EU law, which was put into practice in *Bergaderm* (ECJ 2000),[3] following *Brasserie du Pêcheur* (ECJ 1996).[4] The basic assumption for this study was that albeit Member State liability had been subject to a considerable number of contributions in the doctrine, an approach axised on convergence of the two systems could bring some added value. In addition, it was thought that following the restatement of liability law in *Bergaderm*, the time would be ripe for such a parallel analysis, which could help to mutually fill the gaps between the two systems and enrich them.

One of the purposes of comparison between the two systems was to give an overview of the essential elements of the two liability systems. Despite the idea of convergence, it appears that a simple presentation of the structural features of the case-law exposes the differences between the systems for which the Court intends convergence to apply.

As to the differences between the two systems, there appears to be five that are worth mentioning. First of all, the *aim* of the EU liability system seems to have been, since the beginning, to ensure a minimum liability following the transfer of competences from Member States to the EU, whereas the key reason behind the Member State liability has been to ensure the effectiveness of EU law. Second, the *role of the*

[1] See ch 5, s II and ch 6, s II.
[2] See ch 5, s III and ch 6 s III.
[3] ECJ Case C-352/98 P *Bergaderm and Goupil v Commission* (appeal dismissed) [2000] ECR I-5291.
[4] ECJ Joined Cases C-46/93 and C-48/93 *Brasserie du Pêcheur and Factortame* [1996] ECR I-1029.

EU courts is different: for EU liability all three of them exercise full jurisdiction and take the final decision on whether damages are awarded or not; for Member State liability only the ECJ is involved through the preliminary rulings procedure and all final decisions are taken by the national courts. This also relates to the third difference: the EU liability system is *closed* in the sense that the questions are resolved purely on the basis of EU law, while for Member State liability national law is always involved, both in procedural and substantive terms. Fourth issue is that the *areas of liability* are often different as the EU is rendered liable mainly for areas that it administers directly (eg agriculture) whereas Member States are liable for indirectly administered areas, which are often regulated through directives. Finally, the *entity liable* is naturally different: payment and prescription of liability claims against the EU are thus regulated through EU law while claims against Member States are regulated by national law and procedure.

Table 7.1 Comparison of Structural Aspects of Liability of the European Union and of the Member States for Breaches of EU Law

Aspect	**Liability of the European Union (ch 5)** ('*Schöppenstedt/Bergaderm*')	**Liability of Member States (ch 6)** ('*Francovich/Brasserie/Factortame*')
Development	Established in 1950s; original conditions put in place in 1970s; revised in 2000	Established in 1991; revised in 1996/2000
Aims of liability system	To ensure minimum liability as regards powers transferred from Member States to the Union	To ensure effectiveness of EU law
Source of rules governing liability	Essentially European courts' case-law; three provisions in the founding treaties	Purely European courts' case-law
Competent courts	All case-law centralised to Luxembourg courts	All case-law decentralised to Member State courts, save ECJ preliminary rulings
Finding law	Almost all case-law available on line, in at least two EU languages (GC, ECJ)	ECJ preliminary rulings available in all EU languages; national case-law available at national sources in procedural language
Jurisdiction	Sole jurisdiction of EU courts; final judgment given by EU courts; application of EU law only	National court which can/must ask for a preliminary ruling from ECJ concerning interpretation or validity of EU law
Appeal	Appeal from GC to ECJ Appeal from CST to GC	Appeal in accordance with the national system

Table 7.1 (*cont.*)

Alternative remedies	Within the EU system: action for annulment and plea of illegality	Defined in national administrative and procedural law
Nature of the system	Closed: issues resolved purely on the basis of EU law	Open: liability system functions in interaction with national law
Institutional coverage	All EU institutions, agencies and external bodies (ECB, EIB) save former EU II/III pillar agencies	All Member State public authorities applying EU law
Sectors of liability (eg)	Directly administered EU law, eg agriculture, public procurement	Indirectly administered EU law, eg internal market; four freedoms
Applicants	Companies, economic operators Staff members of the institutions	Private persons Economic operators
Heads of damage	All defined by EU law	All defined by national law
Who will pay	European Union institution	Member State

II. CONVERGENCE REGARDING 'GRANTING OF RIGHTS TO INDIVIDUALS'

Examination of convergence concerning the criteria relating to 'granting of rights to individuals' took place under two different frameworks, namely non-Hohfeldian for EU liability and Hohfeldian for Member State liability. It now appears that due to the difference between the liability situations and in particular the sources and natures of rights granted to individuals, it is difficult to claim that any full convergence in absolute terms has been achieved, or even that it would be attainable. The principal finding concerning rights of which breach can lead to liability of the European Union and of its Member States could be summarised as follows.

The first finding concerns *application* of the new criteria. For Community liability, a considerable change took place from *Zuckerfabrik Schöppenstedt* (ECJ 1971)[5] to *Bergaderm* (ECJ 2000),[6] as regards rights criteria. The EU courts seem to have applied the new criteria in a fairly systematic fashion, and references to 'superior rules of law for the protection of the individual' from the 'old' case-law seem to have disappeared almost completely. One notable exception can be found, though, in *FIAMM* (ECJ 2008) where the Court was discussing the existence and conditions of strict liability and refers to *Schöppenstedt*. However, that reference would not appear to mean a return to pre-*Bergaderm* conditions in general.[7] In contrast, application of

[5] ECJ Case 5/71 *Zuckerfabrik Schöppenstedt v Council* (damages claim dismissed) [1971] ECR 975 [11].

[6] ECJ *Bergaderm and Goupil* (n 3).

[7] ECJ Joined Cases C-120/06 P and C-121/06 P *FIAMM and Fedon v Council and Commission* (appeal dismissed) [2008] ECR I-6513 [171]–[173].

the new rights criteria following *Bergaderm* to Member State liability did not require a decisive change. In fact, the rights criteria were not subject to adjustment from *Francovich* through *Brasserie du Pêcheur* to *Bergaderm*. Although *Bergaderm* eliminated the requirement of a superior rule of law for the protection of the individual, that did not matter so much as it had not been applied in a consistent manner in the earlier liability cases. This modification, apparently, has not considerably enlarged liability situations.

The second issue relates to the *source* of rights invoked in the two systems. It appears clearly from the case-law that 'rights' protected (as to their source), or at least invoked so far in the light of the existing case-law, are very different. As regards rights for Union liability, liability has been mainly based on breaches of general principles of law. Therefore, and so far, the principles which have remained preponderant in the case-law are sources of rights granted to individuals. This finding is of course again diluted with certain exceptions, as more and more references to concrete positive rights (articles) can be found.[8] In contrast, for Member State liability the provisions invoked are typically those contained in treaty provisions, legislation (rather more directives than regulations), or a combination of the two. The rights invoked for Member State liability are rarely legal principles (in ECJ case-law at least), as the provisions invoked have been more concrete norms. Again, despite this general trend, some exceptions can be found.[9] In addition, when the two issues are compared, one could see some parallel with the division between rules and principles: for Member State liability, the case-law mainly deals with breaches of rules, while for Community liability the breaches relate to principles.

The third observation is that the method or *way of invoking rights* is different. For Union liability, the applicant typically invokes a number of rules of law that the applicant considers to have been breached. The applicant attempts to invoke every possible right which could come into question for assessment of breach. Normally only one or two of these are accepted by the court. For Member State liability, as far as cases come to the ECJ, the preliminary questions have been 'filtered and focused': the right allegedly breached has already been specified by the national court and the question of the applicable right has been limited to one or two sources.

The fourth issue concerns the *grant of rights*. In Union liability, the issue as to whom rights are actually granted very seldom arises. In contrast, for Member State liability the question of grant of rights is central: for whom are the rights identified actually designed? Especially for Member State liability, non-explicit rights in particular have to be read in conjunction with other provisions, or in context, to

[8] eg, CFI Case T-212/03 *MyTravel v Commission* (damages action dismissed, no appeal) [2008] ECR II-1967, where the rights were based on a number of provisions of Council Regulation (EEC) No 4064/89/EEC of 21 December 1989 on the control of concentrations between undertakings [1989] OJ L395/1, corr. [1990] OJ L257/13, read together with the duty of diligence, see [50] and GC Case T-429/05 *Artegodan v Commission* (damages action, dismissed, appealed C-221/10 P, pending) [2010] ECR II-0000 (judgment of 3 March 2010) for Art 11 of Council Directive 65/65/EEC on the approximation of provisions laid down by law, regulation or administrative action relating to medicinal products [1965-1966] English Spec Ed OJ/20.

[9] ECJ Case C-300/04 *Eman and Sevinger* [2006] ECR I-8055 (principle of equal treatment).

discern their essential content, which makes it more difficult to ascertain whether they actually grant rights or not.[10]

Fifth, as regards the *nature of the rights invoked* in general, there seem to be more similarities between the two regimes. In both systems, rights typically invoked are situated within economic rights, ie rights with a 'monetary' connection, or readily quantifiable economic loss (eg losses resulting from obstacles to beer imports or from obstacles for establishment of Spanish fishermen). 'Personal rights', or more generally, fundamental rights, have also been invoked, but they do not necessarily lend themselves well to traditional damages claims. For example, the CFI established in *Sison* (2007) that the rights of defence of the applicant had been breached when the Council had included the applicant in the so-called EU terrorism list, and consequently annulled that act. However, on the damages issue it considered that there was no need to make the institutions pay damages at all, because of the procedural nature of the right breached.[11] Therefore, in the circumstances of the case, annulment of the contested act constituted adequate compensation for the damage caused by that breach.

Moreover, it seems that rights discussion in the damages context, in so far as convergence of rights is considered, requires that new avenues and mutual influence should be addressed. Albeit fundamental rights would appear to have been somewhat in the margins of the rights discussion in damages cases so far, in particular as regards Member State liability, this situation is likely to evolve with the Lisbon Treaty, where these rights are adopted in positive law and where a legal basis is created for accession of the Union to the ECHR.

Another new avenue for the rights discussion is that rights for breach of which damages are claimed are developing. The case-law may be moving from examining breach of a single legal provision, or a single legal instrument, to examining whether the 'legally protected position' of a person has been infringed. This would mean that rights granted to individuals are construed on the basis of several provisions, or instruments, possibly combined with a legal principle. For example, as regards Member State liability, in *Danske Slagterier* (ECJ 2009), the Court noted that the right conferred by Article 28 EC (now Article 34 TFEU) is detailed further and given concrete expression by two directives.[12] Equally, the rights breached in *MyTravel* (CFI 2008) were based on a number of provisions of the Merger Regulation, read together with the duty of diligence.[13]

As to mutual influences for liability of the European Union, it would seem possible that norms allegedly breached will remain general, but they can be concretised, as has been the case with the principle of sound administration. Undoubtedly, such

[10] Snell has pointed out that it may be very difficult for an individual to prove the infringement of Art 28 EC (now Art 34 TFEU), in conjunction with Art 10 EC (replaced in substance by Art 4(3) TEU). See J Snell, Goods and Services in EC Law – A Study of the Relationship Between the Freedoms (Oxford, Oxford University Press, 2002) 158.

[11] CFI Case T-47/03 *Sison v Council* (liability conditions fulfilled, annulment sufficient compensation, no appeal) [2007] ECR II-73*, Summ.pub. (judgment of 11 July 2007) [241].

[12] ECJ Case C-445/06 *Danske Slagterier* [2009] ECR I-2119 [23].

[13] CFI *MyTravel v Commission* (n 8).

norms may also in the future include concrete legislated rights, as well as traditional and general principles of law. While Member State liability could be possible for breaches of rights emanating from external sources (as in *Kondova*), considerable reluctance will remain to accept such external sources (Community agreements, or even WTO agreements) as sources of rights. A potential opening for an external source could be the ECHR and the rights guaranteed therein.

As to mutual influences, as regards Member State liability it seems that one possible line of development could be that breach of legal principles would be invoked more often as a basis for liability. A suitable candidate could be a principle that has already become sufficiently concrete, such as the right to effective judicial protection. As in *Sison*, cited above, it is still possible that even in the Member State damages context the court could consider that annulment could be a sufficient reparation. This position could be reconsidered in the context of the ECHR. It should also be recalled that in *Eman*, cited above, a breach of principle of equal treatment formed the basis for Member State liability.

This section has presented some concluding observations in tracing some common features of the rights protected under the two damages liability systems. On reflection, it seems that some common traces can be found, but there is still no coherent system of rights: it appears that rather than convergent and harmonious, they are happily divergent. A word of consolation may be available from Michael Dougan, though. He has attempted to bring some systemic coherence to use of the concept of direct effect and Community law rights operating in a Member State. His conclusion is that it may not be a very tempting task even within that system, which leads us to conclude that between two systems, it can be insurmountable.[14]

> But 'primacy', 'trigger' or whatever other model one subscribes to, it hardly seems so painful, being forced to acknowledge that the search for a theoretically respectable, watertight descriptive account of the fractured, fumbling case law on the direct effect of directives is a task fit only for masochists.

Be that as it may, the question of protection of EU law rights, within one system or within the two systems will remain on the agenda of the European Union for future developments.

III. CONVERGENCE REGARDING 'SUFFICIENTLY SERIOUS BREACH'

As regards convergence of the criteria relating to 'sufficiently serious breach' for the liability of the European Union and of the Member States, it is probably fair to claim that this is the most essential of the three liability criteria. It is on the basis of this criterion that the following essential question was to be assessed: what action or inaction by institutions of the Union or the Member States should trigger damages

[14] M Dougan, 'When worlds collide! Competing visions of the relationship between direct effect and supremacy' (2007) *Common Market Law Review* 931–63, 963.

liability, and what should not, and how grave should it be? In this respect qualification of the breach is an essential question. As has already been noted, the concept of 'fault', present in national systems, should not be used in EU law, where the concept of 'sufficiently serious breach' is an autonomous concept. In chapter five, section III and chapter six, section III an attempt has been made to set out the law as it stands. It should be noted regarding convergence and divergence for this criterion that it may be easier to point out some divergences than to find common lines. The two systems are rather different, as regards assessment of breach.

Overall, concerning mutual influence, as regards *the liability of the Union*, it should be analysed whether any elements from the Member State liability system could be transposed to Union liability. What help, if any, could *Francovich* case-law provide if a future Mr Adams invokes *Brasserie* in his case, as regards breach?

The most fundamental effect of *Francovich* (ECJ 1991) has already taken place: it was *Francovich* that triggered the development towards more lenient conditions of Union liability. It was *Francovich* that eliminated the division – or even dichotomy – between administrative and legislative measures from the liability conditions. However, it appears that the departure from type of acts is not that definitive. This typology still underlies all liability discussion, but it is not the cornerstone of reasoning. *Francovich* has had the effect on liability of the Union that it is now more than a theoretical possibility to get damages eg in anti-dumping cases: before it was in practice excluded, as it concerned a measure classified as 'legislative'.[15]

It is clear from the case-law that there is no automatic link between illegality and damages liability. Yet, illegality is, though, the *condition sine qua non* for Member State liability: without illegality, without breach of its EU law obligations, a Member State cannot currently incur damages liability. The same goes for EU liability. It seems that this issue was resolved by the ECJ in *FIAMM*. Apparently there was no reference to Member State liability, but rather to the origins of public liability in Member States: as this did not exist there, then nor should it exist in the liability of the European Union.

Concerning mutual influence, as regards *Member State liability*, one essential question is whether elements from the liability system of the European Union could be transposed to Member State liability. As shown above, the courts' analysis of seriousness of breach is, by nature, much more detailed in the case-law regarding liability of the European Union. In that sense it can be said that the case-law could provide potentially useful elements to assess all aspects of liability, including seriousness of breach. The difficulty is, however, that the two liability forms are different in nature. The question is whether they are far too different, or could it be claimed that certain elements of liability of the European Union could be used, by analogy if not otherwise, in the framework of liability of the Member States? The objective of convergence would speak in favour.

[15] CFI Case T-178/98 *Fresh Marine v Commission* (damages awarded, appealed C-472/00 P) [2000] ECR II-3331; ECJ Case C-472/00 P *Commission v Fresh Marine* (damages upheld to NOK 431,000) [2003] ECR I-7541.

What can be said at least is that the case-law applicable to Union liability confirms the importance of discretion even if this issue was only rather implicit in *Francovich* for liability of Member States. Indeed, illegality as such never leads automatically to liability.[16] An infringement by a Member State established by the Court under Article 258 TFEU does not automatically cause liability, as little as an EU act annulled by the General Court under Article 267 TFEU. However, any of them may be a strong indication of sufficiently serious breach.

The convergence argument can also be used to set aside the idea that no-fault liability might exist in Member State liability. Some authors took up this idea after the CFI judgment in *FIAMM* (CFI 2000)[17] where that court found in principle in favour of no fault liability in the Community context.[18] This, after the ECJ judgment on appeal, is no longer relevant (ECJ 2008).[19]

The case-law regarding breach has been summed up on sliding scales in Figure 5.1 for EU liability and in Figure 6.1 for Member State liability. The matrix in Figure 7.1 on 'sufficiently serious breach' is an attempt to set out the existing case-law on seriousness of breach, both for liability of the Member States and for that of the Union. Any matrix is by nature a simplification and this one does not purport to be any exception to that rule. In addition, it is certainly incomplete (and will inevitably become even more so with development of case-law). However, for what it is worth, it might assist the reader to locate current case-law, 'to put it on the map' and help in identifying the 'location' of any potential future liability situations, as regards sufficient seriousness of breach.

The *horizontal axis* represents seriousness of breach discussed in the previous sections. From the left, it starts with the situation where there is no breach and ends, on the right, with 'clearly serious breach'. In this left half of the picture we have situations where breach is either non-existent or not sufficiently serious. The right half of the picture contains situations where breach has reached the degree of sufficiently serious breach.

[16] *cf* CFI *MyTravel* (n 8) [43]: 'Because of the need to have regard to such an effect [the inhibiting effect that the risk of having to bear the losses alleged by the undertakings concerned might have on the control of concentrations], which is contrary to the general Community interest, a failure to fulfil a legal obligation, which, regrettable though it may be, can be explained by the objective constraints to which the institution and its officials are subject in the control of concentrations, cannot be held to constitute a breach of Community law which is sufficiently serious to give rise to the non-contractual liability of the Community. Conversely, the right to compensation for damage resulting from the conduct of the institution becomes available where such conduct takes the form of action manifestly contrary to the rule of law and seriously detrimental to the interests of persons outside the institution and cannot be justified or accounted for by the particular constraints to which the staff of the institution, operating normally, are objectively subject'.

[17] CFI Case T-69/00 *FIAMM and FIAMM Technologies v Council and Commission* (dismissed, appealed C-120/06 P) [2005] ECR II-5393.

[18] G Betlem, 'Beyond Francovich: Completing the Unified Member State and EU Liability Regime. A Comment on the Jan Jans Contribution', in D Obradovic and N Lavranos (eds), *Interface between EU Law and National Law* (Groningen, Europa Law Publishing, 2007) 300–01.

[19] ECJ *FIAMM*, (n 7).

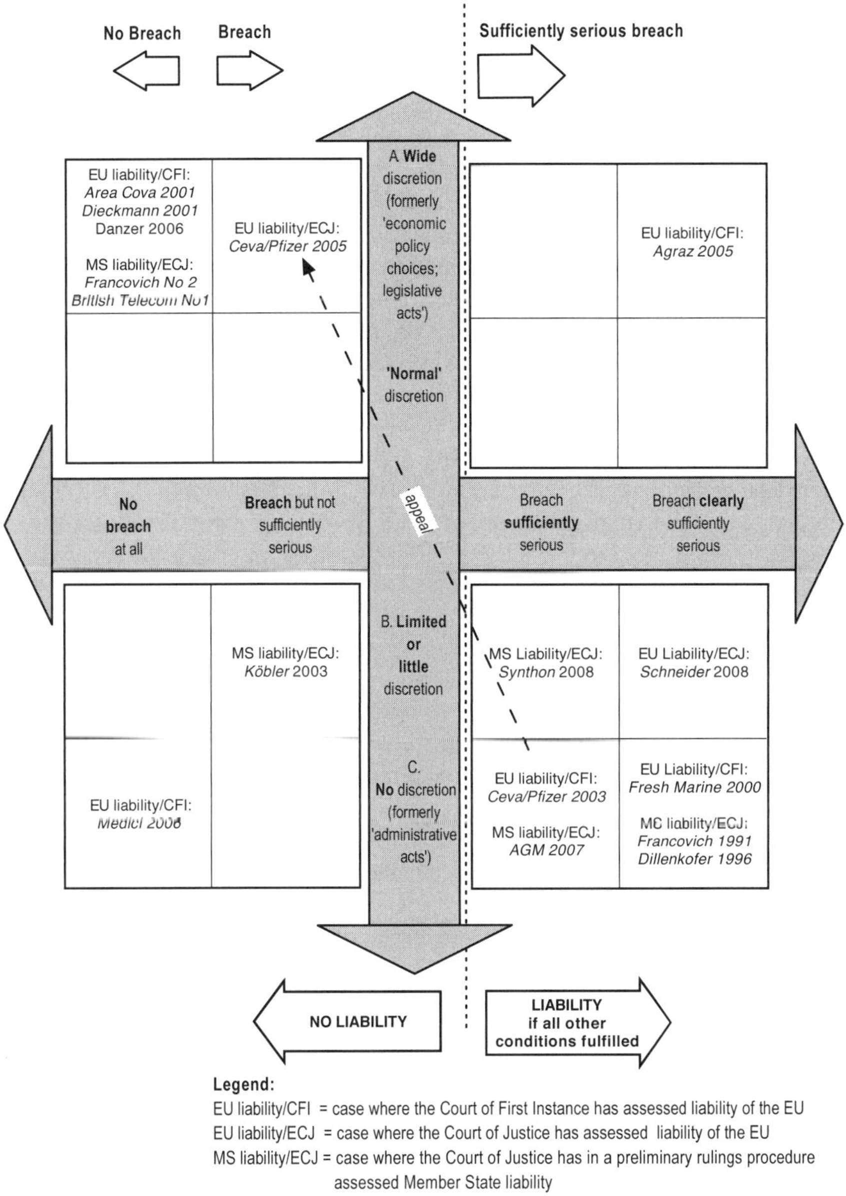

Figure 7.1 Matrix of Sufficiently Serious Breach

A *vertical axis* has been added to this figure, representing the discretion available to the Member State or the EU institution concerned. It stretches from 'wide discretion' at the top to 'no discretion' at the bottom, and accommodates the 'limited/little discretion' in the middle. On the basis of the case-law the first issue to be defined is *the extent of the discretion, ie locate where the case is on the vertical axis*, whether it is in zone A, B or C. Thereafter the possible breach should be qualified. It may be that there is no breach at all or that even in the presence of breach, it is not sufficiently serious. The two other options are that the breach is indeed sufficiently serious for damages liability to be incurred, either as 'simply sufficiently serious' or as 'flagrantly' serious.

Two cases can be used to illustrate the functioning of the matrix. For example, in *Medici* (CFI 2006),[20] the CFI first established that indeed, the Council had no discretion. So for the purposes of the matrix, the case is situated in Zone C. When the Court pursued the analysis further, it came to the conclusion that there was no breach at all. Conversely, in *Agraz* (CFI 2005) the CFI found that the Commission's discretion under basic regulation was wide. Despite this finding – the fact that the Commission was acting in a situation of wide discretion – it had, so held the CFI, breached the limits of its discretion.[21]

All in all, for convergence concerning sufficiently serious breach, it seems that more lessons can, again, be learnt for Member State liability from the liability of the European Union, than the other way around.

IV. ESSENTIAL FINDINGS ON CONVERGENCE

A. Convergence: Brought About by all Means other than Legislation

The first feature is that the impetus for convergence in the area of public liability for breaches of EU law was brought about by all means other than legislation. The requirement of convergence was triggered by legal doctrine and convergence was implemented by the ECJ in principle and by the CFI in practice. As already indicated in a previous chapter, not all legal changes can or have to be brought about by legislation. The case-law of the Court, albeit not 'legislation', is not 'soft law' either.

Indeed, the transition by the ECJ in *Bergaderm* from the dichotomy between administrative and legislative acts was a step in the right direction, but does that correspond to the reality, or was it rather a choice between two second best options? The change was a shift, a refinement, rather than a replacement. The new criterion appears to be more operational in varying liability situations than the preceding rigid dichotomy. Introduction of the new criteria also contributed to modernisation of the liability conditions of the Union. The old criteria were no longer appropriate and had already shown weaknesses: this meant in practice that for example in public procurement procedures almost any breach could qualify for liability, whereas in respect of legislative acts in anti-dumping liability was quasi-absent.

[20] CFI Case T-364/03 *Medici Grimm v Council* (damages claim dismissed, no appeal) [2006] ECR II-79 [84].

[21] CFI Case T-285/03 *Agraz and others v Commission (No 1)* (damage not certain, dismissed, appealed C-243/05 P) [2005] ECR II-1063 [47]. On appeal the ECJ returned the matter to the CFI, as it had wrongly held that damage was not certain, see ECJ Case C-243/05 P *Agraz v Commission* (referred back to CFI) [2006] ECR I-10833.

B. Convergence: a Laudable Objective, but Reasons for it are Understated in the Case-law

It was noted in chapters two, three and four that reasonable convergence between the two systems brings about certain positive effects. Enhancing convergence of the constituent legal systems of the European Union is amongst the fundamental aims of the whole integration process, and striving for sufficient convergence has also been the underlying aim of the internal market programme.

The decision to change liability conditions was taken by the Court, not the legislator. When the process leading to alignment in *Bergaderm* (ECJ 2000)[22] was discussed in chapter four, it appeared that the actual change brought about in that case was not motivated in exceedingly great detail. In addition, when subsequent case-law is analysed, the argument for convergence between the two systems comes up only very rarely and some authors, most notably Hilson, have already found traces that the convergence trumpeted in *Bergaderm* would already be unravelling.[23]

One could ask whether the reasons for convergence were so clear to everybody that they did not need to be discussed, not then and not now. At least in terms of acceptance it seems that this aspect of the case-law has not been much contested. What has been more contested in recent developments is the absence of strict liability, as confirmed by the ECJ in *FIAMM* (ECJ 2007).[24] Perhaps convergence is something very natural. Perhaps the underlying values are so evident that they do not have to be expressed in more detail.

C. Case-law as Source for Convergence

This study has highlighted various aspects of having case-law as a primary legal source for EU public liability law in damages. It must be recognised that a virtue of case-law is that it is indeed a flexible source of law, which can easily be adapted. It is well-suited for gradual changes. However, it should also be said that it represents a challenge for judges, both at EU and national level. For national judges the challenge of using case-law as a source is somewhat alleviated by fact that national liability laws also often heavily rely on case-law, this time national.

One could also ask whether this area represents 'judge-made law', or is it still rather a habitual interpretation by judges: assembling the law from the existing reference pieces? It seems that for EU law public law liability, the pointers would go to the latter. *FIAMM* (ECJ 2008)[25] could even be cited as a counter-example to

[22] ECJ *Bergaderm* (n 6).

[23] See C Hilson, 'The Role of Discretion in EC Law on Non-Contractual Liability' (2005) *Common Market Law Review* 677–95, 691.

[24] See eg, A Steinbach, 'EC Liability for Non-compliance with Decisions of the WTO DSB: The Lack of Judicial Protection Persists' (2009) *Journal of World Trade* 1047–69, and with more detailed analysis A Steinbach, *Die Haftung der EG und ihrer Mitgliedsstaaten für WTO-Rechtsverletzungen aus rechtswissenschaftlicher und ökonomischer Perspektive* (Berlin, Duncker & Humblot, 2009).

[25] ECJ *FIAMM* (n 7).

judicial activism: there the Court did not find that strict liability for legislative acts was a common principle to the Member States so that it should have been adopted for liability of the EU, too.

Another question is: how should a system be appreciated where in the damages liability systems all the choices, including policy choices, are made by judges? For case-law this may look very normal, and even traditional. However, it can be contrasted with certain developments in EU legislative practices.

For example, in the framework of the EU's Better Regulation Programmes an impact assessment procedure has been established for any future Commission proposals. The purpose is to analyse the potential economic, social and environmental consequences of proposals beforehand, and thus prepare evidence for political decision-makers on the advantages and disadvantages of various policy options available. For certain instruments already adopted, the instrument itself foresees that the Commission should draft a report some years after its application in order to assess its functioning. Such an assessment may be made alongside annual reports on the operation of the instrument.[26] These documents are made publicly available and transmitted to the institutions concerned for information and further assessment.

The purpose here is of course not to suggest that the Court should make a public impact assessment every time it intends to distinguish a case from previous case-law, or that the Court should publish specific annual reports on damages cases. It is rather to point out that contrary to developments in the field of legislation, analysis and public debate of damages case-law is largely absent, at least in an institutionalised form, unlike the case of legislation. The contrast may become even sharper when compared to developments in 'private liability', ie the various efforts to find a common core for national private non-contractual liability rules.[27] Moreover, it should be noted that although the domain is different, the Commission has been very active in contributing to the private enforcement debate.[28] There seems to be no reason why such a discussion could not be initiated for EU public liability law, especially now when, due to constitutionalisation, liability has been extended to the whole of the European Union.

D. 'Haphazard' Convergence by Case-law?

The fact that convergence has been built by case-law has of course had important implications. The Union courts take no initiatives to attract new cases to be judged;

[26] eg, see the various reports relating to Regulation (EC) No 1049/2001 of the European Parliament and of the Council of 30 May 2001 regarding public access to European Parliament, Council and Commission documents [2001] OJ L145/43, available at http://ec.europa.eu/transparency/access_documents/index_en.htm.

[27] See ch 3, s IV.

[28] See COM(2005) 672. Green Paper – Damages actions for breach of the EC antitrust rules, 19.12.2005 and COM(2008) 165. White Paper on Damages Actions for Breach of the EC antitrust rules, 2.4.2008; the latter also included an impact assessment and public consultation, and lead to a European Parliament resolution and an opinion of the European and Social Committee.

decisions to introduce cases have been taken by other persons. For EU liability, decisions to sue the Union are taken by individual applicants. For Member State liability, decisions to initiate preliminary rulings procedure before the ECJ are always taken by national courts. It is therefore not without importance from which courts and countries the references have come. It appears that United Kingdom courts are particularly well-represented, alongside the German and Italian Courts.[29] The Austrian courts have also been very active.[30] Some references can also be found from Spain, The Netherlands, Finland and Denmark. The number of references can be affected by procedural reasons or by the fact that the courts in some Member States more readily make references, for example due to national legal traditions and practice. However, what is striking is that there seem to be no references concerning Member State liability from France. Nor do there appear to be any damages references from Portugal, Luxembourg or Ireland, nor again from the twelve new Member States that joined the European Union in 2003 and 2007. However, it seems unlikely that in all these Member States there would never be damages cases against the Member State for a breach of EU law. This finding highlights the fact that certain Member States, or even certain courts, have de facto been setting the agenda of the ECJ for Member State damages liability case-law.

It should also be noted that much of the case-law could have been (very) different on slightly different factual or procedural grounds. In other words, as in case-law in general, the outcome in a number of cases has depended on almost haphazard issues. The existence of a series of *Test Claimants* cases[31] was largely dependent on national procedural rules and a national court willing and ready to craft and send detailed references for preliminary ruling. On the other hand, procedural rules were the reason why the issue of possible no-fault liability of the Union in WTO context kept floating for years even after the appeal in *Biret* (ECJ 2003),[32] as the Court was

[29] For references from UK courts, see eg, ECJ *Brasserie du Pêcheur and Factortame* (n 4); ECJ Case C-5/94 *Hedley Lomas* [1996] ECR I-2553; ECJ Case C-66/95 *Sutton* [1997] ECR I-2163; ECJ Case C-63/01 *Evans* [2003] ECR I-14447; ECJ Case C-452/06 *Synthon* [2008] ECR I-7681 and the Test Claimants cases: ECJ Case C-446/04 *Test Claimants in the FII Group Litigation* [2006] ECR I-11753, ECJ Case C-374/04 *Test Claimants in Class IV of the ACT Group Litigation* [2006] ECR I-11673, ECJ Case C-524/04 *Test Claimants in the Thin Cap Group Litigation* [2007] ECR I-2107, ECJ Case C-201/05 *Test Claimants in the CFC and Dividend Group Litigation* [2008] ECR I-2875.

For references from German courts, see in particular, ECJ *Brasserie du Pêcheur and Factortame* (n 4); ECJ Joined Cases C-283/94, C-291/94 and C-292/94 *Denkavit Internationaal and others v Bundesamt für Finanzen* [1996] ECR I-5063; ECJ Joined Cases C-178/94, C-179/94, C-188/94, C-189/94 and C-190/94 *Dillenkofer and others v Bundesrepublik Deutschland* [1996] ECR I-4845; ECJ Case C-222/02 *Paul and others* [2004] ECR I-9425 and ECJ *Danske Slagterier* (n 12).

For references from Italian courts, see eg, ECJ Joined Cases C-6/90 and C-9/90 *Francovich and Bonifaci* [1991] ECR I-5357; ECJ Joined Cases C-94/95 and C-95/95 *Bonifaci and others and Berto and others v INPS* [1997] ECR I-3969; ECJ Case C-261/95 *Palmisani v INPS* [1997] ECR I-4025; ECJ Case C-373/95 *Maso and others v INPS and Repubblica italiana* [1997] ECR I-405 and ECJ Case C-173/03 *Traghetti del Mediterraneo* [2006] ECR I-5177.

[30] For references from Austrian courts, see eg, ECJ Case C-111/97 *EvoBus Austria* [1998] ECR I-5411; ECJ Case C-140/97 *Rechberger and others* [1999] ECR I-3499, ECJ Case C-302/97 *Konle* [1999] ECR I-3099; ECJ Case C-112/00 *Schmidberger* [2003] ECR I-5659; ECJ Case C-224/01 *Köbler* [2003] ECR I-10239.

[31] See n 29.

[32] ECJ Case C-93/02 P *Biret International v Council* (appeal dismissed) [2003] ECR I-10497.

not in a position to examine an issue which was put forward only on appeal. The clear-cut 'no' came years later from the ECJ in *FIAMM* (ECJ 2008).[33]

As for further convergence, one approach which should be kept in mind is the division of issues to be converged – and those to be left outside. It has been noted regarding private law liability that certain sectoral questions are more receptive and suitable for harmonisation than others.[34] Already in current liability for breaches of EU law, certain questions have been left by the ECJ to national law as regards Member State liability.

E. National Implementation – a Threat for Convergence?

A dedicated EU law fundamentalist could be tempted to see the national implementation of Member State liability as a hindrance or obstacle to the application of Member State liability for breaches of EU law. Problems in that implementation could also be seen as potentially endangering any convergence established by the Court.

The complex environment of national application of EU law can be broken down to variables, which are to be taken into account when assessing application. There appear to be five legal variables in 'Europeanised national law'.[35] They include the following: (1) national law and its sources; (2) EU law and its sources; (3) principles of hierarchy of norms in national law; (4) principles of hierarchy of norms in EU law and (5) principles governing the relationship between national law and EU law (principles stemming from EU law). The challenges originate from the 'intrusion' of EU law into the national system. That marriage is, however, an essential part of the functioning of the whole EU legal system and its legitimacy. This relation is in constant development, including the relationship between the ECJ and national courts.[36]

National implementation of Member State liability should rather be seen as a valuable resource. It gives certain leeway to the national court in taking account of policy and co-ordination of the two systems. If the effectiveness of Member State liability needs to be enhanced, it seems that there are two ways available, as the basic structure (ie the fact that it is the national courts that rule on this issue) cannot be changed. The ECJ makes a de facto choice in each ruling it hands down in damages cases as to how clear or detailed guidance it wishes to give to the national courts – to the court that has asked for the preliminary ruling and all the other courts

[33] ECJ *FIAMM* (n 7).

[34] WH van Boom, 'European tort law: an integrated or compartmentalized approach?' in A Vaquer (ed), *European private law beyond the Common Frame of Reference: essays in honour of Reinhard Zimmermann* (Groningen, Europa Law Publishing, 2008).

[35] See N Jääskinen, *Eurooppalaistuvan oikeuden oikeusteoreettisia ongelmia [The Europeanisation of Law – Jurisprudential Problems]* (Helsinki, 2008) 154, who builds here on analysis by Harris.

[36] See ECJ Case C-453/00 *Kühne & Heitz* [2004] ECR I-837; ECJ Case C-234/04 *Kapferer* [2006] ECR I-2585; ECJ Case C-2/06 *Kempter* [2008] ECR I-411; ECJ Case C-2/08 *Fallimento Olimpiclub* [2009] ECR I-7501 and ECJ Case C-173/09 *Elchinov* [2010] ECR I-0000.

which will (when the time comes) examine its case-law in order to find the law. The nature and tone of this judicial dialogue remains essential: how well can the ECJ convince the judges that are to apply its judgments? An additional and vital way to enhance the passing of messages from the ECJ are academia and doctrine analysing and presenting ECJ case-law. Ideally, such presentations should be adapted to each national system in order to make them more easily accessible to national judges.[37]

F. Convergence in Context: Findings to Help National and EU Judges

One finding of this study is that neither of the EU law public liability systems – that for breaches by the Union or that for breaches by Member States – should be seen as individual, isolated phenomena, either in relation to each other, or in relation to other remedies. There are two aspects here.

The first aspect relates to finding law for convergence purposes. In this respect the task of the Luxembourg judge working on the liability of the Union is easier: it would mean that the Luxembourg judge should explore, when needed, Member State liability case-law to find guidance. In practical terms, this means that the General Court, when examining liability cases against the Union, should examine the case-law of the ECJ on Member State liability. As such, this should not be very difficult. The problem is rather as regards Member State liability in cases where the national judge should thus examine not only Member State liability case-law from Luxembourg, but also another set of Luxembourg case-law, namely the liability case-law of the Union, to find additional sources of law. This polycentric approach can become rather demanding for national judges, who already have to combine EU law and national law for Member State liability for breaches of EU law.

The second aspect is more systemic in nature. The convergence established in case-law has its origins in a refined and elaborate system of mutual influences between public liability laws at various levels. The 'unintended' effects are of special interest. Convergence will inevitably lead to some spill-over effects. Why do they appear, and what effect will they have? The presence of a spill-over effect has been noted by national judges while applying the EU law based liability of the Member States and national public liability law for Member State liability. It was possible to get compensation, in a similar situation, under one scheme, but not under the other. As EU public liability law is closely linked with the national public liability law of the 27 Member States, it is thus inevitably linked to general national liability and private tort law. But it is also linked to European-level tort law and related projects. These findings apparently contributed to certain legislative initiatives in

[37] In this context, see for example R Gordon, *EC Law in Judicial Review* (Oxford, Oxford University Press, 2007). In this work the author explains, in Part I, the functioning of EC law in judicial review (the part includes a section on state liability, 157–78). In Part II, the author sets out the underlying general principles in EC law judicial review challenges and in Part III he presents how the EC law and judicial review in England operate in practice in different areas, such as state aid and competition law, environmental challenges, and public procurement.

the area of public liability in certain Member States, as in many Member States the changes carried out were finally implemented by the legislator. It is submitted that codification by enactment to national law of some principles stemming from ECJ case-law may not in the end be a very good idea: such an action would canonise case-law which is basically subject to change by its author at any time.[38]

Convergence also contributes to increased predictability within the two systems. Incidentally, enhanced clarity of the two systems could lead to better drafting of damages actions, thus leading arguably to more complete and more informative judgments. Coherence would also mean easier recourse to the 'other' half of the case-law.

G. Appearance and Effects of Convergence – Has it Meant 'Progress' for EU Public Liability Law?

How has convergence then appeared? How can progress in 'convergence' be measured? In formal terms, one might be searching for mutual references in the case-law between the two liability systems. These express cross-references are largely absent, but this can be explained by other reasons, namely by the fact there are two different courts which bear the primary responsibility of day-to-day operation of each of the two systems, ie the GC (CFI) for the liability of the European Union and the ECJ for Member State liability, together with the Member State courts. The ECJ appears rarely to refer to GC case-law in general, and even if it were in a position to do so, the bulk of EU liability case-law by the GC is already considerable and ECJ case-law on Member State liability is much less extensive. Thus progress cannot be established from mutual references in case-law, or from the absence of such references.

Convergence ideology has started to deploy its effects, and the liability criteria have been opened up. Yet, on the basis of the findings of this study, it is submitted that the case-law on public liability for breaches of EU law has been – and still is – rather restrictive.

This impression is intensified by a procedural reason. Indeed, when looking at the 'complete solutions' given at EU level, one gets the impression that the liability system for the Union is exceedingly restrictive, in particular when compared to each individual 'positive newsflash' coming in the framework of Member State liability. *Francovich* looks more promising: it is a kind of good news from Luxembourg, but in actual fact, when all the elements of national law are applied by the national court, it may well be, it is submitted, that it is no more open or advantageous for the applicant who has suffered from a breach of EU law rights on the part of a Member

[38] For example, in Finland, at the time of accession to the European Union, it was discussed whether the concepts of direct effect or primacy of community law should be enshrined and defined in Finnish legislation. At the end, this was not done. See, in general, H Kanninen, 'EY-oikeuden soveltamisesta korkeimmassa hallinto-oikeudessa [Application of EC Law in the Supreme Administrative Court]' (2003) *Lakimies* 1253–72, 1255.

State. The replies given by the ECJ – which by definition in the framework of the preliminary rulings procedure are limited and leave the final analysis to the national court – may give rise to hopes for applicants in national procedures, but when all the elements are put into place, the result may be disappointing.

This idea of false 'positive newsflashes' from Luxembourg to individuals and economic operators may be illustrated by recalling the difference between the judgments in *Francovich I* and *Francovich II*. In *Francovich I* (ECJ 1991),[39] the Court boldly established the principle of state liability. In *Francovich II* (ECJ 1995)[40] the Court replied to a new question by the national court that indeed Mr Francovich himself was not covered by the principle bearing his name. The question is now: should the focus be on *Francovich I* or *Francovich II*? In other words: should we focus on *Brasserie du Pêcheur* before the ECJ or the German national case, where damages were finally not awarded, as the breach was not 'sufficiently serious', according to the national court?[41] Both names – *Francovich* and *Brasserie du Pêcheur* – are understood as shorthand for a promising or even formidable 'new' remedy that is to repair infringements individuals have suffered by Member State action. With a shift of vantage point from EU level to national level, they become code names for publicly celebrated, but in actual fact probably deeply disappointed applicants, left with rejected damages claims after years of litigation. A Pyrrhic victory, ruinous for the applicant?

With hindsight, it seems that the recent developments for the liability of the EU[42] and the liability of the Member States have not in actual fact been very progressive or revolutionary, at least when compared to some other areas with recent development, such as, for example, access to documents held by EU institutions. Here, following administrative practices created voluntarily by the institutions, a specific access to documents regulation was adopted by the legislator, following the introduction of a legal basis in the EC Treaty by the Treaty of Amsterdam. The new Regulation and the interpretation given by the CFI and appeals judgments by the ECJ in particular have indeed forced the institutions to further change their policy and procedures in the field of public access to documents, sometimes after long

[39] ECJ Case *Francovich and Bonifaci* (n 29).

[40] ECJ Case C-479/93 *Francovich v Italy (No 2)* [1995] ECR I-3843.

[41] Bundesgerichtshof (Federal Supereme Court). Urteil vom 24.10.1996 (III ZR 127/91) – Brasserie du Pêcheur. Reported in English in [1997] 1 Common Market Law Reports 971 and A Oppenheimer (ed) *The Relationship between European Community law and national law: the cases. Volume 2* (Cambridge, Cambridge University Press 2003) 588–96. Whereas in the case of Andrea Francovich the result was finally largely a result of his individual position, the rejection of the Brasserie du Pêcheur claim before BGH was based on systemic arguments. See eg, G Wilms, 'Le droit allemand' in G Vandersanden and M Dony (eds), *La responsabilité des États membres en cas de violation du droit communautaire. Études de droit communautaire et de droit national comparé* (Brussels, Bruylant, 1997), 82–86.

[42] See eg, J Wakefield, 'Retrench and Reform: The Action for Damages' in P Eeckhout and T Tridimas (eds), *28 Yearbook of European Law 2009* (Oxford, Oxford University Press, 2010) 432ff and D Ritleng, 'De l'irresponsabilité extracontractuelle de la Communauté' in J-C Masclet and H Ruiz Fabri et al (eds), *L'Union européenne – Union de droit, union des droits. Mélanges en l'honneur du Professeur Philippe Manin* (Paris, Pedone, 2010) 922ff.

legal battles.[43] In contrast, neither for the damages liability of the EU, nor for the damages liability of the Member States, has the number of (successful) damages actions dramatically risen since *Bergaderm*. Be that as it may, the explanation given above may not be the only one and no hasty conclusions should be drawn. It can be that the contained number of successful damages cases can be explained by assuming that there are better processes to avoid damages, thus less damages. It is also possible that damages situations arise, but that they are settled by the institutions.

All in all, even if the duty to mitigate loss (ie duty to take all necessary action to minimise harmful effects, including an action of annulment) did not exist, the case-law in both systems remains restrictive so that anyone threatened with damages had better look first for other remedies in a timely manner. This is not always possible, eg in cases where the existence of a breach is only discovered or established afterwards.[44]

H. Convergence and Joint Liability

The convergence of Member State and EU liability criteria has contributed, in principle, to clarification of the conditions to be applied for joint liability. However, it has not harmonised in any way the procedural differences in claiming damages in the EU and in national systems. Even if the conditions were to become increasingly harmonised, the Member States must be sued in a Member State court and the Union in the General Court in Luxembourg: two separate sets of proceedings are still needed.[45]

In particular for joint liability situations, the limitation periods for damages actions are another important issue. In terms of protection of rights and access to justice, the convergent criteria assessed in this study must finally be coupled with all of the other applicable liability criteria that must be fulfilled for damages liability to become operational.[46] In particular, for joint liability one could claim that the deadline of five years for liability of the Union, in situations where Member State liability may also apply, is rather short, maybe even too short. It seems fairly reasonable for cases where only the liability of the European Union is involved. However, for a situation where liability appears to be joint, or when it only appears at a later stage that the liability claimed originally against a Member State is exclusively that of the EU, the five-year period can turn out to be almost unreasonably short.

[43] *cf* eg ECJ Case C-353/99 P *Council v Hautala* (CFI judgment set aside) [2001] ECR I-9565; ECJ Case C-353/01 P *Mattila v Council and Commission* (CFI judgment set aside) [2004] ECR I-1073; ECJ Case C-64/05 P *Sweden v Commission ('IFAW')* (CFI judgment set aside) [2007] ECR I-11389 and ECJ Joined Cases C-39/05 P and C-52/05 P *Sweden and Turco v Council* (CFI judgment set aside) [2008] ECR I-4723.

[44] ECJ Case *Kühne & Heitz* (n 36).

[45] See AWH Meij, 'Article 215(2) EC and Local Remedies' in T Heukels and A McDonnell (eds), *The Action for Damages in Community Law* (The Hague, Kluwer Law International, 1997).

[46] On joint liability, see W Wils, 'Concurrent Liability of the Community and a Member State' (1992) *European Law Review* 191–206 and P Oliver, 'Joint Liability of the Community and the Member States' in T Heukels and A McDonnell (eds), *The Action for Damages in Community Law* (The Hague, Kluwer Law International, 1997).

The importance of timely (ie early) damages litigation has been underlined in a rather convergent manner in two recent cases concerning EU liability and Member State liability. In *Dolianova*, the applicant had originally sued Italy in the national court, and when those proceedings reached the court of final instance in Italy, it held that Italy was not the correct respondent, but it should rather have been the Community. The applicant thus sued the Commission before the CFI, which found that the liability conditions were fulfilled and awarded damages (CFI 2004).[47] However, the Commission appealed to the ECJ, pointing to the limitation period. Advocate General Sharpston proposed that the reading of that criterion should in this case be more open and that the case should have been qualified as exceptional and that the damages award should be upheld.[48] The ECJ did not agree and gave a strict ruling, following an appeal by the Commission (ECJ 2008).[49] This can be assessed alongside *Danske Slagterier* (ECJ 2009),[50] where the ECJ accepted that three years can be accepted for the time limit for Member State liability. This considerably affected the potential damages award in that case.

It thus appears that there are some converging elements in the limitation periods in the two systems which are to be interpreted strictly. It is probable that there are trends in Member States to shorten the time limits.

Therefore, in the current situation the only way of ensuring protection of rights in a situation where joint liability is present or potentially present, is to initiate litigation right away against both the Member State and the European Union. Dual litigation will increase the costs and cost risk for the applicant and will inevitably have a dissuasive effect. It will also make litigation an interesting option only for cases where the monetary interests of the case are considerable: litigation for minor matters becomes too risky.

It is submitted that this point in law may require revising. It seems that in cases of concurrent or sequential liability, this can be an area where the legal rules and their application are, to quote Judge Mancini, letting the citizen down again. It should be explored on a case by case basis whether the EU should consider settling such cases even after expiry of the five-year period.[51] A case by case approach would not necessarily open the floodgates of litigation, but it would make a reasonable outcome possible. Amending the time limit would not require changing the Treaty, but amending statute, which is easier to carry out.

[47] CFI Case T-166/98 *Cantina sociale di Dolianova and Others v Commission* (liability established; appealed C-51/05 P) [2004] ECR II-3991

[48] ECJ Case C-51/05 P *Opinion of Advocate General Sharpston – Commission v Cantina sociale di Dolianova and Others* [2008] ECR I-5341.

[49] ECJ Case C-51/05 P *Commission v Cantina sociale di Dolianova and Others* (CFI judgment set aside; damages action dismissed as inadmissible) [2008] ECR I-5341.

[50] ECJ Case *Danske Slagterier* (n 12). In the national proceedings, after the preliminary ruling the case was sent back from BGH to the court below, see Germany 2009 Bundesgerichtshof (Federal Supereme Court). Urteil des III. Zivilsenats vom 4.6.2009 - III ZR 144/05 (*Danske Slagterier*).

[51] Taking into account, of course, the rules concerning sound financial management and in particular Council Regulation (EC, Euratom) No 1605/2002 of 25 June 2002 on the Financial Regulation applicable to the general budget of the European Communities [2002] OJ L248/1, as amended.

V. OUTLOOK BEYOND CONVERGENCE

There are six issues which may be of interest for future developments. The first would be the liability of the Union for acts of the courts of the European Union. The way forward here has already been paved by *Köbler* and *Traghetti*. Such liability would not, when considering reparation in monetary terms, be very important for the budget of the European Union, but the importance lies in the issue of principle.[52] In practice, such liability would primarily concern only the court of final instance, that is, the ECJ, or in staff cases, the General Court.[53] However, it may be difficult to see many other areas than breach of fundamental rights guaranteed by the ECHR where such liability could be activated.

The second concerns the strict liability of the European Union. Albeit this was excluded in the WTO context in rather clear terms in 2008 by the ECJ, sitting in Grand Chamber in *FIAMM*, this issue will certainly remain on the table. It might become something like horizontal direct effect of directives after *Faccini Dori* (ECJ 1994):[54] 'obviously' it does not exist, but the discussion will go on.

Thirdly, Treaty changes in the Union are always a challenge, but Lisbon has been a particular case, not least because it was planned to 'quickly' remedy the Constitutional Treaty, which was rejected by two referenda. The Lisbon Treaty brought about many rather fundamental changes and in many ways it is comparable to the Maastricht Treaty.[55] As regards public liability issues, the following changes merit particular attention.

In the first place, the collapse of the pillar structure is important. The former third pillar (co-operation in police matters and criminal law) became fully integrated into the TFEU. This is essential for Member State liability in particular. An open question in this area is the effects in time, ie, what, for liability purposes, will be the role of the 'old' III pillar legislation, including provisions declaring that there can be no direct effect for certain current III pillar instruments?[56] There appears to be no express provision on the issue of liability as regards past instruments.[57] On the other hand, the area covered by the former second pillar, the Common Foreign and Security Policy (CFSP), will remain with some exceptions outside the jurisdiction of the Court.[58] No express provision is included in the Treaties for liability and

[52] As underlined in ECJ Opinion 1/09 *Draft Agreement on the creation of a European and Community Patent Court* [2011] ECR I-0000 (Opinion of 8 March 2011).

[53] When it is the appeal court from the Civil Service Tribunal and no re-examination procedure is initiated by the ECJ.

[54] ECJ Case C-91/92 *Faccini Dori v Recreb* [1994] ECR I-3325.

[55] For a concise analysis, see M Dougan, 'The Treaty of Lisbon 2007: winning minds, not hearts' (2008) *Common Market Law Review* 617–703.

[56] See however ECJ Case C-105/03 *Pupino* [2005] ECR I-5285, on interpretation in conformity.

[57] The powers of the Court of Justice are limited in respect of instruments adopted before the entry into force of the Lisbon Treaty; these limitations will cease to apply at the latest five years after entry into force of the Treaty, see Treaty of Lisbon, Protocol (no 36) on transitional provisions.

[58] See Art 275 TFEU and *cf* CFI Case T-338/02 *Segi and Others v Council* (dismissed, appealed C-355/04 P) [2004] ECR II-1647; ECJ Case C-355/04 P *Segi* (appeal dismissed) [2007] ECR I-1657.

jurisdiction for Union liability for CFSP. Be that as it may, it is clear that liability of the Union for the implementing measures adopted in the framework of the TFEU (former EC Treaty) is maintained.[59]

Moreover, when the 'Community of law' was replaced by a 'Union of law', also as regards the liability subject, this enlarged the scope of functions potentially giving rise to liability. Regarding rights granted and guaranteed by EU law, the future accession of the European Union to the European Convention of Human Rights (ECHR), foreseen in Article 6(2) TEU, will undoubtedly lead to enhanced human rights protection, including in respect of damages liability.[60]

Fourthly, as the basis of the EU liability system is principles common to the Member States, the EU liability system could further examine whether new types of compensation mechanisms should be envisaged, in certain sectors, for example. It can be recalled that in the milk quota cases specific Community compensation schemes were established through legislation. There are two systems which would be worth further consideration. The first would be the designation of an independent EU authority which would initially examine a first request for compensation in the first place, with a view to an amicable settlement, before court proceedings are initiated. In Sweden, for example, a request for damages resulting from the activities of public administrative authorities is first made to a government authority[61] thus ensuring either 'no-hassle' compensation or in case of a negative decision, at least an administrative pre-treatment phase of the case to clarify the scope of the claim before any court proceedings.[62] The second system worth considering would be to establish compensation funds in certain specific cases.[63] Even if such ideas might sound remote or impracticable for the time being, it seems useful to mention them. The liability system is in no way static, and sudden developments may call for new solutions sooner than expected.

Fifthly, one aspect which has become clear during the research is the willingness of applicants to resort to damages action, in particular against the European Union. It is some kind of 'damages reflex' in a compensation culture. In a way, the

[59] On this question, see CFI *Sison v Council* (n 11).

[60] See ECJ Case C-185/95 P *Baustahlgewebe v Commission* (reasonable satisfaction for excessive duration of proceedings – €50000 in fine reduction) [1998] ECR I-8417; ECJ Case C-385/07 P *Der Grüne Punkt– Duales System Deutschland v Commission* (appeal dismissed) [2009] ECR I-6155 and CST Joined Cases F-124/05 and F-96/06 *A and G v Commission* (damages awarded €30000, no appeal) [2010] ECR (judgment of 13 January 2010).

[61] Swedish 'justitiekansler', Chancellor of Justice. See the analysis as to the functioning of Member State liability in Sweden in J Engström, *The Europeanisation of Remedies and Procedures through Judge-Made Law. Can a Trojan Horse Achieve Effectiveness?* (Florence, European University Institute, 2009) 487–514.

[62] Such an administrative preparatory phase is not unknown in EU law, see Art 90 of the EU Staff rules (Regulation (EEC, Euratom, ECSC) No 259/68 of the Council of 29 February 1968 laying down the Staff Regulations of Officials and the Conditions of Employment of Other Servants of the European Communities and instituting special measures temporarily applicable to officials of the Commission (Staff Regulations of Officials), as amended [1968] OJ English Spec. Ed. Ser. I Ch. 1968(I)/30) and Art 258 TFEU (ex-Art 226 EC) laying down the compulsory administrative phase in infringement proceedings against Member States.

[63] See on this issue in France, eg A Frank, *Le droit de la responsabilité administrative à l'épreuve des fonds d'indemnisation* (Paris, L'Harmattan, 2008) 39ff.

relevant Treaty provisions and a superficial look at the basic conditions may create the impression that obtaining damages would be a relatively easy task. It is true, at least in comparison to direct actions under the TFEU, that applicants get their case examined more easily, in that the procedural hurdles for admissibility are lower. In reality the probability of actually receiving compensation is rather low. A damages action should, however, never be seen as the only or even the primary remedy; it is a remedy which is particularly fitted for situations where everything else has already failed, or where no other effective remedies are available.

The sixth issue relates to reconnecting to different contexts and constitutionalisation. EU public liability law cannot be surgically extracted from the surrounding world. Private tort law liability is the essentially underlying layer for public liability, even if it has been criticised, too.[64] The actual convergence movement which has been either set in motion by *Bergaderm* or to which *Bergaderm* has contributed, is far more overarching. Lawyers interested in public liability in Member States have started to go international. Since *Francovich*, *Brasserie du Pêcheur* and *Bergaderm* public liability questions have been set to the agendas of seminars, and lawyers have been gradually starting to think about these issues in a wider international perspective. Therefore, the movement to which Bergaderm belongs is clearly part of a larger trend.

In conclusion, one of the underlying aims of this study has been that, by attempting to bring about some systemic clarification to the damages liability conditions of the two systems and their application, this study would contribute to diminishing of liability cases, among other things by encouraging the relevant authorities, EU and national, to properly apply EU law. How far the implicit or explicit creation of liability situation is behaviour which can be deterred, is another question.[65]

In this study, one small yet important piece of EU law, the liability of public authorities for breaches of EU law, has been explored. Rolling back in time, the turning point for all the development was *Francovich* in 1991. Indeed, if one attempted to capture in one key word the trigger for convergent developments in public liability in EU law, '*Francovich*' would be a fairly good candidate.

There appears to be so much more than meets the eye in *Francovich*. True, *Francovich* is often cited as the original authority for Member State liability. It is equally true, however, that it was the imbalance created by *Francovich* that triggered the modification and alignment of the criteria for liability of the Union that was carried out in *Brasserie du Pêcheur/Bergaderm* 1996/2000. These two developments led to issues of implementation of *Francovich* at national level. These, in turn, have

[64] D Edward and W Robinson, 'Is there a Place for Private Law Principles in Community Law?' in T Heukels and A McDonnell (eds), *The Action for Damages in Community Law* (The Hague, Kluwer Law International, 1997).

[65] When analysing the effects of *Francvich* case-law, Baquero Cruz seems to be somewhat disappointed for the functioning of its preventive effect, while for Harlow this is behaviour which cannot be deterred; see J Baquero Cruz, '*Francovich* and Imperfect Law' in M Poiares Maduro and L Azoulai (eds), *The past and Future of EU Law. The Classics of EU Law Revisited on the 50th Anniversary of the Rome Treaty* (Oxford, Hart Publishing, 2010) 420ff and C Harlow, *State Liability: Tort Law and Beyond* (Oxford, Oxford University Press, 2004) 22.

set the train in motion and created spill-over effects to other areas of public liability in purely national law.

The convergence effort put into practice since *Bergaderm* will mark the future of European Union public liability regimes for years to come. In this respect, the future of the public liability system is obviously following a more general trend of convergence. Increasing systemic convergence in all areas of law is likely to continue, including private law, private tort law and administrative law. I think the convergence effort as such is a positive development. The key question, to be decided on a case by case basis for all systems, will still remain the same: when should a specific rule be created and applied, and when should convergence be the commonly accepted objective?

The extensive presentation of EU public liability case-law has hopefully convinced the reader that this is an area in active phase. The convergence introduced in *Brasserie du Pêcheur/Factortame* in 1996 and implemented since *Bergaderm* in 2000 has been a cornerstone for the development. It would be daring to say that this is the end of the story. Taken together, the two sets of case-law do form, it is submitted, a critical mass which will usefully serve for a coherent development towards the next phases of public liability system in EU law.

Bibliography

Aalto, P, *Jäsenvaltion vahingonkorvausvastuu EY-oikeudessa [Damages Liability of the Member States in EC Law]* (Helsinki, Kauppakaari, 1999).

——, 'Twelve Years of Francovich in the European Court of Justice: A survey of the Case-law on the Interpretation of the Three Conditions of Liability' in S Moreira de Sousa and W Heusel (eds), *Enforcing Community Law from Francovich to Köbler: Twelve Years of the State Liability Principle* (Cologne, Bundesanzeiger, 2004) 59–77.

——, 'Valtion korvausvastuu yksilölle unionin oikeuden rikkomisesta [State Liability for Individuals for Breaches of Union Law]' in H Kaila et al (eds), *Yksilön oikeusasema Euroopan unionissa – Individens rättsställning inom Europeiska Unionen: Juhlakirja Allan Rosas – Festskrift Allan Rosas* (Turku/Åbo, 2008) 645–58.

Albers, C, *Die Haftung der Bundesrepublik Deutschland für die Nichtumsetzung von EG-Richtlinien* (Baden-Baden, Nomos, 1995).

Allison, JWF, 'Transplantation and Cross-fertilisation' in J Beatson and T Tridimas (eds), *New Directions in European Public Law* (Oxford, Hart Publishing, 1998) 169–82.

Andersson, H, 'Nationell EKMR-skadeståndsrätt – en argumentativ problemsinventeringsskiss' (2007) *Tidskrift utgiven av Juridiska Föreningen i Finland* 377–414.

Arnull, A, *The European Union and its Court of Justice*, 2nd edn (Oxford, Oxford University Press, 2006).

Aubin, P, *Die Haftung der Europäischen Wirtschaftsgemeinschaft und ihrer Mitgliedstaaten bei gemeinschaftsrechtswidrigen nationalen Verwaltungsakten* (Baden-Baden, Nomos, 1982).

Aziz, M, *The Impact of European Rights on National Legal Cultures* (Oxford, Hart Publishing, 2004).

Baquero Cruz, J, '*Francovich* and Imperfect Law' in M Poiares Maduro and L Azoulai (eds), *The past and Future of EU Law. The Classics of EU Law Revisited on the 50th Anniversary of the Rome Treaty* (Oxford, Hart Publishing, 2010) 418–22.

von Bar, C, *The Common European Law of Torts. Volume* One (Oxford, Clarendon, 1998).

——, *The Common European Law of Torts. Volume Two* (Oxford, Clarendon, 2000).

—— (ed), *Principles, Definitions and Model Rules of European Private Law: Draft Common Frame of Reference (Dcfr)*, outline edition (Oxford, Oxford University Press, 2008).

—— (ed), *Principles of European Law: Non-Contractual Liability Arising out of Damage Caused to Another: v. 7 (European Civil Code Series)* (Oxford, Oxford University Press, 2009).

von Bar, C and Clive, E et al (eds), *Principles, definitions and model rules of European private law: Draft Common Frame of Reference (DCFR) / prepared by the Study Group on a European Civil Code and the Research Group on EC Private Law (Acquis Group)* (Munich, Sellier European Law Publishers, 2009).

Barkhuysen, T and van Emmerik, ML, 'Accountability of the Judiciary on the National Level for Violations of the European Convention of Human Rights' in G Canivet et al (eds), *Independence, Accountability and the Judiciary* (London, BIICL, 2006) 419–29.

Barnard, C, 'Introduction: The Constitutional Treaty, the Constitutional Debate and the Constitutional Process' in C Barnard (ed), *The Fundamentals of EU Law Revisited: Assessing the Impact of the Constitutional Debate* (Oxford, Oxford University Press, 2007) 1–11.

Baudenbacher, C, 'If Not EEA State Liability, Then What? Reflections Ten Years after the EFTA Court's Sveinbjörnsdóttir Ruling', in S Katuoka (ed) *Law in the Changing Europe: Liber Amicorum Pranas Kuris* 545–68 (Vilnius, Mykolo Romerio Universitetas, 2008).

Beaumont, P and Lyons, C et al (eds), *Convergence and Divergence in European Public Law* (Oxford, Hart, 2002).

Bebr, G, 'Case Comment Francovich' (1992) *Common Market Law Review* 557–84.

——, 'The Non-contractual Liability of the European Coal and Steel Community' in T Heukels and A McDonnell (eds), *The Action for Damages in Community Law* (The Hague, Kluwer Law International, 1997) 71–88.

Beljin, S, *Staatshaftung im Europarecht. Konturen des Haftungsinstituts, Mitgliedstaaliche Pflichen und subjektive Gemeinschaftsrechte, Innerstaatliche Durchführung* (Cologne, Carl Heymanns Verlag KG, 2000).

——, 'Rights in EU Law', in S Prechal and B van Roermund (eds), *Coherence in EU Law. The Search for Unity in Divergent Concepts* (Oxford, Oxford University Press, 2008) 91–122.

Bell, J, 'Mechanisms for Cross-fertilisation of Administrative Law in Europe' in J Beatson and T Tridimas (eds), *New Directions in European Public Law* (Oxford, Hart Publishing, 1998) 147–67.

——, 'Introduction' in D Fairgrieve et al (eds), *Tort Liability of Public Authorities in Comparative Perspective* (London, BIICL, 2002) xv–xxvi.

Bell, J and Bradley, AW (eds), *Governmental Liability: A Comparative Study* (London, The United Kingdom National Committee of Comparative Law, 1991).

Bengoetxea, J and Jääskinen, N, 'Rights and Diverse Effects in EC law: a Hohfeldian Approach to the Doctrine of Direct Effect of Directives' in R Banakar (ed), *Rights in Context: Law and Justice in Late Modern Society* (Farnham, Ashgate, 2010), 277–99.

Bengtsson, B, *Skadestånd vid myndighetsutötvning I* (Stockholm, Norstedts, 1976).

——, *Det allmännas ansvar enligt skadeståndslagen. Andra upplagan* (Stockholm, Norstedts, 1996).

Bergmann, K-O and Schumacher, H, *Die Kommunalhaftung. Ein Handbuch des Staatshaftungsrechts* (Cologne, Carl Heymanns Verlag, 2007).

Berrod, F, 'Plaidoyer pour une Union de droit dans la diversité des systèmes judiciaires nationaux', in *Chemins d'Europe. Mélanges en l'honneur de Jean Paul Jacqué* (Paris, LGDJ, 2010) 81–101.

Bertelmann, H, *Die Europäisierung des Staatshaftungsrechts* (Frankfurt, Lang, 2005).

Betlem, G, 'Beyond Francovich: Completing the Unified Member State and EU Liability Regime. A Comment on the Jan Jans Contribution' in D Obradovic and N Lavranos (eds), *Interface between EU Law and National Law* (Groningen, Europa Law Publishing, 2007) 299–309.

Biernat, S and Pilaszewicz-Kulikowska, M et al, Consequences of Incompatibility with EC Law for Final Administrative Decisions and Final Judgments of Administrative Courts in the Member States (Warsaw, Naczelny Sad Administracyjny, 2008).

Binder, J-H, 'Cutting Back State Liability for Regulatory Negligence: The ECJ's decision in *Paul and Others v. Germany*' (2005) *Banking and Insurance Law Review* 133–49.

Biondi, A and Farley, P, *The Right to Damages in European Law* (Alphen aan der Rijn, Kluwer Law International, 2009).

Birkinshaw, P, *European Public Law* (London, Butterworths, 2003).

Bitans, A, 'Latvia', in H Koziol and BC Steininger (eds), *European Tort Law 2005* (Vienna, SpringerWienNewYork, 2006) 380.

Böhme, M, *Staatshaftung für fehlerhafte Bankenaufsicht nach deutschem und europäischem Recht* (Baden-Baden, Nomos, 2009).

Booth QC, C and Squires, D, *The Negligence Liability of Public Authorities* (Oxford, Oxford University Press, 2006).

Broyelle, C, *La responsabilité de l'Etat du fait des lois (*Paris, LGDJ, 2003).

Burrows, N and Greaves, R, *The Advocate General and EC Law* (Oxford, Oxford University Press, 2007).

Caranta, R, 'On Discretion' in S Prechal and B van Roermund (eds), *Coherence in EU Law. The Search for Unity in Divergent Concepts* (Oxford, Oxford University Press, 2008) 186–215.

Castillo de la Torre, F, 'Tribunal Supremo (Spanish Supreme Court), Administrative Law Chamber, judgment of 12 June 2003, Canal Satélite Digital (Case 46/1999)' (2004) *Common Market Law Review* 1717–34.

——, 'Interim measures in Community courts: recent trends' (2007) *Common Market Law Review* 273–353.

Collins, H, *The European Civil Code: The Way Forward* (Cambridge, Cambridge University Press, 2008).

Cornford, T, *Towards a Public Law of Tort* (Aldershot, Ashgate, 2008).

Cornils, M, *Der gemeinschaftsrechtliche Staatshaftungsanspruch. Rechtsnatur und Legitimität eines richterrechtlichen Haftunginstituts* (Baden-Baden, Nomos, 1995).

Costa, J-P, 'The Provision of Compensation under Article 41 of the European Convention on Human Rights' in D Fairgrieve et al (eds), *Tort Liability of Public Authorities in Comparative Perspective* (London, BIICL, 2002) 3–16.

Coutron, L, 'Style des arrêts de la Cour de justice et normativité de la jurisprudence communautaire' (2009) *Revue trimestrielle de droit européen* 643–675.

Craig, P, '*Francovich*, Remedies and the Scope of Damages Liability' (1993) *Law Quarterly Review* 595–621.

——, 'The Domestic Liability of Public Authorities in Damages: Lessons from the European Community?' in J Beatson and T Tridimas (eds), *New Directions in European Public Law* (Oxford, Hart Publishing, 1998) 75–90.

——, *EU Administrative law* (Oxford, Oxford University Press, 2006).

Crawford, J, The International Law Commission's Articles on State Responsibility. Introduction, Text and Commentaries (Cambridge, 2002).

Crawford, J and Pellet, A et al (eds), *The Law of International Responsibility* (Oxford, Oxford University Press, 2010).

Crawford Lichtenstein, C, 'Public Liability in U.S. Courts and *Brasserie du Pêcheur and Factortame* in the European Court' in D O'Keeffe (ed), *Judicial Review in European Union Law. Liber Amicorum in Honour of Lord Slynn of Hadley.* Volume 1 (The Hague, Kluwer Law International, 2000) 287–302.

Cujo, E, 'L'autonomie du recours en indemnité par rapport au recours en annulation – évolutions jurisprudentielles' (1999) *Revue du Marché Commun et de l'Union Européenne* 414–20.

Czaja, A, *Die Außervertragliche Haftung der EG für ihre Organe* (Baden-Baden, Nomos, 1996).

Dalle-Crode, S, *Le fonctionnaire communautaire: droits, obligations et régime disciplinaire* (Brussels, Bruylant, 2008).

von Danwitz, T, *Europäisches Verwaltungsrecht* (Berlin Heidelberg, Springer, 2009).
de Witte, B, 'Direct Effect, Primacy and the Nature of Legal Order' in P Craig and G de Búrca (eds), *The Evolution of EC Law,* 2nd edn (Oxford, Oxford University Press, 2011) 323–62.
Delaunay, B, *La faute de l'administration* (Paris, LGDJ, 2007).
Di Federico, G, 'The Distinction between Legislative and Non-Legislative Acts in the Constitutional Treaty and its Possible Impact on Locus Standi and Non-Contractual Liability. Some Suggestions on the Necessary Adaptations Required by the Treaty Reform Process' in M Dony and S Rossi (eds), *Démocracie, cohérence et transparence. Vers une constitutionallisation de l'Union européenne?* (Brussels, Éditions de l'Université de Bruxelles, 2008) 13–36.
Dias Pereira, AG, 'Portugal' in H Koziol and BC Steininger (eds), *European Tort Law 2007* (Vienna, SpringerWienNewYork, 2008) 476.
Dougan, M, 'When worlds collide! Competing visions of the relationship between direct effect and supremacy' (2007) *Common Market Law Review* 931–63.
——, 'The Intention to Confer Rights under the Francovich Case Law: Still Waters Run Deep' (UKAEL Seminar 'Damages Claims in EU Law', London, 22 February 2008) (unpublished presentation).
——, 'The Treaty of Lisbon 2007: winning minds, not hearts' (2008) *Common Market Law Review* 617–703.
——, 'The Vicissitudes of Life at the Coalface: Remedies and Procedures for Enforcing Union Law before the National Courts' in P Craig and G de Búrca (eds), *The Evolution of EC Law,* 2nd edn (Oxford, Oxford University Press, 2011) 407–38.
Dufwa, BW, 'Horizontal Effect of the European Convention: Swedish Case law' in A Colombi Ciacchi et al (eds), *Haftungsrecht im dritten Millenium – Liability in the Third Millenium: Liber Amicorum Gert Brüggemeier* (Baden-Baden, Nomos, 2009) 85–109.
Durant, IC, 'Causation' in H Koziol and R Schulze (eds), *Tort Law of the European Community* (Vienna, SpringerWienNewYork, 2008) 47–79.
Edward, D and Robinson, W, 'Is there a Place for Private Law Principles in Community Law?' in T Heukels and A McDonnell (eds), *The Action for Damages in Community Law* (The Hague, Kluwer Law International, 1997) 339–50.
Eilmansberger, T, 'The Relationship between Rights and Remedies in EC Law: In Search of the Missing Link' (2004) *Common Market Law Review* 1199–246.
——, 'The Green Paper on Damages Actions for Breach of the EC Antitrust Rules and Beyond; Reflections on the Utility and Feasibility of Stimulating Private Enforcement through Legislative Action' (2007) *Common Market Law Review* 431–78.
Eliantonio, M, *Europeanisation of Administrative Justice. The Influence of the ECJ's Case Law in Italy, Germany and England* (Groningen, Europa Law Publishing, 2008).
Emsinghoff, JF, *Entschädigung für Eigentumseingriffe infolge rechtmäßiger Rechtsetzungsakte der Europäischen Gemeinschaft* (Baden-Baden, Nomos, 2009).
Engström, J, *The Europeanisation of Remedies and Procedures through Judge-Made Law. Can a Trojan Horse Achieve Effectiveness?* (Florence, European University Institute, 2009).
European Tort Law Group (ed) *Principles of European Tort Law: text and commentary* (Vienna, Springer, 2005).
Everling, U, 'Reflections on the Reasoning in the Judgements of the Court of Justice of the European Communities', *Festskrift til Ole Due* (Copenhagen, Gads Forlag, 1994) 55–74.
——, 'On the Judge-Made Law of the European Community's Courts' in D O'Keeffe (ed), *Judicial Review in European Union Law. Liber Amicorum in Honour of Lord Slynn of Hadley. Volume 1* (The Hague, Kluwer Law International, 2000) 29–44.

Eyjólfsson, M, 'Case comment Case E-9/97, Sveinbjörnsdottir v Iceland' (2000) *Common Market Law Review* 191–211.

Fairgrieve, D, *State Liability in Tort. A Comparative Law Study* (Oxford, Oxford University Press, 2003).

Fairgrieve, D and Andenas, M et al (eds), *Tort Liability of Public Authorities in Comparative Perspective* (London, BIICL, 2002).

Fartunova, M, 'Le dialogue des juges. Les interactions entre le TPICE et la Cour' in P Mbongo and A Vauchez (eds), *Dans la fabrique du droit européen. Scènes, acteurs et publics de la Cour de justice des Communautés européennes* (Brussels, Bruylant, 2009) 31–52.

Favret, J-M, *Les influences réciproques du droit communautaire et du droit national de la responsabilité publique extracontractuelle* (Paris, Pedone, 2000).

Fenger, N, *Forvaltning & Faelleskab. Om EU-rettens betydning for den almindelige forvaltningsret: Konfrontation og frugtbar sameksistens* (Copenhagen, Jurist- og Økonomforbundets Forlag, 2004).

Fetzer, R, *Die Haftung des Staates für legislatives Unrecht: zugleich ein Beitrag zum Staatshaftungsrecht der Europäischen Gemeinschaften, der EG-Mitgliedstaaten, der Schweiz und Österreichs* (Berlin, Duncker & Humblot, 1994).

Fines, F, *Étude de la responsabilité extracontractuelle de la Communauté économique européenne* (Paris, LGDJ, 1990).

——, 'A General Analytical Perspective on Community Liability' in T Heukels and A McDonnell (eds), *The Action for Damages in Community Law* (The Hague, Kluwer Law International, 1997) 11–39.

Frank, A, *Le droit de la responsabilité administrative à l'épreuve des fonds d'indemnisation* (Paris, L'Harmattan, 2008).

Freeman, MDA, *Lloyd's Introduction to Jurisprudence. Seventh Edition* (London, Sweet & Maxwell, 2005(2001)).

Giegerich, T, 'Another Incoming Tide? Tort Liability in Public International Law' in A Colombi Ciacchi et al (eds), *Haftungsrecht im dritten Millenium – Liability in the Third Millenium: Liber Amicorum Gert Bruggemeier* (Baden-Baden, Nomos, 2009) 577–606.

Giliker, P, 'European Tort Law: Five Key Questions for Debate' (2009) *European Review of Private Law* 285–304.

Gordon, R, *EC Law in Judicial Review* (Oxford, Oxford University Press, 2007).

Granger, M-PF, 'National applications of *Francovich* and the construction of a European administrative *ius commune*' (2007) *European Law Review* 157–92.

Gratias, M, *Staatshaftung für fehlerhafte Banken- und Versicherungsaufsicht im Europäischen Binnenmarkt* (Baden-Baden, Nomos, 1999).

Grossrieder Tissot, S, 'La responsabilité de la Communauté européenne du fait de l'activité normative de la Commission' (2001) *Revue trimestrielle de droit européen* 91–121.

Guimaraes-Purokoski, A, *Vertikaalinen toimivallanjako EU-oikeudessa [The Vertical Division of Competences in EU Law]* (Jyväskylä, Suomalainen Lakimiesyhdistys, 2009).

Görgens, S, *Die außervertragliche Haftung der Europäischen Gemeinschaft für Verletzungen des WTO-Rechts durch ihre Organe. Die Haftung bei Nichtumsetzung von Entscheidungen des Streitbeilegungsgremiums der WTO* (Berlin, Duncker & Humblot, 2005).

Hakalehto-Wainio, S, *Valta ja vahinko. Julkisen vallan käyttäjän vastuu vahingonkorvauslaissa [Power and Liability. Tort Liability of the Public Authorities under the Tort Liability Act]* (Hämeenlinna, Talentum, 2008).

——, 'Strasbourgista Suomeen – Ihmisoikeusloukkauksen korvaaminen Euroopan ihmisoikeustuomioistuimen käytännössä ja kansallisella tasolla [Von Strassburg nach

Finnland – die Entschädigung für Verletzung eines Menschenrechtes in der Praxis des Europäischen Gerichtshofes für Menschenrechte und auf der nationalen Ebene]' (2010) *Defensor Legis* 747–63.

Hancher, L, 'Issues of Non-Contractual Liability under the EAEC Treaty' in T Heukels and A McDonnell (eds), *The Action for Damages in Community Law* (The Hague, Kluwer Law International, 1997) 41–69.

Harlow, C, 'Francovich and the Problem of the Disobedient State' (1996) (3) *European Law Journal* 199–225.

——, 'The Current State of State Liability' (2002) (4) *Rivista trimestrale di diritto pubblico* 915–33.

——, 'Voices of Difference in a Plural Community' in P Beaumont et al (eds), *Convergence and Divergence in European Public Law* (Oxford, Hart Publishing, 2002) 199–224.

——, *State Liability: Tort Law and Beyond* (Oxford, Oxford University Press, 2004).

——, 'Three Phases in the Evolution of EU Administrative Law' in P Craig and G de Búrca (eds), *The Evolution of EC Law*, 2nd edn (Oxford, Oxford University Press, 2011) 439–64.

Hartkamp, A and Hesselink, M et al (eds), *Towards a European Civil Code. Third Fully Revised and Expanded Edition* (The Hague, Kluwer Law International, 2004).

Held, S, *Die Haftung der EG für die Verletzung von WTO-Recht* (Tübingen, Mohr Siebeck, 2006).

Hemmo, M, Vahingonkorvausoikeus [Law of Damages] (Porvoo, 2006).

Henrichs, C, *Haftung der EG-mitgliedstaaten für Verletzung von Gemeinschaftsrecht* (Baden-Baden, Nomos, 1995).

Hettne, J, *Rättsprinciper som styrmedel: Allmänna rättsprinciper i EU:s domstol* (Stockholm, Norstedts Juridik, 2008).

Hettne, J and Otken Eriksson, I (eds), *EU-rättslig metod: teori och genomslag i svensk rättstillämpning* (Stockholm, Norstedts juridik, 2005).

Heukels, T, 'The Contractual Liability of the European Community Revisited' in T Heukels and A McDonnell (eds), *The Action for Damages in Community Law* (The Hague, Kluwer Law International, 1997) 89–108.

Heukels, T and McDonnell, A (eds), *The Action for Damages in Community Law* (The Hague, Kluwer Law International, 1997).

Hidien, JW, *Die Gemeinschaftsrechtliche Staatshaftung der EU-Mitgliedstaaten* (Baden-Baden, Nomos, 1999).

Hilson, C, 'Liability of Member States in Damages: The Place of Discretion' (1997) *International and Comparative Law Quarterly* 941–47.

——, 'The Role of Discretion in EC Law on Non-Contractual Liability' (2005) *Common Market Law Review* 677–95.

Hilson, C and Downes, T, 'Making Sense of Rights: Community Rights in E.C. Law' (1999) *European Law Review* 121–38.

Hix, J-P, 'Zur ausservertragliche Haftung der Gemeinschaft' in S Moreira de Sousa and W Heusel (eds), *Enforcing Community Law from Francovich to Köbler: Twelve Years of the State Liability Principle* (Cologne, Bundesanzeiger, 2004) 199–223.

Hogg, PW and Monahan, PJ, *Liability of the Crown*, 3rd edn (Toronto, Carswell Thomson Professional Publishing, 2000).

Hohfeld, WN, *Fundamental Legal Conceptions as applied in judicial reasoning and other legal essays* (New Haven, Yale University Press (digital version at www.archive.org), 1920).

Huglo, J-G, 'Fasc. 371 – Cour de justice – Responsabilité extracontractuelle – Conditions de fonde du recours en indemnité – Décision de la Cour (à jour au 28 avril 2004)', *Jurisclasseur Europe Traité*, 2004),

Höher, K, *Die Haftung der Europäischen Gemeinschaft für Verstöße gegen das WTO-Recht: eine Untersuchung am Beispiel des WTO-Bananenstreitverfahrens* (Baden-Baden, Nomos, 2006).

Jans, JH, 'State Liability: In Search of a Dividing Line between National and European Law' in D Obradovic and N Lavranos (eds), *Interface between EU Law and National Law* (Groningen, Europa Law Publishing, 2007) 279–96.

Jans, JH and de Lange, R et al (eds), *Europeanisation of Public Law* (Groningen, Europa Law Publishing, 2007).

Jaaskinen, N, 'Kolme aaltoa – miten Suomen oikeusjärjestys eurooppalaistui?' (2001) *Defensor Legis* 603–19.

——, *Euroopan unioni – oikeudelliset perusteet [European Union - Legal Foundations]* (Jyväskylä, Talentum, 2007).

——, *Eurooppalaistuvan oikeuden oikeusteoreettisia ongelmia [The Europeanisation of Law – Jurisprudential Problems]* (Helsinki, 2008).

——, 'Back to the *Begriffshimmel?* A Plea for an Analytical Perspective in European Law' in S Prechal and B van Roermund (eds), *Coherence in EU Law. The Search for Unity in Divergent Concepts* (Oxford, Oxford University Press, 2008) 451–61.

——, 'EU ja Hohfeld' in H Kanninen et al (eds), *Puhuri käy. Muuttuva suomalainen ja eurooppalainen valtiosääntömme. Heikki Karapuu 30.12.1944 – 15.6.2006* (Helsinki, Edita, 2009) 245–302.

Kanninen, H, 'EY-oikeuden soveltamisesta korkeimmassa hallinto-oikeudessa' [Application of EC Law in the Supreme Administrative Court] (2003) *Lakimies* 1253–72.

Klauer, I, *Die Europäisierung des Privatrechts. Der EuGH als Zivilrichter* (Baden-Baden, Nomos, 1998).

Koziol, H (ed) *Unification of Tort Law: Wrongfulness* (The Hague, Kluwer Law International, 1998).

Koziol, H and Schulze, R (eds), *Tort Law of the European Community* (Vienna, SpringerWienNewYork, 2008).

Krümmel, T and D'Sa, RM, 'Implementation by German Courts of the Jurisprudence of the European Court of Justice on State Liability for Breach of Community Law as Developed in Francovich and subsequent cases' (2009) *European Business Law Review* 273–86.

Kulla, H, 'The Responsibility of the State as Legislator' in T Modeen (ed), *Finnish National Reports to the XVTH Congress of the International Academy of Comparative Law (Bristol, July 26 – August 1, 1998)* (Helsinki, 1998) 201–14.

Kvjatkovski, V, 'What is an 'Emanation of the State'? An Educated Guess' (1997) *European Public Law* 329–38.

Ladenburger, C, 'Evolution oder Kodifikation eines allgemeinen Verwaltungsrechts in der EU' in H-H Trute et al (eds), *Allgemeines Verwaltungsrecht – zur Tragfähigkeit eines Konzepts* (Tübingen, Mohr Siebeck, 2008) 109–33.

Lahe, J and Kull, I, 'Estonia' in H Koziol and BC Steininger (eds), *European Tort Law 2006* (Vienna, SpringerWienNewYork, 2008) 178.

Lando, O and Beale, H (eds), *Principles of European Contract Law. Parts I and II (Combined and Revised)* (The Hague, Kluwer Law International, 2000).

Leczykiewicz, D, 'Private Party Liability in EU Law: In Search of the General Regime' in C Barnard and O Odudu (eds), *Cambridge Yearbook of European Legal Studies. Vol 12, 2009-2010* (Oxford, Hart Publishing, 2010) 257–82.

Legrand, P, 'European Legal Systems Are Not Converging' (1996) *International and Comparative Law Quarterly* 52–81.

——, 'A Diabolical Idea' in A Hartkamp et al (eds), *Towards a European Civil Code. Third Fully Revised and Expanded Edition* (The Hague, Kluwer Law International, 2004) 245–72.

Lehto, M, *Indirect responsibility for terrorist acts: redefinition of the concept of terrorism beyond violent acts* (Leiden, Martinus Nijhoff, 2009).

Lenaerts, K and van Aerschot, P et al, *Constitutional Law of the European Union*, 2nd edn (London, Sweet and Maxwell, 2005).

Lever, J, 'Mutual Permeation of Community and National Tort Rules' in J Wouters et al (eds), *Principles of Proper Conduct for Supranational, State and Private Actors in the European Union: Towards a Ius Commune. Essays in Honour of Walter van Gerven* (Antwerp, Intersentia, 2001) 91–110.

Lukas, M, 'Fault Liability' in H Koziol and R Schulze (eds), *Tort Law of the European Community* (Wien, SpringerWienNewYork, 2008) 81–102.

Lyons, C, 'Perspectives on Convergence Within the Theatre of European Integration' in P Beaumont et al (eds), *Convergence and Divergence in European Public Law* (Oxford, Hart Publishing, 2002) 79–96.

Lysén, G, *The Non-Contractual and Contractual Liability of the European Economic Communities* (Uppsala, 1976).

——, *EU Framework decisions: Who is liable to pay compensation for the violation of the rights of the individual. A public international law approach* (Uppsala, Iustus, 2006).

Mabrito, J, 'The American and EC Approaches to Member State Liability and the Possibility of State Officer Liability in the EC' in P Eeckhout and T Tridimas (eds), *26 Yearbook of European Law 2007* (Oxford, Oxford University Press, 2008) 219–54.

MacCormick, N, *Rhetoric and the Rule of Law. A Theory of Legal Reasoning* (Oxford, Oxford University Press, 2005).

MacCormick, N and Summers, RS (eds), *Interpreting Precedents. A Comparative Study* (Ashgate, 1997).

Magnus, U (ed), *Unification of Tort Law: Damages* (The Hague, Kluwer Law International, 2000).

Mancini, F, *Democracy and constitutionalism in the European Union: Collected Essays* (Oxford, Hart Publishing, 1999).

Markesinis, BS, 'Learning from Europe and Learning in Europe' in BS Markesinis (ed), *The Gradual Convergence: Foreign Ideas, Foreign Influences and English Law on the Eve of the 21st Century* (Oxford, Clarendon, 1994) 1–32.

Markesinis, BS and Lorenz, W et al, *The German Law of Obligations. Volume II. The Law of Torts: A Comparative Introduction*, 3rd edn with corrections and additions (Oxford, Clarendon, 1997).

Maunu, A, 'Direktiivin yksityisiä velvoittava vaikutus täsmentyy yhteisöjen tuomioistuimen Delena Wells -ratkaisussa (EYTI C-201/02)' (2004) *Defensor Legis* 302.

——, 'Direktiivien oikeusvaikutukset kansallisissa tuomioistuimissa: oireet, diagnoosi ja hoitokeinot' in H Kaila et al (eds), *Yksilön oikeusasema Euroopan unionissa – Individens rättsställning inom Europeiska Unionen: Juhlakirja Allan Rosas – Festskrift Allan Rosas* (Turku/Åbo, 2008) 595–621.

Meij, AWH, 'Article 215(2) EC and Local Remedies' in T Heukels and A McDonnell (eds), *The Action for Damages in Community Law* (The Hague, Kluwer Law International, 1997) 273–84.

Méndez-Pinedo, E, *EC and EEA Law. A Comparative Study of the Effectiveness of European Law* (Groningen, Europa Law Publishing, 2009).

Mulders, L, 'Translation at the Court of Justice of the European Communities', in S Prechal and B van Roermund (eds), *Coherence in EU Law. The Search for Unity in Divergent Concepts* (Oxford, Oxford University Press, 2008) 45–59.

Müller, F and Christensen, R, Juristische Methodik. Band II. Europarecht. Zweite, neu bearbeitete und stark erweiterte Auflage (Berlin, Duncker & Humblot, 2007).

Mylly, T, *Intellectual Property and European Economic Constitutional Law – The Trouble with Private Informational Power* (Vaajakoski, IPR University Center, 2009).

Mäenpää, O, 'Hyvä hallinto oikeutena ja yleisenä oikeusperiaatteena' in H Kaila et al (eds), *Yksilön oikeusasema Euroopan unionissa – Individens rättsställning inom Europeiska Unionen: Juhlakirja Allan Rosas – Festskrift Allan Rosas* (Turku/Åbo, 2008) 465–74.

——, Eurooppalainen hallinto-oikeus (3. painos) (Helsinki, Talentum, 2011).

Nacimiento, P, *Gemeinschaftsrechtliche und nationale Staatshaftung in Deutschland, Italien und Frankreich* (Baden-Baden, Nomos, 2006).

Nebbia, P, 'Damages actions for the infringement of EC competition law: compensation or deterrence?' (2008) *European Law Review* 23–43.

Nergelius, J, *The Constitutional Dilemma of the European Union* (Groningen, Europa Law Publishing, 2009).

Ojanen, T, *The European Way. The Structure of National Court Obligation under EC Law* (Saarijärvi, 1998).

——, 'The Changing Concept of Direct Effect of European Law' (2000) *European Review of Public Law* 1253–70.

——, 'Perus- ja ihmisoikeudet – eurooppalaisen konstitutionalismin Akilleen kantapää?' (2009) *Lakimies* 1106–21.

Oliver, P, 'Joint Liability of the Community and the Member States' in T Heukels and A McDonnell (eds), *The Action for Damages in Community Law* (The Hague, Kluwer Law International, 1997) 285–309.

——, 'State Liability in Damages following Factortame III: A Remedy Seen in Context' in J Beatson and T Tridimas (eds), *New Directions in European Public Law* (Oxford, Hart Publishing, 1998) 49–61.

Ossenbühl, F, *Staatshaftungsrecht. 5., neu bearbeitete und erweiterte Auflage* (Munich, Beck, 1998).

——,'Anmerkungen zur Hoheitshaftung in Europarecht', in J Ipsen and B Stüer (eds), *Europa in Wandel. Festschrift für Hans-Werner Rengeling* (Cologne, Carl Heymanns Verlag, 2008), 369–82.

Paasilehto, S, Constellations – A New Approach to Legal Culture and European Integration of Private Law (Helsinki, 2002).

Paasivirta, E and Kuijper, PJ, 'Does one size fit all? The European Community and the responsibility of international organizations' *Netherlands Yearbook of International Law Vol XXXVI – 2005* (Netherlands, 2007) 169–226.

Patrão, A, *Responsabilidade Extracontratual da Comunidade Europeia* (Coimbra, Almedina, 2008).

Pescatore, P, 'Responsabilité des États membres en cas de manquement aux règles communautaires' (1972) (Parta Quarta) *Il Foro Padano* 9–24.

Pfander, JE, 'Member State Liability and Constitutional Change in the United States and Europe' (2003) (2) *American Journal of Comparative Law* 237–74.

Picod, F and Coutron, L, 'La responsabilité de la Communauté européenne du fait de son activité administrative' in J-B Auby and J Dutheil de la Rochère (eds), *Droit administratif européen* (Brussels, Bruylant, 2007) 171–211.

Poiares Maduro, M, 'Contrapunctual Law: Europe's Constitutional Pluralism in Action' in N Walker (ed), *Sovereignity in Transition* (Oxford, Hart Publishing, 2003) 501–37.

——, 'European Constitutionalism and Three Models of Social Europe' in M Hesselink (ed), *The Politics of a European Civil Code* (The Hague, Kluwer Law International, 2006) 125–41.

Potteau, A, 'A propos d'un pis-aller: la responsabilité des États membres pour l'incompatibilité du droit de l'Union avec la convention européenne des droits de l'homme' (2009) *Revue trimestrielle de droit européen* 697–716.

Prechal, S, 'Member State liability and direct effect: what's the difference after all?' (2007) *European Business Law Review* 299–316.

——, 'Protection of Rights: How Far?' in S Prechal and B van Roermund (eds), *Coherence in EU Law. The Search for Unity in Divergent Concepts* (Oxford, Oxford University Press, 2008) 155–82.

Prechal, S and van Roermund, B, 'Binding Unity in EU Legal Order: An Introduction' in S Prechal and B van Roermund (eds), *Coherence in EU Law. The Search for Unity in Divergent Concepts* (Oxford, Oxford University Press, 2008) 1–20.

Prinssen, JM and Schrauwen, A (eds), *Direct Effect – Rethinking a Classic of EC Legal Doctrine* (Groningen, Europa Law Publishing, 2002).

Raitio, J, 'Mistä EY:n jäsenvaltion vahingonkorvausvastuu jäsenvelvoitteidensa rikkomisesta yksityisille aihetuneista vahingoista voidaan johtaa?' (1998) *Lakimies* 630–50.

——, *The principle of legal certainty in EC law* (Dordrecht, Kluwer Academic Publishers, 2003).

——, 'Eurooppaoikeus on kehittyvä oikeudenala' (2006) *Lakimies* 813–17.

——, 'Eurooppaoikeus, tieto ja sivistys' (2008) *Lakimies* 288–93.

Rebhahn, R, 'Public Liability in Comparison – England, France, Germany' in H Koziol and BC Steininger (ed), *European Tort law 2005* (Vienna, SpringerWienNewYork, 2006) 68–93.

Reich, N, '"System der subjektiven öffentlichen Rechte" in the Union: A European Constitution for Citizens of Bits and Pieces', *Collected Courses of the Academy of European Law. Volume VI, Book I (1995). European Community law* (The Hague, Kluwer Law International, 1998) 157–235.

——, 'Horizontal Liability in EC Law: Hybridization of Remedies for Compensation in case of Breaches of EC Rights' (2007) *Common Market Law Review* 705–42.

——, 'Rights without duties? Reflections on the state of liability law in the multilevel governance system of the Community: Is there a need for a more coherent approach in European private law?' (2009) *Tidskrift utgiven av Juridiska Föreningen i Finland* 492.

Reichel, J, *God förvaltning i EU och i Sverige* (Stockholm, Jure, 2006).

Ritleng, D, 'De l'irresponsabilité extracontractuelle de la Communauté' in J-C Masclet et al (eds), *L'Union européenne – Union de droit, union des droits. Mélanges en l'honneur du Professeur Philippe Manin* (Paris, Pedone, 2010) 921–32.

Rosas, A, 'State responsibility and liability under civil liability regimes' in O Bring and S Mahmoudi (eds), *Current international law issues: Nordic perspectives : essays in honour of Jerzy Sztucki* (Stockholm, Springer, 1994) 161–82.

Rosas, A and Armati, L, *EU Constitutional Law* (Oxford, Hart Publishing, 2010).

Routamo, E and Ståhlberg, P et al, *Suomen vahingonkorvausoikeus [Finnish Law of Damages]* (Helsinki, 2006).

Saarikoski, M, 'EY-oikeuden vaikutuksesta keskeiseen vahingonkorvaus- ja vakuutusoikeuteen – Esimerkkinä matkustajan myötävaikutus liikennevahinkoon' (2007) *Defensor Legis* 22–36.

Salminen, J, 'Euroopan yhteisöjen tuomioistuimen tuomio asiassa C-224/01, Gerhard Köbler vastaan Itävallan tasavalta – Lisiä oppiin unionin jäsenvaltion vahingonkorvausvastuusta yhteisön oikeuden rikkomisesta?' (2004) *Lakimies* 1125–35.

Schermers, HG and Waelbroeck, DF, *Judicial Protection in the European Communities*, 6th edn (The Hague, Kluwer Law International, 2001).

Scherr, KM, 'Public Liability for Administrative Acts under French Law' (2008) (2) *European Public Law* 213–36.

——, *The Principle of State Liability for Judicial Breaches. The case Gerhard Köbler v. Austria under European Community Law and from a comparative national law perspective* (Florence, European University Institute, 2008).

Schockweiler, F and Vivenes, G et al, 'Le régime de la responsabilité extra-contractuelle du fait d'actes juridiques dans la Communauté européenne' (1990) *Revue trimestrielle de droit européen* 27–74.

Schoißwohl, B, *Staatshaftung wegen Gemeinschaftsrechtsverletzung: Anspruchsgrundlage und materielle Voraussetzungen (f. Österreich)* (Vienna, Springer, 2002).

Scholl, K, Haftung zwischen den EG-Mitgliedstaaten bei Verletzung von Gemeinschaftsrecht. Begründung eines zwischenstaatlichen Schadensersatzanspruchs (Munich, Beck, 2005).

Schuck, P, *Suing Government* (New Haven, Yale University Press, 1983).

Schwarze, J, *European Administrative Law*, revised 1st edn (London, Sweet and Maxell, 2006).

——, 'Rechtstaatliche Grundsätze für das Verwaltungshandeln in der "alten" und "neuen" Europäischen Union' in J Iliopoulos-Strangas and H Bauer (eds), *Die Neue Europäische Union* (Athens, Ant. N. Sakkoulas, 2006) 165–97.

Seltenreich, S, *Die Francovich-Rechtsprechung des EuGH und ihre Auswirkungen auf das deutsche Staatshaftungsrecht: ein Rückblick fünf Jahre nach dem Ergehen des Francovich-Urteils* (Konstanz, Hartung-Gorre, 1997).

Senkovic, P, *L'évolution de la responsabilite de l'État législateur sous l'influence du droit communautaire* (Brussels, Bruylant, 2000).

Sevón, L and Johansson, M, 'The protection of the rights of individuals under the EEA Agreement' (1999) *European Law Review* 373–86.

Sharpston, E, 'Milk Lakes, SLOMs and Legitimate Expectations' in D O'Keeffe (ed), *Judicial Review in European Union Law. Liber Amicorum in Honour of Lord Slynn of Hadley. Volume 1* (The Hague, Kluwer Law International, 2000) 557–67.

Shelton, D, *Remedies in International Human Rights Law* (Oxford, Oxford University Press, 1999).

Siltala, R, *A Theory of Precedent. From analytical positivism to a post-analytical philosophy of law* (Oxford, Hart Publishing, 2000).

Simma, B and Pulkowski, D, 'Leges Speciales and Self-Contained Regimes' in J Crawford et al (eds), *The Law of International Responsibility* (Oxford, Oxford University Press, 2010) 139–63.

Simon, D, 'The Sanction of Member States' Serious Violations of Community Law' in D O'Keeffe (ed), *Judicial Review in European Union Law. Liber Amicorum in Honour of Lord Slynn of Hadley. Volume 1* (The Hague, Kluwer Law International, 2000) 275–86.

Simon, D and Barav, A, 'La responsabilité de l'administration nationale en cas de violation du droit communautaire' (1987) *Revue du Marché Commun et de l'Union Européenne* 165–74.

Sirinelli, J, *La transformation du droit administratif par le droit de l'Union européenne - Une contribution à l'étude du droit administratif européen* (Paris, LGDJ, 2011).

Sisula-Tulokas, L, 'To be or not to be – harmonisering av den europeiska avtalsrätten' (2001) *Tidskrift utgiven av Juridiska Föreningen i Finland* 708–20.

——, 'Europeisering av vår skadeståndsrätt . . . que será, será' in H Lindfors et al (eds), *Kovia aikoja: riitoja ja maksukyvyttömyyttä - Juhlakirja Risto Koulu 60 vuotta* (Helsinki, COMI & Edita, 2009) 571–90.

——, 'Att ge och ta – ansvar för rena ekonomiska skador vid myndighetsutövning' (2010) *Tidskrift utgiven av Juridiska Föreningen i Finland* 291–321.

Slaughter, A-M and Stone Sweet, A et al (eds), *The European Court and National Courts – Doctrine and Jurisprudence. Legal Change in Its Social Context* (Oxford, Hart Publishing, 1998).

Smith, F and Woods, L, 'Causation in *Francovich*: The Neglected Problem' (1997) *International and Comparative Law Quarterly* 925–41.

Snell, J, *Goods and Services in EC Law – A Study of the Relationship Between the Freedoms* (Oxford, Oxford University Press, 2002).

Snyder, F, 'The Effectiveness of European Community Law: Institutions, Processes, Tools and Techniques' (1993) *Modern Law Review* 19–54.

——, 'The unfinished constitution of the European Union: principles, processes and culture' in JHH Weiler and M Wind (eds), *European Constitutionalism Beyond the State* (Cambridge, Cambridge University Press, 2003) 55–73.

Stefanou, C and Xanthaki, H, *A Legal and Political Interpretation of Article 215(2) [new Article 288(2)] of the Treaty of Rome. The Individual Strikes Back* (Aldershot, Ashgate, 2000).

Stein, E, *Thoughts from a Bridge. A Retrospective of Writings on New Europe and American Federalism* (Ann Arbor, The University of Michigan Press, 2000).

Steinbach, A, *Die Haftung der EG und ihrer Mitgliedsstaaten für WTO-Rechtsverletzungen aus rechtswissenschaftlicher und ökonomischer Perspektive* (Berlin, Duncker & Humblot, 2009).

——, 'EC Liability for Non-compliance with Decisions of the WTO DSB: The Lack of Judicial Protection Persists' (2009) (5) *Journal of World Trade* 1047–69.

Suviranta, O, *Virkamiehen ratkaisutoiminta ja Euroopan yhteisön oikeus [Das Entscheiden des Verwaltungsbeamten unter dem Aspekt des Europäischen Gemeinschaftsrechts]* (Vammala, 1996).

Säuberlich, U, *Die außervertragliche Haftung im Gemeinschaftsrecht: Eine Untersuchung der Mehrpersonenverhältnisse* (Berlin, Springer, 2005).

Tammi-Salminen, E, 'Kansainvälistyminen ja varallisuusoikeuden kansalliset opit' (2004) *Lakimies* 1340–54.

Teubner, G, 'Legal Irritants: Good Faith in British Law or How Unifying Law Ends Up in New Divergences' (1998) *Modern Law Review* 11–32.

Thies, A, 'The Impact of General Principles of EC Law on its Liability Regime Towards Retaliation Victims after FIAMM' (2009) *European Law Review* 889–913.

——, *The Liability of the European Community for Conduct in the Context of International Trade Disputes* (Munich, 2009).

Tison, M, 'Do not attack the watchdog! Banking supervisor's liability after *Peter Paul*' (2005) *Common Market Law Review* 639–75.

Toner, H, 'Thinking the Unthinkable? State Liability for Judicial Acts after *Factortame III*', *17 Yearbook of European Law 1997* (Oxford, Clarendon, 1999) 165–89.

Toth, AG, 'The Concepts of Damage and Causality as Elements of Non-Contractual Liability' in T Heukels and A McDonnell (eds), *The Action for Damages in Community Law* (The Hague, Kluwer Law International, 1997) 179–98.

Tuori, K, *Oikeuden ratio ja voluntas* (Vantaa, WSOYpro, 2007).

——, 'The Many Constitutions of Europe' in K Tuori and S Sankari (eds), *The Many Constitutions of Europe* (Farnham, Ashgate, 2010) 3–30.

van Boom, WH, 'European tort law: an integrated or compartmentalized approach?' in A Vaquer (ed), *European private law beyond the Common Frame of Reference: essays in honour of Reinhard Zimmermann* (Groningen, Europa Law Publishing, 2008) 131–49.

Van Dam, C, *European Tort Law* (Oxford, Oxford University Press, 2006).

——, 'European Tort Law and the Many Cultures of Europe' in T Wilhelmsson et al (eds), *Private law and the many cultures of Europe* (The Hague, Kluwer, 2006) 57–80.

Van Der Woude, MH, 'Liability for Administrative Acts under Article 215(2) EC' in T Heukels, and A McDonnell (eds), *The Action for Damages in Community Law* (The Hague, Kluwer Law International, 1997) 109–28.

van Gerven, W, 'Bridging the Unbridgeable: Community and National Tort Laws after Francovich and Brasserie' (1996) *International and Comparative Law Quarterly* 507–44.

——, 'Non-contractual Liability of Member States, Community Institutions and Individuals for Breaches of Community Law with a View to a Common Law for Europe' in W van Gerven and M Zuleeg (eds), *Remedies and Sanctions for the Enforcement of Community Law* (Cologne, Bundesanzeiger, 1996) 29–54.

——, 'Mutual Permeation of Public and Private Law at the National and Supranational Level' (1998) *Maastricht Journal of European and Comparative Law* 7–24.

——, 'Of Rights, Remedies and Procedures' (2000) *Common Market Law Review* 501–36.

——, 'The ECJ Case Law as a Means of Unification of Private Law?' in A Hartkamp et al (eds), *Towards a European Civil Code. Third Fully Revised and Expanded Edition* (The Hague, Kluwer Law International, 2004) 101–23.

——, 'Courage v Crehan and the Way Ahead' in M Johansson et al (eds), *Liber Amicorum in Honour of Sven Norberg – A European for all seasons* (Brussels, Bruylant, 2006) 485–509.

——, 'Two Twin Principles of EU Law: Democracy and Accountability, Consistency and Convergence' in U Bernitz et al (eds), General principles of EC law in a process of development : reports from a conference in Stockholm, 23-24 March 2007, organised by the Swedish Network for European Legal Studies (Alphen aan den Rijn, Kluwer Law International, 2008) 25–46.

——, 'Judicial Convergence of Laws and Minds in European Tort law and Related Matters' in A Colombi Ciacchi A et al (eds), *Haftungsrecht im dritten Millenium – Liability in the Third Millenium: Liber Amicorum Gert Brüggemeier* (Baden-Baden, Nomos, 2009) 29–47.

van Gerven, W and Lever, J et al, Cases, Materials and Text on National, Supranational and International Tort Law (Oxford, Hart Publishing, 2000).

Vandersanden, G and Dony, M (eds), *La responsabilité des États membres en cas de violation du droit communautaire. Études de droit communautaire et de droit national comparé* (Brussels, Bruylant, 1997).

Varney, M and Birkinshaw, P, 'Public Liability: European Influence and Domestic Change' in C Kombos (ed) *Studies in European Public Law: Thematic, National and Post-National Perspectives* (Athens–Thessaloniki, Sakkoulas Publications, 2010) 149–96.

Vaughan, D, '*Factortame* and After: A Fishy Story' (2005) *European Business Law Review* 511–17.

Wakefield, J, *Judicial Protection through the Use of Article 288(2) EC* (The Hague, Kluwer Law International, 2002).

——, 'Retrench and Reform: The Action for Damages' in P Eeckhout and T Tridimas (eds), *28 Yearbook of European Law 2009* (Oxford, Oxford University Press, 2010) 390–434.

Walker, N (ed), *Sovereignty in Transition* (Oxford, Hart Publishing, 2003).

Walker, N, 'Culture, Democracy and the Convergence of Public Law: Some Scepticisms about Scepticism' in N Walker (ed), *Convergence and Divergence in European Public Law* (Oxford, Hart Publishing, 2002) 257–71.

Ward, A, *Judicial Review and the Rights of Private Parties in EU Law, 2nd edn* (Oxford, Oxford University Press, 2007).

Ward, I, *A Critical Introduction to European Law* (London, Butterworths, 1996).

Wathelet, M and Van Raepenbusch, S, 'La responsabilité des États membres en cas de violation du droit communautaire. Vers un alignement de l'état sur celle de la Communauté ou l'inverse?' (1997) *Cahiers de droit européen* 13–65.

Weiler, JHH, 'The Transformation of Europe' (1991) *Yale Law Journal* 2403–83.

——, *The Constitution of Europe. 'Do the New Clothes Have an Emperor?' and Other Essays on European Integration* (Cambridge, Cambridge University Press, 1999).

Weiler, JHH and Lockhart, NJS, '"Taking Rights Seriously" Seriously: The European Court and its Fundamental Rights Jurisprudence I' (1995) *Common Market Law Review* 51–94.

——, '"Taking Rights Seriously" Seriously: The European Court and its Fundamental Rights Jurisprudence II' (1995) *Common Market Law Review* 579–627.

Wilhelmsson, T, 'Ole Landon kyydissä kohti eurooppalaista sopimusoikeutta' (2000) (3) *Defensor Legis* 440–51.

Wilhelmsson, T and Paunio, E et al, *Private law and the many cultures of Europe* (The Hague, Kluwer, 2006).

Williams, R, *Unjust Enrichment and Public Law. A Comparative Study of England, France and the EU* (Oxford, Hart Publishing, 2010).

Wilms, G, 'Le droit allemand' in G Vandersanden and M Dony (eds), *La responsabilité des États membres en cas de violation du droit communautaire. Études de droit communautaire et de droit national comparé* (Brussels, Bruylant, 1997) 65–93.

Wils, W, 'Concurrent Liability of the Community and a Member State' (1992) *European Law Review* 191–206.

Wollbrandt, J, *Gemeinschaftshaftung für judikatives Unrecht* (Osnabrück, dissertation.de, 2005).

Wouters, J and Verhey, L et al (eds), *European Constitutionalism Beyond Lisbon* (Antwerp, Intersentia, 2009).

Wurmnest, W, *Grundzüge eines europäischen Haftungsrechts: eine rechtsvergleichende Untersuchung des Gemeinschaftsrechts* (Tübingen, Mohr Siebeck, 2003).

Zenner, M, *Die Haftung der EG-Mitgliedstaaten für die Anwendung europarechtswidriger Rechtsnormen* (Munich, V. Florenz, 1995).

Zweigert, K and Kötz, H, *An Introduction to Comparative Law*, 3rd revised edn (Oxford, Clarendon, 1998).

Index